Disability, Work and Cash Benefits

Jerry L. Mashaw
Virginia Reno
Richard V. Burkhauser
Monroe Berkowitz
Editors

1996

W.E. Upjohn Institute for Employment Research
Kalamazoo, Michigan

Library of Congress Cataloging-in-Publication Data

Disability, work and cash benefits / Jerry L. Mashaw . . . [et al.],
    editors.
        p. cm.
        Papers presented at a conference on disability, work and cash benefits held
December 8-10, 1994 in Santa Monica, California, jointly sponsored by National
Academy of Social Insurance and the National Institute for Disability and
Rehabilitation Research of the U.S. Department of Education.
        Includes bibliographical references and index.
        ISBN 0–88099–168–2 (alk. paper). — ISBN 0–88099–167–4 (pbk. : alk. paper)
        1. Handicapped—Employment—United States—Congress. 2. Insurance,
Disability—United States—Congress. 3. Social security—United States—
Congresses. 4. Vocational rehabilitation—United States—Congress. 5. Sheltered
workshops—United States—Congress. 6. Employee fringe benefits—United
States—Congress. 7. Labor market—United States—Congress. 8. Handicapped—
Employment—Law and legislation—United States—Congress. I. Mashaw, Jerry
L. II. National Academy of Social Insurance (U.S.) III. National Institute for
Disability and Rehabilitation Research (U.S.)
H7256.U5D565   1996
331.5'9'0973—dc20

96–22377
CIP

The facts presented in this study and the observations and viewpoints expressed are
the sole responsibility of the authors. They do not necessarily represent positions of
the W. E. Upjohn Institute for Employment Research.

Cover design by J. R. Underhill
Index prepared by Shirley Kessel.
Printed in the United States of America.

Preface

Katherine D. Seelman
Peter A. Diamond

The workshop on *Disability, Work and Cash Benefits* convened some 50-60 of the nation's leading scholars in disability studies, income security policy, labor economics, and rehabilitation to explore the overarching policy question before the workshop: How might we alter public policy to promote employment, where feasible, as well as foster community integration and economic self-sufficiency of working-age Americans who find themselves, through illness, injury, aging, birth, or environmental barriers, to be counted among the nation's persons with disabilities.

The workshop, held December 8-10, 1994, in Santa Monica, California, was jointly sponsored by the National Institute of Disability and Rehabilitation Research (NIDRR) of the U.S. Department of Education and the National Academy of Social Insurance (the Academy). It proved to be a highly productive collaboration between our two organizations' complementary roles in promoting research and understanding of disability policy.

The mission of NIDRR is to promote the independence of persons who have disabilities by seeking improved systems, products, and practices in the rehabilitation process. It does this by funding research and training in medical or vocational rehabilitation, the development of assistive technology, and policy research on issues of particular importance to persons with disabilities. Its support of this workshop aptly fits within this mission.

The Academy encourages research, understanding, and sound policy for the nation's social insurance programs -- the largest of which is Social Security, or Old-Age, Survivors and Disability Insurance. In the United States, as in other industrialized countries, social insurance programs have the common purpose of protecting workers and their families against the risk of severe financial hardship when they lose income from work because of insured-against events. In the United States those include work injury (workers' compensation), involuntary job loss (unemployment insurance) or retirement, death of a family worker or severe long-term work disability (Social Security). Coverage under social insurance programs is broadly based, generally pooling the risk of wage loss that all workers share by covering workers across the occupational, earnings, and age spectra. Such programs are closely tied to work. They are financed by contributions from earnings while people are employed, and they provide income continuity to workers and their families when earnings are lost for reasons beyond the worker's control.

Because of its expertise in social insurance, the Academy in 1991 was asked by the Chairman of the Committee on Ways and Means of the U. S.

House of Representatives and the Chairman of its Subcommittee on Social Security to undertake a comprehensive review of the Social Security disability programs, with a special emphasis on disability and work. In particular, the Academy was asked: Can an emphasis on rehabilitation and work be incorporated into the disability income programs without greatly expanding costs or weakening the right to benefits for those who cannot work? Are there ways to encourage beneficiaries to use their residual work capacity? In answering these questions, the Academy was encouraged to take into account experience in the private sector and in foreign disability income programs.

Given the Academy's on-going task, it was particularly appropriate for the Academy to collaborate with NIDRR in commissioning papers for this workshop. The purpose was to bring together current research on a range of topics that ultimately affect employment prospects for persons with work disabilities. Relevant topics include analyses of the size and composition of the working-age population who have work disabilities (variously defined), the implications of broader economic and labor market trends for the opportunities and barriers to employment that persons with disabilities face, lessons learned from varied models of linking rehabilitation to cash benefit programs, including historical experience in the United States, approaches adopted in the social insurance programs in other countries, and innovations tested by private employers and insurers in the United States. Further analyses emphasized the role of health care and personal assistance services in reducing barriers to employment in the United States.

The collaboration between our two organizations brings a rich and varied blend of perspectives to research questions related to disability income and work. NIDRR brings broad experience with how diverse policies weave together to affect the lives of Americans with disabilities. Disability policy broadly construed extends well beyond income support and rehabilitation to include education and training, technology, transportation, civil rights, job accommodations and public access. Further, the changing universe of disability highlights the close connection between new risks of work disability and social and economic conditions. The Academy brings a breadth of expertise in the design and financing of income support and health care financing through social insurance, assistance, and private insurance that includes but is not limited to disability policy. Its membership includes social insurance experts from a variety of disciplines and professions -- including actuarial science, economics, health policy, law, medicine, philosophy, political science, public administration, social work, and sociology.

The papers in this volume constitute an important companion to the Academy's report, *Balancing Security and Opportunity: The Challenge of Disability Income Policy,* which is being issued in 1996. More important, this volume stands on its own as a valuable resource for students of social policy and university faculty who offer cross-disciplinary approach to the teaching of economics, social sciences, rehabilitation and disability policy. Policy makers, journalists, and other participants in debates on disability and income security policy will gain from the papers that follow an understanding of the breadth and diversity of the population of persons with disabilities and the need for equally broadly based interventions to foster their economic security and full participation in American life.

Katherine D. Seelman, Ph.D.
Director
National Institute of Disability and Rehabilitation Research
Office of Special Education and Rehabilitation Services
U.S. Department of Education

Peter A. Diamond
Paul A. Samuelson Professor of Economics
Massachusetts Institute of Technology

President
National Academy of Social Insurance

CONTENTS

Overview   1
   Jerry L. Mashaw
   Yale University
   Virginia P. Reno
   National Academy of Social Insurance

**The Contemporary Labor Market and the Employment Prospects
of Persons with Disabilities**   33
   Edward Yelin
   Miriam Cisternas
   University of California, San Francisco

**Employment and Economic Well-Being Following
the Onset of a Disability
The Role for Public Policy**   59
   Richard V. Burkhauser
   Mary C. Daly
   Syracuse University

Employment and Benefits for People with Diverse Disabilities   103
   Walter Y. Oi
   University of Rochester

European Experiences with Disability Policy   129
   Leo J.M. Aarts
   Leiden University, the Netherlands
   Philip R. de Jong
   Erasmus University, Rotterdam and Leiden University

**Patterns of Return to Work in a Cohort
of Disabled-Worker Beneficiaries**   169
   Martynas A. Yčas
   Social Security Administration

**The Effectiveness of Financial Work Incentives in Social Security
Disability Insurance and Supplemental Security Income
Lessons from Other Transfer Programs**   189
   Hilary Williamson Hoynes
   University of California, Berkeley
   Robert Moffitt
   Johns Hopkins University

**Lessons from the Vocational Rehabilitation/Social Security
Administration Experience**   **223**
Edward Berkowitz
George Washington University
David Dean
University of Richmond

Disability and Work
Lessons from the Private Sector   **245**
H. Allan Hunt
W.E. Upjohn Institute for Employment Research
Rochelle V. Habeck
Michigan State University
Patricia Owens
UNUM Insurance Company
David Vandergoot
Center for Essential Management Services

**Quantitative Outcomes of the Transitional Employment
Training Demonstration**
Summary of Net Impacts   **273**
Aaron J. Prero
Social Security Administration

**Policies for People with Disabilities in U.S. Employment
and Training Programs**   **297**
Burt S. Barnow
Johns Hopkins University

**Improving the Return to Work of Social Security
Disability Beneficiaries**   **331**
Monroe Berkowitz
Rutgers University

People with Disabilities
Access to Health Care and Related Benefits   **357**
Robert B. Friedland
Alison Evans
National Academy on Aging

Health Care, Personal Assistance and Assistive Technology
**Are In-Kind Benefits Key to Independence
or Dependence for People with Disabilities?**   **389**
Andrew I. Batavia
*McDermott, Will and Emery
and Georgetown University School of Medicine*
Index   **413**

Disability, Work
and
Cash Benefits

BK title:

Overview

USA
I12
J15
J21
J28

Jerry L. Mashaw
Yale University
Virginia P. Reno
National Academy of Social Insurance

The papers in this volume are devoted to the analysis of disability, work, and cash benefits. The authors seek to understand the causes of work disability and the types of interventions that might enable individuals to remain at work, return to work, or enter the workforce for the first time, despite having chronic health conditions or impairments. There are several reasons for this interest, and these concerns form the backdrop for the studies included here.

First, all would agree that a life of productive employment, when it is practical, is far more desirable for individuals with disabilities and for their families and society at large than a life of relying on cash benefits as a substitute for wages. Moreover, even when persons with disabilities cannot be fully self-supporting, there may be major gains in family economic welfare and substantial contribution to aggregate productivity when impairments can be ameliorated or accommodated to permit some paid work.

Second, after a period of stability in the last half of the 1980s, the cost of Social Security disability benefits grew rapidly in the early 1990s, prompting concern about the long-term future of these programs. In 1994, Congress provided temporary additional funding for Social Security Disability Insurance (DI), but called for research to determine whether the recent growth in applications and allowances was a temporary phenomenon or a long-term trend, and, if the latter, what should be done about it.

Third, the main disability policy initiative in the 1980s focused on civil rights and culminated in the enactment of the Americans with Disabilities Act (ADA) of 1990. The Act rests on the belief that low employment rates among people with disabilities are due to prejudice and environmental barriers in public access and accommodation. Since

1

passage of the law, however, employment rates have not significantly increased, leading to new questions about what is needed to improve employment outcomes.

Finally, the rates of Social Security benefit terminations due to medical recovery or return to work have always been modest, but have reached all-time lows. This has prompted calls for new approaches to link beneficiaries to the services that will enable them to earn enough to leave the public assistance rolls completely.

These concerns form the backdrop for the discussion in this volume. The papers were presented at a conference on Disability, Work, and Cash Benefits held December 8-10, 1994 in Santa Monica, California. The conference was jointly sponsored by the private, nonprofit National Academy of Social Insurance and the National Institute for Disability and Rehabilitation Research of the U.S. Department of Education.

Who Are the Work Disabled?

A recurrent theme of all the papers is the vast diversity within the population of persons with disabilities. That diversity results not just from the range of physical or mental impairments but also from variations in age, education, prior work experience, and existing social supports, and in the possibilities for accommodation of differing impairments in distinct work environments.

At one level, determining the population of persons with work disabilities seems relatively straightforward. The work disabled are those persons who have significant physical or mental impairments that prevent these individuals from earning enough to support themselves at a decent standard of living. At another level, however, determining who has disabilities is an enormously complicated question to which a large range of responses might be given.[1] We, therefore, devote some consideration to how those with work disabilities might be categorized.

If we were concerned with everyone who has some chronic health condition or impairment that might impose a limitation on their functioning, our research would involve perhaps one-half of the entire population of the United States, including the elderly and children. If we narrow our focus to those whose impairments or health conditions limit their major activity—such as work or housework for working-age adults, activities of daily living for the elderly, and playing or attending school for children—then about 36 million would be counted, based on estimates of the household population from the National Health Interview Survey (HIS), and of the institutionalized population (LaPlante 1991, 1992; National Academy of Social Insurance (NASI) 1994).

For this volume on work and disability, our interest centers on the working-age population. If we consider working-age people who have any of a broad range of functional limitations, or disabilities, that include but are not limited to work,[2] then nearly 30 million or almost one in five Americans aged 15-64 would be counted, according to the 1991-1992 Survey of Income and Program Participation (SIPP). On the other hand, if we were concentrating only on those who have the most significant functional limitations—for example, persons who require assistance with one or more of the basic activities of daily living—we would be interested in about 1.5 million persons in the household population, or less than 1 percent of those aged 15-64; if we narrowed our focus to only those who use wheelchairs, then about 500,000 persons would be of interest (McNeil 1993).

There might be perfectly sound policy reasons to study either these very large or very small groups of "persons with disabilities." Our concern with work disability policies, however, is one that focuses on persons who have relatively severe impairments that put them at considerable risk of serious disadvantage in the labor market. These are people whose impairments pose a substantial threat to their economic well-being, but who nevertheless *might* work.

A relatively narrow subset of the work disabled consists of those who are receiving either DI or Supplemental Security Income (SSI) disability benefits. As of December 1993, this group comprised about 6.7 million working-age Americans. By statutory definition, the individuals in this group have an impairment that, when considered in light of their age, education, and work experience, makes them unable—for at least a year—to engage in substantial gainful employment (that is, with earnings of more than $500 per month). Note that while this is a severely impaired population, the receipt of cash benefits does not necessarily imply that persons who receive DI or SSI assistance cannot

work at all or that they will never again work at a level that might produce substantial income.

The cash benefit programs of interest, DI and SSI, provide modest
substitutes for wages that, on their face, would seem to make work a
preferred alternative. Social insurance payments from DI replace a disabled worker's prior earnings under a sliding scale, with lower replacement rates for higher earners. For average earners and above, the
benefits replace far less than half of what the worker had earned while
working. For low earners, whose replacement rates approach half the
worker's prior earnings, the benefits nonetheless provide a level of living that is less than the poverty threshold for an individual (figure 1).
Studies of replacement needs across the earnings range indicate that
about 70-80 percent of prior earnings is required to yield a comparable
level of living (Palmer 1994). The estimates take account of the difference in tax treatment of various sources of income and the absence of
work-related expenses. These estimates are for reasonably healthy
retirees and do not take account of the added cost associated with disability.

Figure 1. Social Security Provides Only Partial Earnings Replacement
Percent of Prior Earnings Replaced by Social Security Benefits, 1993

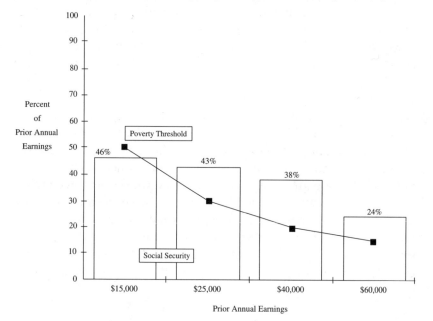

SSI provides means-tested benefits for disabled persons with little or no other income or financial assets. The full federal benefit, $458 a month in 1995, amounts to 71 percent of the poverty threshold for an individual.[3] For some, SSI supplements very low benefits from DI. Others who receive SSI do not qualify for DI because they lack the covered work experience needed before the onset of their disability. In brief, while these two programs provide a critical safety net of cash support for those who are unable to work, the modest level of benefits makes work a far preferable alternative for those who have the capacity to do so. Hence, several of the papers focus particularly on the work prospects for this population, or for some part of it (Monroe Berkowitz, Edward Berkowitz and David Dean, H. Allan Hunt et al., and Martynas A. Yčas).

We must remember, nevertheless, that there is great diversity even among the 3.8 million disabled-worker beneficiaries in the DI program, all of whom must have had significant work records before the onset of their disability. Some have life-threatening diseases such as cancer or AIDS. The majority are older workers—just over half are over the age of 50—and they tend to have impairments or diseases that are associated with aging, such as cardiovascular or respiratory illnesses, complications of diabetes or arthritis, or other musculoskeletal impairments. Over the past two decades, however, there has been an increase in the number with mental illness as their primary diagnosis, from about 11-12 percent in the 1970s to about 25 percent today; these individuals tend to be workers in their thirties and forties (U.S. Department of Health and Human Services, Social Security Administration (SSA) 1994; NASI 1994).

Working-age adults who receive SSI benefits because of disability or blindness, who numbered 3.1 million at the end of 1993, are also a very diverse group. They include about 0.6 million whose SSI benefits supplement DI; the rest do not qualify for DI because their disabilities began before they had sufficient work records (NASI 1994). Many have disabilities that started in childhood or early adulthood. Just over a quarter have mental retardation as their primary diagnosis, and an additional quarter have other mental disorders as their primary diagnosis. The paper by Aaron Prero focuses on young adults with mental retardation who receive SSI and on their experience with transitional employment services to aid their entry into the workforce.

Other authors in this volume defined the group of interest as considerably broader than those in current DI or SSI payment status, by including those who self-report in household surveys that they have a physical, mental, or other health condition that limits the kind or amount of work they can do or that prevents them from working altogether. This increases the population of concern to something between 16 and 17 million persons, approximately 10-11 percent of the working-age population, according to the 1993 Current Population Survey and the 1991-1992 SIPP (U.S. Bureau of the Census 1993; McNeil 1993).

Those who report that they have work disabilities are of special concern because a number of these individuals are not receiving cash benefits yet are at a particular disadvantage in the labor market. Consequently, they are at a high risk of having inadequate incomes and of needing to rely on some form of cash support.

Persons who report themselves as having work disabilities are more than twice as likely as other workers to be unemployed, that is, without jobs but in the labor force actively seeking work. In March 1993, when the unemployment rate for workers without disabilities was 7.3 percent, it was 16.4 percent for those aged 16-64 with work disabilities. Viewed in another way, the unemployment figures show the particular challenges faced by job seekers with disabilities: for each one who was looking for work, there were ten other persons without disabilities also seeking work. Further, the job seekers without disabilities were, on average, younger than the job seekers with disabilities (U.S. Bureau of the Census 1995).

Perhaps it should not be surprising that persons with work disabilities are far more likely than other workers to be out of the workforce altogether. That was the case in March 1993, when fully 66 percent of those with work disabilities were neither employed nor looking for work, compared to about 16 percent of other persons aged 25-64 (U.S. Bureau of the Census 1995). Similar disparities existed in past years, when the economy was stronger and overall unemployment was lower. For example, in 1988, 70 percent of persons with work disabilities and 17 percent of other persons aged 25-64 were out of the workforce (Bennefield and McNeill 1989).

Because employment is the primary means of support for most Americans, these differentials translate easily into much higher risks of poverty for persons with a work disability. Nearly 30 percent of people with a work disability had incomes below the poverty level in 1992, as compared with 10 percent of the working-age population without a disability (U.S. Bureau of the Census 1993).

Within the working-age population, both age and educational attainment are strong predictors of work disability (table 1). The risk of work disability rises sharply with age, with persons aged 55-64 being four times as likely to have a work disability (22 percent) as persons aged 16-24 (under 5 percent). The sharp increase in disability with age also indicates that the onset of work disability usually occurs during the work life—often relatively late in the work life—rather than before.

Table 1. Prevalence of Work Disability, by Age and Educational Attainment, March 1993

| | | Educational attainment | | | | |
| | | Elementary only, | High school | | College | |
Age	Total	0-8 years	1-3 years	4 years	1-3 years	4 years or more
Percentage reporting a work disability						
Total, aged 16-64	9.5	27.3	13.3	10.0	7.3	4.1
16-24	4.5	9.8	5.9	5.2	2.4	1.0
25-34	6.6	18.4	12.8	7.2	5.6	2.0
35-44	8.6	23.0	17.3	9.2	8.3	3.5
45-54	12.1	31.0	22.6	12.0	10.6	5.1
55-64	21.7	41.9	31.7	18.1	17.4	11.1
Distribution of educational attainment of total population						
Aged 25-64	100	6	9	35	26	24

SOURCE: Unpublished tabulations from the Current Population Survey, March 1993, U.S. Bureau of the Census.

The minority of working-age Americans over 25 years old who did not enter high school (6 percent) or did not complete it (9 percent) are at great risk of work disability, a risk that rises with age. On the other hand, the advantages of post-secondary education in averting or compensating for the disabling consequences of chronic health conditions are evident among workers in all age categories.

African-Americans and Hispanics also are more likely to have severe work disabilities than nonminorities. Some level of work disability was reported for 14 percent of African-Americans aged 16-64 and for about 9 percent of Hispanics and of whites. Severe work disabilities, which generally means the persons are prevented from working by their condition, were reported for 10 percent of African-Americans, 6 percent of Hispanics, and 5 percent of whites (U.S. Bureau of the Census 1993).

At the same time, according to the SIPP, a narrow majority (52 percent) of 21-64 year-olds with functional limitations were employed (McNeil 1993 p. 62). Furthermore, some persons reporting quite substantial limitations had jobs. For example, 46 percent of persons with difficulty seeing normal newsprint even with corrective lenses were employed, as were 26 percent of those unable to see newsprint, 58 percent of those unable to hear a normal conversation even with a hearing aid, 31 percent of those with difficulty walking three city blocks, and 20 percent of those requiring personal assistance in keeping track of money and bills (McNeil 1993).

These data suggest that the population of persons with work disabilities is extraordinarily heterogeneous. Individuals' work limitations result from a wide variety of medical problems that have differential impacts on success in the labor market. People have varying levels of education and radically different levels of social supports to assist them in coping with their impairments. Equally important, the employment of persons with functional limitations shows that workplaces can accommodate and individuals can adapt to quite significant disabilities under some circumstances. The question is whether and how such adaptations and accommodations can be broadened.

Changes in the labor market will obviously affect this diverse population in different ways. The progressive shift from manual labor to service and "mind work" may reduce the barriers to successful employment for those with serious physical limitations but with high intelligence and educational levels. On the other hand, the same developments disadvantage those with lower educational attainment, limited cognitive ability, and mental disorders that make it difficult for them to work in customer- or team-oriented employment situations. Hence, an overall theme of the conference proceedings was that, given the heterogeneity of the population with work disabilities and the shifting nature of the job market, there was no magic policy "bullet" that would improve employment prospects for all persons with disabilities. Any single solution, however generally available, is likely in practice to be a partial solution with respect to a subset of the total population of concern.

The Plan of the Volume

The papers have been organized into three major groupings. The introductory section concerns work disability as a function of the economic and programmatic environment and considers the ways in which labor market changes, policy interventions, and individual choices shape the workforce participation of those with disabilities. The authors in the first section emphasize different aspects of this complex interaction, drawing on both national and cross-national experience.

The second section analyzes return-to-work policies provided by both the public and the private sectors for persons with disabilities. Although the workforce participation rate for all persons with any form of chronic health condition is quite high, it drops sharply for those with a work disability and much more sharply for those with severely disabling conditions. The emphasis in this section is on the latter two groups and on various strategies for preventing a severing of workplace ties or for promoting return to work after a period of disability.

Finally, the last two papers in the volume focus on particular needs of persons with disabilities that strongly affect their workforce participation. These needs include access to health care, to personal assistance, and to assistive technologies. The policy concerns in the last section shift from specific attempts at improving return-to-work outcomes to the broader social interventions that may be the necessary preconditions for the success of more targeted return-to-work efforts.

Work Disability and the Economic and Programmatic Environment

The volume leads off with a paper by Edward Yelin and Miriam Cisternas entitled "The Contemporary Labor Market and the Employment Prospects of Persons with Disabilities." The authors' interest is in the similarities and differences between the workforce experience of those with and without a disability, given these workers' other characteristics and changes in the labor market itself. As do all the authors, Yelin and Cisternas find that workers with disabilities are quite heterogeneous in terms of their age, gender, prior work history, education, and skill levels. Generally, these characteristics are predictors of labor force success, so they should be expected to have similar effects for those with disabilities. Indeed, that is the authors' finding. On the other hand, it is clear from the data that persons with disabilities are uniquely disadvantaged in labor market competition. With respect to either cyclical or structural changes in the economy, individuals with disabilities seem to be the leading edge out of the labor market, and they lag behind other workers in returning to work.

These results are particularly strong for certain workers, such as males over 50, but are less strong for other groups, such as young females entering the labor market. Disability thus seems to amplify negative effects for those who are already disadvantaged by changes in the contemporary labor market. Conversely, disability may have a lesser effect on those who have been entering the labor market in increasing numbers. Yelin and Cisternas caution that we currently have relatively poor models of how the labor market is shifting. Moreover, no one has yet analyzed data concerning persons with disabilities in relation to newer descriptions of the characteristics of the labor force, such as the increasingly important distinction between "core" and "peripheral" workers.

In their paper, "Employment and Economic Well-Being Following the Onset of a Disability: The Role for Public Policy," Richard V. Burkhauser and Mary C. Daly take a different cut at understanding the workforce participation rates of persons with disabilities. Through careful manipulation of data from the Panel Study of Income Dynamics (PSID), they are able to trace the employment history of persons who have an onset of a work disability and to analyze the transition out of and back into work by these persons. The authors find that first, most persons who report the onset of work limitations are employed after that onset, with only the most severe conditions leading to an ultimate transition entirely out of the workforce. Second, the transition out of the workforce is relatively slow. Most persons who experience a disabling event still have significant attachment to the workforce during the first five years following that event.

Third, those who are never forced to sever their ties to the workforce completely have considerably better success in maintaining their position in it. There is substantial return to work by even those persons who spend a year out of the workforce, but never leaving seems to be strongly associated with longer-term retention. Burkhauser and Daly thus stress the importance of accommodation and early intervention in preventing long-term work disability. They urge a renewed emphasis on policy interventions that would reenforce both accommodation and the worker's desire to maintain attachment to a job.

In his paper, "Employment and Benefits for People with Diverse Disabilities," Walter Oi underlines both the diversity of persons with impairments and the poor labor force results of those with a work disability. He is particularly concerned with the policy environment within which such persons must determine whether to remain in the workforce or to move into a relatively permanent benefit status. Oi is critical of both the existing major cash benefit programs and of the ADA for their failure to focus explicitly on the diversity of the population that they serve.

In analyzing the work decisions individuals face from the perspective of economic theory, Oi observes that poor health tips the work-leisure trade-off on several dimensions. First, it makes work more difficult, thereby reducing the individual's preference for employment; it can lower the individual's wage rate, thereby decreasing the financial return from work; and finally, disability steals time by requiring more attention to "maintaining the human agent," leaving less time for work, leisure, or both.

Attributes of the disabling condition also influence whether work is an economically rational outcome for the individual or for society at large, according to Oi. The severity of the impairment clearly is a factor. Other considerations are the age at onset, the anticipated duration of the condition, and its impact on life expectancy. Both age at onset and life expectancy influence the returns that can be anticipated from investment in human capital, such as training or preparation for a new career. Duration of an impairment is often difficult to predict but is critical to the worker's response to its onset. If the duration is believed, or hoped, to be only temporary, the rational investment might be in curing or in reversing the condition by having the individual remain away from work to rest and recuperate. On the other hand, persons who have conditions with early onset, which are expected to be permanent but not life-threatening, are the best candidates for investment in human capital, training, and return-to-work efforts. Oi observes that recipients of DI and SSI tend to be older and to have more serious, life-threatening conditions. They are not representative of the larger population reported in surveys to have a work disability, and they are not particularly good candidates for return-to-work efforts. He concludes that disability policy needs to draw proper distinctions in order to target the remedies offered by income support, training, wage subsidies, and accommodations to the particular subsets of the population for whom they are appropriate. To be treated fairly, people in different circumstances have to be treated differently.

In the last paper of this section, "European Experiences with Disability Policy," Leo J.M. Aarts and Philip R. de Jong provide a masterful and concise description of four different European systems. Because this chapter gives us both an historical account and a cross-sectional comparison, it is difficult to summarize in a few words. Four points appear to be particularly salient. First, our West European neighbors—the Netherlands, the United Kingdom, Germany, and Sweden—have experimented with a number of different approaches to disability policy. This is true both within individual systems and across the four systems studied. Second, the data suggest that all four of these systems have higher public expenditures for disability programs than does the United States, whether measured in terms of the prevalence of disability benefit receipt or the share of gross domestic product allocated to disability benefits, rehabilitation, and employment programs. Third, these higher disability benefit expenditures occur despite policies that emphasize rehabilitation, public-sector jobs, private employer quotas or subsidies, and partial pensions to encourage employment. Finally, in evaluating the consequences of disability income policy, incentives matter, not just those faced by workers with chronic health conditions, but those faced by employers, by disability adjudicators, and by those offering services to workers with disabilities.

Return-to-Work Policy

In the first paper in this section, "Patterns of Return to Work in a Cohort of Disabled-Worker Beneficiaries," Martynas Yčas analyzes data from the New Beneficiary Survey and from subsequent samples sometimes characterized as the "New Beneficiary Data System." He cautions that his particular analysis is limited to persons who survived about a decade after entering the DI rolls. As such, it excludes about four in ten of the original group, because they had died. Relying on his own analysis and that of others, Yčas seeks to understand who among the survivors might have been prime candidates for return to work after they entered the disability benefit rolls.

Yčas' results are complex, nuanced, and tentative, but several findings stand out in fairly sharp relief and buttress Oi's conceptual approach. First, when the results are controlled for age, reported health status seems to be the primary determinant of labor market participation. Second, age is strongly predictive of the likely return to work or of the substantial labor force participation of beneficiaries. Workers over age 50 or 55 seem to be poor candidates for return-to-work intervention, while the (considerably smaller) group of comparatively young workers has much better prospects.

These findings are not terribly surprising, but they support certain policy conclusions. On one hand, these data suggest that current policy—making qualification for benefits somewhat easier for workers over age 50—is probably justified. Yčas suggests that the criteria should perhaps be relaxed somewhat further. These older workers are more like "retirees" than they are like younger disabled workers. By contrast, the failure to pursue the prospects for medical recovery or return to work with respect to younger beneficiaries may be overlooking a substantial pool of potential labor force returnees.

The paper by Hilary Williamson Hoynes and Robert Moffitt is entitled "The Effectiveness of Financial Work Incentives in Social Security Disability Insurance and Supplemental Security Income: Lessons from Other Transfer Programs." The lessons that Hoynes and Moffitt give us are highly cautionary. Work incentives designed to lower the marginal tax rate on earnings of existing beneficiaries have theoretically ambiguous net effects on program participation and on work effort. The empirical literature suggests that net increases in employment, if any, are quite small overall. The ambiguity results from the fact that lower marginal tax rates increase the incentives for work effort by those already on the rolls but simultaneously may attract new entrants and forestall exit by those who could then earn more without losing their benefit status. Numerous studies in nondisability programs suggest that these offsetting effects make standard work incentive provisions relatively ineffective in either increasing employment or reducing program participation.

Hoynes and Moffitt are careful to point out that the population of persons with disabilities may be different from that in other cash support programs, and that the complex rules in the DI and SSI programs present somewhat different incentive structures from provisions found in Aid to Families with Dependent Children, the Food Stamp program, or a negative income tax. Nevertheless, the data concerning work incentives related to receipt of disability benefits also suggest modest responsiveness by disabled beneficiaries to changes in the economic incentives built into the programs. Given these sobering findings, Hoynes and Moffitt suggest that new policy instruments, such as the Earned Income Tax Credit, might have significantly greater effects in increasing work effort among all income transfer program beneficiaries, including those receiving disability benefits.

Edward Berkowitz and David Dean have a somewhat similar story to tell in their paper, "Lessons from the Vocational Rehabilitation Link for DI Beneficiaries." While virtually everyone agrees that rehabilitation and return to work are preferred to labor force nonparticipation and receipt of disability benefits, there is little evidence to suggest that rehabilitation policy has been or can be made effective for a large segment of the population with such significant work disabilities that they receive DI benefits.

Although there have been strong proponents of incorporating rehabilitation into the DI program dating back to the earliest proposals for public disability insurance, both politics and objective factors have prevented a fruitful marriage between DI and vocational rehabilitation (VR). As a matter of disability policy, Congress has stipulated that DI trust funds could be used to finance rehabilitation only for beneficiaries, not for applicants or denied applicants. Yet it is an article of faith in the rehabilitation community that early intervention holds the best prospects for promoting return to work. Further, the legislative rationale for spending DI trust funds for rehabilitation is to reduce trust fund expenditures. Hence, the cost of rehabilitation should not exceed the benefit savings that accrue when beneficiaries leave the rolls and return to work. Since 1981, DI has paid only retrospectively for VR successes among beneficiaries, and the number of successes has been small.

On the other hand, the problem is not just the micro-politics of program finance. On average, persons with significant work disabilities who receive DI benefits are not particularly good candidates for vocational rehabilitation services. Hence, it is not obvious that large numbers would be successfully returned to work by vocational rehabilitation activities, even if potential beneficiaries could be targeted before obtaining beneficiary status. Still, dramatic program shifts in the direction of the rehabilitation ideal might have substantial impacts, particularly with respect to younger workers.

The team of H. Allan Hunt, Rochelle V. Habeck, Patricia Owens, and David Vandergoot, has a much more encouraging story to tell in "Disability and Work: Lessons from the Private Sector." Through the review of case studies of private-sector interventions, these authors find that an aggressive approach to managing disability claims has significant payoffs in maintaining employees in their current jobs or in some job with their present employer. Firms use a multitude of strategies, but each successful strategy is characterized by (1) early intervention, (2) a commitment to the twin goals of illness and injury prevention and return to work, and (3) continuous attention to the medical, vocational rehabilitation, and accommodation needs of their disabled workers. As this study recognizes, private sector employers have major advantages in carrying out these aggressive return-to-work strategies in comparison to public programs like DI or SSI. Indeed, the authors note that these public programs provide places for firms to lay part of their potential long-term disability burdens in the cases where a return to work is not achieved.

Nevertheless, these authors are optimistic that public policy could be reshaped to provide incentives for return to work, early intervention, and strong case management. They are under no illusions that this could be accomplished without major changes in public policy, including, among other things, the elimination of waiting periods, the provision of partial disability payments, and enormous increases in services and supports to those at risk of long-term disability. These would be costly interventions, but, in these authors' views, would be appropriate public policy by comparison with the system that now sorts individuals into two lumpy baskets: the disabled who receive an entitlement to long-term benefits and the nondisabled who receive virtually nothing.

The uncertain returns to focused public interventions to promote work are underlined by Aaron Prero's paper, "Quantitative Outcomes of the Transitional Employment Training Demonstration: Summary of Net Impacts." Prero provides a retrospective analysis of a transitional employment training demonstration program for mentally retarded adults sponsored by the Social Security Administration (SSA). The demonstration was conducted as a formal experiment with randomly assigned participants and control group members. At issue was the effect of placement in real jobs in the community, with training by job coaches, on the earnings and SSI outcomes of a cohort of SSI recipients, ranging from 18 to 40 years of age. The six-year experiment showed a small decline in receipt of SSI, but the dollar savings from that decline were much smaller than the costs of the training provided. There was a similar result for earnings. The author cautions that these negative findings should not be over-interpreted. When the benefits of training were measured only in terms of savings in SSI payments, they were less than the cost of the training. Nonetheless, the trainees' employment rate, earnings, and income did increase as a result of their participation, suggesting positive outcomes by measures other than SSI program savings. Moreover, the study cannot exclude the possibility that more precisely targeting services to groups where gains are likely to be large might produce better results in terms of program savings.

In "Policies for People with Disabilities in U.S. Employment and Training Programs," Burt Barnow looks at a broader range of initiatives to improve work outcomes for persons with disabilities. Included in his review are vocational rehabilitation funded through the Rehabilitation Services Administration; vocational education funded under the Perkins Act; the Job Training Partnership Act, Title II, training for economically disadvantaged adults and youth; labor exchange activities; the Targeted Jobs Tax Credit and testing programs run by the U.S.

Employment Service; and the Special Minimum Wage Program for people with disabilities administered by the Employment Standards Administration. In general, Barnow finds very modest effects from any of these interventions.

It is not clear whether these results flow from the inherent difficulty of the task or from the structure of the programs. The employment service, for example, has a very low application rate by disabled individuals for its programs, but when disabled individuals do apply, they receive greater-than-average services and their placement rates are above the average for all applicants. On the other hand, programs like the Targeted Jobs Tax Credit seem to serve very few people with disabilities and almost certainly could be allowed to expire with no adverse effects. In general, Barnow finds that there is no overall strategy for assessing the employment and training needs of the population of persons with disabilities or for developing a comprehensive approach to serving that population. Little serious work has been done in evaluating the capacity of existing programs to help those with a disability. Barnow concludes, therefore, that there is currently no way of ascertaining whether sufficient resources are being devoted to improving the workforce participation rate of persons with work disabilities.

The section concludes with a paper by Monroe Berkowitz, "Improving the Return to Work of Social Security Disability Beneficiaries," which proposes an entirely new approach to involving the private sector in return-to-work efforts. Berkowitz suggests that the creative energies of the private sector be harnessed by providing substantial incentives to successful return-to-work activity. Providers who manage to return beneficiaries to work and to eliminate the need for further DI payments would receive a percentage of the long-term savings to the trust fund attributable to their efforts. A novel aspect of the Berkowitz proposal is the incentive to maintain prior beneficiaries in the workforce by making compensation payments to providers on an annual basis, conditional upon the recipient of services remaining off the DI program rolls. Given the high risks involved, it is uncertain how many providers could be attracted by this proposal or what percentage of the population could be served effectively. On the other hand, given the extremely low success rates of current return-to-work interventions and its provision for paying providers only after benefit savings accrue, the Berkowitz proposal has obvious attractions.

The Role of Health Care and In-Kind Benefits in Promoting Work

In "People with Disabilities: Access to Health Care and Related Benefits," the findings of Robert Friedland and Alison Evans suggest that our current arrangements are not "work friendly," but that they may be quite difficult to change. Persons with disabilities face substantial barriers to obtaining health care coverage in private markets. This situation makes these individuals difficult to hire and retain and increases their incentive to participate in public programs with relatively comprehensive attachments for health care coverage—Medicaid for SSI recipients and Medicare for DI beneficiaries after a 24-month waiting period. The recent failure of comprehensive health care reform is particularly salient from this perspective.

The authors discuss a wide range of piecemeal reforms to the regulation of health insurance practices and modifications of the current Medicaid and Medicare programs. However, these initiatives hold out modest prospects for assisting persons with disabilities to maintain needed coverage while returning to the workforce. Even if available, employment-based coverage frequently does not provide the range of services required by those with significant disabilities. Moreover, a number of the incremental reforms discussed might exacerbate work disincentives, perpetuate inequities across different groups, or accelerate the decline of the availability of private insurance for the nondisabled. Recent state initiatives seem designed more to spread a thin public health care dollar over a greater number of eligible people than to provide the chronic care or long-term care coverage options that are often most needed by persons with disabilities. In short, if the goal is to uncouple health care provision from cash benefits entitlement, and thus to eliminate incentives to seek cash benefits in order to get needed health care, we seem to be making little progress.

Andrew Batavia attacks these work disincentives through a different route in "Health Care, Personal Assistance, and Assistive Technology: Are In-Kind Benefits Key to Independence for People with Disabilities?" Batavia postulates that the objective of disability policy is to permit independent living by persons with a disability. He recognizes, however, that this objective consists of two potentially conflicting subordinate goals: (1) assisting disabled individuals to live in their communities (the support goal), and (2) assisting disabled individuals to live self-sufficiently (the employment goal). In his view, the linking of in-kind benefits such as health care, personal assistance, and assistive technology to participation in cash benefit programs may promote the support goal but is likely to have the negative effects that Friedland and Evans postulate on the employment goal. Batavia's solution is to uncouple in-kind benefits from cash payments by providing benefits through cash equivalents, such as vouchers or refundable tax credits, not tied to eligibility for income support. The cash equivalents would be phased out incrementally as incomes rise. Hence, Batavia would provide benefits to people with disabilities regardless of their employment status. Assuming that administrative and fiscal difficulties could be surmounted, a major assumption, Batavia argues that such programs would give persons with disabilities greater control in achieving their twin goals of living in their communities while remaining self-supporting.

Policy Implications

We now return to the policy issues that are the backdrop for our discussion: the rising cost of cash benefit programs; the limited success to date of attempts to improve employment of persons with disabilities through legal remedies called for in the ADA; and the all-time low in the rate at which persons are leaving cash benefit rolls because of medical recovery or return to work.

Balancing Policy Goals: Income Support and Work

We started with the fundamental belief that productive employment, when it is feasible, is the optimal outcome for both individuals with disabilities and for society at large. At the same time, income support during periods of long-term work incapacity is an essential element of disability policy. Virtually all industrialized countries have some type of social insurance system for ensuring income support to workers who have lost their earning capacity due to illness, injury, or chronic health conditions. Most also provide social assistance for those who do not achieve a basic minimum income from either work or social insurance benefits. Initiatives, therefore, must necessarily strive for a balance between policies that facilitate employment and those that ensure a fair and decent level of income support during periods of work incapacity. Further, that balance has to be found in an environment where new public spending for social welfare purposes is sharply constrained.

The paper by Aarts and de Jong offers a cross-national perspective for evaluating U.S. disability policy. Several observations emerge. First, if the success of disability policy is equated with low national spending on cash support for disabled workers (an equation that some would dispute), then the United States is highly successful when compared with its European neighbors. Among the five countries reviewed, federal spending for long-term disability benefits in 1991 was lowest in the United States, at 0.7 percent of gross domestic product (GDP). This compared with 1.9 percent in the United Kingdom, which has strict eligibility rules and relatively low benefits; 2 percent in Germany, which is notable for its emphasis on "rehabilitation before disability pensions"; 3.3 percent in Sweden, a mature welfare state that emphasizes both rehabilitation and publicly financed employment; and a whopping 4.6 percent in the Netherlands, which generally serves as a model of runaway disability costs not to be emulated elsewhere. When federal spending for vocational rehabilitation and employment programs for persons with disabilities is added to benefit spending, the United States remains the most frugal, with total disability spending of 0.75 percent of GDP compared to 2.22 percent in Germany, for example, where both rehabilitation and private sector employment are more strongly emphasized and subsidized.

The relatively low spending on long-term disability benefits in the United States is even more noteworthy because, as Aarts and de Jong point out, the United States does not have other policy instruments in place that reduce pressure on disability pensions. All of the other countries studied have systems that aid in preventing reliance on long-term disability benefits, such as universal short-term sickness benefits, which provide support while rehabilitation and return to work are tried; national health care coverage for all residents regardless of changes in their disability or employment status; and comprehensive programs to help pay for long-term supports such as personal assistance or assistive technology and devices. As Batavia and Friedland and Evans discuss, the lack of secure financing of health care and related long-term supports poses severe constraints on the employment choices people with disabilities face in the United States. To date, efforts to remedy this problem through comprehensive health care reform have not been successful. Incremental reforms that target particular subgroups may have better prospects.

However, the fact that the United States spends less than other industrialized countries on disability remedies does not, in itself, suggest obvious reforms in a period of tight budget constraints. It also does not answer other important questions. What caused the rapid growth in Social Security disability benefit claims and allowances during the early 1990s? Is it a temporary phenomenon or a long-term trend? What can be done to improve the employment outlook for workers with disabilities? In particular, how might we improve the return-to-work prospects of those who receive benefits?

Cyclical Changes in the Economy

"The economy matters" is the clear message in the papers by Yelin and Cisternas, Oi, Burkhauser and Daly, and others. Cyclical changes—periods of economic expansion and recessions—alter the choices available to both employers and people with disabilities. When the economy is growing and firms are expanding, employers are in a much better position to accommodate workers with disabilities. Employers' assessment of what constitutes a reasonable accommodation may be more expansive when firms are competing for skilled workers and they have valued employees that they do not want to lose. On the other hand, when firms are laying off employees, opportunities decline for workers with disabilities along with the prospects for other workers, according to Yelin and Cisternas. They also find that people with disabilities—particularly older workers—are less likely to return to work when the economy improves.

For these kinds of reasons, cyclical changes in the economy affect the number of people claiming and receiving Social Security disability benefits. In fact, the recent, unexpected growth in DI claims and allowances coincided with an economic recession in 1990-1991. The number of people applying for and being allowed benefits reached an all-time high in 1992. Since then, the number of new entrants to the DI rolls has leveled off and declined. The number of people receiving benefits, however, continues to grow because more people are being added to the benefit rolls than are leaving. Policy approaches to address the low rate of terminations from the benefit rolls are discussed subsequently.

The condition of the economy also influences the effectiveness of the ADA because it alters the environment in which decisions about reasonable accommodation are made. Momentum for enacting the ADA built during a period of sustained economic growth during the 1980s. The actual implementation of the ADA, however, fell on the heels of the recession of 1990-1991. Perhaps it should not be surprising that the beneficial effects of the ADA on employment of people with disabilities are being realized more slowly than had been hoped during its development and enactment.

Structural Changes in Employment and Wage Differentials

Structural changes in the economy over the past two decades have also differentially affected opportunities for workers with disabilities. Technological advancements and the decline in physically demanding jobs may bring better prospects for skilled workers with physical impairments. On the other hand, increased emphasis on intellect, advanced education, and flexibility may make cognitive limitations or mental illness greater impediments to work. In general, changes in the demand for workers with different aptitudes and education have brought about increased disparity in opportunities and earnings between highly educated and less-skilled workers (NASI 1994). This disparity is also likely to become evident within the highly diverse population of people with disabilities. In noting the great diversity within the disabled population, Oi's analysis suggests that the ADA remedies—banning discrimination, requiring reasonable accommodation, and breaking down architectural barriers—will be most effective for highly skilled workers who have faced these obstructions in the past. However, workers who face the double disadvantages of low skills and physical or mental impairments may need other remedies.

Burkhauser and Daly offer a solution for the problem faced by low-skilled workers with disabilities. They propose a wage subsidy built on the concept of the Earned Income Tax Credit, but one that is targeted at workers with disabilities. The subsidy is seen as a way to encourage entry into the workforce among young persons and to delay withdrawal from the workforce among older workers. For young workers with developmental disabilities, a wage subsidy encourages employment, even part-time or at low pay, that over the long run can improve human capital through on-the-job experience. Burkhauser and Daly also view the subsidy as a means of encouraging older workers with disabilities to remain at work even if their hours of employment or wage rates decline.

Hoynes and Moffitt's analysis lends support to the wage-subsidy proposal. Hoynes and Moffitt suggest that a wage subsidy—modeled after the EITC for workers with disabilities—might be more cost effective than adding new work incentives to the DI program. They note that expanding DI by offering a partial benefit offset to those who return to work is likely to increase program expenditures and to yield ambiguous results, at best, in terms of net increases in labor supply.

Oi observes that, because disability steals time, part-time or flexible work schedules may be the kinds of accommodations some employees need. If such adjustments are accompanied by lower wages for workers in general, that result is likely to occur for workers with disabilities as well. A publicly financed wage subsidy, like that proposed by Burkhauser and Daly, is one way to alleviate these effects.

Oi also argues for a wholly different approach to cash support, which he offers as a substitute for DI. This alternative is based on the veterans' compensation concept of paying individuals based on their impairments, irrespective of the impairments' effects on earning capacity. While this approach was not specifically modeled by Hoynes and Moffitt, it appears to hold many of the same risks of increased program participation. The eligible population of benefit recipients would be significantly expanded even if eligibility were limited to persons with an impairment rating of 50 percent or more on the scale used for veterans' compensation. Paying benefits to a larger population of persons with disabilities, regardless of their ability to work, would significantly raise benefit costs unless current benefits were substantially reduced, and it would clearly result in more workers among the benefit recipients. As far as increasing the amount of labor supplied by the target population, Hoynes and Moffitt's analysis suggests that the outcomes, at best, would be ambiguous. Oi's proposal, however, for targeting return-to-work efforts on young persons with disabilities is consistent with that of Monroe Berkowitz, as discussed in the following section.

Rehabilitation and Return-to-Work Services

Prero's analysis raises important issues about the purpose and financing of rehabilitation services. One obvious goal is that of improving the quality of life and the community integration of persons who receive services. That, clearly, is among the objectives of the federal/state vocational rehabilitation program. The program is required by law to give first priority to persons with the most significant impediments to employment, and it is permitted to define rehabilitation success as placement in either competitive or sheltered employment or in unpaid homemaking activities.

As Prero notes, a different rationale has been used to justify the financing of rehabilitation services out of funds earmarked for cash benefit programs. In this case, the purpose is to reduce benefit expenditures. The measure of success is whether the client returns to work at a level of earnings that results in savings in cash benefits exceeding the cost of rehabilitation provided. To this end, services would be appropriately targeted on those with the best prospects of leaving the benefit rolls because of those services. This is the rationale used by private insurers, according to Hunt et al.

Monroe Berkowitz proposes a radical new approach to linking DI beneficiaries with return-to-work services, based on this latter rationale. The plan offers consumers a choice in selecting their private or public provider of services; it enlists private sector providers in the task of returning DI beneficiaries to work; and it offers them incentives to produce that result by basing their payment, not on the cost of services they give, but on their success as measured by their clients' return to work and departure from the benefit rolls. Providers would be paid only after their success had been documented, and the amounts would be based on savings to the trust funds (from benefits not paid) as those savings accrue.

This reimbursement mechanism encourages service providers to select clients with the best long-term prospects for employment. It naturally targets those identified by Yčas and Oi as being good candidates for return-to-work efforts—the small, but growing, minority of DI beneficiaries who are relatively young and have stable impairments that are not life-threatening.

Because service providers are paid for their results, not for their inputs, they would have incentives to use whatever other resources they are able to locate. This strategy could include negotiating accommodations with an employer, or assisting clients in gaining access to the complex array of existing vocational education, training, and employment programs described by Barnow. Presumably, rehabilitation providers would build on the lessons learned from private sector employers and insurers about successful return-to-work methods, which are discussed by Hunt et al.

A question remains as to whether private sector rehabilitation providers would choose to participate in a system in which they would be expected to assume the financial risks and would be paid only after success had been demonstrated. Some payments to providers may be needed as their clients achieve milestones along the way toward fully withdrawing from the benefit rolls.

In their paper, Edward Berkowitz and David Dean recount the sometimes fitful marriage between DI and publicly financed vocational rehabilitation services. However, a glimmer of good news exists in their findings about the cost-effectiveness of investing in rehabilitation services for beneficiaries. Between 1965 and 1980, the Social Security Act provided for allocating up to 1.5 percent of DI benefit expenditures for vocational rehabilitation services to return DI beneficiaries to employment. There were few strings attached to the way in which public VR agencies expended the funds, and guidelines for their use were not strictly enforced. Audits by the General Accounting Office concluded that the monies were not well-managed, and the policy was abandoned in 1981. Nevertheless, even the most critical of the cost-benefit evaluations of that program, poorly managed as it may have been, found that it returned savings to the DI trust fund of about $1.15 for each $1.00 spent for rehabilitation services. Subsequent and more refined cost-benefit analyses found savings ranging from about $1.40 to $2.70 for each $1.00 spent (McManus 1981). These studies suggest that there are savings to be gained by financing rehabilitation services from DI trust funds. With the proper mix of incentives and with accountability for service providers, some payment to providers for milestones their clients reach on the road to leaving the benefit rolls could be justified on cost-benefit grounds.

Administration and Disability Management

Aarts and de Jong emphasize that administrative accountability matters. They attribute part of the runaway cost of disability benefits in Holland to an administrative structure where adjudicators—disability boards made up of employer and labor representatives—are not accountable for the public costs of the decisions they make to allow benefits. In the United States, SSA, which administers the DI and SSI programs, is directly accountable.

There is, nevertheless, a parallel to this problem in American budget policy. Congressional policy makers work under a set of rules whereby disability cash benefits themselves are outside of a budgetary cap (as they are in other European countries studied), but the funds used to administer those benefits must compete with all other "discretionary" spending, which is sharply constrained. Still, private sector experience, recounted by Hunt et al., shows that sound disability management more than pays for itself. Some types of disability management initiatives available to private employers and insurers are not available to SSA without costly changes in policy; such initiatives include the elimination of the five-month waiting period for cash benefits or of first-day coverage under Medicare. However, other steps would be possible; these would include individualized attention in order to correctly decide who is eligible for benefits, who should be referred for rehabilitation, and who should be subject to periodic review of continuing eligibility, and in order to make accurate and fair decisions on the outcome of those reviews. The United States currently spends about 2.6 percent of DI outlays on administration, considerably less than the percentage for private insurers. Both the backlogs of pending applications and appeals and the shortfall in conducting the number of continuing disability reviews required by law suggest that the United States is not investing enough in administration. SSA's actuaries estimate that investments in continuing disability reviews, even when only a small proportion result in benefit terminations, pay for themselves in benefit savings.

Conclusions

Some answers emerge to the questions raised earlier. What caused the recent rapid growth in disability benefit costs? Is it a temporary phenomenon or a long-term trend? What can be done to improve the employment opportunities of workers with disabilities? In particular, how might we improve the return-to-work prospects of those who receive benefits?

First, the economy matters. The economic recession of 1990-1991 contributed to the growth in claims and allowances. The number of new benefit awards reached an all-time high in 1992 and has since declined As such, the surge in benefit awards appears to be a wave rather than a long-term trend.

The number of people receiving benefits, however, continues to grow because more people are entering the rolls than are leaving. There are four reasons people leave the rolls: they die; they reach age 65, when they are shifted to the retirement benefit rolls; they medically recover; or they return to work despite the continuation of their impairments. The last two reasons have always accounted for a small portion of benefit terminations, but they are now at a record low. Benefit termination rates because of retirement also are down. Part of the explanation is that more people are entering the rolls at younger ages, that is, under age 50. This is due, in part, to population changes (NASI 1994). The baby boom is now in the 35-to-50 age range. Just as these individuals swell the ranks of the labor force, they add to the ranks of the disability rolls when they become disabled. In addition, as more women are in the paid workforce, they qualify for social insurance benefits when they become disabled. Had they been housewives, as many of their mothers were, they would not have had disability income protection. To the extent that the low rate of terminations is due to the bulge of the baby boom cohort, it is a temporary phenomenon rather than a long-term trend. In the next decade, as the baby boom ages, we can expect more entrants to the disability rolls to be over 50 years old and therefore to have relatively shorter duration on these rolls.

The historically low rate of benefit terminations due to return to work or medical recovery may be more amenable to policy prescriptions. First, the innovative proposal for enlisting private sector providers in offering return-to-work services to DI beneficiaries could improve employment outcomes for some subset of beneficiaries, particularly those who are relatively young and have stable, nonfatal impairments.

In addition, as discussed by several authors, a wage subsidy for disabled persons, patterned after the EITC, would improve returns to work for persons attempting to leave the benefit rolls. Perhaps more importantly, it could reduce entries onto the cash benefit rolls, first, by encouraging young workers to enter the labor force, and second, by encouraging older workers to delay their exit from the labor force even though their hours of work or wage rates decline because of the onset of a chronic health condition. The wage subsidy also could help increase the effectiveness of the ADA in promoting employment and accommodations for young or low-skilled workers with disabilities.

Finally, the rate of benefit terminations due to medical recovery is expected to be relatively low because of the nature of the strict test of long-term disability that is used. But SSA's own estimates indicate that this rate could be improved if more continuing reviews were conducted. Further, the effectiveness of both return to work and medical reviews could be enhanced by better disability management when claims are first allowed. Sorting new beneficiaries according to their prospects for either medical improvement or return to work and informing individuals of those expectations seem to be easily transferable lessons from private sector disability management. Allocating adequate resources to more fine-tuned management of initial disability awards and conducting ongoing disability reviews are expected to more than pay for themselves through benefit savings. To date, however, obstacles to allocating those resources through the federal budget process have proven insurmountable.

The volume's overarching theme is that the population of working-age persons with disabilities is extraordinarily diverse. Therefore, disability policy, broadly construed, has to match that diversity with a wide range of remedies appropriate for different subsets of the population. Those diverse remedies include the following: access to health care and related services, which is highly problematic for some persons with disabilities in the United States; civil rights protections and employer accommodations, as called for in the ADA; wage subsidies for low-income workers with disabilities; and access to appropriate rehabilitation, which may be financed from different sources, such as the federal/state VR program, employers, insurers, or public cash benefit programs, for different subsets of the population. More generalized education and employment policies also can be considered as part of disability policy. To the extent that such approaches enable Americans to gain and maintain the ability to compete in today's labor market, they aid in preventing even quite significant impairments from resulting in work disability. Finally, cash support programs—social insurance and social assistance—remain critical elements of disability policy for those who experience periods of work incapacity.

NOTES

1. See particularly LaPlante (1992), and LaPlante, Miller, and Miller (1992).

2. The functional limitations are defined in the 1991-1992 Survey of Income and Program Participation to include the following: a work disability; a functional limitation in seeing, hearing, speaking, lifting, climbing stairs, or walking; a limitation in activities of daily living that include bathing, eating, toileting, getting around inside the home, getting in or out of bed or a chair; or instrumental activities of daily living that include going outside the home, keeping track of money and bills, preparing meals, doing light housework, or using the telephone; or a mental or emotional disability.

3. The poverty threshold for an individual under age 65 was $7,357 in 1993, while federal SSI benefits were $434 a month. Both are adjusted each year by changes in the Consumer Price Index.

References

Bennefield, Robert L., and John M. McNeil. 1989. "Labor Force Status and Other Characteristics of Persons with a Work Disability: 1981 to 1988." U.S. Bureau of the Census, Current Population Reports Series, P-23, No. 160, July.

LaPlante, Mitchell P. 1991. "The Demographics of Disability." In *The Americans with Disabilities Act: From Policy to Practice*, Jane West, ed. New York: Milbank Memorial Fund.

_____. 1992. "How Many Americans Have a Disability?" *Disability Statistics Abstract,* No. 5. National Institute on Disability and Rehabilitation Research, U.S. Department of Education, December.

LaPlante, Mitchell P., Shawn Miller, and Karen Miller. 1992. "People with Work Disability in the U.S.," *Disability Statistics Abstract*, No. 4. National Institute on Disability and Rehabilitation Research, U.S. Department of Education, May.

McManus, Leo A. 1981. "Evaluation of Disability Insurance Savings Due to Beneficiary Rehabilitation," *Social Security Bulletin* (February): 19-26.

McNeil, John M. 1993. "Americans with Disabilities: 1991-1992, Data from the Survey of Income and Program Participation." U.S. Bureau of the Census, Current Population Reports Series P70-33, December.

National Academy of Social Insurance. 1994. *Preliminary Status Report of the Disability Policy Panel. Rethinking Disability Policy: The Role of Income, Health Care, Rehabilitation and Related Services in Fostering Independence*. Washington, DC: NASI.

Palmer, Bruce A. 1994. "Retirement Income Replacement Ratios: An Update," *Benefits Quarterly* (Second Quarter): 59-75.

_____. 1993. "Poverty in the United States: 1992." Current Population Reports Series, P60-185, September.

_____. 1995. Unpublished tabulations of the 1993 and 1994 Current Population Surveys.

U.S. Department of Health and Human Services. Social Security Administration. 1993a. *Annual Statistical Supplement to the Social Security Bulletin*.

_____. 1993b. "Statistical Notes from the New Beneficiary Data System," *Social Security Bulletin* (Fall): 88-94.

_____. 1994. *Annual Statistical Supplement to the Social Security Bulletin*.

Work Disability and the Economic and Programmatic Environment

The Contemporary Labor Market and the Employment Prospects of Persons with Disabilities

USA
I,2
J/S
J21

Edward Yelin
Miriam Cisternas   J28
University of California, San Francisco

The employment of persons with disabilities is a central focus of disability policy, for the positive reason that the Americans with Disabilities Act of 1990 (ADA) targets increasing jobs (Jones 1991) and for the negative reason that the rise in the number of beneficiaries has jeopardized the fiscal integrity of public and private disability insurance programs (Stapleton, Barnow, Coleman, Furman, and Antonelli 1994). In trying to project the work prospects of persons with disabilities in the near future, the labor market dynamics of the recent past may be our best guide. While major discontinuities in long-term patterns do occur, and cyclical downturns interrupt the patterns, overall employment trends are remarkably stable.

There have only been two major discontinuities in the past fifty years, the first occurring with the end of World War II, when all the Rosie the Riveters went home to take care of their children and were replaced by men returning from the war, and the last occurring with the energy crisis of 1973, when declining real wages spawned an increase in the proportion of women working (Evans and Nelson 1989; Levy 1987). Few of those observing the labor market in the late 1960s foresaw the end of the rapid increase in the standard of living that occurred in the early 1970s. Similarly, few writing now foresee a major disruption of the principal forces shaping the contemporary labor market. The trends in the labor market since 1973, particularly stagnant wages accompanied by the increase in labor force participation among women, have been so strong that, in the absence of a major shift in employment patterns, one can state with a fair degree of certainty what the patterns in the near future will be.

In this paper, then, we will review the overall labor market trends for the last two decades to show the extent to which the employment of persons with disabilities fits these more general developments. In addition, we will describe some of what is known about the characteristics of persons with disabilities that affect the probability that they will be able to find work if unemployed and to stay employed if already in the labor force. Our goal is to show the basic parameters for job prospects for individuals with disabilities and the likely success of efforts to alter those prospects.

Our research draws upon analyses of data from two surveys, the National Health Interview Survey (Kovar and Poe 1985) and the March supplement to the Current Population Survey (U.S. Bureau of the Census 1993a). The National Health Interview Survey (HIS) is the principal survey evaluating the health status of the noninstitutionalized population. We use data from the 1970 through 1992 HIS to trace the trends in labor force participation among persons with disabilities. In the HIS, respondents are asked if they are unable to do their major activity or are limited in the amount or kind of their major or outside activities. For the purposes of the analyses reported here, persons who report one of these forms of limitation are said to have a disability.

The Current Population Survey (CPS) is the principal survey evaluating the labor market behavior of the U.S. population. However, since 1981, the March supplement to the CPS has asked whether respondents have a health condition that prevents work or limits the amount or kind of work. For this study, persons who report one of these forms of work limitation are said to have a disability. We use data from the 1981 through 1993 March supplement to compare trends in the length of the workweek among persons with and without disabilities and to trace the pattern of transitions into and out of the labor force among the two groups.

Labor Force Participation Since 1970

In the 25 years between the end of World War II and 1970, labor force participation rates appeared to match the stereotype for the American family. Men had consistently high labor force participation rates, somewhat reduced in time of recession, and women generally had low participation rates, with the exceptions that most young women worked prior to having children and some older women returned to work after their children had grown (Levy 1987). Most men worked full-time, and most had long tenures on the job. The economic situation in the U.S. reinforced the stereotype. Relatively rapid growth in real wages enabled most families to do well on one full-time income. Indeed, the expectation of rising wages allowed Americans to plan for large families, which, in turn, reinforced the decision that most women would not work outside the home. Women were needed in the home economy, if not remunerated for that role.

In reality, the postwar period might better be viewed as an aberration in long-term trends, since women had had relatively high labor force participation rates at several points prior to that time (Evans and Nelson 1989). The stereotype did not even fit the postwar period perfectly. During the 1960s, at the height of American prosperity, women in every age group experienced increasing labor force participation rates (U.S. Bureau of the Census 1981). Indeed, in 1970, about half of all working-age women were in the labor force, an increase of more than 15 percent relative to 1960, and the sectors of the economy in which they took jobs were those in which they have always been well represented. Thus, the entry of women into the labor force in the ensuing two-and-a-half decades may represent less of a break with historical precedent and more of a quickening of trends already underway.

The employment trends among men after 1970, however, do represent a major change from the immediate postwar period, both because their overall labor force participation rates fell and because they experienced a shift in the kind of jobs held and in the working conditions at those jobs. Figure 1 traces the labor force participation rates among men 18-44, 45-54, and 55-64 from 1970 through 1992. The sharpest fall in labor force participation rates was among men 55-64, with most of that decline occurring early in the period under study. Thus, in 1970, 79 percent of men in this age group were in the labor force, but by 1983, their labor force participation rate had fallen to 65 percent, or by about 18 percent in relative terms, before leveling off. In contrast, labor force participation rates held relatively steady among men 45-54, only declining from 91 to 86 percent over the entire period, and among men 18-44 there was almost no net change in labor force participation, although such men experienced greater volatility in employment than their older counterparts as a result of short-term economic cycles.

Figure 1. Labor Force Participation of Men, by Age, 1970-1992

SOURCE: Authors' analysis of the National Health Interview Survey.

The employment trends among women are almost the exact opposite of those affecting men (figure 2). Labor force participation rates among women 18-44 and 45-54 have risen substantially since 1970, pausing only during economic downturns. Overall, women aged 18-44 saw their labor force participation rates rise from 48 to 69 percent during this time, or by about 44 percent in relative terms, whereas women 45-54 experienced about a 37 percent increase. While men 55-64 had a precipitous fall in employment in the 1970s, followed by relatively stagnant labor force participation rates in the interim, women in this age group had relatively stagnant rates in the 1970s, before experiencing a substantial and steady increase after 1982.

Figure 3 summarizes the labor market dynamics of the period from 1970 through 1992. Rapidly growing labor force participation rates among women, interrupted only by the recession in the early 1980s, more than offset a slight decline in labor force participation among men, in the process radically increasing the proportion of all working-

Figure 2. Labor Force Participation of Women, by Age, 1970-1992

SOURCE: Authors' analysis of the National Health Interview Survey.

Figure 3. Labor Force Participation, by Gender, 1970-1992

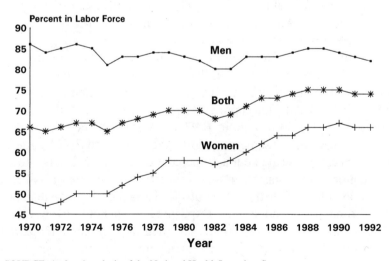

SOURCE: Authors' analysis of the National Health Interview Survey.

age adults in the labor force. Thus, in 1970, 66 percent of all persons 18-64 were in the labor force, but by 1992, that proportion had risen to 74 percent, or by more than 12 percent in relative terms. This increase is all the more remarkable because, due to the baby boom generation, the number of adults 18-64 swelled during the period. The U.S. labor market accommodated a rising proportion of a rapidly growing working-age population, resulting in the addition of more than 10 million to the workforce than would have been the case had the 1970 labor force participation rates continued.

Persons with Disabilities and the Labor Market

How did the surge of women into the labor force and the flow of men out of the labor force affect persons with disabilities? The short answer is that men with disabilities fared much more poorly than men without them, experiencing a far greater decrease in labor force participation rates. In contrast, women with disabilities fared almost as well as women without them, sustaining only a slightly smaller increase in labor force participation rates than all working-age women without disabilities and, among young women, actually registering a larger proportional increase (Yelin and Katz 1994a). Nevertheless, for both genders, the labor market trends of persons with disabilities were similar to those affecting persons without disabilities.

Thus, older men with disabilities sustained a rapid decline in labor force participation rates from 1970 through 1982, and have experienced relative stasis since then (figure 4). Overall, men aged 55-64 with disabilities saw their labor force participation rates fall from 52 percent in 1970 to 33 percent in 1992, or by about 37 percent in relative terms. During the same period of time, men aged 55-64 without disabilities experienced about a 16 percent decline in their labor force participation rates (data not in figure). Similarly, while men 18-44 and 45-54 years old sustained only about 1 and 3 percent relative declines in labor force participation rates, respectively (data not in figure), men with disabilities in both age groups saw their labor force participation rates fall by about 17 percent. Older men with disabilities experienced a disproportionate decline in their access to employment relative to older men without them, and younger men with disabilities, unlike younger men without disabilities, sustained *significant* reductions in their labor force participation rates.

Figure 4. Labor Force Participation of Men with Disabilities, by Age, 1970-1992

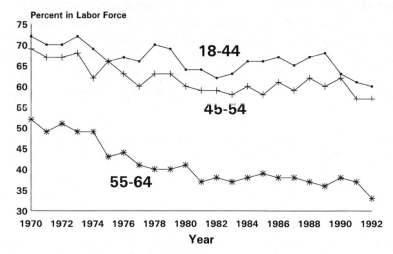

SOURCE: Authors' analysis of the National Health Interview Survey.

Among women with disabilities, those 55-64 years old held their ground, with labor force participation rates about the same in 1992 as in 1970 (figure 5). Middle-aged and young women with disabilities, however, sustained substantial increases in labor force participation over this time span, with the exception of the severe recession of the early 1980s and, among women aged 18-44, during the recession just ended. The gains among women aged 18-44 with disabilities are particularly striking, with their labor force participation rates increasing by 50 percent in relative terms, from slightly over one-third to more than half. These increases occurred while the number of young women with disabilities was expanding rapidly. In 1970, fewer than 900,000 women 18-44 years old of the more than 2.6 million such women with disabilities were in the labor force; by 1992, this proportion had increased to 2.7 million out of more than 5.3 million.

Table 1 summarizes the employment dynamics among persons with and without disabilities over the 23 years ending in 1992. While the market was accommodating an increase of 12.2 percent in the proportion of working-age adults in the labor force, persons with disabilities experienced a slight decline in their overall labor force participation rates, while those without disabilities experienced a 14.7 percent increase. The slight net decrease in labor force participation rates among persons with disabilities is the net result of a substantial decline among men with disabilities (16.6 percent) and a substantial increase among women with disabilities (32.4 percent). Men with disabilities experienced more than eight times as large a decrease in labor force participation rates as men without disabilities. Meanwhile, women with disabilities saw their labor force participation rates increase by 84 percent as much as women without disabilities (32.4 versus 38.6 percent).

**Figure 5. Labor Force Participation of Women with Disabilities,
by Age, 1970-1992**

SOURCE: Authors' analysis of the National Health Interview Survey.

Clearly, persons with disabilities, like members of racial minorities, have become one of the principal ways the labor market accommodates change. Men with disabilities are the leading edge of the decline in labor force participation rates among older men, while women with disabilities follow just behind other young women in gaining increased

Table 1. Labor Force Participation Rates of Persons 18-64 with and without Disability, U.S., by Gender, 1970 and 1992

	Participation rate (percent)								
	Men			Women			Total		
Year	With disability	Without disability	Total	With disability	Without disability	Total	With disability	Without disability	Total
1970	69.7	93.3	90.1	34.3	53.7	51.5	52.5	72.2	69.8
1992	58.1	91.4	86.8	45.4	74.4	70.2	51.5	82.8	78.3
Percent change	-16.6	-2.0	-3.7	32.4	38.6	36.3	-1.9	14.7	12.2

SOURCE: Authors' analysis of the National Health Interview Survey.

access to the labor force. Indeed, race and disability interact, with older minority men with disabilities experiencing a larger proportional decline in labor force participation rates than such white men. Similarly, minority women with disabilities have experienced smaller proportional gains in their labor force participation rates than such white women, in part because minority women had higher labor force participation rates in the past (Yelin 1989).

The exit of men, particularly older men, and the entrance of women, especially young women, do not course evenly throughout the economy. Instead, these changes are part and parcel of the gradual economic transformation from the production of goods to the provision of services. In the next section, we show how disability interacts with these occupational and industrial shifts.

Disability and the Shifting Mix of Occupations and Industries

The transformation of the American economy was described more than a decade ago as a process of de-industrialization (Bluestone and Harrison 1982). Since then, American manufacturing has undergone a type of renaissance, as some old industries (e.g., automobiles) have become more efficient and some relatively new ones (e.g., computer chips) have successfully recaptured markets thought lost forever (Jablonski 1994). However, by and large, these improvements in the prospects for manufacturing have not stanched the employment declines in occupations and industries related to this sector (Kutscher 1993). Instead, older manufacturing concerns have learned to operate with fewer workers, sometimes making current employees work longer hours, while newer ones have been founded with the goal of minimizing the amount of labor required. Thus, notwithstanding the cyclical increase that comes with the end of recession, the decline in manufacturing-related employment continues, along with the expansion of service-related employment.

While many analysts were concerned with the impact of de-industrialization on the overall economy, others argued that de-industrialization might lead to a proletarianization of the workforce, with more of us in low-skill, low-pay service sector jobs (Wright and Singleman

Table 2. Mix of Occupations by Disability Status, U.S., 1970 and 1992

	Percentage distribution								
	With disability			Without disability			Total		
Occupation	1970	1992	Percent change	1970	1992	Percent change	1970	1992	Percent change
Professionals	12.6	17.2	36.5	15.3	18.8	22.9	15.0	18.7	24.7
Farm occupations	4.6	2.8	–39.1	2.8	2.6	–7.1	3.0	2.6	–13.3
Managers	11.6	13.3	14.7	10.8	14.3	32.4	10.9	14.3	31.2
Clerical	15.0	14.9	–0.7	18.4	15.1	–17.9	18.1	15.0	–17.1
Sales	7.1	11.6	63.4	5.9	11.4	93.2	6.0	11.4	90.0
Crafts	14.8	9.6	–35.1	13.7	10.9	–20.4	13.8	10.8	–21.7
Operatives	16.9	11.2	–33.7	18.0	10.7	–40.6	17.9	10.8	–39.7
Service	13.6	16.1	18.4	11.3	12.4	9.7	11.5	12.8	11.3
Laborers	3.9	3.3	–15.4	3.8	3.8	0	3.8	3.7	–2.6
Total	100.0	100.0	--	100.0	100.0	--	100.0	100.0	--

SOURCE: Authors' analysis of the National Health Interview Survey.
NOTE: Totals of items may not equal 100 due to rounding.

Table 3. Mix of Industries by Disability Status, U.S., 1970 and 1992

Industry	With disability			Without disability			Total		
	1970	1992	Percent change	1970	1992	Percent change	1970	1992	Percent change
Agriculture, forestry, mining	6.0	3.2	-46.7	4.0	3.3	-17.5	4.2	3.3	-21.4
Construction	6.7	5.2	-22.4	6.6	6.4	-3.0	6.6	6.3	-4.6
Manufacturing	24.0	15.8	-34.2	27.2	17.8	-34.6	26.9	17.7	-34.2
Transportation, utilities	6.4	7.2	12.5	7.2	7.3	1.4	7.1	7.3	2.8
Wholesale/retail trade	19.1	19.2	0.5	18.4	19.2	4.3	18.5	19.2	3.8
Finance, insurance, real estate	4.8	6.0	25.0	5.4	6.7	24.1	5.3	6.6	24.5
Service	26.1	37.3	42.9	25.3	34.6	36.8	25.3	34.8	37.6
Public administration	7.0	6.2	-11.4	6.1	4.8	-21.3	6.2	4.9	-21.0

SOURCE: Authors' analysis of the National Health Interview Survey.

1982). The fears about the nature of jobs proved unfounded. The number of service jobs increased, and many of them were poor jobs, but many of them were high-wage, professional jobs in such sectors as research organizations or financial services (Nasar 1994). Just as the loss of manufacturing employment did not signify the demise of manufacturing, the rise of service employment did not signify the demise of high-wage labor.

However complex employment dynamics have become, the same set of forces have affected persons with and without disabilities alike. Between 1970 and 1992, the two groups experienced similar rates of increase in the growth occupations and industries and similar rates of decrease in most of the declining sectors of the economy (tables 2 and 3). Thus, as the demand for craft workers and machine operatives sagged, persons with and without disabilities experienced a decline in the proportion of jobs in these occupations (table 2). In contrast, both groups sustained substantial increases in the proportion of jobs in professional, managerial, sales, and service occupations. The growth in professional and managerial job categories was particularly gratifying, since it indicated that as the economy shifted away from craft and machine operative occupations, persons with disabilities were not consigned to low-paying jobs, disproportionately located in services.

The data on the proportion of jobs in various industries tells a similar story (table 3). Persons with and without disabilities saw their share of jobs in agriculture and extractive industries, construction, manufacturing, and public administration decline, and their share of jobs in finance, insurance, and real estate, and in services increase. Again, persons with disabilities were able to gain proportionate access to growth sectors with good jobs, such as finance, insurance, and real estate, and they did not sustain a disproportionate share of the losses in the well-paying manufacturing sector.

Disability and the Workweek

As the proportion of all working-age adults in the labor force increased and as a growing fraction of the employed moved from goods to service production, persons with and without disabilities experienced these changes in tandem. However, their experience diverged on the other major trend in employment, the length of the workweek (table 4).[1] Persons with disabilities sustained a much larger decline in the proportion working full-time than did those without disabilities. They experienced a much sharper increase in the proportion working part-time for economic reasons, and, unlike persons without disabilities, they also experienced a rapid increase in the proportion stating that they worked part-time for noneconomic reasons. Thus, while the average workweek increased by 1.2 hours among persons without disabilities, it declined by 2.2 hours among persons with them.

The disproportionate increase in part-time work, especially involuntary part-time work, among persons with disabilities suggests that when employers foresee downturns in the economy, they shift a larger percentage of employees with disabilities to part-time work and that when employers foresee upturns in the economy, they hire a greater percentage of persons with disabilities in part-time jobs. Alternatively, persons with disabilities may seek part-time work as a way of protecting jobs when they fear impending work loss, and they may seek part-time work when they are trying to find employment.

Overall, however, persons with disabilities experienced both the positive and negative trends in the labor market in roughly the same way as persons without disabilities (Yelin 1992), with older men shedding jobs in manufacturing and younger women obtaining them in the service sector. In the next section, we study the factors affecting transitions into and out of the labor force in greater detail, focusing on the impact of the specific work history of individuals on their labor market prospects.

Transitions Into and Out of Work

Static measures, such as the labor force participation rate or average workweek, mask the extent to which individuals flow into and out of jobs. The ability to retain jobs is particularly important to persons with disabilities because they may be subjected to the preexisting condition clauses in health insurance policies should they have to change jobs and because employers are more likely to provide long-term workers

Table 4. Workweek of Persons with and without Disabilities, 1981 and 1993

| | Percentage of persons employed | | | | | | Hours per week | |
| | Full-time | | Part-time, economic reasons | | Part-time, noneconomic reasons | | | |
Year	With disability	Without disability	With disability	Without disability	With disability	Without disability	With disability	Without disability
1981	72.1	83.3	6.3	4.3	21.6	12.4	37.2	40.8
1993	65.9	82.8	9.7	5.3	24.5	12.0	36.4	41.3
Percent change	-8.6	-0.6	54.0	23.3	13.4	-3.2	-2.2	1.2

SOURCE: Authors' analysis of the March supplement to the Current Population Survey.

with flexibility in how they perform their work. Moreover, with the passage of the ADA, increasing the proportion of persons with disabilities in the labor market has become a central tenet of public policy, making such transitions all the more important.

In 1993, slightly more than 8 percent of persons without disabilities who had not worked in the preceding year reported being employed in the week prior to the interview for the March supplement (table 5).[2] Persons with disabilities who had not worked in the previous year fared much more poorly, with only about 2 percent reporting that they had worked in the week prior to the interview. For both groups, persons who had a history of labor force participation at some point in the past were much more likely to be employed. Among persons with disabilities, 6.5 percent of those with a work history but only 1.8 percent of those without one had found employment; among persons without disabilities, 24.3 and 7.9 percent of those with and without work histories, respectively, found employment.

Table 5. Transitions into and out of Employment among Persons with and without Disabilities, 1992-1993

| | Percentage of persons | | |
Transitions in work status	With disability	Without disability	Total
Employed: Did not work prior year, worked prior week	1.9	8.3	5.9
Without previous work history	1.8	7.9	5.6
With previous work history	6.5	24.3	18.2
Best combination of occupation and industry	8.7	30.4	23.2
Worst combination of occupation and industry	0.3	1.1	0.7
Unemployed: Worked in prior year, did not work in prior week	56.2	24.7	25.6
Best combination of occupation and industry	36.5	12.8	13.4
Worst combination of occupation and industry	98.3	93.6	93.8

SOURCE: Adopted from Yelin and Katz (1994b, tables 3 and 4).

The *specific* work history also affects the probability of finding work. Whereas 8.7 percent of persons with disabilities with a work history in the combination of occupations and industries most conducive to finding work were employed in the week prior to the interview, only 0.3 percent in the worst combination had found jobs, a 29-fold difference. Thus, although the prospect that an individual with a disability will enter the labor force in any one year appears small even in the best circumstances, those who had established a work history and especially those who had established a history in occupations and industries with growth potential were much more likely to find work. In contrast, for those with a history in occupations and industries rapidly shedding workers, finding work was almost unprecedented.

The specific work history of individuals also profoundly affects whether they will be able to retain jobs. In 1993, slightly less than 26 percent of the respondents to the March CPS reported that they had worked at some point in the year preceding the survey but were not working in the prior week. Among persons with disabilities, about 56 percent reported having worked in the past year but not in the past week. Of those persons with disabilities in the combination of occupations and industries most conducive to the maintenance of employment, 36.5 percent stopped working, while among those in the combinations least conducive, fully 98.3 percent stopped working. Interestingly, persons without disabilities with a history of employment in the combination of occupations and industries least conducive to the maintenance of employment did not fare much better, with 93.6 percent reporting that they stopped working. Thus, the presence of a disability is more of a hindrance in the combination of occupations and industries less likely to shed workers, while in the industries more likely to shed them, even good health will not preclude losing one's job.

Overall, persons with disabilities were less likely than those without disabilities to find work, and they were more likely to stop working. Nevertheless, those with a work history prior to disability fared much better than those without a work history prior to disability in finding work, and such persons with a history of work in the combination of occupations and industries most conducive to the maintenance of employment fared much better in staying employed than those with a history in the least conducive combinations.

Is It the Disability or the Characteristics of Persons with Disabilities?

The labor market difficulties of persons with disabilities extend far beyond the conditions themselves (Burkhauser and Daly 1994). While the media sometimes focuses on the well-educated, relatively young population with congenital problems or impairments arising from trauma, the majority of persons with disabilities have an onset of chronic conditions in the mid-to-late stages of working ages (LaPlante 1988). These individuals have less education than persons without disabilities and are more likely to reside in rural, particularly southern, areas and to live in families in which the other workers have low wages. Thus, although some of the gap in employment between persons with and without disabilities is due to the condition itself, much is due to differences between the two groups in demographic characteristics and work history. Moreover, when persons with disabilities do have jobs, they earn about 40 percent less than those without disabilities. Indeed, almost half of employed persons with disabilities earn less than the poverty level income for their family size (Yelin and Katz 1994b).

In addition, the population of persons with disabilities is shifting, with dramatic increases in the number of young persons, including those with congenital conditions that were previously fatal prior to adulthood and those with a history of mental illness or substance abuse problems (Chirikos 1993; Stapleton, Barnow, Coleman, Furman, and Antonelli 1994). Recall that having established a work history is one of the most important determinants of current employment status. Persons whose onset of conditions was at an early age are much less likely to have established a work history prior to the development of disability, a problem amplified by the discrimination those with conditions such as mental disorders face in the labor market. The population of persons disabled by the onset of chronic conditions in middle age or later is very different from the population without disabilities, making them less likely to succeed in the labor market even in the absence of disability (Yelin and Katz 1994b). However, when the onset of disability is at an early age, establishing a significant work history is difficult to accomplish and is made even more so by the kinds of conditions prevalent among younger adults.

Qualitative Changes in Working Conditions

During most of the twentieth century, employment could be divided neatly into two groups: those paid a salary to design and monitor other's work and, perhaps, to sell the fruits of this labor, and those paid a wage to do the actual production (Osterman 1988). The first group was accorded greater rewards and security than the second group and relative autonomy to carry out tasks. The second group was expected to complete tasks without exercising much autonomy, because in the successful industrial system that evolved in the U.S., production was designed away from the shop floor and any variation was thought to undermine productivity (Hirschhorn 1984). In time, the combination of unionization and productivity increases enabled wages and benefits to rise and a measure of security to be provided, in effect allowing prosperity (or its prospect) to offset the absence of autonomy (Levy 1987). The system worked so well that salaried workers frequently earned less than those paid hourly wages. Incomes grew increasingly more equal as the 1950s and 1960s unfolded (Burtless 1990).

After 1973, the slowdown in productivity growth led many analysts to bemoan the American system of manufacture and to argue that the distinction between those designing and those completing production processes was outmoded (Zuboff 1988). The success of our Japanese and European competitors who opted for flatter hierarchies and the lack of success for American firms using more traditional methods of work provided some evidence that the demarcation between design and implementation was no longer working. In the last decade or so, American firms have increasingly adopted the methods of continuous improvement manufacturing, reducing the number of layers in the employment hierarchy so that communication is eased between those designing production processes and those implementing them. In this way, production workers are involved in the improvement, if not the original design, of those processes.

Paradoxically, as production workers are given more autonomy, blurring the distinction in actual work between salary and wage earners, employment conditions of salaried workers have grown to resemble those of production workers, with smaller proportions having health insurance or pension coverage (Yelin 1992; U.S. Bureau of the Census 1993b), with temporary layoffs becoming more common (Gardner 1994), and with permanent displacement of white collar workers occurring more frequently (Gardner 1993). Indeed, there have been substantial increases in the proportion of employees displaced from managerial and professional occupations over the last decade, while the displacement rate has actually declined for craft workers and operatives. Equally surprising, the fastest increase in the displacement rate has occurred in the growth sectors of the economy, including the financial, insurance, and real estate, and wholesale and retail sectors (Gardner 1993).

As the proportion of all workers with permanent, secure jobs has declined, the proportion of workers hired temporarily has increased (Blank 1990) as have the mechanisms to accomplish this (Belous 1989; Polivka and Nardone 1989). Temporary employees can be part-time, impermanent personnel or independent contractors of the hiring firm or they can work for a temporary agency or on the permanent staff of another subcontracting firm. The separation between those designing and those implementing production processes has been blurred. However, this distinction has been replaced by another: that between a core group hired permanently by successful firms, and given wages or salaries and benefits befitting that success, and a peripheral group hired in a temporary manner to work alongside the core employees when needed or to work in other organizations, albeit in close interaction with the firm's core employees (Osterman 1988).

Information on many dimensions of the shift in the nature of work is difficult to obtain. We know that persons with disabilities experienced a disproportionate amount of the increase in part-time work, and we suspect that employers' concerns about the impact of persons with disabilities on health insurance premiums have reduced these individuals' access to jobs. However, we do not know the extent to which the fear of jeopardizing their Medicare or Medicaid benefits keeps persons with disabilities from venturing into the labor market. We also do not know the extent to which they have made inroads into the core group of

workers with permanent positions or have been disproportionately relegated to the peripheral group. Contemporary labor market surveys do
not fully reflect the changes in the nature of work that have occurred in
the last decade or so (Bregger and Dippo 1993), making it impossible
to assess the costs and benefits of the current employment scene for
persons with disabilities.

In the absence of information about the extent of the changes that
have occurred, it becomes easy to lament the loss of job security and to
fear the prospects of this trend continuing into the future. However,
persons with disabilities might profit from the flexibility inherent in
temporary and part-time work (Blank 1990), especially if significant
health reform enables them to purchase health insurance without the
albatross of their preexisting conditions. Armed with health insurance,
they become less risky to potential employers, and, in turn, they can
choose to trade increased flexibility in when and how they work for a
decrease in security of employment.

Nevertheless, the power and rewards come to those in the core group
of permanent employees. That being so, we need much better tools to
assess the extent to which persons with disabilities are relegated invol-
untarily to the secondary labor market, or choose such employment
because of a better fit between job requirements and the limitations
imposed by the disabilities. We need to know who will retain employment in good times and bad and who will be central to the mission of
the organization as it attempts to succeed in uncertain circumstances.
Tenure is no longer a good proxy for future work, and individuals on
part-time status are but a small fraction of those whose prospects for
secure employment are poor. Even objective measures of skill levels
have proven an imperfect guide to success in the labor market, as the
displacement of professionals and managers in successful firms attests.
Thus, although we know that being at the core of a firm's mission is
probably the key to one's job outlook, current labor market surveys do
not gauge this characteristic.

Summary of the Impact of Recent Labor Market Trends on Persons with Disabilities

There can be no doubt that the employment prospects of persons with disabilities are tied to the general trends in the labor market, favorable and unfavorable. Indeed, persons with disabilities would appear to be at the leading edge of some of these trends. As older men generally withdrew from the labor market, older men with disabilities withdrew in greater proportions. As young women generally entered the labor force, young women with disabilities followed, their labor force participation rate rising in tandem. As the share of all workers declined in goods production and rose in services, the share of workers with disabilities did so as well. Finally, as the proportion of the labor force in part-time work increased, persons with disabilities experienced a disproportionate amount of this increase.

The tie between general trends in the labor market and the fate of persons with disabilities is underscored by the importance of the specific work history of individuals in determining whether they were able to find work if unemployed or to retain work if employed. Those with a history in the best combination of occupations and industries were able to ride the positive trends in the labor market and to avoid being harmed by the negative ones.

Despite growing inequality of incomes and relatively stagnant average earnings among those in the labor force, the U.S. economy has generated millions of well-paying jobs in the last decade (Nasar 1994), in the process disproving fears that the manufacturing sector would die or that proletarianization of the workforce would occur. There do not appear to be any major discontinuities in labor market trends in the offing. Projections call for continued erosion of manufacturing employment and for further gains in the service sector. On the high end, managerial and professional specialty occupations appear targeted for more growth, and, on the low end, so do service occupations (Franklin 1993; Silvestri 1993).

Thus, the trends of the last few years will probably be the best guide to the immediate future for employment among persons with disabilities. We know that the recent past has taken older men out of the labor force, albeit at a slower rate than in the 1970s, and put younger women in it, that these dynamics were related to the shift from manufacturing to services, and that they affected persons with and without disabilities alike. We know, too, that smaller proportions of the entire labor force are in secure, permanent positions with good benefits and that larger proportions are in peripheral positions. What we do not know is whether persons with disabilities are increasingly relegated to peripheral jobs within both the growing and declining sectors of the economy or whether, instead, they get the kinds of jobs and the working conditions they want and in which they and their workplaces can succeed.

When the ADA was passed, providing equal employment opportunities for persons with disabilities became a central tenet of public policy. We hardly have the means to assess the extent to which persons with disabilities are finding employment possibilities in *quantitative* terms. To fully implement the ADA, we must develop the tools to measure the potential for *quality* employment. In the mid-1990s, equal employment opportunity means access to a proportionate share of jobs with good working conditions and good prospects, not just an equal quantity of jobs.

NOTES

The authors acknowledge the support for this paper provided by grant AR-20684 from the National Institute of Arthritis, Musculoskeletal, and Skin Diseases.

1. The previous analyses used the National Health Interview Survey and covered the period from 1970 through 1992. In the remainder of this section and in the next one, we draw upon analyses of the March supplement to the Current Population Survey for the period 1981 through 1993.

2. In the March supplement to the CPS, respondents report on their employment in the entire year prior to the interview as well as in the past week. This creates an asymmetry in the time frames covered by the present study's proxy measures for finding and retaining work. The number reporting that they stopped working between the prior year and the prior week is necessarily greater than the number finding employment, since the former includes any individuals who worked at all in the past year and were not working in the past week, while the latter includes only the few who did not work at all in the past year and who were working in the past week. The CPS also includes many who did not work in the past year who may not have worked for even longer periods.

References

Belous, Richard. 1989. *The Contingent Economy: The Growth of the Temporary, Part-Time, and Subcontracted Workforce.* Washington, DC: National Planning Association.

Blank, Rebecca. 1990. "Are Part-Time Jobs Bad Jobs?" In *A Future of Lousy Jobs? Changing Structure of U.S. Wages*, Gary Burtless, ed. Washington, DC: Brookings Institution.

Bluestone, Barry, and Bennett Harrison. 1982. *De-Industrialization of America: Plant Closings, Community Abandonment, and the Dismantling of Basic Industry.* New York: Basic Books.

Bregger, John E., and Cathryn S. Dippo. 1993. "Overhauling the Current Population Survey: Why Is It Necessary to Change?" *Monthly Labor Review* (September): 3-9.

Burkhauser, Richard V., and Mary C. Daly. 1994. "The Economic Consequences of Disability," *Journal of Disability Policy Studies* 5, 1: 25-52.

Burtless, Gary. 1990. "Earnings Inequality Over the Business and Demographic Cycles." In *A Future of Lousy Jobs? Changing Structure of U.S. Wages,* Gary Burtless, ed. Washington, DC: Brookings Institution.

Chirikos, Thomas N. 1993. "The Composition of Disability Beneficiary Populations: Trends and Policy Implications." Washington, DC: U.S. Department of Health and Human Services, Office of the Assistant Secretary for Planning and Evaluation.

Evans, Sara M., and Barbara J. Nelson. 1989. *Wage Justice: Comparable Worth and the Paradox of Technocratic Reform.* Chicago: University of Chicago Press.

Franklin, James C. 1993. "Industry Output and Employment," *Monthly Labor Review* (November): 41-57.

Gardner, Jennifer M. 1993. "Recession Swells Count of Displaced Workers," *Monthly Labor Review* (June): 14-23.

_____. 1994. "The 1990-1991 Recession: How Bad Was the Labor Market?" *Monthly Labor Review* (June): 3-11.

Hirschhorn, Larry. 1984. *Beyond Mechanization: Work and Technology in a Postindustrial Age.* Cambridge, MA: MIT Press.

Jablonski, Mary. 1994. "Productivity in Industry and Government, 1973-1992," *Monthly Labor Review* (October): 49-56.

Jones, Nancy L. 1991. "Essential Requirements of the Act: A Short History and Overview." In *The Americans with Disabilities Act: From Policy to Practice*, Jane West, ed. New York: Milbank Memorial Fund.

Kovar, Mary G., and Gail S. Poe. 1985. "The National Health Interview Survey Design, 1973-1984, and Procedures, 1975-1983," *Vital and Health Statistics,* Series 1, No. 18. Washington, DC: Government Printing Office.

Kutscher, Ronald E. 1993. "The American Work Force, 1992-2005: Historical Trends, 1950-1992 and Current Uncertainties," *Monthly Labor Review* (November): 3-10.

LaPlante, Mitchell P. 1988. "Data on Disability from the National Health Interview Survey, 1983-1985." Washington, DC: National Institute for Disability and Rehabilitation Research.

Levy, Frank. 1987. *Dollars and Dreams: The Changing American Income Distribution.* New York: Russell Sage Foundation.

Nasar, Sylvia. 1994. "Statistics Reveal Bulk of New Jobs Pay Over Average: Managers and Professionals Dominate Hiring, Raising Overall Level of Wages," *New York Times,* October 17.

Osterman, Paul. 1988. *Employment Futures: Reorganization, Dislocation, and Public Policy.* New York: Oxford University Press.

Polivka, Anne E., and Thomas Nardone. 1989. "On the Definition of Contingent Work," *Monthly Labor Review* (December): 9-16.

Silvestri, George T. 1993. "Occupational Employment: Wide Variations in Growth," *Monthly Labor Review* (November): 58-86.

Stapleton, David, Burt Barnow, Kevin Coleman, Jeff Furman, and Angela Antonelli. 1994. "Labor Market Conditions, Socioeconomic Factors, and the Growth of Applications and Awards for SSDI and SSI Disability Benefits." Report prepared for the Department of Health and Human Services, Office of the Assistant Secretary for Planning and Evaluation, under Contract No. 100-0012.

U.S. Bureau of the Census. 1981. *Statistical Abstract of the United States, 1981.*Washington, DC: Government Printing Office.

_____. 1993a. *Current Population Survey: Technical Documentation.* Washington, DC: Government Printing Office.

_____. 1993b. *Statistical Abstract of the United States, 1993.* Washington, DC: Government Printing Office.

Wright, Erik O., and Joachim Singleman. 1982. "Proletarianization in the American Class Structure." In *Marxist Inquiries,* Michael Buroway and Theda Skocpol, eds., *American Journal of Sociology* 88 (Supplement): 176-209.

Yelin, Edward H. 1989. "Displaced Concern: The Social Context of the Work Disability Problem," *Milbank Quarterly* 67, Supplement 2, Part 1: 114-165.

_____. 1992. *Disability and the Displaced Worker.* New Brunswick, NJ: Rutgers University Press.

Yelin, Edward H., and Patricia P. Katz. 1994a. "Labor Force Trends of Persons With and Without Disabilities," *Monthly Labor Review* (October): 36-42.

_____. 1994b. "Making Work More Central to Work Disability Policy," *Milbank Quarterly* 72 (4): 593-619.

Zuboff, Shoshana. 1988. *In the Age of the Smart Machine: The Future of Work and Power.* Cambridge, MA: MIT Press.

Employment and Economic Well-Being Following the Onset of a Disability

The Role for Public Policy

Richard V. Burkhauser
Mary C. Daly
Syracuse University

USA
I12   J28
J15
J21

Work in the marketplace is the principal source of income in all modern societies, and, for people of working age, it is the key to financial independence.[1] For this reason, a critical objective of those interested in the economic independence of people with disabilities is their full access to and participation in market work. The Americans with Disabilities Act of 1990 (ADA) is the most recent example of federal legislation aimed at ensuring that this goal is achieved. Title I of the ADA requires employers to make reasonable accommodations for workers with disabilities unless this would cause undue hardship to the operation of business. One of the hopes underlying the ADA is that accommodation at the onset of a health impairment will delay job exit and subsequent movement onto the disability rolls. Yet, before the ADA was enacted and even now, in 1996, little is known about the labor force experiences of people with disabilities and how they and their employers respond when a health condition begins to affect work.

Most studies of the work experience of people with disabilities have concentrated on the "official" disability transfer population and have thus restricted the analysis to individuals who, at the present time, are either not working or are working less than full-time. While this is a reasonable approach for evaluating how public policy might return such people to full-time work, for those interested in a broader menu of public policy initiatives, it is important to recognize that the transition onto the disability transfer rolls may neither be swift nor certain for the majority of those with disabilities. To see the role that employment plays in the lives of people with disabilities and to begin to understand the paths that people take following the onset of a health condition, we must look at the entire population with disabilities, including those who are full-time workers. To do otherwise would be to ignore the "successful" work outcomes that policies such as the ADA seek to promote. In addition, we must expand our analysis across time and observe the changes in work and economic well-being that follow the onset of a health condition. Since the vast majority of those with disabilities are not born with them, understanding the transition into disability and the changes in well-being and work that it entails is critical to developing successful and supportive public policies.[2]

In this paper, we first look at the broad population with disabilities, including those working full-time and part-time who are not currently receiving government transfers, and compare their labor force activities and economic well-being to those without disabilities in 1988 and 1989, the years just prior to the passage of the ADA. We then focus on the transition into disability for men and women who became disabled at some time between 1970 and 1988. We trace their economic well-being and work experience over the years before and after the onset of their disability. We use our multiperiod data to see, among other things, how long after the disability begins a person first stops working, receives disability transfers, or recovers. We conclude with a discussion of the importance of accommodations on job retention and of the policies that might encourage additional accommodation and employment for people with disabilities.

Defining the Population with Disabilities

The ADA defines disability as a physical or mental impairment that substantially limits one or more major life activities, a record of such an impairment, or being regarded as having such an impairment.[3] This definition of disability is much broader than the widely accepted measure developed by Nagi (1965, 1969, 1991).

The Nagi measure, the dominant one in the literature, distinguishes among three states of diminished health. The first state describes the existence of a pathology, the presence of a physical or mental malfunction and/or the interruption of normal process. The second level, an impairment, combines a pathology with functional requirements— physiological, anatomical, or mental loss or abnormality that limits a person's capacity and level of function. The final state, disability, is then defined as an inability or limitation in performing roles and tasks that are socially expected. For men and, increasingly, for women of working age, market work is a socially expected role.

What is most controversial about Nagi's definition is the relative importance of pathology and environment in determining how a given pathology results in an impairment that then leads to disability. Less controversial is the recognition that the definition gives to "disability" as a dynamic process in which individual pathology and the socioeconomic environment interact. This measure of "disability" is more limited than the ADA measure in that it ignores the broader "population with disabilities" that has successfully integrated into society as well as those who are not integrated because of perceptions concerning an impairment that does not exist.

In our analysis, we want to examine the changes that follow the onset of health-related impairments. To do so, we must expand the Nagi definition to one more in line with the broader ADA concept by including the portion of the population with disabilities that is successfully integrated into the workforce.

An Empirical Estimate of the Working-Age Population with Disabilities

In most surveys of income and employment, the data available on health are self-reported and are couched in terms of work limitations. The problems inherent in these types of data are well documented (see Parsons 1980, 1982; Bazzoli 1985; Bound 1991). Still, researchers have shown these measures to be highly correlated with more objective assessments of health (see Bound 1991 and Stern 1989) and, as discussed more fully in the appendix, we believe such data are capable of identifying people with serious pathologies.

In the Panel Study of Income Dynamics (PSID), which we use in this paper, the population with disabilities is defined by a survey question that asks respondents, "Do you have any physical or nervous condition that limits the type or the amount of work that you can do?" By including in our sample only those individuals who report a limitation for two consecutive years, we eliminate from our analysis those individuals whose health limitations are short term. In this way, the analysis is restricted to the population with long-term impairments. In the appendix, we provide a comparison of this measure of disability and of more objective health and functional measures asked of PSID respondents in the 1986 Health Supplement.

Throughout this paper, we rely on data from the PSID to examine the population with disabilities and the patterns of individuals with transitions into and out of a state of disability. Although the PSID is not commonly used for studies of disability, its long history and consistently asked core questionnaire make it a useful data source for studying the employment behavior, transfer receipt, and economic well-being of individuals before and after a spell of disability. Since 1968, the PSID has interviewed annually a representative sample of some 5,000 families. At least one member of each family was either part of the original families interviewed in 1968 or born to a member of one of these families. In this paper, we use data from the 1989 PSID response-nonresponse file to represent the noninstitutionalized U.S. population of household heads and their spouses.[4] For a more complete discussion of these data, see Hill (1992).

To place the population with disabilities that we will use in our analysis in the context of those described with other data sets, in table 1 we report the prevalence of disability within age and gender groups in the United States in studies using data from the PSID, the Current Population Survey (CPS), and the Survey of Income and Program Participation (SIPP). All three data sets have a self-reported health question that can be used as a disability marker. In addition to this question, the SIPP has self-reported questions relating to function. These questions are also reported in table 1.

Using the PSID and our two-year definition of disability, we estimate the disability prevalence for men and women of prime working age (25 to 61 years old) and for older men and women (62 years old and over).[5] We find that 9.2 percent of working-age males and 10.6 percent of working-age females have a disability. These rates lie between estimates based on the CPS and SIPP data. Using 1990 CPS data, we find that 8.1 percent of working-age men and 7.8 percent of working-age women have a disability. In contrast, McNeil (1993), using the 1991 SIPP, finds higher prevalence rates of 11.7 and 11.6 percent for

Table 1. Cross-Sectional Estimates of the Population with Disabilities across Data Sources

Data	Year	Survey questions	Population	Percent of population with disabilities
PSID[a]	1989	Do you have any nervous or physical condition that limits the type or the amount of work you can do? (Must have responded yes in both 1988 and 1989.)	Aged 25 to 61 Men Women Aged 62 and over Men Women	 9.2 10.6 23.0 38.1
CPS[b]	1990	Do you have a health problem or disability which prevents you from working or which limits the kind or the amount of work you can do? or Main reason did not work in 1989 was ill or disabled; or Current activity reason not looking for work ill or disabled.	Aged 25 to 61 Men Women	 8.1 7.8
SIPP[c]	1990	Do you have a physical, mental, or other health condition which limits the kind or amount of work you can do?	Aged 21 to 64 Men Women	 11.7 11.6
		Do you have difficulty with one or more ADLs or IADLs, or have a learning disability, Alzheimers/dementia, an emotional condition, or use a wheelchair?[d]	Aged 65 and over Men Women	 50.9 56.0
		Severely disabled are the subset of yes respondents to the question above who are unable to perform one or more of the ADL or IADL activities.[d]	Aged 65 and over Men Women	 29.1 37.4

a. Panel Study of Income Dynamics (PSID).
b. Current Population Survey (CPS).
c. Survey of Income and Program Participation (SIPP) as reported in McNeil (1993).
d. Activities of Daily Living (ADLs) include tasks such as walking, eating, and bathing; Instrumental Activities of Daily Living (IADLs) include tasks such as shopping and working.

men and women, respectively, aged 21 to 64.[6] Unlike the PSID or CPS survey question, the SIPP explicitly includes mental health as a work-limiting condition, as can be seen in table 1. This more explicit question might explain why the population captured by the SIPP is larger.

Our prevalence rate calculations for those aged 62 and older are also based on the single PSID work-limit question. Thus, we would expect our estimates of disability among those aged 62 and older to be lower than those from the SIPP, where more general questions about health and functional status are asked. Among men aged 62 and over, we estimate that 23 percent have a disability. McNeil (1993), using a broader health- and function-limitation question in the SIPP, estimates a 50.9 percent prevalence rate among men aged 65 and over, of whom 29.1 percent are "severely" disabled. Our estimate seems to correspond to McNeil's severe measure. The same pattern holds for women.

Although estimates of the size of this population fluctuate across data sets, the PSID seems to capture a population with disabilities between those defined by the CPS and SIPP data. These results suggest that the PSID is a reasonable source of data for studying the effects of disability on working-age adults.

The Importance of Employment to the Working-Age Population with Disabilities

A Cross-Sectional View

To understand the impact of employment policies on the diverse population with disabilities, it is important to see how successfully people of working age with disabilities are integrated into the labor force. Table 2 uses data from the 1989 PSID response-nonresponse file to measure labor force participation and public disability or retirement transfer receipt of people with disabilities prior to the passage of the ADA. Past studies of the "disabled" population have concentrated on that part of the population with disabilities receiving Social Security benefits or working less than full-time because of a health-related impairment. (See, for example, Haveman and Wolfe 1990; Burkhauser, Haveman, and Wolfe 1993.) Table 2 shows that, in 1988, this definition would have excluded over a third of the male population with disabilities, who both worked full-time and received no disability-related transfers [43.0 * (1-.159)] and more than one-sixth of the female population. It is only among the older population, where full-time work among people with disabilities is rare, that such limited definitions capture the majority of people with disabilities.

While full-time work remains less common among the working-age population with disabilities than it is among those without disabilities using our broader definition, we still find that it is an extremely important activity that belies the notion that people with disabilities do not work. Among working age men with disabilities, two of every three worked in the labor market, and 43 percent worked full-time in 1988. Even among the men with disabilities who worked part-time, there was a major commitment to work. The average hours worked by men with disabilities employed part time was over 1,000 per year. Only 38 percent of men with disabilities received a disability transfer payment. The patterns are similar for women. In 1988, more than one-half of women with disabilities worked. Comparing those with and without disabilities, table 2 verifies that people with disabilities worked less, but it also shows that, even prior to the passage of the ADA, a majority of both men and women (aged 25 to 61) with disabilities worked at least part time and a large fraction worked full time.

However, this finding does not suggest that pathologies cannot result in serious employment limitations or that health never prevents work. Approximately one-third of working-age men and almost one-half of working-age women with a disability had no labor earnings in 1988. Among this subgroup of the population with disabilities, nearly 70 percent of men and 43 percent of women received a disability transfer payment in that year.

In table 3, we look more closely at the differences in economic well-being and work between the populations with and without disabilities. Since we are interested in examining the relative position of those with disabilities within the context of public policy, we measure economic status both in the absence of government taxes and transfers (before government income) and in their presence (after government income).[7] We compute household income by combining all sources available to the household. To account for differences in family size, we apply the equivalence scale weighting factor contained in the U.S. Bureau of the

66

Table 2. Labor Force Participation and Transfer Receipt among People with and without Disabilities in 1988

| | Aged 25 to 61 | | | | Aged 62 and above | | | |
| | Men | | Women | | Men | | Women | |
	With disabilities[a]	Without disabilities	With disabilities[a]	Without disabilities	With disabilities[a]	Without disabilities	With disabilities[a]	Without disabilities
Total population[b]	4,778,859	46,999,206	6,491,730	54,845,708	4,686,946	9,084,164	7,735,634	12,572,785
Percent of total population:	9.2	90.8	10.6	89.4	34.0	66.0	38.1	61.9
Percent receiving public disability or retirement transfers[c]	38.0	2.9	25.8	4.4	95.4	79.0	95.7	87.1
Percent working	65.0	97.5	52.1	80.5	13.4	38.1	5.4	21.1
Labor force activity:								
Percent engaged in full-time work[d]	43.0	83.6	18.7	42.5	3.5	19.1	1.5	4.5
Average hours	2,263	2,398	2,224	2,195	2,583	2,334	2,323	2,069
Percent receiving public disability or retirement transfers[c]	15.9	2.5	8.7	3.3	37.5	25.8	41.6	27.0
Percent engaged in part-time work[e]	22.0	13.9	33.4	38.0	9.9	19.0	3.9	16.7
Average hours	1,094	1,267	1,025	1,141	727	870	768	896
Percent receiving public disability or retirement transfers[c]	33.6	4.5	11.1	4.7	88.7	84.9	79.0	70.2
Percent not working[f]	35.0	2.5	47.9	19.5	86.6	61.9	94.6	78.8

Percent receiving public disability or retirement transfers[c]							
68.0	9.2	42.8	6.4	98.5	93.6	97.2	94.1

SOURCE: 1989 response-nonresponse file of the Panel Study of Income Dynamics (PSID). Sample is weighted to reflect population values.

a. People who reported a physical or nervous condition that limits the type of work or the amount of work they could do in both 1988 and 1989.

b. Population is limited to those aged 25 and older who were either household heads or spouses and were so in both the 1988 and 1989 PSID surveys.

c. Public transfers include Social Security Disability Insurance, Supplemental Security Income, Veterans Disability Benefits, Workers' Compensation, and Social Security Retirement Insurance.

d. People who worked at least 1,820 hours in 1988 (35 hours per week).

e. People who worked at least 52 hours but no more than 1,820 hours in 1988.

f. People who worked less than 52 hours in 1988.

Table 3. Economic Well-Being and Employment of Working-Age Men and Women with and without Disabilities

	Men[a]			Women[a]		
	With disabilities[b]	Without disabilities	Ratio	With disabilities[b]	Without disabilities	Ratio
Percent working positive hours[c]	65.0	97.5	0.67	52.1	80.5	0.65
Median labor earnings[d]	11,513	32,237	0.36	576	12,664	0.05
Median before government income[a]	20,307	31,635	0.64	18,786	27,600	0.68
Median after government income[e]	20,343	27,069	0.75	18,705	24,102	0.78
Income-to-needs ratio of median person[f]	2.93	3.90	0.75	2.70	3.48	0.78
Number of observations	366	3,524		433	4,111	

SOURCE: 1989 response-nonresponse file of the Panel Study of Income Dynamics (PSID). Sample is weighted to reflect population values.

a. Population is limited to those aged 25 to 61 who were either household heads or spouses in 1988 and 1989.

b. People who reported a physical or nervous condition that limits the type of work or the amount of work they could do in both 1988 and 1989.

c. People who worked at least 52 hours in 1988.

d. Median labor earnings includes zero earnings. Earnings are in 1991 dollars.

e. Before and after government incomes are adjusted for household size using the equivalence scale implied by the U.S. poverty line. Income is in 1991 dollars. See appendix table 1 for the weights by household size.

f. The income-to-needs ratio is computed as equivalence-weighted postgovernment household income divided by the 1991 one-person poverty threshold of $6,932.

Census poverty measures to each individual household income (see appendix table 1 for the weighting factors). Labor earnings include all income from labor market sources, including primary and secondary jobs, professional practices, and bonus income.[8]

As reported previously, in table 3 we find that both men and women with disabilities work less than those without disabilities but that work, nonetheless, is still very common. Both working-age men and women with disabilities were about two-thirds as likely to have been employed in 1988 as their counterparts without disabilities. Because men with disabilities are less likely to have a job, and more likely to be employed part-time when working, the median working-age male with a disability in the United States received only 36 percent of the labor earnings of his able-bodied counterpart. The median working-age woman with a disability had an even smaller ratio, 5 percent. Hence, other private sources of income, as well as government taxes and transfers, have a substantial gap to fill in order to assure that the household economic well-being of those with disabilities does not fall below that of their counterparts without disabilities.

As can be seen in row 3, the before government household-size-adjusted income of both men and women with disabilities was about two-thirds that of their counterparts without disabilities.[9] This shows that, prior to accounting for government policy, other sources of household income have made up a large part of the initial gap caused by differences in labor earnings. Government policy then narrows the remaining income gap. When taxes are removed and government transfers included, the gap narrows to around 25 percent.[10] These findings suggest that, on average, the economic well-being of working-age men and women with disabilities in the United States is substantially improved by other private sources of household income as well as by government tax and transfer policies but that the large difference in labor earnings between those with and without disabilities is not fully offset.[11]

A Multiperiod View

The previous tables show substantial differences between the labor earnings and economic well-being of working-age people with and without disabilities in 1988. However, such cross-sectional analysis may not accurately portray the impact that a disability has on individuals. First, cross-sectional analysis cannot distinguish between differences caused by the onset of a work-limiting health condition and differences that may have existed prior to onset. From the perspective of policy makers, this distinction is important. Economic disparities that exist prior to the onset of a disability may not be eliminated by disability-based programs. In addition, cross-sectional "snapshots" of the population with disabilities reveal little about the transition to disability, the opportunities for intervention, or the time frame during which individual economic well-being declines. Finally, as Bane and Ellwood (1986) have shown, cross-sectional data oversample "long-stayers." Thus, any cross section of people with disabilities will have a disproportionate percentage of individuals whose disability occurred long ago. If work and economic well-being deteriorate as a spell of disability lengthens, then cross-sectional samples may overstate the impact that disability initially has on economic well-being.[12]

In table 4, we try to address these points by providing a multiperiod view of disability. We use the 1970-to-1989 waves of the PSID to follow the life course of men and women with an onset of disability after their 25th but before their 61st birthday. The onset of disability is captured by requiring individuals to have two periods of no reported disability followed by at least two periods of disability. Applying these criteria over 20 years of PSID data, we collected a sample of 725 men and 303 women.[13] Each of these men and women experienced the onset of a disability between 1970 and 1988. Some members of our sample experienced multiple spells of disability over the 20 years. However, since we are trying to capture experiences following the first occurrence of a disability, we excluded subsequent spells from our analysis.[14] We use this longitudinal sample to examine the labor market activity and economic well-being of individuals prior to, during, and after disability onset. By examining these transitions, we hope to get a more accurate picture of the impact that the initial onset of disability has on work and on individual and family economic well-being.

As table 4 shows, two years prior to the onset of their health-related work limitation, 90.4 percent of men and 67.3 percent of women worked. In subsequent rows, we see that, after the onset of the disability, there is a decline in work. As was true in table 3, labor earnings are more seriously affected. For men, median labor earnings fall from

Table 4. Economic Changes Following the Onset of a Disability among Working-Age Men and Women in the United States, 1970-1989

	Men[a,b]				Women[a,b]			
			Equivalent median 1991 dollars[d]				Equivalent median 1991 dollars[d]	
Onset of disability	Percent working positive hours	Median labor earnings[c]	Before government income	After government income	Percent working positive hours	Median labor earnings[c]	Before government income	After government income
Two years prior	90.4	21,215	17,347	16,224	67.3	5,063	18,247	16,842
One year prior	90.8	21,543	18,381	16,812	68.0	6,582	19,921	17,370
Year of disability event	87.2	18,760	16,434	16,160	70.0	5,995	19,827	17,923
One year after	72.3	13,220	14,567	15,739	63.6	3,277	18,446	17,859
Two years after	68.2	11,798	13,930	15,406	57.6	1,699	20,251	18,537
Median percentage changes from								
One year prior to one year after disability		-24.0	-9.7	-2.6		-41.0	1.7	5.0
One year prior to two years after disability		-31.0	-12.1	-3.7		-61.7	5.5	7.6

SOURCE: 1989 response-nonresponse file of the Panel Study of Income Dynamics (PSID).

a. The sample is based upon data from the 1970-1989 waves of the PSID. The sample includes household heads and spouses who reported two consecutive periods of no disability followed by two consecutive periods of disability, who were between the ages of 25 and 61 at onset. A period of disability is one in which the respondent reported that a physical or nervous condition limits the type of work or the amount of work that he/she can do.

b. The sample size for men in the first four periods is 725. It is 677 in the fifth period (two years after onset). The sample size for women in the first four periods is 303. It is 236 in the fifth period (two years after onset). The sample size is smaller for women because the PSID did not ask about spouses' disability status until 1981.

c. Median labor earnings includes zero earnings. Earnings are in 1991 dollars.

d. Before and after government incomes are adjusted for household size using the equivalence scale implied by the U.S. poverty line. See appendix table 1 for the weights by household size. Income-to-needs ratios can be computed by dividing equivalent median income by the 1991 one-person poverty threshold of $6,932.

$21,543 the year before onset to $13,220 the year following onset. Among women, median labor earnings fall from $6,582 one year prior to onset to $3,277 one year after onset. The final two rows of table 3 show the median percentage change in labor earnings and family income between one year prior and one and two years after the onset of disability. The median change in labor earnings for men is a decline of 24 percent one year after onset and 31 percent two years after onset. For women, the median drops are even larger. However, while employment falls following the onset of a disability, the median man or woman experiences a much smaller drop in labor earnings than is implied by the cross-sectional results in table 3.

Moreover, the drops in labor earnings that are observed after onset do not carry over to household income. We find median real household-size-adjusted income does not fall by the same amount as labor earnings for either men or women immediately following the onset of a disability. This is true for both before and after government income. For men, before government income drops from $18,381 one year before onset to $14,567 one year after onset.[15] For women, the values are $19,921 and $18,446, respectively. After government income, changes are even smaller. When we look at the median percentage change, which describes the change in income for the median individual, we find that among men, before government income falls by 9.7 percent and after government income falls by 2.6 percent during the period one year before and one year after onset. Over this time, the median percentage change for women is positive, with an increase in before government income of 1.7 percent and an increase in after government income of 5 percent. These results suggest that the picture cast by cross-sectional data, one in which individuals and their families face precipitous declines in economic well-being following the onset of a disability, do not represent the short-term consequences of disability for the typical individual.

In table 5, we use our longitudinal PSID sample to further examine the pattern of work and economic well-being of men and women following the onset of a disability. We report the cumulative "risk" of occurrence of certain events after the start of a disability.[16] Since our findings were not significantly different when we segmented our sample by gender, we combine men and women and separate the sample by age at disability onset.

Table 5. Cumulative Occurrence of Economic Consequences Following the Onset of a Disability

Years since onset of a disability	Stop working[a] Age		Return to work[a] Age		Fall into poverty[b] Age		Economic recovery[c] Age		Recovery from disability[d] Age		Receive transfers[e] Age	
	25-50	51-61	25-50	51-61	25-50	51-61	25-50	51-61	25-50	51-61	25-50	51-61
1	0.15 (0.013)	0.24 (0.023)	0.28 (0.025)	0.14 (0.021)	0.08 (0.019)	0.08 (0.012)	0.46 (0.016)	0.46 (0.022)	f	f	0.14 (0.016)	0.19 (0.021)
2	0.26 (0.016)	0.35 (0.026)	0.46 (0.029)	0.19 (0.025)	0.13 (0.012)	0.13 (0.016)	0.63 (0.016)	0.57 (0.022)	0.02 (0.005)	0.01 (0.003)	0.22 (0.019)	0.29 (0.024)
3	0.32 (0.017)	0.42 (0.027)	0.52 (0.030)	0.22 (0.027)	0.17 (0.013)	0.17 (0.018)	0.72 (0.016)	0.64 (0.023)	0.04 (0.007)	0.02 (0.006)	0.30 (0.022)	0.40 (0.027)
4	0.38 (0.019)	0.49 (0.028)	0.58 (0.031)	0.24 (0.028)	0.20 (0.015)	0.20 (0.019)	0.77 (0.016)	0.69 (0.023)	0.13 (0.013)	0.07 (0.012)	0.36 (0.024)	0.53 (0.029)
5	0.44 (0.019)	0.53 (0.028)	0.61 (0.032)	0.28 (0.031)	0.22 (0.016)	0.22 (0.020)	0.84 (0.016)	0.75 (0.024)	0.13 (0.013)	0.07 (0.013)	0.45 (0.027)	0.70 (0.029)
Median years to outcome	5+	5	3	5+	5+	5+	2	2	5+	5+	5+	4

SOURCE: Panel Study of Income Dynamics (PSID).

NOTE: Values represent the probability that an outcome has occurred by time *t*. Values in parentheses are standard errors assuming simple random sampling. Sample is based upon data from the 1970-1989 waves of the PSID. Sample includes household heads and spouses who reported two consecutive periods of no disability followed by two consecutive periods of disability and who were between the ages of 25 and 61 at onset. A period of disability is one in which the respondent reported that a physical or nervous condition limits the type of work or the amount of work that he/she can do.

a. Excludes individuals who were not working one year before onset. Stop working means not working for one full year.

b. Poverty calculated using the U.S. poverty thresholds and the official income definition.

c. Includes individuals who experience no loss of income at the onset of a disability.

d. Recovery occurs when a respondent reports that he/she does not have a physical or nervous condition that limits work.

e. Excludes individuals who receive transfers in the year before onset. Transfers include Social Security Disability Insurance, Supplemental Security Income, Veterans Disability Benefits, Workers' Compensation, and Social Security Retirement Insurance.

f. Not applicable.

In the first two data columns of table 5, we track the subsequent employment history of men and women who were employed in the year before the onset of their disability. We disaggregate our sample by the age of individuals when they first experienced their disability. Our younger group was aged 25 to 50 at onset. Our older group was aged 51 to 61. The values in columns 1 and 2 show how many years elapse before members of these age groups first experience an entire year of not working following onset of a disability.[17] (As in our other tables, our definition of not working includes anyone working fewer than 52 hours per year.) In the first year following the onset of a disability, 15 percent of people between the ages of 25 and 50 have experienced a year of not working. In our older sample, this holds true for nearly one-quarter. After two years, 26 percent of our younger sample and 35 percent of our older sample have experienced a year of not working. At the end of five years, nearly 45 percent of younger workers and over 50 percent of older workers have had a year of no work since the onset of disability.

Such findings suggest that the onset of a disability does have a substantial impact on subsequent employment. For older workers, the risk of experiencing a year of not working is significantly higher than for younger workers. The median or typical older person in our sample will have experienced at least one year of not working five years after the onset of his or her disability. For younger workers, however, the median person has maintained yearly employment over the entire five years.

While 44 percent of younger workers have not worked for at least one year in the five years following disability onset, some of these workers may have returned to work. Columns 3 and 4 of data in table 5 show the share of those in our sample who stop working for at least one year and return to work. Among younger workers who stop work for one year after onset, more than one-quarter return to work the next year, and nearly one-half return to work after two years. The pattern is very different among older workers. Only about one-quarter have ever returned to work five years following their initial employment stoppage. While the median younger person who leaves work for at least one year following a disability has returned to market work three years later, the median older worker is still not working five years later and may have moved permanently onto the disability or retirement transfer rolls.

The patterns in the first four data columns of table 5 suggest that the majority of workers maintain a link to the labor force for several years after a disability begins. In the next section, we will speculate on the effectiveness of public policies aimed at extending the period of work following the onset of a disability.

The consequences of the onset of a disability on economic well-being are measured in the next two columns, which report the number of years following a disability before younger and older individuals fall into poverty, excluding those who were in poverty the year before onset. Although poverty experience increases over time, less than one-quarter of the population ever experiences it. Only about 8 percent of the populations of older and younger workers fall into poverty in the first year following disability onset. Moreover, fewer than one in four do so after five years. The drops in employment traced out in columns 1 and 2 do not translate into poverty for the majority of individuals who experience a disability. Still, five years following onset of a disability, about one-quarter of our population has had at least one year of poverty.

Table 5 shows that a substantial proportion of people experience a work reduction and/or poverty spell at some point following the onset of a disability even though the median experience with respect to income loss (as reported in table 4) following onset is relatively modest. Columns 7 and 8 in table 5 suggest an explanation for these small changes in median income. Fully 46 percent of our sample of younger and older workers have at least as much income in the year following the onset of a disability as they had in the year prior to the disability. By the second year following onset, more than one-half have experienced a year of household income at least as high as in the year before onset of their disabilities. Five years after onset, nearly 85 percent of younger workers and 75 percent of older workers have had a year of household income better than or equal to their pre-onset income.

To sort out part of the heterogeneous patterns of income and work following the onset of a disability, we look at two other trends for this population. The first is recovery from disability. Since our definition requires individuals to report having a health condition that affects their ability to work for two consecutive years, no one recovers in the first year following onset of a disability. However, recovery is possible thereafter. Subsequent recovery can explain only a small part of the experience of economic recovery reported in the previous columns. Only 2 percent of our younger sample and 1 percent of our older sample recover in the second year following onset. After five years, only 13 percent of our younger sample and 7 percent of our older sample have experienced a recovery year.

A more important reason for economic recovery is the growth in the receipt of government transfer payments. In the first year following onset, 14 percent of our younger sample and 19 percent of our older sample begin to receive disability or retirement transfers. This closely matches the share of our samples who stop working in that first year after onset. After five years, 45 percent of our younger sample and 70 percent of our older sample are receiving transfers. Because at onset a large number of our older population is within five years of age 62, the earliest age for Social Security retirement benefits, undoubtedly many of the older transfer recipients are receiving early retirement rather than disability payments.

Table 5 shows that patterns of work stoppage, poverty, and transfer receipt following the onset of a disability are relatively complex. The vast majority of people with disabilities do not stop working immediately following the onset of a disability. A majority of younger workers and almost one-half of older workers are continuously employed during the five years following onset. The transition onto government transfer programs is also not instantaneous. Less than 20 percent of people with disabilities receive such transfers one year after onset, and a majority of younger workers do not do so even after five years. However, the great majority of older workers who experience the onset of a disability are receiving either retirement or disability transfers five years later.

Once one has a disability, it is relatively rare to experience a health recovery. Only about 13 percent of younger workers and 7 percent of older workers have done so after five years. Somewhat surprisingly, while it is normal for people to continue working for several years following the onset of a disability, it is also common for younger individuals to return to work after a year of not working. In contrast, only a minority of older people return to work after not working for at least one year.

Economic well-being is even more complex. The vast majority of people who experience a disability are able to match or improve their economic well-being in the year before onset at least once over the first five years following onset: the majority do so after two years. However, some individuals also experience substantial drops in economic well-being at some time following onset, with over 20 percent falling into poverty for at least one year of the five-year period.

All of this suggests that the time period between onset of a health condition and either exit from the labor market or admittance onto the disability or retirement rolls is longer than first imagined. What is less clear is whether the time between these events is completely health driven or whether it can be influenced by employee and employer actions and, even more importantly from a policy perspective, by government actions.

Consequently, in order to address these questions, we shift our focus in the next section from an analysis of work and economic well-being to an evaluation of the existing research on the impact of the ADA. To assess the impact that this legislation might have on the population with disabilities, we combine data from the Health and Retirement Survey (HRS) regarding the pre-ADA prevalence of employer accommodations with research on the influence of accommodation on post-onset employment duration.

Maintaining People with Disabilities in the Workforce

In the previous section, we report that the onset of a disability is synonymous neither with a long absence from the workforce (at least one year) nor, at least for younger workers, with permanent withdrawal from work following an absence. In this section, we review the evidence on what prolongs duration on the job and then suggest ways government policy may affect employment. As was the case in our other sections, all of the experiences reported here occurred prior to the passage of the ADA.

When a pathology begins to affect one's ability to work, important job-related decisions must be made by both the worker and his or her employer. These decisions may also be influenced by government policies. The relative rewards of continued work versus applying for transfer benefits will be considered by the worker. In like manner, an employer's willingness to accommodate the worker will be influenced by the social institutions and legal mandates within which the firm must operate.This is not to suggest that all workers can or will transform themselves into candidates for disability transfer benefits. However, those with some work limitation who are having difficulty with their current job or who are no longer working will be influenced by the relative rewards provided by the disability or retirement transfer system in deciding whether to try to remain in the labor force or to apply for such benefits.

We are also not suggesting that all those with disabilities can continue to work. Some have work limitations so severe that continued employment is impossible and a movement onto the transfer rolls is inevitable. However, for others who experience a pathology that affects their ability to work, the length of time they stay on the job depends on the social institutions that are in place as well as on their specific condition. It is this subset of the population with disabilities that public policy can influence. Pro-work measures such as accommodation or rehabilitation can affect an individual's ability and desire to continue working, as opposed to becoming additions to the disability benefit or welfare systems.

The Americans with Disabilities Act of 1990

In the spirit of the civil rights legislation of the 1960s, the ADA attempts to provide people with disabilities the same access to employment as people without disabilities, thus extending protection from employment discrimination to those with disabilities. Title I of the ADA requires employers to make reasonable accommodations to workers with disabilities unless this would cause an undue hardship on the operation of business. On July 26, 1992, all employers of 25 or more workers were subject to its rules. On July 26, 1994, the standards of antidiscrimination were extended to all employers of 15 or more workers. However, when considering the actual influence of this Act on the work of people with disabilities, it is important to recognize when the law is most likely to be used and by whom.

It is unlikely that any of the 3.9 million persons receiving disability benefits or the 3.3 million blind or disabled adults under age 65 receiving Supplemental Security Income (SSI) benefits in December 1994 will return to work (U.S. Social Security Administration 1995). Despite some efforts to encourage reentry into the labor market, by extending the eligibility period for Medicaid and Medicare benefits and allowing labor earnings during a transitionary period before ineligibility occurs, only a tiny percentage of those who go into these programs ever return to the workforce.[18]

The same is likely to be the case for those who have applied for disability insurance or welfare programs and have been denied entrance. The legal process to official disability can be lengthy. Both those who succeed and those who fail to gain entrance to the disability rolls have already traveled a long road. To be eligible for benefits, a worker must not have performed any "substantial gainful activity" for at least five months and must be expected not to do so for at least a year. However, lack of work for five months or more is only the beginning of the process.

A combination of reductions in disability determination staff, from 13,302 in 1986 to 11,168 in 1991, and the growth in applications fueled by the recession of the early 1990s increased the time needed to process claims, from 64 days in 1989 to 91 days in April 1992. Access time has been estimated at 213 days, as of fiscal year 1993 (Beedon 1993). This is only the first step in the elimination process, and it does not include delays in a final determination attributable to appeals. Before all potential appeals are exhausted, the ultimate eligibility outcome for those who are denied benefits at every step can take several years to unfold. Of course, reapplication is then possible.

For individuals with disabilities who are not employed throughout this process, a return to work may be quite unlikely, even if they are ultimately rejected by the system (see Parsons 1991 for a fuller discussion). Hence, deciding to remain on the job after a health condition first affects performance may bear little resemblance to the decision to work of those who have long since left the job they held when their work impairment began. For those who have already left employment, it will be difficult to return even with the ADA. The hope provided by the ADA is that intervention at the point when a health condition starts to affect job performance will delay job exit, as well as application for disability benefits. Thus, the ADA will actively reduce transfer dependency, not so much by increasing exits from the disability rolls, but by reducing the risk at any moment that the onset of a pathology will lead to job loss and entrance onto the disability rolls.

Does Accommodation Prolong Work?

Since the initial effective date for the employment provisions of the ADA was July 26, 1992, it is far too early to determine the law's influence on accommodation. However, an important new data set begun in 1992 provides a glimpse of how workers with disabilities in that year were accommodated when their health condition first affected their ability to work.

Tables 6 and 7 use data from the HRS to show the pattern of disability onset and accommodation experience of a random sample of men and women aged 51 to 61 in 1992. The population of people with disabilities, as before, is based on self-reported work-limitation questions. As is the case with the PSID, the HRS asks respondents, "Do you have any impairment or health problem that limits the kind or amount of paid work you can do?" Because in 1995 only one wave of data was available to researchers, we are unable to apply our cross-sectional rule, two consecutive years of reported disability, to distinguish short-term from long-term health problems. Our alternative approach is to exclude "short-term" health problems by not including respondents who report that their disability just began. Thus, our sample of people with disabilities from the HRS includes all individuals who answer yes to the work-limits question and report retrospectively that the onset of disability was at least one year ago. Using this definition, we have a sample of 2,076 individuals with disabilities, consisting of 947 men and 1,129 women. Most importantly, while all of these individuals had a health condition that affected their ability to work in 1992, the onset of their impairments and their employers' responses to them predate the implementation of the ADA.

As previously noted, the ADA is likely to be of greater benefit to those individuals employed at the onset of their impairment. However, as the data in table 6 show, this includes most people with disabilities.

Nearly 70 percent of the men and women in the HRS with a disability in 1992 report that their impairment began during their work life. Moreover, as the results in table 2 show, the majority of working-age people with disabilities remain in the labor market and do not receive disability transfers. These percentages suggest that, for a large fraction of people with disabilities, the ADA may be able to extend work life and to delay entry onto disability rolls.

Table 6. The Timing of the Onset of Work-Limiting Health Impairments

	Total	Men	Women
Number of observations	2,076	947	1,129
Onset of impairment		(percentage)	
Before work life	12.3	9.5	14.6
During work life	68.4	81.0	57.7
After work life	8.2	4.5	11.3
Never worked	11.1	5.0	16.4
Total	100.0	100.0	100.0

SOURCE: Beta Release of the Health and Retirement Survey (HRS) 1992. Sample is weighted to reflect population values.
NOTE: Includes persons in the HRS sample born between January 1, 1931, and December 31, 1941, who reported that they are currently impaired and have been so for at least one year.

In table 7, we examine the incidence of accommodation prior to the implementation of the ADA among individuals who were employed at the onset of their impairment.[19] In this pre-ADA sample, about one person in five was accommodated by his or her employer at the time health first began affecting the individual's ability to work. Better-educated workers were significantly more likely to be accommodated than less well-educated workers. Somewhat surprisingly, older workers were more likely to be accommodated than younger workers (34.9 percent versus 19.3 percent). However, no significant differences are observed by gender or firm size.

Direct employer accommodation most frequently came in the form of a change in job duties or schedule and someone to help, but varied by firm size and, to a lesser extent, by gender and education. Accommodated workers in small firms (fewer than 15 employees) were more likely to receive changes in schedule and shorter work days and less

82

Table 7. Incidence of Employer Accommodation Following the Onset of a Health Impairment

	Total	Gender		Age at onset		Education		Firm size		
		Men	Women	Younger than 50	50 and older	High school dropout	High school graduate	1 to 14	15 to 499	500 and over
Number of observations	1,209	659	550	993	216	431	778	232	112	865
Percent accommodated	22.2	22.1	22.4	19.3**	34.9**	18.2**	24.1**	21.8	22.6	22.3
Percent of those accommodated by type of policy:										
Someone to help	38.4	37.5	39.4	37.8	39.7	46.6**	35.4	39.9	44.6	37.1
Shorter work day	31.2	30.9	31.5	30.5	32.8	26.7	32.8	45.8**	27.0	27.7
Change in schedule	33.6	31.8	35.8	32.5	36.2	32.5	34.0	53.6**	29.7	28.6
More breaks	38.5	39.2	37.7	38.0	39.7	31.6	41.0	48.4	45.9	34.8
Special transportation	4.9	4.7	5.1	5.1	4.3	5.8	4.5	5.2	0.0	5.4
Different job duties	46.5	51.9*	40.0	46.8	45.7	50.0	45.2	32.7**	58.1	48.7*
Training or new skills	12.7	10.4*	15.5	13.3	11.2	14.6	12.0	9.2	13.5	13.6
Special equipment	11.7	13.2	9.9	9.7	16.4	15.0	10.5	6.5*	8.1	13.6
Assistance with tasks	5.6	6.6	4.5	4.4	8.6	6.8	5.2	7.8	8.1	4.7
Emotional support	2.1	1.4	2.8	1.5	3.4	1.0	2.4	2.6	0.0	2.2
Medical care	6.3	7.8	4.5	7.5**	3.4	4.4	7.0	6.5	1.4	6.9
Medical leave	2.2	1.0	3.7	1.8	3.0	1.0	2.6	1.0	8.1	1.8
Time off	4.1	3.8	4.5	4.4	3.4	1.9	4.9	2.6	8.1	4.0
Parking	1.5	0.0*	3.4	1.5	1.7	0.0	2.1	0.0	0.0	2.2

SOURCE: Beta Release of the Health and Retirement Survey (1992). Sample is weighted to reflect population values.
NOTE: Sample includes all persons aged 51 to 61 in 1992 currently impaired and impaired while employed by someone other than themselves.
*Statistically significant at the .05 level.
**Statistically significant at the .10 level.

likely to receive different job duties. Workers with less than a high school education were more frequently provided with someone to help them than were those with at least a high school degree. Finally, men were more likely than women to get different job duties following an impairment but were less likely to receive training or new skills. Other forms of accommodation, such as special equipment or special transportation, were less likely to be provided to any group or in any setting.

In other research, Burkhauser, Butler, and Kim (1995) used data from the 1978 Survey of Disability and Work to investigate the extent to which individuals continued with their employer following the onset of a health condition that limited their ability to work. The authors found that 30 percent of men with disabilities in 1978 had been accommodated by employers subsequent to the development of a work-limiting health condition. By simulating the results of their hazard model for an otherwise average worker who was accommodated, the researchers estimated that the worker would continue on the job another 7.5 years. For the same worker who was not accommodated, they estimated a continued tenure of 2.6 years. Table 8, which comes from Burkhauser, Butler, and Kim (1995), shows the simulated distribution of employment exits that their hazard model predicts for men after the development of health conditions. For those without accommodation, the prediction is for 76.7 percent to exit within three years. In contrast, it takes more than nine years before three-quarters of those with accommodation leave their employer. The results from these two pre-ADA samples suggest that employers do make accommodations for their employees and that this accommodation does prolong work life following the onset of a health condition.

The Power of Policy Intervention

Indications are that accommodation can extend employment for people with disabilities. The dimensions of this impact, however, must be put in perspective. The median age at onset of the health condition that limited work in the HRS sample in table 7 was 49. Age 62 is the earliest year of eligibility for Social Security benefits. Hence, even if accommodation nearly triples postdisability work life to 7.5 years, as reported by Burkhauser, Butler, and Kim (1995), this will not keep the average person in the workforce until the Social Security early retirement age.

Table 8. Distribution of Expected Job Exits for the Average Male Worker with and without Accommodation

Years on the job following onset	With accommodation	Without accommodation
1	0.134	0.386
2	0.116	0.236
3	0.100	0.145
4	0.087	0.089
5	0.075	0.055
6	0.065	0.034
7	0.056	0.021
8	0.049	0.013
9	0.042	0.008
10	0.037	0.005
More than 10	0.239	0.008

SOURCE: Burkhauser, Butler, and Kim (1995).

In addition, for at least two reasons, the Burkhauser, Butler, and Kim results probably represent the upper limit of the effect of ADA-enforced accommodation. It is unlikely that, prior to the ADA, employers randomly chose whom they accommodated. In the absence of the ADA, a profit-maximizing firm would be more likely to assist those whose chance of success per dollar spent on accommodation was highest. If successful, the ADA, which requires accommodation unless it imposes an undue hardship on the employer, is anticipated to widen the scope of accommodation to workers with more significant conditions and lower expected success rates. (See Chirikos 1991 for a review of the literature on accommodation prior to the passage of the ADA.)

A second, and potentially more important, concern is whether the law will, in fact, increase accommodation significantly from its previous levels. In 1992, 1.3 million people applied for Social Security Disability Insurance (DI) benefits, and 0.6 million benefits were awarded. In that same year, the adult population on the Blind and Disabled SSI program increased by 344,000 or 9.4 percent. In the first 13 months of the ADA's existence, July 1992 to August 1993, 14,334 charges were filed with the Equal Employment Opportunity Commission (EEOC). While those numbers do not provide a systematic comparison of the relative importance of the ADA, their orders of magnitude suggest that more than the ADA will be needed to keep people with disabilities on the job.

Conclusions and Policy Considerations

Applying the fuller ADA-based definition, which includes people with health impairments and functional limitations regardless of their labor market activity or disability benefit receipt, we find that a majority of men and women of working age with disabilities are employed. In 1988, over 40 percent of these men and nearly 20 percent of these women worked full-time. More men with disabilities worked full-time than received disability transfers.

Furthermore, analyses using cross-sectional data tend to understate the successful integration into the labor market of people with disabilities. Cross-sectional analyses are limited to comparisons of those with and without disabilities at a given moment in time. Using multiperiod data for those individuals who first experience a disability after age 25, we find much smaller average declines in economic well-being or in employment than simple cross-sectional comparisons would imply. Our findings suggest that, even before the passage of the ADA, the majority of working-age people first experiencing disabilities were able to stay in the labor force for four years without a long spell of not working (not working for an entire calendar year). The transition onto disability transfer rolls was also of about this same duration, at least for younger persons. More importantly, even among those who experienced a full year of not working following the onset of a disability, a majority were able to return to work.

Such findings suggest that, for the majority of people who experience a disability, work continues for a significant period thereafter. One possible avenue for reducing the disability transfer rolls in the long run may be to put more resources into keeping people with disabilities in the labor force rather than into returning those already on the disability rolls to work. This suggests shifting to policies that attack the employment problem before individuals begin to receive disability transfers.

The ADA is an important example of this focus. It will most likely be used to ensure the accommodation of people with disabilities in the workforce at the time of disability onset. As we have seen, however, accommodation existed before the passage of the ADA, and it is unclear how successful this legislation will be in increasing accommodation.

The policy options sketched below are not meant to represent a specific legislative agenda but to provide a sample of the kind of creative pro-work changes in government policy that would increase the likelihood of employment for people with disabilities. Some proposals are marginal, while others are radical. Unlike the ADA, all would directly affect the government budget, but each is likely to affect employment at least as much as the ADA.

Direct Government Subsidies for Accommodation

Prior to passage of the ADA, section 190 of the Internal Revenue Code permitted businesses to deduct up to $35,000 for expenses incurred in removing physical barriers to access by handicapped and elderly individuals. In a revenue-neutral move following passage of the ADA, section 190 deductions were reduced to a maximum of $15,000, but an "access credit" was permitted, which enables small businesses to claim a credit against taxes for one-half of their first $10,000 of eligible costs of complying with the ADA. This extremely modest credit was expected to result in an annual revenue loss to the Treasury of less than $10 million. (See Schaffer 1991 for a fuller discussion.) This is a trivial government expenditure when compared to transfer payments or even to current rehabilitation programs. A more controversial strategy for increasing accommodation would be for the United States to follow the example of European countries where employers who provide accommodation and training to workers with handicaps receive generous government-funded reimbursements. Making government, rather than employers, primarily responsible for financing the costs of accommodation would shift public policy from the stick of ADA mandates to the carrot of accommodation tax credits.

The Earned Income Tax Credit

Expansion of the Earned Income Tax Credit (EITC) was the single most important piece of welfare legislation passed in the first years of the Clinton administration. It effectively raised the hourly pay of a minimum wage earner with two children in 1996 from $4.25 per hour to $5.95 per hour. (See Burkhauser, Couch, and Glenn forthcoming for a more detailed treatment.) Expanding EITC eligibility to people with disabilities who live in low-income households would increase their reward for work. This would target government funding to those with disabilities and poor job skills, whose current productivity in the private sector is not great enough to command wages sufficient for their families to reach a minimum living standard.

Education and Job Training

The EITC is an effective method of providing low-wage workers who live in or near poverty with greater income until they acquire the education, skills, and training to earn higher wages on their own. For those with disabilities and low job skills who are capable of work, transfer payments tied to wages offer a pro-work alternative to SSI. In the longer run, however, the road to higher wages for people with disabilities and low job skills is the same as for those without disabilities but with poor job skills. In developing new job and welfare programs, policy makers must recognize that most people with disabilities are capable of work and should have the same access to job programs and the same responsibility to leave the welfare rolls as other Americans.

Rehabilitation

More substantive changes would shift current U.S. disability policy from one primarily driven by transfers to one with a return to work as the primary goal. An example of such change would be to require all DI or SSI applicants to go through a temporary benefit phase in which they were evaluated for rehabilitation, as is done in Sweden and Germany. Linking rehabilitation to federal disability transfer programs is especially important given the drop in age and the changing mix of conditions of new beneficiaries.

It is beyond the scope of this paper to specify the optimal mix of policies and programs to best integrate people with disabilities into society. What this paper does recognize is that the goals of economic independence and full participation in market employment are significant and that accommodation will extend the work life of those with disabilities. It is far from clear if the mere passage of the ADA will ensure the achievement of these important social goals. It is more likely that some mix of pro-work policies will prove necessary to supplement current approaches.

Appendix

Equivalence Weights

Appendix table 1 lists the equivalence weights used in our estimations of the relative economic well-being of people with and without disabilities. These weights are derived from the official U.S. Department of Commerce poverty thresholds for families of different sizes.

Appendix Table 1. U.S. Equivalence Weights for Adjusting Household Income

Household size	Weight
Single person	1.00
Couple	1.29
Couple plus child	1.55
Couple plus two children	1.95
Couple plus three children	2.29
Couple plus four children	2.57
Couple plus five children	2.88
Couple plus six children	3.16
Couple plus seven children	3.87

NOTE: The equivalence weights for the United States are derived from the Bureau of the Census poverty thresholds, U.S. Department of Commerce (1991).

Spell Lengths From a Cross-Sectional Draw

As Bane and Ellwood (1986) point out, cross-sectional draws from a population will oversample individuals in the midst of longer spells. In appendix table 2, we show the proportion of individuals captured in our 1989 cross-sectional estimates whose spell of disability began in 1988, 18.7 percent for men and 31.6 percent for women, and the percentage whose spells began at some earlier point in time. More than 80 percent of men and about 70 percent of women in the cross-sectional sample had spells of disability that began earlier than 1988. Overall, about 40 percent of the men and 30 percent of the women in our cross-sectional sample reported spells of disability of more than five years. The average spell length for persons in this sample is 6.6 years for men and 4.8 years for women. If the patterns of work and economic well-being change over the course of a disability spell, cross-sectional estimates will not accurately portray the experiences of the average individual after the onset of a disability.

Appendix Table 2.   Distribution of Spells among the Population with Disabilities Captured by the Cross-Sectional Definition from Table 2

	Population with disabilities[a]	
	Men	**Women**[b]
Number of observations	336	443
Spell length (years)	(percent)	
2	18.7	31.6
3 - 5	39.3	38.8
6 - 10	19.8	24.7
More than 10	22.2	4.9
Average spell length[c]	6.6	4.8

SOURCE: Panel Study of Income Dynamics.
a. Answered yes to the question, "Do you have a nervous or physical condition that limits the amount or type of work you can do?" in 1988 and 1989.
b. The distribution of spell lengths for women is influenced by the fact that, prior to 1981, the PSID did not regularly ask health-related questions about spouses.
c. The actual spell length may be longer since none of the spells we observed in 1989 are completed.

Measuring Disability

In most surveys of income and employment, the data available on health come from a small set of questions that ask respondents to assess whether their health limits the kind or amount of work that they can perform. Other questions ask respondents to rate their health relative to others in their age group. Researchers have been suspicious of these measures for a number of reasons. First, self-evaluated health is a subjective measure that may not be comparable across respondents. Second, these indicators may not be independent of the observed variables one wants to explain, such as economic well-being, employment status, or family structure. Third, since social pressures make it undesirable to retire before certain ages, reasonably healthy individuals who wish to exit the labor force prematurely may use poor health as their excuse (Parsons 1980, 1982; Bazzoli 1985). Finally, in the United States, federal disability transfer benefits are available only to those judged unable to perform any substantial gainful activity, so individuals with some health problems may have a financial incentive to identify themselves as incapable of work because of their health. Misclassification based on self-reported health can underestimate the true number of persons who suffer from a particular condition and overestimate the negative effects of health impairments on economic well-being. Such problems are exacerbated when these measures are used to track changes in the population with disabilities over time.

Although the problems inherent in disability measures based on self-evaluated health have led some researchers (Myers 1982, 1983) to conclude that no useful information can be gained from such data, objective measures of health, which are much less available, also suffer from inherent biases (Bound 1991). Moreover, as Bound and Waidman (1992) show, even when a clear relationship between changes in public policy and changes in disability prevalence rates is demonstrated, it does not imply that those who come under the disability classification are erroneously classified. The information available in most microdata sources does not allow us to determine the extent to which changes in pathology have contributed to changes in the prevalence of disability. However, it is possible to inform the debate about the relationship between health, employment, and public policy by consistently applying a definition of disability and by being cautious when interpreting the results.

In the PSID, the population with disabilities is defined using a survey question that asks respondents, "Do you have any physical or nervous condition that limits the type or the amount of work that you can do?" In our cross-sectional analysis, we eliminate individuals from our sample whose health limitations are short term by classifying as disabled only those people who report a limitation for two consecutive years. In our longitudinal analysis, where we are examining the effects of the onset of a disability, we define as having a disability only those individuals who report two consecutive years of no health-related work limitations followed by two consecutive years of such limitations.

To assess whether these measures of the population with disabilities accurately capture a group of people in poorer health or with more functional limitations than the remaining population, we use data from the 1986 PSID Health Supplement. Using these data, we compare the health and functional status of our sample of individuals with disabilities with the status of other groups in the population. The 1986 Health Supplement is the most recent detailed look at the health and functional status of respondents available in the PSID.

To evaluate our cross-sectional measure, we define four mutually exclusive groups: (1) individuals who report having no health-related work limitation in both 1985 and 1986; (2) individuals who report having a limitation in 1985 but not in 1986; (3) individuals who report having a limitation in 1986 but not in 1985; (4) individuals who report having a limitation in both 1985 and 1986 (our definition of a disability). We begin by comparing these groups over the set of health-related questions asked in the 1986 Health Supplement. The Supplement includes questions about current health status; current health compared to health two years ago; expected health in two years; functional limitations in activities such as walking and climbing, bending, lifting, and stooping, or driving a car; as well as questions about general health limitations and minor health problems. We then compare the labor force status and economic well-being of these four groups. Finally, we examine the responses to these questions for the subset of our cross section that would be included in our longitudinal definition: individuals who report a work-limiting condition in both 1985 and 1986 and who report no limitation in both 1983 and 1984 (group 5). If our disability measures are consistent, we should find group (4), those with a health-related work limitation in both 1985 and 1986, to be in poorer health and to have more functional limitations than any of the other cross-sectional groups. In addition, if our cross-sectional sample overrepresents those in the midst of a long spell of disability, then we should find group (5) to be better off than group (4).

In appendix table 3, we report the results of these comparisons separately for men and for women. In both cases, the findings are consistent with our expectations; those captured by our cross-sectional definition of disability (column 4) are in worse health than the remaining three cross-sectional groups. Moreover, a large fraction of the individuals classified as having a disability under our definition indicate that they are in relatively poor health and/or have some functional limitation. For example, 54.2 percent of men and 67 percent of women whom we defined as having a disability report that their health relative to others in their age group is fair or poor. In contrast, among those who have no health-related work disabilities in both 1985 and 1986, only 5.2 percent of men and 6 percent of women say that they are in fair or poor health relative to others. Looking at changes and expected changes in health over time, a similar pattern emerges. Among those we classify as having a disability, only one in ten men reported that his health improved between 1984 and 1986, and fewer that two in ten men expected their health to improve in the next two years.

The most dramatic differences among these four groups are in the measures of functional ability. More than one-half of men we classify as having a disability have difficulty in walking or climbing stairs and nearly two-thirds report difficulty in bending, lifting, or stooping. For women, the percentages are even

Appendix Table 3. Consistency of Multiperiod Measures of Disability with Other Measures of Disability

Groups[a]	No limitation in either 1985 or 1986 (1)	Limitation in 1985, not in 1986 (2)	Limitation in 1986, not in 1985 (3)	Limitation in 1985, 1986 (4)	No limitation in 1983, 1984; disability in 1985, 1986 (5)
			Men		
Number of observations	3,154	175	151	269	46
Health status compared to others your age:					
Excellent/very good	72.3	47.6	30.8	21.1	18.2
Good	22.4	28.2	22.6	24.8	29.5
Fair/poor	5.2	24.2	46.7	54.2	52.3
Health compared to two years ago:					
Better	14.9	17.1	17.1	10.4	0.0
Same	75.2	66.0	38.7	46.7	34.4
Worse	9.9	16.8	44.2	43.0	65.6
Expected health in two years:					
Better	18.2	20.0	30.8	17.4	33.9
Same	79.4	73.1	55.3	67.4	58.9
Worse	2.4	6.9	13.9	15.2	7.2
Limitations:					
Walking/climbing	2.8	23.9	30.2	54.4	45.7
Bending/lifting/stooping	4.4	33.1	47.6	61.7	59.2

(continued)

Appendix Table 3. (continued)

Groups[a]	Men				
	No limitation in either 1985 or 1986 (1)	Limitation in 1985, not in 1986 (2)	Limitation in 1986, not in 1985 (3)	Limitation in 1985, 1986 (4)	No limitation in 1983, 1984; disability in 1985, 1986 (5)
Driving a car	0.2	2.4	8.9	17.2	18.2
Traveling unassisted	0.1	0.0	4.2	10.1	4.8
Confined indoors	0.2	1.4	5.2	12.7	10.1
Confined chair/bed	0.0	0.0	5.5	11.9	4.8
Uncorrectable eye trouble	1.7	8.5	7.2	11.1	2.1
Minor health problems	12.8	24.9	23.4	43.2	14.0
Health limits physical activity	5.2	25.4	56.7	78.4	70.7
Outcomes:					
Labor force status					
Full-time	81.3	68.6	61.5	36.9	47.1
Part-time	16.3	24.2	27.1	26.6	30.7
No work	2.4	7.3	11.4	36.6	22.2
Economic well-being					
Median labor earnings	$33,544	$22,784	$22,658	$9,493	$15,569
Median before government income	$29,456	$24,785	$22,611	$18,949	$22,991
Median after government income	$25,406	$21,416	$19,332	$19,666	$19,666

Appendix Table 3. (continued)

Groups[a]	Women				
	No limitation in either 1985 or 1986 (1)	Limitation in 1985, not in 1986 (2)	Limitation in 1986, not in 1985 (3)	Limitation in 1985, 1986 (4)	No limitation in 1983, 1984; disability in 1985, 1986 (5)
Number of observations	3,472	304	186	339	70
Health status compared to others:					
Excellent/very good	62.8	28.1	34.4	10.4	24.9
Good	31.2	46.7	30.9	22.6	36.0
Fair/poor	6.0	25.2	34.8	67.0	39.2
Health compared to two years ago:					
Better	17.4	20.0	19.0	12.5	11.0
Same	74.9	61.1	52.9	36.4	40.5
Worse	7.7	18.9	28.1	51.1	48.5
Expected health in two years:					
Better	18.8	23.1	36.5	23.0	48.0
Same	79.4	71.3	53.5	56.4	44.0
Worse	1.8	5.6	10.0	20.6	8.0
Limitations:					
Walking/climbing	6.5	28.1	43.7	72.9	56.0
Bending/lifting/stooping	7.4	30.8	45.1	71.6	62.6
Driving a car	0.1	4.6	4.2	21.8	5.0
Traveling unassisted	0.1	1.3	3.0	17.6	1.3

(continued)

Appendix Table 3. (continued)

	Women				
Groups[a]	No limitation in either 1985 or 1986 (1)	Limitation in 1985, not in 1986 (2)	Limitation in 1986, not in 1985 (3)	Limitation in 1985, 1986 (4)	No limitation in 1983, 1984; disability in 1985, 1986 (5)
Confined indoors	0.3	0.9	1.8	15.7	0.7
Confined chair/bed	0.1	0.8	4.0	14.6	0.7
Uncorrectable eye trouble	1.8	5.1	5.2	13.0	7.7
Minor health problems	11.3	38.1	46.9	59.8	53.4
Health limits physical activity	9.2	26.9	47.6	66.1	44.8
Outcomes:					
Labor force status					
Full-time	39.7	25.4	31.0	14.0	22.4
Part-time	40.6	37.7	45.7	30.3	53.8
No work	19.7	36.9	23.3	55.8	23.7
Economic well-being					
Median labor earnings	$12,658	$3,797	$6,962	$0	$5,696
Median before government income	$27,117	$22,484	$24,043	$17,415	$21,891
Median after government	$23,514	$20,291	$22,616	$16,331	$19,106

SOURCE: 1989 response-nonresponse file of the Panel Study of Income Dynamics (PSID).

NOTE: Population is limited to those aged 25 to 61 in 1986 who were either household heads or spouses in both the 1985 and 1986 PSID surveys.

a. Group 1: Individuals who reported no health-related work limitations in both 1985 or 1986. Group 2: Individuals who reported a health-related work limitation in 1985 but not in 1986. Group 3: Individuals who reported a health-related work limitation in 1986 but not in 1985. Group 4: Individuals who reported a health-related work limitation in both 1985 and 1986. Group 5: Individuals who reported no health-related work limitation in 1983 and 1984 but reported such limitations in both 1985 and 1986.

larger. For the population of individuals who report having no health-related work limitations in this time period, less than 5 percent report limitations in walking or climbing or in bending, lifting, or stooping. The same pattern of results holds for our other measures of functional status. About 20 percent of those we classify as having a disability have trouble driving a car, about 12 percent are confined to a chair or bed, and more than 10 percent need assistance in traveling. Among the remaining population, including those with shorter-term health-related work constraints, the percentages with functional limitations are significantly lower.

Finally, in column 5 of appendix table 3, we record the responses for individuals who satisfy our longitudinal definition. As expected, we find that in general these individuals are in worse health and have more functional limitations than groups (1), (2), and (3), but are in better health than those in group (4). In general, this pattern holds for the outcome measures of labor market activity and economic well-being. We expect group (5) people to be in worse health and to have more functional limitations than groups (1), (2), and (3) because, by 1986, those in column 5 have been in the state of disability longer than the other groups. We expect persons in the last column, because they have been in the state of disability for a shorter period, to be in better health and to have fewer functional limitations than group (4).

The results from these questions indicate that individuals who report having two years of consecutive health-related work limitations are in poorer health and are more likely to have functional limitations than either individuals who do not report work limitations or individuals who reported limitations only in 1986. Moreover, examining the labor force status and economic well-being of these individuals, we find that those with longer-term health-related work limitations are less likely to work and have lower median labor earnings and lower household income than do other groups. These patterns hold for both men and women. These findings support the idea that our two measures of disability, while not perfect, are able to identify, both in the cross section and dynamically, populations with substantial differences in health status and functional limitations.

NOTES

1. Because Social Security retirement benefits based on past wage earnings and employer pensions based on past service with a firm dominate the income of older people, it is also true that past work is the principal source of income for older Americans.

2. As we will discuss later, using data from the Health and Retirement Survey, we find that about 70 percent of the population of men and women aged 51 to 61 with a work-limiting health condition reported that it originated during their work life.

3. LaPlante (1991) provides a useful discussion of various methods that can be used to estimate this population.

4. The PSID does not ask about the health of all household members. Hence, this sample will exclude adults aged 25 and over who live in a household in which they are neither a head nor a spouse. It is likely that a disproportionate percentage of such people will have a work limitation.

5. The choice of "working age" is somewhat arbitrary. We chose age 25 because that is generally the age when women and men have fully experienced the transition out of school and into the permanent workforce and have established their own household. We chose age 61 because it is the last year before eligibility for Social Security retirement benefits.

6. Bennefield and McNeil (1989) report that estimates from the CPS are lower than estimates from both the SIPP and the National Health Interview Survey (HIS).

7. In developing our after government measure, we used the tax estimates supplied on the PSID public release file.

8. To estimate labor earnings, we used the annual hours worked and annual labor market income variables provided in the PSID.

9. After government income is based on actual income data from the PSID. Before government income is a "counterfactual" concept, which makes the strong assumption that behavior does not change in the absence of government. This is clearly only an approximation of what would actually occur without government. Hence, our before government values are best thought of as a means of showing to whom current benefits go, given present government policy, rather than as a measure of what would actually occur in the absence of government. To account for families of different sizes, family income was adjusted by using the equivalence scale in the official poverty measures.

10. These results hold for the mean as well as for the median individual. Tables using mean values are available from the authors.

11. Pre- and post-government income is adjusted for family size and reported in 1991 dollars. To compute the income-to-needs ratio for the median person, one can simply divide median post-government household income by the 1992 one-person poverty threshold of $6,932. This would not alter the relative position of such persons in the income distribution and our ratio values (columns 4 and 7) would not change.

12. For a fuller discussion of the differences between our cross-sectional and longitudinal samples, see the appendix, in which we show that the average spell duration in the disability state of our cross-sectional sample is quite long and that income and economic well-being are reduced for long-stayers.

13. The sample size is smaller for women because the PSID did not ask about spouses' disability until 1981, therefore we only have nine years of data on disability for married women compared to almost twenty years of data for men.

14. Our sample is a proxy for first occurrence. The PSID does not ask respondents about previous disabilities. Therefore, we only have an individual's first spell of disability recorded in the survey. This may not be an individual's first spell over a lifetime, if an individual had a spell of disability prior to becoming a PSID respondent.

15. This represents a reduction in income-to-needs from 2.65 to 2.10, obtained by dividing the median values by the 1991 one-person poverty threshold of $6,932.

16. The "event history" analysis in table 5 shows the cumulative share of the population that had experienced an event of not working for one year, returning to work after not working for one year, falling into poverty, experiencing a year of economic well-being as high or higher than in the year prior to onset, or of recovering from disability in each of the five years of our analysis. Note that this does not imply that these are all "absorbing" states. That is, for instance, while we show that 22 percent of the younger population experienced a drop into poverty after five years of onset,

some may have escaped poverty thereafter. Thus, this table *does not* report how many people are in poverty five years after onset.

17. The results in table 5 were computed using the Kaplan-Meier method, which accounts for right-censored observations, or observations that have not experienced the event in question by the end of the survey period. We report the values from the cumulative distribution function, which is simply the probability that a person experiences the outcome in question by time t. Results were computed using the SAS life test procedure, Version 6.2.

18. Hennessey and Dykacz (1993) compared recovery termination rates (based on those who leave the program because they are judged able to engage in substantial gainful activity) of Social Security Disability Insurance beneficiaries entitled in 1972 and 1985 and found that, after four years, 7.7 percent of new beneficiaries in 1972 recovered while only 3.9 percent of new beneficiaries in 1985 recovered after four years. Bound (1989, 1991) showed that the prognosis is not much better for those who apply for Social Security Disability Insurance benefits but are rejected. Using data from the 1978 Survey of the Disabled, he found that fewer than 50 percent of rejected applicants in the 1970s were employed in 1978 and only about two-fifths of that 50 percent were working full-time.

19. To obtain this sample, we exclude all individuals who experienced the onset of their current impairment prior to or after work life, as well as those who never worked. In addition, we exclude all those individuals who were not employed or were self-employed when the impairment began. This leaves us with a sample of 1,209. Of these, 659 are men and 550 are women.

References

Bane, Mary J., and David Ellwood. 1986. "Slipping Into and Out of Poverty," *Journal of Human Resources* 21, 1: 1-23.

Bazzoli, Gloria J. 1985. "Evidence on the Influence of Health," *Journal of Human Resources* 20, 2: 214-234.

Beedon, Laurel E. 1993. "Changing Social Security Disability Insurance." AARP Public Policy Institute Working Paper No. 9302. Washington, DC: AARP.

Bennefield, Robert L., and John M. McNeil. 1989. "Labor Force Status and Other Characteristics of Persons with Work Disabilities: 1981 to 1988." U.S. Bureau of the Census, Current Population Reports, Special Series No. 160, July.

Bound, John. 1989. "The Health and Earnings of Rejected Disability Insurance Applicants," *American Economic Review* 81, 5: 1427-1434.

_____. 1991. "Self-Reported Versus Objective Measures of Health in Retirement Models," *Journal of Human Resources* 26, 1: 106-138.

Bound, John, and Timothy Waidman. 1992. "Disability Transfers, Self-Reported Health, and the Labor Force Attachment of Older Men: Evidence from the Historical Record," *Quarterly Journal of Economics* 107, 4: 1393-1419.

Burkhauser, Richard V., J.S. Butler, and Yang Woo Kim. 1995. "The Importance of Employer Accommodation on the Job Duration of Workers with Disabilities: A Hazard Model Approach," *Labour Economics* 3, 1 (June): 1-22.

Burkhauser, Richard V., Kenneth A. Couch, and Andrew J. Glenn. Forthcoming. "Public Policies for the Working Poor: The Earned Income Tax Credit Versus Minimum Wage Legislation." In *Research in Labor Economics*, Sol Polacheck, ed. Greenwich, CT: JAI Press.

Burkhauser, Richard V., Robert H. Haveman, and Barbara L. Wolfe. 1993. "How People with Disabilities Fare When Public Policies Change," *Journal of Policy Analysis and Management* 12, 2: 251-269.

Chirikos, Thomas N. 1991. "The Economics of Employment (Title I of the Americans with Disabilities Act)." In *The Americans with Disabilities Act: From Policy to Practice*, Jane West, ed. New York: Milbank Memorial Fund.

Haveman, Robert H., and Barbara L. Wolfe. 1990. "The Economic Well-Being of the Disabled, 1962-1984," *Journal of Human Resources* 25, 1: 32-55.

Hennessey, John, and Janice M. Dykacz. 1993. "A Comparison of the Recovery Termination Rates of Disabled Worker Beneficiaries Entitled in 1972 and 1985," *Social Security Bulletin* 56, 2: 58-69.

Hill, Martha S. 1992. *The Panel Study of Income Dynamics: A User's Guide.* Beverly Hills, CA: Sage Publications.

LaPlante, Mitchell P. 1991. "The Demographics of Disability." In *The Americans with Disabilities Act: From Policy to Practice*, Jane West, ed. New York: Milbank Memorial Fund.

McNeil, John M. 1993. "Americans with Disabilities: 1991-1992." Bureau of the Census, Current Population Reports, Household Economic Studies P70-33.

Myers, Robert J. 1982. "Why Do People Retire from Work Early?" *Aging and Work* 5: 83-91.

_____. 1983. "Further Controversies on Early Retirement Study," *Aging and Work* 6: 105-109.

Nagi, Saad. 1965. "Some Conceptual Issues in Disability and Rehabilitation." In *Sociology and Rehabilitation*, M.B. Sussman, ed. Washington, DC: American Sociological Association.

_____. 1969. *Disability and Rehabilitation: Legal, Clinical and Self-Concepts of Measurement.* Columbus: Ohio State University Press.

_____. 1991. "Disability Concepts Revisited: Implications to Prevention." In *Disability in America: Toward A National Agenda for Prevention*, A.M. Pope and A.R. Tarlove, eds. Washington, DC: National Academy Press.

Parsons, Donald O. 1980. "The Decline in Male Labor Force Participation," *Journal of Political Economy* 88, 1: 117-134.

_____. 1982. "The Male Labor Force Participation Decision: Health, Reported Health, and Economic Incentives," *Econometrica* 49: 81-91.

_____. 1991. "The Health and Earnings of Rejected Disability Insurance Applicants: Comment," *American Economic Review* 81, 5: 1419-1426.

Schaffer, Daniel C. 1991. "Tax Incentives." In *The Americans with Disabilities Act: From Policy to Practice*, Jane West, ed. New York: Milbank Memorial Fund.

Stern, Steven. 1989. "Measuring the Effect of Disability on Labor Force Participation," *Journal of Human Resources* 24, 3 (Spring): 301-395.

U.S. Department of Commerce, Bureau of the Census. 1991. "Poverty in the United States, 1990." Current Population Reports, Series P-60, No. 175.

U.S. Social Security Administration. 1995. *Social Security Bulletin*, Annual Statistical Supplement.

Employment and Benefits for People with Diverse Disabilities

Walter Y. Oi
University of Rochester

The Americans with Disabilities Act (the ADA or, simply, the Act) became the law of the land over four years ago and was supposed to improve the lives of 43 million disabled individuals. It has not produced the anticipated growth in employment. There are proportionally more persons getting disability benefits from the Social Security Administration (SSA) today. Employers are reluctant to talk about the ADA, and the Equal Employment Opportunity Commission (EEOC) has reported a sharp increase in the number of lawsuits filed by disgruntled workers charging that employers are violating the law. The problem can be traced to the fact that the ADA embraced a civil rights approach to achieve its employment goal. As stated by Nancy Lee Jones:

> Seldom do race, sex, or national origin present any obstacle to an individual in performing a job or participating in a program. Disabilities by their very nature, however, may make certain jobs or types of participation impossible (Jones 1991).

Insufficient attention was paid to the nature of a disabling condition and to the wide diversity of such conditions. This paper tries to develop a theory of the labor market for people with disabilities, recognizing the great range and instability of disabling conditions. Work is not the preferred path to a higher level of satisfaction for all disabled persons. The employment goal of the ADA should be coordinated with a larger policy portfolio providing training, income transfers, and medical care to people with disabilities. Further, these policies should recognize the wide differences across individuals identified by the age at onset and the impairment. Not everyone ought to get the same monthly benefit or access to training and job placement services. It is surely true that if you want to treat people fairly, you have to treat them differently.

A Person with a Disability

The ADA implies that there is a minority distinguishable from a majority of nondisabled persons. A large body of literature deals with the concept of disability and its measurement. Johnson and Lambrinos (1985) turned to the definitions set forth by the World Health Organization to distinguish among three terms.

> *Impairment* is a psychological, anatomical, or mental loss or some other abnormality. *Disability* is a restriction on or lack (resulting from an impairment) of an ability to perform an activity in the manner or within the range considered normal. *Handicap* is a disadvantage resulting from an impairment or disability (p. 265, emphasis added).

Policy makers seem to prefer a definition based on functional limitations. A problem arises because the definition for a substantial limitation, "an inability to perform an activity in the manner or within the range considered normal," depends on the activity and the environment. An inability to reach or to lift may be a seriously disabling condition for a lobster fisherman but only a nuisance for a preacher. The latter might not even report such a limitation in a survey. The language of the Act sets forth the following definition.

> *Disability* means with respect to an individual (1) a physical or mental *impairment* that substantially *limits* one or more of the *major life activities* of such individual, (2) a record of such an *impairment*, or (3) being regarded as having such an *impairment*.

> *Major life activities* means functions such as caring for oneself, performing manual tasks, walking, seeing, hearing, speaking, breathing, learning, and working. There is no requirement for a medical certification of the impairment, a record or being regarded as having such an impairment is sufficient. The interpretative guidance to the Act argues that the ADA is intended to establish a process wherein disability will be determined on an individual basis.

> This case by case approach is essential if qualified individuals of varying abilities are to receive equal opportunities to compete for an infinitely diverse range of jobs. For this reason, neither the ADA nor this regulation can supply the *correct* answer in advance

for each employment decision concerning an individual with a disability (emphasis added).

According to the EEOC regulations, *disability* would seem to be a highly subjective state that defies quantification.

The surveys that have been undertaken mainly rely on self-reporting of functional limitations, activities of daily living (ADL), and impairments or chronic disabling conditions. They yield varying estimates of the overall prevalence of disability but show agreement on differences in the relative incidence rates due to age, race, gender, and education. Based on data from the March 1988 Current Population Survey (CPS), Bennefield and McNeil (1989) estimated that there were 13.4 million working-age Americans (8.6 percent) with a work disability. The proportion with a reported disability is higher in surveys conducted to ascertain health and program participation status; 11.5 percent of working-age adults were disabled in the 1984 Survey of Income and Program Participation (SIPP) and 11.3 percent in the 1983 National Health Interview Survey (HIS). LaPlante (1988) reported that orthopedic impairments were the leading factor, accounting for 29 percent of the 17.4 million adults with a work disability in 1983-1985.[1] The elements of the health capital vector A deteriorate at different rates, with sharply rising incidence rates for cancers, digestive, and circulatory impairments. Only 11.4 percent of work limitations reported by adults 18-44 years old were caused by these three conditions, but this figure climbs to 32 percent for the group aged 45-69. The shorter life expectancy of mentally retarded persons is responsible for the declining importance of mental conditions as a cause for work limitations.

Table 1 presents the LaPlante estimates in relation to the age-specific U.S. populations. Some 5.8 percent of Americans 18-44 years old reported a work limitation, and this incidence rate rose to 21 percent for the group aged 45-69, a 3.6-fold increase in the work disability rate. The work disability rate due to orthopedic impairments rose from 2.4 to 4.8 percent. The functional limitations associated with ulcers are different from those due to hypertension or from partial paralysis of the lower extremities, and these differences will surely affect the kinds and costs of reasonable workplace accommodations.

From an analytic viewpoint, *disability* ought to be described by both the functional limitation and by the impairment. A person's manual

Table 1. Incidence of Work Limitations by Age and Sex

Both sexes	Percentage of U.S. Population		
	All ages	18-44 years	45-69 years
All causes	11.07	5.82	20.98
Percentage caused by:			
Musculoskeletal	1.46	0.39	3.49
Orthopedic impairments	3.21	2.38	4.78
Blind and visually impaired	0.38	0.22	0.68
Deaf and hearing impaired	0.20	0.15	0.30
Digestive	0.35	0.15	0.73
Circulatory	2.10	0.42	5.29
Respiratory	0.76	0.38	1.49
Miscellaneous	1.46	0.89	2.52
Cancer	0.29	0.09	0.67
Mental	0.84	0.76	1.01
Male			
All causes	10.98	5.96	21.00
Percentage caused by:			
Musculoskeletal	1.00	0.30	2.41
Orthopedic impairments	3.63	2.69	5.50
Blind and visually impaired	0.43	0.29	0.71
Deaf and hearing impaired	0.21	0.16	0.31
Digestive	0.29	0.15	0.57
Circulatory	2.19	0.33	5.91
Respiratory	0.83	0.33	1.81
Miscellaneous	1.25	0.80	2.14
Cancer	0.27	0.07	0.66
Mental	0.88	0.83	0.98
Female			
All causes	11.15	5.69	20.95
Percentage caused by:			
Musculoskeletal	1.90	0.47	4.46
Orthopedic impairments	2.81	2.07	4.14
Blind and visually impaired	0.33	0.15	0.66
Deaf and hearing impaired	0.19	0.14	0.28
Digestive	0.42	0.16	0.88
Circulatory	2.02	0.50	4.74
Respiratory	0.70	0.42	1.20
Miscellaneous	1.66	0.99	2.86
Cancer	0.32	0.11	0.69
Mental	0.81	0.68	1.04

SOURCE: Derived from data in LaPlante (1988, table 1A).
NOTE: Percentages may not sum precisely to totals due to rounding.

dexterity might be constrained by an injury to a muscle or by the development of arthritis. As Yelin (1991) points out, on a bad day, an arthritic individual may need more time in the morning to get started, but the person with the muscle injury may be permanently limited. The former may need a flextime work schedule for his or her accommodation, while the latter may require special equipment. Additionally, knowledge about both the impairment and functional proficiency conveys more information with respect to the length of the remaining work life.

Supplying Time to the Labor Market

Over two-thirds of working-age adults with a disability are out of the labor force or unemployed. According to Bennefield and McNeil (1989), only 27.8 percent of disabled men were gainfully employed in March 1988, as compared to 74.4 percent of nondisabled men. Disabled men earned only $15,497 a year, 64 percent of the annual earnings of nondisabled men. A third of the disabled respondents to the 1983 HIS and 44 percent of disabled persons in the Louis Harris poll who were not employed indicated that they wanted to work. Brown (1989) analyzed the HIS data and found that persons with three or more functional limitations expressed a far stronger preference for work than persons with one or two limitations.

The familiar model of Sir Lionel Robbins (1930) serves as a useful point of departure. The utility maximizing supply of work hours H (the difference between a time endowment T and the demand for leisure hours L; $H = T\text{-}L$), is determined by tastes (for a consumption good and leisure) and a budget constraint describing the opportunity set. The equilibrium depicted in figure 1 satisfies two equations, a budget constraint and an equality of the marginal rate of substitution (MRS) to the wage rate:

$$X + wL = F = wT + Y \text{ and MRS} = U_L/U_X = w$$

where w is the hourly wage, Y is nonwage income, and F is full income. (X stands for consumption, U_L and U_X denote the marginal utilities of leisure and consumption.)

Figure 1

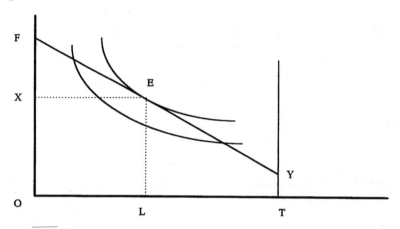

The onset of a disabling condition can displace the equilibrium in three ways. First, poor health is likely to affect tastes by raising the marginal value of leisure time, meaning a larger MRS. The adjustment involves an increase in the demand for leisure and reduces the supply of work hours, possibly to zero if the person is pushed to the corner at point Y in figure 1. Second, the disability might reduce the person's productivity, implying a decrease in the hourly wage w which he or she can command in the market. The disability pushes the individual to a lower indifference curve, but its impact on the supply of labor time H depends on the strengths of the opposing substitution and income effects. Third, *disability steals time*. We all get the same endowment of calendar time, $T^* = 168$ hours a week, but the time required for maintenance of the human agent varies. Stafford and Duncan (1980) discovered that individuals with lower wages devoted more time to sleep. A rigorous model of the demand for sleep was developed by Biddle and Hamermesh (1990). Time for medical and personal care ought also to be included in maintenance time T_m. The pertinent discretionary time endowment that can be allocated to work and leisure, $T = T^*-T_m$, is surely a function of the individual's stock of health capital.[2] A disabling condition can be expected to shove T to the left, which unambiguously reduces work hours H (= T–L). Some disabled persons may choose to accept part-time employment, while others may opt to withdraw from the labor force. That disabled individuals supply less time to the labor market can be explained in the context of the Robbins model, where disability can affect tastes, wages, or discretionary time endowments.

Equal Employment Opportunities

The hearings before the House and Senate committees preceding the passage of the ADA supported the following findings:

- Historically, society has tended to isolate and segregate individuals with disabilities and such discrimination continues to be a serious and pervasive social problem.

- Discrimination persists in such areas as employment, housing, public accommodations, education, transportation.

- Unlike individuals who face discrimination on the basis of race, color, or sex, people with disabilities have often had no legal recourse to redress such discrimination.

- Census data have documented that people with disabilities as a group occupy an inferior status in our society and are severely disadvantaged.

- The nation's goals are to assure equality of opportunity, full participation, independent living, and economic self-sufficiency.

These findings were mainly supported by testimony involving cases in which individuals were denied access to places, housing, and, most importantly, to jobs because of their disabilities. In a 1972 survey, the average hourly wages of handicapped workers were some 44.5 percent below the average for nondisabled men. Johnson and Lambrinos (1985) estimated that 15.2 percentage points of this differential could be attributed to discrimination in the labor market.[3] The ADA was enacted to guarantee equal employment opportunities, but to do so, it had to define what constituted labor market discrimination.

In section 1630.g of the Regulations, the ADA adopts a three-pronged approach. First, a person is said to have a *disability* if he or she has "an impairment that substantially limits one or more of the major life activities of such individuals." Whether the substantial activity limitation or limitations affect the capacity to do the work is to be determined by the concept of "a qualified person with a disability." This qualification is to be determined in two steps: (a) whether the individual has the requisite skills, experience, education, licenses, etc., and (b) whether the individual can perform the *essential functions* with or without accommodations, the two remaining prongs in the three-pronged approach. The EEOC has apparently embraced a fuzzy criterion, namely, a threshold hiring standard that will be determined by the *essential functions* of the job.[4] If a job is narrowly described (e.g., proofreading aloud, lifting, etc.), it will be easier to ascertain if a person is qualified. The "interpretative guidance" contained one example in which an applicant might be asked for a driver's license because, in some exceptional instances, the person might be asked to drive. If driving is a *marginal function* of the main job, and if there are enough other employees with licenses among whom to distribute any driving chores, the employer could not deny employment because the applicant had no driver's license. The set of *essential functions* associated with a job will be smaller, the larger the size of the employer's workforce. If a clerk at a garden store is occasionally required to lift 100-pound bags of fertilizer, *lifting* would be *essential* in that position for a store hiring only two clerks but not for a store with twelve clerks. If a requirement is defined by a work load (e.g., typing 75 words a minute or standing for eight hours), the employer must demonstrate that the standard was not set to exclude a disabled person.

The phrase "with or without *accommodations*" is crucial in the process of determining who is "a *qualified* person with a *disability*." An employer will voluntarily invest in training, superior equipment, and a more pleasant workplace if such investments raise labor productivity by more than the cost. The argument in Becker (1964) and Oi (1962) is that, if training increases productivity in all employment, its costs will be borne by the worker who receives a lower wage during the training period. If, however, the increased productivity is firm-specific, Hashimoto and Yu (1980) have shown that it is optimal to share the costs. According to the EEOC regulations,

> In general, an *accommodation* is any change in the work environment or the way things are customarily done that enables an individual with a disability to enjoy equal employment opportunities (a) . . . in the application process, (b) . . . that permit the person to perform the *essential functions* and (c) . . . to enjoy equal benefits and privileges of employment as are enjoyed by employees without disabilities (emphasis added).

An employer would have voluntarily made the accommodation if it raised the individual's productivity by more than the cost. With the passage of the ADA, the decision is no longer left to discretion but is instead imposed as an obligation: "[covered] Employers are required to make *reasonable accommodations* to the known physical or mental limitations of an otherwise *qualified* individual unless to do so would impose an undue hardship" (emphasis added).

The effect on demand will depend on what is construed to be a *reasonable accommodation* and on what penalties are placed on employers for noncompliance.[5] The undue hardship defense favors the smaller employer with a shallow pocket. The burden of providing jobs for the disabled is likely to be borne by the large employers, who both have the wherewithal to assume the accommodation costs and who have big enough workforces to reduce the number of *essential functions* that have to be performed by qualified persons with a disability.

If job restructuring and part-time and part-year work schedules are accepted as *reasonable accommodations*, the employer faces a difficult problem in the equitable treatment of all employees. In most firms, part-time employees are paid at a lower hourly rate than are full-time employees in the "same" job. The hourly wage discount for part-time work is larger in manufacturing industries, but it is still observed in sales, service, and clerical occupations because the part-time employee typically receives less "on-the-job" training, has less work experience, and is asked to perform fewer tasks than his/her full-time counterpart. The existing part-time wage discounts would thus seem to reflect a compensating difference reflecting the lower productivity of the part-time employee. If disabled persons need modified work schedules because of their physical/mental impairments, should they be entitled to the same pay as full-time employees? The correct answer is no if we want to discourage nondisabled persons interested in part-time jobs from claiming that they are disabled to avoid the part-time wage discount. In short, accommodations that affect worker productivity should be accompanied by compensating wage differences.

There are at least two serious problems with this civil rights approach to disability policy. First, it forces employers to adopt a *satisficing* employment policy. A qualified person with a disability who needs only a *reasonable accommodation* has as much right to a job as any other applicant. The employer is discouraged from searching for the most highly qualified individual. The efficiency loss from such a satisficing strategy might be small if the variance in performance across job applicants is small. If, however, the variance is large, as it is perceived to be when recruiting for a highly skilled position, an obligation to accept an applicant who meets the minimal job requirements could result in a significant opportunity cost to the employer.

Second, *disability* is not an easy state to define or to determine; the *essential functions* that have to be performed can vary depending on the size of the workforce and on the nature of the job. The efficacy of *reasonable accommodations* is uncertain, and the legislation and the enforcement agencies cannot promulgate clear-cut guidelines. The ADA is intended to establish a *process*.

The intent of the Act is to promote employment by placing an obligation upon *covered employers* to make job offers to *qualified* persons with a disability and to provide them with *reasonable accommodations*. Failure to do so puts the employer in a position where he or she can be sued for discrimination. Enforcement of the law is likely to be left to civil litigation.[6]

Disability: Its Duration and Impact on the Length of Life

Disabling conditions are not all alike. Severity is surely an important dimension, which might be measured by the capacity to perform the various activities of daily living or by the disadvantage that accompanies such limitations. In addition to severity, a disability can be described by (1) the age at onset, (2) the anticipated duration of the condition, and (3) the impact of the condition on the expected length of life. Disability is rarely congenital. It can sometimes be linked to a specific event, an accident, or illness, but it is usually a by-product of aging. The age at onset is rarely reported, but the nature of the disabling condition (the diagnostic group) serves as an imperfect proxy. For example, mental retardation and mental illness occur relatively early in life, while disabilities related to cancers and to circulatory and digestive impairments have a later onset.

The difficulty in identifying the target population derives from the fact that disability is usually a transitory state. Some 13 percent of 1,760 white male, married household heads in 1972 reported that they had a work disability, but only about 5 percent said that they had a disability in each of the five consecutive years, 1968-1972.[7] At onset, there is uncertainty about the anticipated duration. Functional limitations are unstable and fluctuate from week to week. Workers hope that their loss of sight or difficulty in walking is only temporary. They may wait to ascertain the extent of the limitation before taking the next step—return to work, retrain for a new job, or withdraw from the labor force. Time and money will be spent to see if the condition can be reversed. The individual's response clearly depends on whether the disabling condition is perceived to be temporary or permanent.

The impact of a disability on the length of life depends on the severity and nature of the impairment. Severely disabled individuals who qualify for benefits under the Social Security Administration's Disability Insurance (DI) program experience substantially higher mortality rates. In addition, unsuccessful applicants to the DI program (who were denied benefits) have exhibited death rates higher than those of nondisabled persons (Bound 1989). Bye and Riley (1989) followed the cohort of 18,782 persons who were awarded benefits and enrolled in the DI program in 1972.[8] The percentages of this cohort who died or recovered (and hence were dropped from the program) during the next two years were determined from SSA records. Table 2 reproduces their findings, classified by gender and race, age at entry into the program, years of education, occupation, and diagnostic group. These people were in poor health, as evidenced by the fact that over one-eighth, 12.8 percent, died within two years. Only 5.3 percent recovered and were dropped from the SSA rolls. The two-year mortality rates were higher for men and blacks, rising with age at entry.[9] Education and the two-year mortality rate are positively correlated, but this is likely a result of the interaction between education and age at onset. The more-educated disabled persons probably became disabled after they were 50 or older.

Table 2. Two-Year Death and Recovery Rates for 1972 Entrants to the Social Security Administration's Disability Insurance Program

	1972 cohort		Percentage in the first two years who	
	Number	**Percent**	**Died**	**Recovered**
Total	18,782	100.0	12.8	5.3
Sex and race				
Men	13,150	70.0	13.9	6.0
Women	5,632	30.0	10.4	3.7
White and unknown	15,958	85.0	12.8	5.4
Black	2,617	13.9	13.2	4.7
Other	207	1.1	8.2	5.8
Age in 1972				
Under 40	2,961	15.8	6.7	15.2
40-49	3,602	19.2	13.4	7.9
50-59	9,407	50.1	14.0	2.6
60-61	2,812	14.9	14.8	0.6
Years of education				
None	215	1.1	10.7	1.4
1-8	6,540	34.8	12.2	3.2
9-12	8,180	43.6	14.4	6.7
13 or more	1,459	7.8	15.4	8.4
Unknown	2,388	12.7	8.1	4.7
Occupation				
Professional	1,878	10.0	17.2	9.9
Clerical and sales	2,266	12.1	14.5	9.1
Service	2,656	14.1	12.1	8.1
Farming	757	4.0	10.8	4.4

Table 2 (continued)

	1972 cohort		Percentage in the first two years who	
	Number	**Percent**	**Died**	**Recovered**
Processing	564	3.0	13.3	4.8
Machine	1,632	8.7	12.8	5.8
Benchwork	1,164	6.2	10.3	4.4
Structural	2,220	11.8	12.5	6.1
Miscellaneous	2,847	15.2	12.8	6.4
Unknown	2,798	14.9	11.2	5.6
Diagnostic group				
Infectious	319	1.7	7.2	23.2
Neoplasms	1,582	8.4	64.5	1.9
Endocrine	613	3.3	12.6	1.6
Mental	1,736	9.2	3.3	4.7
Nervous	681	3.6	6.3	2.8
Eye and ear	385	2.0	4.2	4.9
Circulatory	5,321	28.3	12.3	2.5
Respiratory	1,163	6.2	10.2	1.0
Digestive	542	2.9	22.5	4.2
Genitourinary	128	0.7	25.0	6.3
Musculoskeletal	2,883	15.3	2.7	6.8
Traumatic	1,260	6.7	2.5	22.1
Other	2,179	11.6	6.6	5.2

SOURCE: Bye and Riley (1989).

The surprising finding is the wide variance in death rates by diagnostic group. Nearly two-thirds, 64.5 percent, of those who were disabled by neoplasms (cancers) passed away within two years of admission to the DI program. High mortality rates were also observed for those with genitourinary and digestive conditions: 25 and 22.5 percent died within two years. People whose disabilities were caused by traumatic injuries had the lowest mortality rate, 2.5 percent, followed by musculoskeletal impairments, at 2.7 percent. Disabled beneficiaries whose limitations were caused by infectious diseases and traumatic injuries reported the highest recovery rates, 23.2 percent and 22.1 percent, respectively.

Disabling conditions are not all alike and ought to be differentiated by severity, age at onset, duration, and longevity. Variations in mortality and recovery rates due to age and the approximate cause of the disability indicate not only the probable returns to policies promoting employment but also the budgetary costs of changing the standards to earn entitlement to DI benefits. We are sure to learn more from the New Beneficiary Survey about how age and diagnosis are related to mortality risks and to the odds of recovery.[10]

Work and Welfare

In designing policies to deal with poverty, we confront the insoluble problem of distinguishing between the deserving and nondeserving poor. Garraty (1978) noted that, in the Middle Ages, doubts arose about the need to supply food to beggars who looked as if they might be able to provide for themselves. The community was unwilling to assist big beggars, malingerers, and free riders. There is no bright line separating the disabled from the nondisabled. More importantly, the target population of people with disabilities is not a stable minority, such as one differentiated by race or gender, but changes from day to day. Additionally, policies have to be designed to recognize the wide diversity among people with disabilities.

Implicit and Explicit Wage Subsidies

Wage subsidies were introduced to reduce teenage unemployment. The Targeted Jobs Tax Credit program is an explicit wage subsidy which reduces the net labor costs for an employer who hires an individual eligible for tax credits. Vocational rehabilitation can be viewed as an implicit subsidy because the agency assumes the cost of counseling, training, and placing the client. The workers' compensation program also offers an implicit wage subsidy for the largest employers. A covered employee who is classified as totally disabled, temporary or permanent, becomes eligible for weekly benefits. Most employers with 500 or more employees are self-insured (except in a few states), and the workers' compensation benefits become a direct cost.

Suppose that the person in question had been earning a weekly wage of $W = \$500$ before the onset of the disability and the mandated workers' compensation weekly benefit $B = \$200$. If the disabling condition reduces this person's productivity so that he or she is worth retaining only at a weekly wage of, for example, $W_1 = \$400$, a self-insured employer has an incentive to retain the worker, pay him or her a wage equal to the pre-injury wage of $W = \$500$, and save the outlay for workers' compensation benefits of $B = \$200$. Indeed, if the worker's net product after the onset of the disabling condition exceeds his or her net wage of $W_n = (W - B) = \$300$, it is in the firm's best interests to retain the disabled worker. This implicit wage subsidy is not available to a small employer who is not self-insured. Casual observations suggest that the implicit wage subsidy under workers' compensation is effective. The workforces of larger firms seem to contain a higher fraction of disabled employees.

Training

At the onset of disability, a worker may be uncertain about how the condition will affect his or her productivity and time endowment. If the condition is perceived to be temporary (a short anticipated duration), the individual is likely to exhibit a high intertemporal elasticity of substitution, sharply cutting back on his or her labor supply until the condition improves.[11] When workers are not recalled by their previous employers and are out of the labor force, they may be eligible for training and vocational rehabilitation. A theory of human capital predicts that the returns to an investment in training will be larger, the greater the increment to earnings due to more human capital and the longer the anticipated period of employment.[12] The odds that individuals will elect to enroll in a training program and to return to work are higher, the younger the age at disability onset. A shorter remaining work life reduces the return to training, but in addition, older workers are less adaptable and experience higher attrition rates in vocational rehabilitation and formal training courses. We want to believe that an individual is unable to find suitable work because she or he lacks the requisite skills that can be taught in a training program, formal or on-the-job. By allocating more resources to training, the problem of underemployment can allegedly be solved, but only for a subset of people with disabilities.

Civil Rights and Accommodations Again

The ADA obligates an employer to offer equal opportunities to "a qualified person with a disability who can perform the essential functions of the job with or without reasonable accommodations." This civil rights approach ignores the *caveat* voiced by Jones, that disability is not like race and gender. Some accommodations, such as the provision of a reader or interpreter, are expensive. Under the ADA, "employers are required to make reasonable accommodations ... unless to do so would impose an undue hardship." Disputes are certain to arise about what are the *essential functions* of a job and what is a *reasonable accommodation*. The EEOC regulations explicitly state that these matters have to be settled on a case-by-case basis because the disabling condition and the requirements of the job can change from day to day or from place to place. Litigation could be reduced by replacing the "undue hardship" criterion with an explicit rule that specifies a cost cap defining what is reasonable.

It is not surprising that many disabled persons ask for flexible, part-time, or part-year schedules. A disability increases both the average maintenance time for sleep and care as well as its variance. The demand for short hours and more "time off" privileges will rise in response to a wider dispersion in the number of physician visits or in the days of restricted activity. The Civil Rights Act calls for "equal pay for equal work." But what is *equal work*? The hourly rate of pay for an employee on a part-time or flexible schedule is usually below that for a full-time worker. The size of the wage discount for an irregular work schedule varies across industries and occupations. If a job has to be restructured or a work schedule shortened to accommodate a disabled person, is the firm obliged to pay that person the same wage as that paid to a full-time nondisabled employee facing different working conditions? If a competitive labor market establishes compensating wage differences for special working arrangements, these differences should also apply to a regulated labor market for disabled workers.

Program Participation

A disabling condition may be so severe and/or the circumstances may be such that work is an infeasible or inferior option. The preferred path could be one in which the individual withdraws from the labor force and applies to the SSA for DI benefits (if the person has the necessary work history) or for Supplemental Security Income (SSI). In deciding on which path to follow, the person has to assess the extent of the health loss, its duration, including the chances for recovery, and the application costs, which entail lengthy waiting periods and delays in the appeal process. The returns to becoming a DI or SSI beneficiary are greater, the older the age at onset and the higher the anticipated mortality rate.

The number of DI/SSI beneficiaries is growing (it is nearly 7 million today), and the median age of new awards is falling; these developments threaten the solvency of the trust funds. A trial work period (TWP) was introduced as an incentive for program participants to return to work; they could exceed the substantial gainful activity (SGA) level of earnings during the TWP and still retain their monthly benefits and Medicare. This incentive was enhanced in 1986 by an extended period of eligibility (EPE), which increased the grace period from 15 to 36 months. Muller (1992) analyzed the New Beneficiary Data System data. Only 10.2 percent of the cohort who were awarded DI benefits in 1981 reported doing "any work," and an even smaller fraction, 2.8 percent, actually left the rolls in the next ten years (see the SGA terminations in table 3). A younger age at entitlement and more years of education raise the odds that a DI beneficiary will recover and leave the rolls.[13] Only about 6 percent of SSI beneficiaries, who are, on average, younger and less educated than DI beneficiaries, reported doing "any work" in the decade of the 1980s. The DI and SSI program participants are older and have more serious life-threatening impairments. They are not representative of the 13-to-18 million working-age adults with an employment disability, and it is not surprising that a majority of them elect to remain out of the workforce.

Table 3.   Work Experience of Disability Insurance Beneficiaries, 1982-1991

Characteristic	Number	Any work (percent)	SGA termination (percent)
Total	192,774	10.2	2.8
Education			
0-8 years	58,580	4.9	0.8
9-11 years	43,038	8.2	1.8
12 years	57,684	11.6	3.0
13 or more years	32,583	19.8	7.2
Age at entitlement			
Under 40	36,335	29.1	9.3
40-49	29,969	12.4	3.0
50-59	94,359	4.8	1.1
60 or older	32,111	2.5	0.2
Family income			
Under $5,000	30,434	15.7	3.6
$5,000-$9,999	56,281	10.1	2.2
$10,000-$19,999	66,495	7.3	2.1
$20,000-$39,999	35,504	11.0	4.2
$40,000 or more	4,060	11.7	4.6

SOURCE: Muller (1992, table 3, pp. 9-10).

A Wider Policy Portfolio

The employment record is dismal, as documented by the finding that only about 28 percent of persons with a work disability in 1988 held a job. In addition, research by Haveman and Wolfe (1990) shows that the well-being of disabled persons (judged by family income) has been declining. Further evidence of the problems of individuals with disabilities is provided by the Harris poll, which in 1984 reported that 44 percent of disabled persons who were out of work wanted a job. Title I of the ADA tries to raise the employment-to-population ratio in two ways. First, it adopts a broad definition of a person with a disability. Second, the Act widens the window of prospective jobs by requiring employers to provide equal employment opportunities to "a *qualified* person with a *disability.*" The essential functions of the job have to be identified to determine if the disabled person is qualified. If an accommodation is needed for the worker to perform the essential functions, the employer has to provide it unless an undue hardship is imposed. The ADA invites litigation, an outcome that I had predicted when the Act was being debated, and the caseload at the EEOC has exploded.

Employment prospects have, if anything, deteriorated since the passage of the ADA. Only 31 percent of disabled individuals held a job last year, down from 33 percent in 1986. The share of disabled SSI beneficiaries with a job has also dropped, from 6.5 to 5.8 percent (Holmes 1994, p. 26).[14] The passage of the ADA was intended to create jobs, thereby promoting a movement out of dependency and idleness. The burden of supplying work and paying for reasonable accommodations was legislatively shifted to employers, a policy labeled by Burkhauser (1990) as "Morality on the Cheap." We have witnessed a sharp increase in the number of lawsuits charging employers with violations of Title I but no significant rise in employment.

Although the diversity and instability of disabling conditions were emphasized in the hearings, the mandate in Title I assumes that gainful work is the way to improve well-being for a majority of people with disabilities. The presumption implies that the target population exhibits a substantial degree of homogeneity in tastes and productive traits, a presumption that is not supported by the data. Training for a new job is neither practical nor desirable for persons who become disabled at older ages, especially when life expectancy is also shortened by the onset of the condition. Some may be eligible for benefits under workers' compensation or private disability insurance, but SSA is the agency to which most turn for income support. Although monthly DI benefits vary depending on the recipient's work history, the dispersion is relatively small. Given the high application costs and the SGA limits on earnings, a person who applies for DI benefits seems to be making a commitment to a more or less permanent withdrawal from the legal labor market. A trial work period is available for up to 36 months to induce individuals to give up their disability benefits and to return to the world of work. The ones already on board are, however, different from other disabled individuals. We may be directing the work incentives to the wrong group.

It is instructive to review the policy of the Department of Veterans Affairs. An individual with a service-connected disability is evaluated and assigned a rating, which fixes the size of the monthly compensation. There is no earnings test; everyone who is entitled to a pension gets it irrespective of his or her earnings in the labor market. Cohany (1987) found that 95.8 percent of Vietnam-era veterans with no disabilities were gainfully employed. The employment rate was 79.9 percent for those with a service-connected disability and was closely related to the disability rating: 92.2 percent with a disability rating of 1-to-30 percent were working, as compared to 79.5 percent for disability ratings of 30-to-60 percent and 34.5 percent for disability ratings of over 60 percent. Although the supply of labor will be inversely related to the size of the pension, I suspect that the data largely reflect a response to the severity of the disabling condition.

The present DI program has the effect of locking in its clients, such that very few voluntarily terminate their monthly benefits to return to work, and should be replaced by a social insurance program that acknowledges the heterogeneity of people with disabilities. The following modifications should be made. First, admission to the program should be based on a medical assessment of the applicant's physical and mental impairments. The waiting period during which the applicant performs no work should be abandoned. Second, monthly benefits should be a function of the applicant's *disability class*, which could be based on the applicant's age and diagnostic group.[15] Third, the earnings test should be abolished, and DI benefits should be subject to income taxation. The youngest DI beneficiaries with the lower mortality risks receive the smallest monthly benefits; they can supplement their monthly disability benefits by working, and the sum of earnings and disability benefits should be subject to income taxation. Fourth, each beneficiary should be obliged to undergo a disability review to confirm that his or her disabling condition still persists and warrants keeping him or her on the DI rolls. The time interval before the scheduled disability review should be shorter for persons with lower disability class rankings. A disabled beneficiary in a low disability class is younger and stronger. The individual is entitled to a smaller monthly disability benefit, which raises the opportunity cost of remaining out of the workforce. Since there is no earnings test, and benefits will continue until the next disability review, the opportunity cost of seeking and obtaining a job is small.

It is unclear if the costs of administering this modified DI program will be higher or lower than those of the present system. The placement of each client into a disability class and a periodic disability review will raise administrative costs, but the proportion requiring appeals is likely to be smaller. My proposal has been questioned by the Panel of the National Academy of Social Insurance on at least two grounds. First, the military relies on a draft to obtain personnel, who are not free to choose their assignments. This is simply not true; conscription was abolished over 20 years ago. Second, risks are allegedly higher in the military, and the recommended changes would lead to inordinately high costs or inadequate benefits. These are conjectures that cannot be resolved without a careful analysis of the proposal.[16]

The current policy portfolio is one in which SSA is mainly responsible for welfare (supplying income and medical care for seriously disabled individuals), workers' compensation provides support for the short-term disabled, and state rehabilitation agencies assist in training and job placement. The earnings and dignity from employment are certainly important. The ADA has adopted a civil rights model, which worked well in reducing the height of employment barriers for women and racial minorities. The burden of creating jobs and paying for accommodations for people with disabilities has been placed on employers. When an accommodation is person-specific (and can be transported from one employer to another), its cost ought to be financed out of general funds rather than placed on an employer.

The ADA has failed to raise the employment-to-population ratio. Individuals with disabilities are a diverse group; not all seek work in the market. As Jones has pointed out, "Disabilities make certain jobs and types of participation impossible." Retirement is a superior option for an older individual who experiences the onset of a condition that seriously limits performance and shortens longevity. The size and availability of disability benefits should be calibrated to the likelihood that the individual can be rehabilitated and returned to the world of work. One income maintenance policy will not be efficient for a population of people with widely different disabling conditions.

NOTES

1. The working-age adult population in the LaPlante study includes persons up to 69 years old. The impairments and chronic conditions identified by LaPlante were combined into 10 groups.

2. The concept of health capital is well developed by Grossman (1972) in the context of a life cycle model.

3. The data came from the 1972 SSA Survey of Disabled and Nondisabled Adults. Separate wage equations were estimated for handicapped workers (using the narrow definition from the World Health Organization classification) and nonhandicapped workers. The validity of this estimate is questionable; a critical review of the methodology is contained in the appendix notes to Oi and Andrews (1992).

4. The language of Title I of the Act spells out what is meant by the *essential functions* of a job. I have taken the liberty of summarizing the basic clauses, as follows: 1. The term pertains to the fundamental duties and excludes the marginal functions of the position. 2. A job function may be considered essential for several reasons: it is the reason for the creation of the position, only a limited number of employees can perform this function, and/or it is highly specialized. 3. The Act spells out what constitutes evidence.

5. To paraphrase the EEOC regulations, (1) the term *reasonable accommodations* means modification of the job application process, modification of the work environment, or modification that allows an employee with a disability to enjoy equal benefits and privileges; (2) reasonable accommodations may include, but are not limited to, equal access, job restructuring including part-time or flexible work schedules, reassignment, acquisition of equipment or devices, appropriate examinations and training materials, provision of readers or interpreters; and (3) it may be necessary to engage in an interactive process with a qualified person with a disability.

6. Chirikos (1991) has reviewed the studies that revealed modest accommodation costs for the comparatively small number of disabled persons who were gainfully employed. These accommodation costs mainly deal with such factors as the acquisition of special equipment, modifying the physical layout, or training procedures. To the best of my knowledge, no attempt is made to estimate the cost of job restructuring, providing a flexible work schedule, or extra leave for physician visits. Chirikos argues that, if the Act is successful in expanding employment, workplace accommodation costs could sharply rise as employers hire individuals with more functional limitations and impairments. The efficiency of placing the cost burden entirely upon employers is questioned by Rosen (1991). If the accommodation is *reasonable* and specific to the particular worker-firm attachment, a strong case can be made to share the costs.

7. The panel data from the Michigan Survey of Income Dynamics, Panel Study of Income Dynamics, were screened to obtain samples of married male household heads. Records with data for five consecutive years were obtained for 1,760 whites and 771 nonwhites. In 1972, 13.1 percent of the whites and 18.3 percent of the nonwhites were disabled. However, only 4.9 and 5.8 percent of these two samples reported a work disability in each of the five years, 1968-1972. Details of these tabulations can be found in Oi (1978).

8. All of these persons were judged under the SSA disability determination process to be so severely disabled that they were unable to work. The DI program imposes a two-year waiting period before a beneficiary is entitled to Medicare benefits. The objective of the Bye and Riley study was to evaluate the merits of eliminating the two-year waiting period.

9. The death rate was 6.7 percent for those under 40 years of age but jumped to 13.4 percent for the 40-49 age group. It continued to climb, but the increment to the oldest age group was only 1.4 percentage points.

10. The survey covered persons who entered the SSA rolls in 1980-1981 as new beneficiaries of the DI, Supplementary Security Income (SSI), or retired worker programs. Follow-up surveys were conducted in 1982 and 1991. Some 42 percent of the DI beneficiaries died in the decade following entitlement; the death rate was highest in the first six months on the DI rolls. The kinds of data included in the New Beneficiaries Data System (NBDS) are described by Yčas (1992). It is my understanding that Howard Iams and Barry Bye are preparing an analysis of the DI sample from the NBDS in a forthcoming article.

11. Lucas and Rapping (1969) showed that the labor supply response to a temporary wage cut will be larger than the response to a permanent wage cut because the worker will substitute current for future leisure. One should expect a similar difference in labor supply responses to disabling conditions that are temporary versus permanent.

12. See Oi (1962), Becker (1964), and Ben-Porath (1967).

13. There are three ways to leave the DI rolls: death, attainment of age 65 (and automatically transferring to the Old Age and Survivors fund), and recovery (SGA termination). In the Muller study, 9.3 percent of those under the age of 40 at entitlement recovered, as compared to only 1.1 percent of those who were 50-59 years of age in 1981. Notice in table 3 that the percentage separated for SGA terminations is only weakly related to family income. The surprising result reported by Muller is the small dispersion across diagnostic groups in the percentage doing "any work," varying from a low of 5.5 percent (respiratory) to a high of 12.8 percent (nervous disorders).

14. Holmes points out that the recession in 1993 may have depressed the employment-to-population ratio.

15. The Veterans Administration rating scheme assigns a score to each applicant that ranges from 0 to 100 percent. Several variables might be consulted to define disability classes for a new DI program: quarters of covered work experience, age, diagnostic group, medical rating of severity, and education. I assume that eligibility will be restricted to persons with X or more quarters of covered employment. A simple plan might identify only four disability classes: (1) under 50 years of age and in diagnostic group DG-A, (2) under 50 and in DG-B, (3) 50 or older and in DG-A, and (4) 50 or older and in DG-B. The classification DG-A includes those diagnostic groups exhibiting low two-year mortality rates, and DG-B includes diagnostic groups with high mortality rates.

16. An excerpt from a memo prepared for the Panel of the National Academy of Social Insurance noted that there were 2.2 million on the VA disability rolls, of which only 9 percent were unable to work. Reference to the SSA's *Annual Statistical Supplement*, 1993 (p. 329) reveals that, in 1992, there were 2,181,000 VA pensioners with service-connected disabilities and that 1,245,000 were under 65 years of age. Only 141,000 VA pensioners were under 65 years of age and had ratings of 70 to 100 percent. In my proposal, the medical assessment would serve as a screen excluding anyone with a rating of under 50 percent. This would have excluded an individual with one eye who would have received a VA disability pension.

References

Becker, Gary S. 1964. *Human Capital*. New York: National Bureau of Economic Research.

Bennefield, Robert L., and John M. McNeil. 1989. "Labor Force Status and Other Characteristics of Persons with a Work Disability: 1981 to 1988." U.S. Bureau of the Census, Current Population Reports, Series P-23, No. 160, July.

Ben-Porath, Y. 1967. "The Production of Human Capital and the Life Cycle of Earnings," *Journal of Political Economy* 75 (August), Part I: 352-365.

Biddle, Jeff E., and Daniel S. Hamermesh. 1990. "Sleep and the Allocation of Time," *Journal of Political Economy* 98 (October): 922-943.

Bound, John. 1989. "The Health and Earnings of Rejected Disability Insurance Applicants," *American Economic Review* 79 (June): 482-503.

Brown, Diane Robinson. 1989. "Work and Health Status Among Older Americans: An Analysis of Race Differences." Discussion Paper No. 877-889. Institute for Research on Poverty, University of Wisconsin, August.

Brown, Scott Campbell. 1993. "Revitalizing Handicap for Disability Research: Developing Tools to Assess Progress in Quality of Life for People with Disabilities," *Journal of Disability Policy Research* 4, 2.

Burkhauser, Richard V. 1990. "Morality on the Cheap: The Americans with Disabilities Act," *Regulation* 13 (Summer): 47-56.

Bye, Barry V., and Gerald F. Riley. 1989. "Eliminating the Medicare Waiting Period for Social Security Disabled Worker Beneficiaries," *Social Security Bulletin* 52 (May): 2-15.

Chirikos, Thomas N. 1991. "The Economics of Employment." In *The Americans with Disabilities Act: From Policy to Practice*, Jane West, ed. New York: Milbank Memorial Fund.

Cohany, Sharon R. 1987. "Labor Force Status of Vietnam-Era Veterans," *Monthly Labor Review* (February): 12-17.

Garraty, J.A. 1978. *Unemployment, A History*. New York: Harper and Row.

Grossman, M. 1972. "On the Concept of Health Capital and the Demand for Health," *Journal of Political Economics* 80 (March): 223-255.

Hashimoto, M., and B. Yu. 1980. "Specific Capital, Employment Contracts, and Wage Rigidities," *Bell Journal of Economics* (Spring): 536-549.

Haveman, Robert H., and Barbara L. Wolfe. 1990. "The Economic Well-Being of the Disabled, 1962 to 1984," *Journal of Human Resources* 25 (February): 32-54.

Holmes, Stephen A. 1994. "In Four Years, Disability Act Has Not Improved Job Rate," *New York Times,* October 23: 26.

Johnson, William G., and James Lambrinos. 1985. "Wage Discrimination Against Handicapped Men and Women," *Journal of Human Resources* 20 (Spring): 264-277.

Jones, Nancy Lee. 1991. "Essential Requirements of the Act: A Short History and Overview." In *The Americans with Disabilities Act: From Policy to Practice*, Jane West, ed. New York: Milbank Memorial Fund.

LaPlante, Mitchell P. 1988. *Data on Disability from the National Health Interview Survey, 1983-85, An In-House Review.* Washington, DC: National Institute on Disability and Rehabilitation Research.

Lucas, R., and L. Rapping. 1969. "Real Wages, Employment and Inflation," *Journal of Political Economics* 77 (September): 721-753.

Muller, L. Scott. 1992. "Disability Beneficiaries Who Work and Their Experience Under Program Work Incentives," *Social Security Bulletin* 55 (June): 2-19.

Oi, Walter Y. 1962. "Labor as a Quasi Fixed Factor," *Journal of Political Economy* 70 (December): 538-555.

_____. 1978. "Three Paths from Disability to Poverty." Technical Analysis Paper No. 57. Washington, DC: U.S. Department of Labor, Assistant Secretary for Policy Evaluation and Research, October.

Oi, Walter Y., and E. Andrews. 1992. "A Theory of Labor Market for People with Disabilities." Photocopy, University of Rochester.

Parsons, Donald O. 1980. "The Decline in Male Labor Force Participation," *Journal of Political Economy* 88 (February): 117-134.

Robbins, Lionel. 1930. "On the Elasticity of Demand for Income in Terms of Effort," *Economica* 10 (June): 123-129.

Rosen, S., 1991. "Disability Accommodations in the Labor Market." In *Disability and Work*, Caroline Weaver, ed. Washington, DC: AEI Press.

Rupp, Kalman, Stephen H. Bell, and Leo A. McManus. 1994. "Design of Project Network Return to Work Experiment for People with Disabilities," *Social Security Bulletin* 57, 2 (Summer): 3-20.

Stafford, Frank, and Greg J. Duncan. 1980. "The Use of Time and Technology by Households in the United States." In *Research in Labor Economics*, Vol. 3, R.G. Ehrenberg, ed. Greenwich, CT: JAI Press.

Weaver, Carolyn L. 1991. *Disability and Work: Incentives, Rights, and Opportunities.* Washington, DC: AEI Press.

Yčas, Martynas A. 1992. "A New Beneficiary Data System: The First Phase," *Social Security Bulletin* 55 (June): 20-35.

Yelin, Edward H. 1991. "The Recent History and Immediate Future of Employment Among Persons with Disabilities." In *The Americans with Disabilities Act: From Policy to Practice*, Jane West, ed. New York: Milbank Memorial Fund.

European Experiences with Disability Policy

Leo J.M. Aarts
Leiden University, the Netherlands
Philip R. de Jong
Erasmus University, Rotterdam
and *Leiden University*

The general aim of public policies toward disability is to share and to contain the associated social cost. Each country develops its own response with respect to disability. National policies typically are a mixture of three main objectives: (1) to ease the burden of impairments and the loss of earning capacity, which Haveman, Halberstadt, and Burkhauser (1984) call the *ameliorative* policy response; (2) to recover the earning capacity and the ability to perform normal social functions, so-called *corrective* policies; and (3) to prevent the occurrence of health impairments and to promote swift restoration of capacities if impairments prove to be irreversible, e.g., by adapting job demands or job conditions, which is the *preventive* approach.

In this paper, we discuss European experiences with disability policy over the last decades and current trends. We do so by presenting four typical national policies, from the Netherlands, Sweden, West Germany, and the United Kingdom. Each of these puts different emphases on compensation levels, on the linkage of ameliorative with corrective approaches, and on employment opportunities for disabled workers.[1] We start by tracking the disability records of the United States in comparison with the other four countries indicated and illustrate how different policy mixtures result in different outcomes. Next, we discuss how these various policy outcomes relate to cross-national approaches to disability insurance and to rehabilitation. We then focus on incentive structures as defined by the design and administration of disability programs and by their broader socioeconomic and policy environment. In the concluding section, we draw some lessons from other nations' experiences that may be relevant for redesigning U.S. disability policy.

Cross-National Comparison of Disability Records

Over the past two decades, virtually all Organization for Economic Cooperation and Development (OECD) countries have been confronted with excess supplies of labor resulting from demographics (the influx of baby boomers) and changed tastes for market work (the increasing participation of married women). Most of these countries have seen substantial declines in older male labor force participation as well as considerable increases in the availability and generosity of disability, and other early retirement, benefits. The concurrence of these tendencies suggests that disability programs have been generally used to achieve more general social policy goals, such as low (youth) unemployment.

In their comprehensive cross-national study of disability policy, Haveman, Halberstadt, and Burkhauser (1984) attribute the generally observed growth of disability income support to faltering economic growth. According to them, it made older workers with more or less serious impairments targets for layoffs while reducing their opportunities to obtain a job if out of work. In response, eligibility criteria for disability were relaxed. The disability option was attractive to older workers, as benefit payments became increasingly more adequate, and relatively little stigma was attached to the receipt of disability transfer income. Employers, likewise, found this development attractive, as it made release of long-term older, low-skilled, or impaired workers less difficult. With large cohorts of better-educated youths and women entering the labor market, replacement of older workers was not difficult. Disability income support programs became an instrument to encourage early retirement.

To the extent that this scenario holds for most Western countries, disability policy, at least in the 1970s, has emphasized income support rather than rehabilitation. A closer comparison of five countries (table 1), however, reveals that the age-specific trends in the number of disability beneficiaries show significant cross-national differences. To contain unemployment, the Netherlands clearly chose the income maintenance option, even for those under 45. Sweden and Germany, on the other hand, largely opted for employment security for ailing workers under 60 and restoration of their earning capacities where possible. Part of the German excess labor supply was captured by relaxing benefit eligibility criteria, both for disabled and able-bodied workers over 60. The United States initially showed a tendency towards the income maintenance option but started to tighten eligibility standards at the end of the 1970s. Considering the full 1970-1990 period, the United States accommodated an excess supply of labor by letting wage rates drop and allowing market forces to create low-productivity employment for impaired workers. After 1990, however, disability transfer recipiency shows a steep increase (for a short description, see U.S. General Accounting Office 1994).

Like the United States, Germany introduced stricter eligibility standards in 1985, which brought the relative size of the 1990 beneficiary volume back to the low level that had prevailed in the 1970s. Note also that the German prevalence rates for younger workers were relatively low over the whole period, and lower in 1990 than in 1970. This suggests that by making older workers redundant, younger workers' employment could be secured. Finally, the United Kingdom has seen disability growth in all age brackets but, contrary to the other countries, only after 1980.

The data in table 1 highlight the unique position of the Netherlands. For those younger than 60, disability prevalence rates have been about three times as high as in other countries (Aarts, Burkhauser, and de Jong 1996). Furthermore, the average Dutch beneficiary age is 49, which compares to 57 in Sweden and Germany. As one can plausibly assume that the Dutch do not have significantly poorer health status and job conditions than other European populations, the difference must be sought in the way disability benefits are being allocated.

Table 1 also shows that, despite having a disability beneficiary volume which is two-to-three times as large as that in comparable welfare states, the Dutch unemployment rate is at about the OECD average level. As a consequence, the employment rate, i.e., employed persons as a percentage of the working-age population, is low, especially among older workers (see OECD 1993). These data on the Dutch labor market suggest that other comparable countries have a stronger capacity to reintegrate, or keep, less productive individuals in the workforce.

**Table 1. Disability Transfer Recipients per Thousand Active Labor Force
Participants by Age, Unemployment Rates, and Older Male
Labor Force Participation Rates, in Five OECD Countries,
1970-1994**

	1970	1975	1980	1985	1990	1994
15-44 years						
The Netherlands	17	32	57	58	62	66
United States	11	17	16	20	23	38
United Kingdom	8	9	11	20	23	
Germany[a]	7	6	7	8	5	5[b]
Sweden	18	20	19	20	21	27
45-59 years						
The Netherlands	113	179	294	305	339	289
United States	33	68	83	71	72	96
United Kingdom	48	46	51	97	119	
Germany[a]	75	64	84	103	75	80[b]
Sweden	66	95	99	108	116	143
60-64 years						
The Netherlands	299	437	1,033	1,283	1,987	1,911
United States	154	265	285	254	250	294
United Kingdom	219	195	209	357	413	
Germany.[a]	419	688	1,348	1,291	1,109	1,064[b]
Sweden	229	382	382	512	577	658
Total population, 15-64 years						
The Netherlands	55	84	138	142	152	151
United States	27	42	41	41	43	62
United Kingdom	29[b]	28	31	56	68[d]	
Germany[a]	51	54	59	72	55	54[b]
Sweden	49	67	68	74	78	97
Unemployment rate (percent)						
The Netherlands	1.0	5.2	6.0	10.6	7.5	7.2
United States	4.8	8.3	7.0	7.1	5.4	6.0
United Kingdom	2.9[c]	3.9	6.4	11.2	6.8	9.6
Germany[a]	0.6	3.6	2.9	7.1	4.8	6.9

**Table 1.   Disability Transfer Recipients per Thousand Active Labor Force
Participants by Age, Unemployment Rates, and Older Male
Labor Force Participation Rates, in Five OECD Countries,
1970-1994**

	1970	1975	1980	1985	1990	1994
Sweden	1.5	1.6	2.0	2.8	1.5	8.0
Labor force participation rates (x 100) for males, 55-64						
The Netherlands	81	72	63	47	46	43
United States	81	76	72	68	68	67
United Kingdom	88[c]	88	82	69	68	66
Germany[a]	80	70	67	60	58	50
Sweden	85	82	79	76	75	73

SOURCE: United Kingdom age-specific data are derived from Lonsdale (1993) and *Employment Gazette* (several issues); U.K. disability beneficiary data for 1993 or 1994 were not available.; other data are updates from Aarts, Burkhauser, and de Jong (1992).
a. German data refer to the former Federal Republic.
b. Figure refers to 1993.
c. Figure refers to 1971.
d. Figure refers to 1991.

Table 2 provides data on "active," or corrective (vocational rehabilitation, work for the disabled), versus "passive," or ameliorative (disability benefits), program expenditures. Of the countries listed, Sweden and Holland devote by far the largest shares of their national resources to both types of disability policies. In these countries, the largest parts of redeployment budgets are used to create jobs outside of the market. While in Sweden only a minority of this budget is allocated to sheltered workshops (see "Cross-National Comparison of Rehabilitation Policies" on p. 141), in Holland, the entire budget is used to keep disabled workers who want jobs out of regular employment. Recent changes in Dutch disability insurance legislation seek to reduce disability benefit dependency and to keep people with disabilities in paid work. The Dutch figures for 1993 suggest that these amendments were unsuccessful; however, the disability volume decreased in 1994, for the first time in an almost 30-year history of relentless growth.

The low U.S. spending on disability as a percentage of Gross Domestic Product suggests that this section relies more than do Western European countries on policies that induce impaired persons to seek private solutions for their employment problems. Germany stands out as a country that emphasizes rehabilitation and spends a moderate proportion on cash benefits, mainly on older workers.

The costs involved with private solutions to the employment problems faced by the disabled depend on regulations such as employment quotas, job protection, and equal opportunity legislation. These types of costs are mainly borne by the employer. Moreover, countries with stringent award policies and low benefit levels shift a larger part of the social cost of disability to the household budgets of people with disabilities. National policies, therefore, not only determine the level of the total, social cost of disability, but also the way in which this cost is shared between the private and public sectors. Countries with comparatively tight budgets for cash benefits are likely to have relatively low social costs, e.g., efficiency losses, and a relatively large share of private costs (to employers and households).

Table 2. Public Expenditures on Labor Market Measures for the Disabled and on Cash Benefits, as a Percentage of GDP, 1991

	Vocational rehabilitation	Work for the disabled	Disability benefits
		(Percent of GDP)	
F.R. Germany	0.13	0.09	2.0
United Kingdom	0.01	0.02	1.9
United States	0.05	a	0.7
Sweden	0.10	0.68	3.3
Netherlands	a	0.64	4.6

SOURCE: OECD (1992, 1993); *Sociale Nota* (1993), and authors' calculations.
a. Less than 0.01 percent.

Cross-National Comparison of Disability Benefit Policies

In this section, we describe several aspects of disability policies as elements of a broader set of income maintenance and labor market programs. We start with an outline of common features of selected social security systems and their divergent underlying philosophies. Specific approaches toward disabled citizens are reflected primarily by differences in the accessibility, generosity, and administration of disability transfer programs. The main characteristics of such programs will be discussed and are summarized in an appendix table. Also important is the broader institutional setting, in which the availability of alternative transfers and the scope of rehabilitation and redeployment programs are crucial elements. At the beginning, and at the end of this section, we therefore devote a few paragraphs to more general aspects of social policy.

Common Features: Social Insurance and Welfare Provisions

European social security systems include both social insurance and social assistance (welfare) programs. Social insurance flows from the vision of Bismark, the German politician who, in the second half of the 19th century, introduced the first legally established insurance funds to cover work injuries. Other types of social insurance, covering wage loss due to temporary sickness, nonwork-related invalidity, old age, and unemployment, followed.

Welfare programs germinated from ideas in the Atlantic Charter, drafted by Churchill and Roosevelt in 1941. This document offered a blueprint for the postwar Keynesian welfare state, which rested on the twin principles of "freedom from want" and "freedom from idleness." For the United Kingdom, this blueprint was elaborated by Beveridge, who proposed a national safety net to protect every citizen against poverty.

Both types of programs are based on the principle of solidarity and on its legal counterpart, the constitutionally established responsibility of the state to protect its residents from poverty. This goal is achieved by two provisions: wage-replacement and minimum income guarantees. Wage-replacement is based on mutual, and intergenerational, solidarity among employees to protect their acquired standards of living. Wage-replacing schemes consist of social insurance covering the loss of earnings due to old age, unemployment, temporary sickness, or permanent disability. Social insurance expenditures are financed by compulsory contributions, and the premiums are determined under a pay-as-you-go system.

Social assistance programs safeguard the subsistence levels of all residents by offering flat-rate, means-tested transfers financed by general revenue and administered by municipalities or local agencies. Statutory, or collectively bargained, minimum wages are intended to protect the livelihood of those who are employed.

Finally, in the European welfare states people have broad access to health care through combinations of public, tax-funded programs, social insurance, and/or regulated private markets. Such arrangements are of prime interest for people with disabilities.

Comparison of these general features of European welfare states with the United States reveals four major differences. First, the United States has no universal safety net provision for those, working or nonworking, below the poverty line. Second, contrary to European systems, temporary sickness is not covered by a statutory sick pay plan that encompasses all those in paid employment. Third, Americans are not universally (or federally) insured against loss of earnings due to unemployment. Fourth, despite the existence of two public, federal programs that cover health costs for target groups (Medicare and Medicaid), universal coverage is not available.

Underlying Philosophies

The common features of European social security systems only indicate the broad principles on which they are based. However, as the data in the two preceding tables suggest, the countries surveyed here differ significantly in their treatment of people with disabilities. These approaches are related to varying perspectives on the disabled and translate into cross-national differences in disability policies and policy outcomes.

Considering the 1970-1990 period, Holland is an exceptional case by its emphasis on "freedom from want" at the expense of "freedom from idleness," which is the overriding principle in Sweden, the United Kingdom, and Germany. Until 1990, when the Swedish economy slipped into its deepest crisis since World War II, the Swedes gave priority to vocational rehabilitation and redeployment of the disabled, mostly through public sector work programs. Since then, job programs have been cut, and unemployment has soared. Nevertheless, swift rehabilitation is still a major goal. Sweden also stresses moderation of income differentials so that both benefit replacement rates and public sector wages are comparatively high and independent of job performance.

Despite sharp differences in disability policy and records, Holland and Sweden share the economic problems attributable to a wasteful welfare state. Both countries are now reevaluating their social systems, to strike more of a balance between equity and efficiency. One of the focal points of this process is the incentive structure in which relevant parties (covered workers, employers, program administrators) operate (see the section entitled "The Importance of Incentive Structures").

In comparison to those in Holland and Sweden, the German system appears to be more manageable. *Rehabilitation bevor Renten* (rehabilitation before pensions) is the often-quoted leading principle of German disability policy and of social policy in general. It implies a public commitment to give priority to preventive and corrective policy responses. Strict admission procedures, mandatory rehabilitation, a quota for employers to provide (market) jobs for the disabled, and a separate disabled worker status in employment are the main instruments to support vocational rehabilitation.

Finally, the United Kingdom contains its disability budget mainly by keeping benefit levels low. Vocational rehabilitation is supported by a set of instruments similar to that in Germany. However, these tools are less effective, as the involvement of employers in shaping and administering social insurance programs is weaker than on the European continent, where the concept of a "social partnership" between labor and management has strong traditional roots and pervades the institutional framework in which the labor market operates.

Accessibility I: Coverage[2]

In European welfare states, all employees are covered by social insurance against the risk of wage loss due to temporary sickness or permanent disablement. Sick pay usually covers all health contingencies, whether objectively assessable or not. If the incapacity has a work-related cause, a separate work injury program may replace wage loss. European work injury plans are similar to the U.S. workers' compensation program, both in design and origin. Work injury programs were the first form of social insurance in all early market economies.

As a consequence of the Industrial Revolution, a large number of individuals became involved in hazardous jobs. Simultaneously, tort law evolved such that employers were increasingly found liable for the financial consequences of job-related diseases and injuries. These parallel trends spurred a common interest among labor and firms in coverage of the financial risks of work injury. As private insurance markets were unable to provide such coverage, this common interest created a broad political platform for the implementation of statutory social insurance plans.

In almost all welfare states, coverage of work injury and related risks is compulsory for private employment. One of the exceptions is Holland, which abolished the distinction between work-related and other causes of incapacity under its disability insurance scheme in 1967. In the United States, small firms, and firms in certain states, may be exempted from mandated coverage.[3]

Most disability transfer programs covering social risks, i.e., non-work-related contingencies, consist of an employment-related, social insurance scheme, like the Social Security Disability Insurance (DI) program, and a separate arrangement for disabled persons without, or with limited, work experience, like Supplemental Security Income (SSI). In Holland and Sweden, compensation for loss of earning capacity due to long-term impairments is provided by a two-tier disability insurance program. The first tier is universal, with eligibility being based on citizenship. These national disability insurance programs typically offer flat-rate benefits that are, of course, earnings-tested but are not tested for other household means. They target those handicapped congenitally, or in early childhood, and provide benefits from age 18 onwards. In Holland, these basic benefits also cover self-employed people. In Germany and the United Kingdom, those with insufficient insurance contribution years have to rely on means-tested social assistance transfers. In the United Kingdom, an additional disability premium may be allowed up to the basic rate under invalidity benefits (see the appendix table). In Germany, employees who become disabled before age 55 enjoy entitlements as if they had worked until age 55.

Eligibility for a supplement is restricted to labor force participants. These second-tier benefits are based on age, or employment history, and wage earnings. In Germany and Sweden, as is the case under the U.S. Social Security system, earnings-related disability insurance is part of the legal pension system. Coverage depends on contribution years. More specifically, at least three years (Sweden) or three out of the five years (Germany) preceding a contingency should have been spent in paid employment. Wage earners are obliged to participate, and the self-employed may participate voluntarily. Holland and the United Kingdom have no contribution requirements for earnings-related benefits in terms of years of covered employment. However, the United Kingdom has a requirement of covered earnings both for statutory sick pay and invalidity benefits, and, in 1993, Holland introduced a system of age-dependent supplemental benefits, which simulate a contribution years requirement.

Accessibility II: Eligibility Requirements and Benefit Levels

By definition, eligibility for disability pensions is based on some measure of (residual) capacity or productivity. The United Kingdom has an all-or-nothing system: after 28 weeks, when sickness benefits have run out, only those fully incapacitated, i.e., more than 80 percent disabled, qualify for invalidity benefits. These are basically flat-rate benefits, which are only distantly related to previous earnings (see the appendix table). Supplements and allowances may be given, depending (inversely) on age and on household situation.

Germany has a dual system, with full benefits for those who lose two-thirds or more of their earning capacity with regard to any job available in the economy and partial benefits for those who are more than 50 percent disabled with regard to their usual occupation. Under the Handicapped Act of 1974, workers having a permanent reduction in their labor capacity of at least 50 percent are entitled to the status of "severely disabled" (*Schwerbehinderte*). Given this status, workers are entitled to extra vacation and enjoy protection against dismissal. Although being recognized as a severely disabled worker does not give access to cash benefits, it allows one to retire at age 60 with a full pension, given sufficient (15) contribution years.[4]

Sweden has a more lenient eligibility standard, as incapacity is measured with regard to commensurate employment instead of any gainful activity. Moreover, the Swedish program has four disability categories, depending on the size of residual capacity, with a corresponding system of full and partial pensions.

The Dutch disability program is unique in that it distinguishes seven disability categories, ranging from less-than-15 percent, 15-25 percent disabled, and so on, to 80-100 percent disabled. The minimum degree of disability yielding entitlement to benefits is 15 percent. The degree of disablement is assessed by consideration of the worker's residual earning capacity. As of 1994, capacity is defined by the earnings flowing from any job commensurate with one's residual capabilities as a percentage of predisability usual earnings. The degree of disablement, then, is the complement of the residual earning capacity and defines the benefit level. Before 1994, only jobs that were compatible with one's training and work history could be taken into consideration. Not only has the definition of suitable work been broadened, but the medical definition of disability has been tightened: under the new ruling, the causal relationship between impairment and disablement has to be objectively assessable.

Administration

The preceding short overview of "the rules of the game" does not say much about how the game is played. It does not explain why different national schemes produce the divergent results recorded by tables 1 and 2. More specifically, the fact that Holland has such a high prevalence of disability transfer payment recipients has more to do with the way in which the rules are applied than with the rules as such.

The Dutch disability plan differs from other national programs, not only because it has no separate work injury scheme and has a more elaborate system of partial benefits, but also because its social insurance programs (disability and unemployment insurance, and sickness benefits) are run by autonomous organizations, which lack direct governmental (political) control. These "Industrial (Insurance) Associations" represent different (19) branches of industry. They are managed by representatives of employers' organizations and trade unions. Membership in one of these associations is obligatory for every employer. The Industrial Associations have discretion to develop autonomous benefit award and rehabilitation policies without having to bear the fiscal consequences of their policy choices, as disability program expenditures are funded by a uniform contribution rate. Thus, administrative autonomy is not balanced by financial responsibility (see the discussion under "The Importance of Incentive Structures").

In Germany and Sweden, disability insurance is part of the national pension program, which is run by an independent, national board that is, however, closely supervised by those who are politically responsible for the operation of the social security system and therefore subject to parliamentary control. These boards monitor disability plans and safeguard uniformity in award policy by issuing rules and guidelines to local agencies. The British administration, being a civil service run by the Department of Social Security, is more similar to the U.S. Social Security Administration. The difference between these countries and Holland, then, is that their disability systems are under some form of budgetary control.

In Holland, disability assessments are made by teams of insurance doctors and vocational experts employed by the administrative offices of the Industrial Associations. These teams also have to examine the rehabilitation potential of disability claimants and to rehabilitate those with sufficient residual capacities. A further potentially important difference with the other European countries, then, is that the Dutch disability assessment teams are legally obliged to examine every benefit claimant personally, not just administratively. This may have spurred a liberal, conflict-avoiding attitude, especially in a setting in which neither the gatekeepers themselves nor their managers are confronted with the financial consequences of award decisions.

Sweden only allows administrative checks of disability claims on the basis of written, medical and other, reports in order to prevent the program gatekeepers from being influenced by self-reports and by the physical presence of claimants. In Germany, too, award decisions are made by using medical reports and by applying uniform decision rules developed by specialists' panels, each covering a diagnostic group. Entry into the British Invalidity Benefit program rests upon the claimant's doctor issuing a statement that advises the person to refrain from work when, in the doctor's opinion, the patient is definitely unable to do so because of a physical or mental disorder or when work would be detrimental to the patient's health. Claimants may be, and often are, referred to doctors of the Benefit Agency's Medical Reference Services. Usually, one in three among those examined by reference doctors is considered fit for either the predisability job or for some other work.

"Hidden" Unemployment

Workers with disabilities have a higher-than-average sensitivity to cyclical downswings. Independent of the operation of disability programs, they are among the first to be made redundant. Both American and British studies show a significant relationship between labor market conditions and disability program participation rates.[5] These studies do not explain the extent to which there may be severely disabled individuals hidden among workers in boom periods or (mildly disabled) unemployed persons hidden among disability benefit recipients in slack periods.

As discussed, European workers who lose their jobs are usually covered by unemployment insurance. Entitlement to earnings-related unemployment insurance benefits is of limited duration and is followed by flat-rate, means-tested social assistance. In Holland, Germany, and Sweden, entitlement durations depend on age, such that workers older than 58 or 60 may keep unemployment insurance until they reach pensionable age (65) or qualify for disability insurance benefits on non-medical, labor market grounds. Improper use of disability benefits as a more generous, and less stigmatizing, alternative to unemployment benefits was quite common in the 1975-1990 period (see the earlier section on disability records). It provided employers with a flexible instrument to reduce the labor force at will and kept official unemployment rates low. The approach was very popular in Sweden until 1992, when the law was changed and disability pensions based solely on unemployment could no longer be awarded.

Holland had similar experiences. Until 1987, the law explicitly recognized the difficulties impaired workers may have in finding commensurate employment by prescribing that the benefit adjudicators should take account of poor labor market opportunities. The administrative interpretation of this so-called labor market consideration was so liberal as to award a full benefit to almost anyone who passed the low threshold of a 15 percent reduction in earnings capacity. The share of unemployed (or "socially disabled") among disability insurance beneficiaries, applying the pre-1994 eligibility standards, is estimated to be 40 percent (see Aarts and de Jong 1992, chapters 5 and 11). The fact that the abolition of this legal provision could not halt the growth in the incidence of disability transfer payment recipients (table 1) induced further amendments in 1992-1994.

Labor market considerations also influence disability determinations in Germany. In 1976, the German Federal Court ruled that if insured persons have limited residual capacities and the Employment Service or the Pension Insurance is unable to find them a commensurate job within one year, they can be awarded a full disability pension retroactively. Because partial disability benefits are based on the availability of commensurate work, certified skilled workers may refuse any job that is not at least semiskilled in nature. A semiskilled worker must only accept unskilled jobs that are prominent in pay and prestige. Unskilled workers who are not eligible for a full disability pension have to resort to unemployment or to social assistance. These regulations, in combination with a slack labor market, have reduced the proportion of partial pensions from 30 percent in 1970 to less than 5 percent in the early 1990s.

Cross-National Comparison of Rehabilitation Policies

Assessment of rehabilitative potential is the counterpart of disability assessment. To contain dependency on transfer payments, impairments should be cured, or their limiting consequences corrected, as soon as possible. The ultimate goal of a vocational rehabilitation plan is work resumption. This involves more than treatment, training, and the provision of corrective devices. It also involves job mediators and employers. Swift rehabilitation and redeployment depend on the willingness of all of these different actors to invest money, time, and/or effort to boost the employment possibilities of impaired workers. The job of some of these participants (doctors, ergonomists, job mediators) is to help people overcome their handicaps. For others, the impaired workers and their employers, it is more or less a matter of choice and, hence, of incentives, as to whether they engage in rehabilitative efforts.

Policies differ with respect to public spending on rehabilitation services and on employment programs for disabled workers (see table 2). Rehabilitation services may consist of (subsidies on) tangible provisions (corrective devices, such as wheelchairs, workplace accommodations, Seeing Eye dogs) or of intangible ones (training, therapy, counseling, job mediation). Given the broad accessibility of health care in European welfare states, there are no serious financial impediments to obtaining medical rehabilitation. Nevertheless, over the past years, as part of the changes in their welfare programs, Sweden and Holland have introduced patient fees for an increasing number of health and rehabilitation services.

National policies also differ in the extent to which they require rehabilitation efforts. Mandatory rehabilitation is a possible outcome of the disability determination process in both Germany and Sweden. Moreover, Germany and the United Kingdom have quotas, stipulating that firms should employ a certain percentage of workers who are registered as handicapped. Dutch and Swedish civil law similar to the Americans with Disabilities Act requires firms to provide commensurate work to employees who have become disabled in their current jobs.

Public Provision of Rehabilitation Services

In addition to cash compensation, Dutch disability insurance offers in-kind provisions covering job accommodation and training costs to promote redeployment of impaired workers. As table 2 indicates, spending in this area is minimal. In 1993, spending on provisions in kind under the Dutch disability insurance program amounted to 0.8 billion guilders. Only 20 million (2.5 percent of provisions expenditures, about 0.1 percent of total disability expenditures) was used for vocational rehabilitation and workplace adjustment. The rest was spent on provisions for general daily activities (mobility, dwelling, etc.). The amount is extremely low simply because very few claims are filed. On a per-capita basis, Germany spends 42 times more than Holland does on vocational rehabilitation.[6]

Various aspects of the disability pension system reflect the German commitment to a corrective policy response. First, a relatively large amount of money is spent on vocational rehabilitation (see table 2). Impaired workers are referred to rehabilitation by the adjudicators of either the sickness insurance system, the disability pensions, or by the local employment agencies. Furthermore, to encourage employment of disabled workers, the Handicapped Act subsidizes employer expenses related to job accommodations.

The Swedish Social Security Administration and its regional and local offices do not have their own rehabilitation personnel or facilities. Instead, they enlist the services of the various medical, vocational, and other professionals in this field. Each county has AMIs (labor market institutes), special centers for vocational rehabilitation and guidance. The centers are operated by the National Labor Market Board through the county labor market boards. Some of them specialize in groups with specific disabilities. The AMIs provide more detailed examinations than are given at the employment offices, in order to determine the work capacity of people with disabilities and to provide general help in developing the capacities necessary to work. However, in most cases, specific occupational training for the disabled is provided under the same programs that train people without disabilities. The AMIs also serve the nondisabled; the share of those in AMI programs who are able-bodied has gradually increased and is now about 50 percent.

Recently, the general policy emphasis in Sweden has been put on early intervention for those receiving sickness benefits and on the coordination of all the parties involved in rehabilitation, i.e., medical professionals, unions, employers, vocational professionals, and employment service administrators, depending on what the case is judged to require. New legislation gives the social insurance offices the responsibility for initiating and coordinating rehabilitation when necessary. This has enabled social insurance administrators to act more as private insurers with a responsibility to contain costs. The government has established cost-reduction goals for all the regional offices regarding sickness and disability payments. In sum, the trend of recent years has been to make more resources available for rehabilitation, while at the same time goals have been set for reducing benefit payments by returning persons to the workplace.

The British Department of Employment, operating under the responsibility of the Secretary of State for Employment, administers a number of programs aimed at rehabilitation and reentry into the labor market. The United Kingdom provides a status to those who qualify to be registered as disabled similar to the official status of *Schwerbehinderte* in Germany. Being on the register enables a person to claim various kinds of assistance aimed at getting a job.

Vocational rehabilitation is provided mainly through 26 Employment Rehabilitation Centres (ERCs). The ERC staff includes individuals such as psychologists, social workers, and technical instructors, who provide fuller assessments of capacity as well as employment rehabilitation and training. Research in 1980 showed that, six months after completing the courses, about half the participants were employed and the other 50 percent were either on sickness benefits or unemployed. To our knowledge, more recent empirical analyses are not available. The present trend is towards privatizing the Employment Rehabilitation Centers.

Employment Policies

Provision of jobs for workers with disabilities can take several forms. One is job creation in the public sector, either as part of an employment policy targeted at a broader population, including the able-bodied unemployed, or via a narrow approach, by creating sheltered workshops as a kind of workfare for the disabled. Another way to promote employment is to hand out wage subsidies to private business. Finally, employers may be forced to make room for handicapped workers by regulations, such as requirements involving special perks for recognized disabled workers, job protection, and employment quotas.

Sheltered Work. Holland, Sweden, and the United Kingdom have forms of sheltered work for the disabled. Holland has a national network of sheltered workshops, employing 88,000 people with disabilities (1.5 percent of total employment). Sweden has 35,000 handicapped workers (0.83 percent of total employment) in sheltered jobs. In both countries, the operating costs of these workshops are almost fully funded by government. On average, wages are higher than disability benefits, and part-time earnings may be combined with partial benefits. Handicapped workers may choose freely whether or not they want to be employed in a sheltered workshop. In the United Kingdom, the range of sheltered employment opportunities goes from large government-supported companies to smaller sheltered workshops that are little more than welfare provision. They all are heavily subsidized by way of grants to cover trading losses and training fees. Quantitatively, the sheltered employment programs are of marginal significance, as only about 20,000 severely disabled people (0.075 percent of total employment) are in sheltered employment. Sheltered placements are increasing, however.

Wage Subsidies and Partial Benefits. Apart from being an insurance device to compensate the exact loss of earning capacity, partial benefits also work as a wage subsidy. In fact, introduction of the fine grid of seven disability categories under Dutch disability insurance was supported by explicitly referring to its rehabilitative aims when the program was enacted in 1967. Partial benefits were intended to help disabled workers find commensurate employment. By liberal application of labor market considerations, it became routine to award full benefits under the presumption of a shortage of employment opportunities. This lenient approach was hoped to have been changed by the 1987 amendments, banning labor considerations, into an administrative practice of accurate assessments of residual capacities. The old routines proved difficult to alter, however, and the amendments did not produce the expected results. At the end of 1993, 77 percent of current disability beneficiaries still had an award based on full disability. Hence, a new series of cuts and changes were introduced in 1993 and 1994.

Like Holland, Sweden and Germany have also seen a growing share of full disability benefits. Currently, 85 percent of Swedish and 95 percent of German beneficiaries (up from a 1965 low of 67 percent) are labeled as fully disabled. These differences suggest that the more stringent the award system, the stronger the pressure to obtain full awards. In Sweden, a separate wage subsidy program was introduced in 1980, replacing two earlier programs. The compensation rate paid to the employer varies depending on the disability, on the duration of employment (compensation is generally higher in the first years after a person is hired; subsidies are not available for already employed persons), on the sector in which the person is employed, and on the person's age (compensation is highest for disabled youth). On average, the compensation rate was 73 percent in July 1992 for those in their first year of support and 61 percent for those assisted for longer periods. These wage subsidies are used by about 1 percent of total employment.

Although the British system does not provide for partial disability benefits, people with severe disabilities are subsidized under the British Sheltered Placement Scheme to work in the open labor market. The wage subsidies are paid to the employers to compensate for the difference in productivity between a disabled and a nondisabled worker. Furthermore, the Disability Working Allowance, a bonus for disability beneficiaries who have found a job, was introduced in 1992. The allowance depends on the wage and on the disabled person's wealth. Claims are adjudicated on the basis of self-assessed disability. The Department of Social Security anticipated an annual number of 50,000 claims. Within six months following its introduction, around 20,000 claims were received; however, 90 percent were denied, mainly because claimants had not yet obtained a job.

Employer Mandates

Quotas. Employment quotas exist in Germany and the United Kingdom. The German Handicapped Act requires that public and private employers with more than 15 employees hire one severely disabled person for every 16 job slots or pay monthly compensation of deutsche mark (DM) 200 ($130) for each unfilled quota position. In 1990, approximately 900,000 severely disabled persons were employed, and 120,000 were unemployed. Despite the carrot of subsidies for workplace adjustments and the stick of monthly fines, disabled persons make up only 4.5 percent of the targeted workforce, well below the 6 percent quota. Only 19 percent of the 122,807 public and private employers subject to the quota have managed to fill it; 44 percent of these enterprises employ some severely disabled persons, although the numbers are lower than required by the Handicapped Act. The remaining 37 percent employ no disabled persons (Sadowski and Frick 1992a). Although German authors are rather critical of the effect of the Handicapped Act and compliance is far from full, the employment rate among disabled workers in the market sector is high by international standards, even by comparison with Sweden.

The British Disabled Persons Act of 1944 places a statutory obligation on employers with 20 or more employees to fulfill a "quota" of at least 3 percent of registered disabled people in the workforce. In theory, noncompliance can lead to a fine or even to imprisonment. In practice, however, the quota regulation is not enforced. Fines have been imposed on only a handful of occasions despite the fact that, for the past 20 years, the majority of employers have stayed well below their quota requirements. In Holland, successive governments have also been reluctant to regulate business in this way, preferring to rely on the promotion of voluntary codes of practice.

Job Protection. Dutch legal regulations oblige employers to provide commensurate work to employees who have become disabled in their current jobs. After the onset of impairment, individuals can only be dismissed if continued employment in one's usual, or alternative, work would put a more-than-reasonable strain upon the employer. An absolute dismissal ban is in force during the first two years of disability. After these two years, the employer is usually granted dismissal permission. Similarly, German workers that are recognized as severely disabled have the right to demand workplace adjustments and to enjoy protection against dismissal.

The Importance of Incentive Structures

Overview

European welfare states are in a phase of reorientation. The negative efficiency impacts of the equity principles upon which these states were built have gradually turned into urgent social policy problems. In countries such as Holland and Sweden, the sentiment is that

> far too many people rely on social benefits, while too few citizens are at work contributing to economic growth and the financing of social welfare expenditure. The benefit rules and the high levels of taxation required to finance the system affect human motivation in a negative direction and may increase the propensity to work unofficially in the "black" economy.[7]

Among other things, the generosity and lack of control of disability benefit programs are now important entries on the agenda for reform. As we have seen, Germany and the United Kingdom have less generous and, therefore, more manageable disability programs.

Among the four countries studied, Germany probably shows the best example of a balanced approach toward disability in that it is the least controversial. However, national policies have their own historical background and are set in a specific political and socioeconomic context. An exact copy of the German system in another national setting could, therefore, yield very different results. What we can learn from varying experiences in different settings is something about the combined effects of, and possible relationships between, disability policies and their social, economic, and political environment.

Every country develops its own set of policy responses, which are typically mixtures of ameliorative, corrective, and preventive elements. More specifically, disability policies are directed at four goals, namely, (1) prevention of, (2) compensation for, and (3) recovery from losses in earning capacity due to functional limitations, and (4) reduction in the waste of human capital, by either retaining people with residual earning capacities within the employing firm or by gainful redeployment through external channels.

In practice, the second and fourth goals often are in conflict. Since adequate compensation may collide with the need to contain benefit expenditures, each national system has to find a balance by setting priorities and by using a number of instruments that are more or less universal across countries, such as

• social insurance benefits;

• assessment instruments and procedures that help in targeting benefits to the most needy and that facilitate timely interventions;

• rehabilitation services (training, medical services) and other in-kind provisions to accommodate functional limitations;

• redeployment services (job mediation), sheltered employment opportunities for those who are not employable in regular jobs, and quotas;

• legal provisions aimed at reducing the risk of work injury and occupational diseases;

• legal employment protection of functionally impaired people to counterbalance their reduced "market value"; and

• wage subsidies, partial benefits, or disability allowances to compensate employees/employers for productivity losses.

Under the European systems reviewed in this paper, most of these policy instruments are available to the administrators of disability programs. In this respect, European policy approaches are similar. Cross-country differences in policy outcomes, therefore, cannot be explained by a lack of tools. The dominant view in Europe, nowadays also shared by traditional supporters of the welfare state in Sweden and the Netherlands, is that the incentive structure implied by the design of national disability policies is crucially inadequate. To illustrate this argument, we will identify the major agents involved in shaping disability practices and the ways in which their behavior is affected by the implicit incentive structure.

Who Are the Agents?

The allocation of disability benefits over the population at risk takes place through the operation of three agents: (1) insured/covered persons, mainly employees, who can claim to be unfit for work because of a physical or mental impairment; (2) their employers, if any, who either may support the claim, or, if held responsible, fight it, or may help in overcoming the limiting consequences of functional impairments; and (3) the intermediaries, i.e., private or social insurers and the curative sector, which have to assess the extent to which claimants are eligible and to which their ailments can be cured or their limitations can be overcome.

Each of these three agents is subject to incentives determining the outcome of a process that starts with the manifestation of the symptoms of an ailment. These incentives are primarily defined by the design of the plans covering disability-related needs. For instance, stringent, and easily and unambiguously applicable, eligibility rules for disability (cash) benefits restrict the discretion of both the gatekeepers of the disability plan and the persons covered. On the other hand, disability eligibility rules that encompass every conceivable health complaint leave a great deal of latitude both to gatekeepers in their disability determinations and, hence, to covered persons in weighing the costs and benefits of program participation.

The greater the room for choice, the stronger the impact of other than health-related factors. Such factors may be program characteristics—benefit size and duration, availability of curative, corrective, or rehabilitative provisions in kind, mandated redeployment—or may be more or less independent of the design and operation of the disability plan. These external influences can be found in different spheres of life—personal, vocational, social—of the individuals covered by the program. These factors, however, may also stem from a broader environment, such as regional labor market circumstances and the availability of alternative cash benefits.[8]

The Employee/Disability Beneficiary

Economic theory posits that workers supply labor according to their preferences with regard to the trade-off between leisure and earnings, available nonwork income, and earning capacities as reflected by wage rates. The stronger one's taste for leisure, the lower the expected wage rate, and the larger the amount of nonwork income, the smaller the expected number of hours supplied. The expected wage rate is the product of the wage rate in a given job and the probability of finding such a job, taken over all jobs in the relevant segment of the labor market, i.e., the wage offer distribution. Similarly, the expected number of hours is the product of the probability of labor force participation and the preferred number of hours, given participation.

Within this theoretical framework, health impairments may reduce labor supply for two reasons. Impairments affect the demand for leisure positively and, depending on the extent of disablement, have a negative impact on the expected wage rate, both by reducing the earning capacity in a given job and by lowering the mean of the wage offer distribution. The negative effect of a lower wage on labor supplied may be reinforced by disability-related income transfers that replace part of the earnings loss. The relevant concept is the *expected benefit* as a function of award stringency and the benefit stream upon award.

In the absence of mandatory rehabilitation and regular reviews of disability status, eligible workers can choose between permanent withdrawal from the labor force, by enrollment in a disability insurance plan, or reentry into the workforce, by, if necessary, enrollment in a rehabilitation program. As described in the preceding two sections, the Dutch disability insurance system typically offers such discretion to workers who are recognized as disabled. Under the German and British programs, benefit dependency is much less of an option. There, the status of being severely disabled is allowed to keep people in employment instead of making them redundant.

Our research on the determinants of disability benefit recipiency in the Netherlands strongly confirms the influence of economic factors on the choice between benefit dependency and work resumption. We found that medical factors, such as the nature and extent of disablement and health history, explain only about one-third of the variation in the probability of entry into the disability insurance benefit system. Of the remaining, nonmedical factors, *financial considerations*, indicated by the present value of the benefit stream relative to the present value of the expected stream of earnings upon work resumption, and *unemployment hazards* derived from labor market records have proved to be particularly influential (see Aarts and de Jong 1992, pp. 299-303).

Despite stricter systems in the United States and the United Kingdom, similar results have been found in studies of these countries (see Leonard 1986 and Aylward and Lonsdale 1992). These findings suggest that an inherently vague concept like work disability always allows some room for discretion. Given the availability and generosity of disability benefits, eligible workers with no (further) career prospects and a weak labor market position appear to prefer benefit dependency rather than returning to the hazards of labor market participation. The results also imply that an increase in award stringency and/or a reduction in benefit generosity may boost the demand for rehabilitative services. In Sweden, disability benefit replacement rates are relatively high; however, sick pay is even higher, and the incentive is to extend the sickness period. With no statutory limits on the length of sickness benefit entitlements, the sickness benefit program has many beneficiaries who would be considered disabled under the Dutch ruling. Vocational rehabilitation is stimulated by entitling participants to 100 percent benefits. By paying market wages in sheltered employment, the interest in reemployment is increased in a similar way. Empirical evidence suggests that the modest size of the disability populations in Germany (except older workers) and the United Kingdom is to some extent the result of relatively low benefit replacement rates in these countries.

The Employer

Employers are agents who affect disability policy in two ways. First, they can directly influence the incidence of work injuries and occupational diseases. Second, by offering job opportunities to functionally impaired employees or to disabled people from outside the firm, employers may contribute to reducing disability benefit dependency.

Workers can be gainfully employed only as long as the value of their productivity covers labor costs. Thus, impaired workers with reduced productivity must be employed in jobs with wages that are substantially below their pre-impairment level, or in jobs where profitability requirements are less pressing, such as public sector employment in general and sheltered work in particular. Private employers can make jobs available to the functionally impaired only if a positive difference between wages and the (marginal) revenue deriving from this labor is covered in one, or more, of the following ways: increased productivity through vocational rehabilitation, partial benefits or disability allowances for diabled workers, or wage subsidies for employers.

A cost-benefit framework may help to unravel the determinants of the firm's willingness to engage in rehabilitation via accommodating workplaces or offering alternative employment. In the short run, given the enterprise's technology and the level of safety provision, the net cost for the employer of an employee entering a disability transfer program primarily depends on the profitability of the job held by the impaired worker. Clearly, the incentive to retain an impaired employee will be very small if the individual's job is redundant. This is one of the reasons why disability transfer payments increase in times of growing unemployment. If the job is not redundant, enrollment into a disability benefit program means hiring a replacement. The cost-benefit approach implies that a firm's inclination to retain and rehabilitate workers who have become functionally impaired depends on the following:

- The value of the impaired employee's productivity. The higher the postadjustment productivity, the more inclined the firm will be to accommodate and retain the worker.

- The labor costs of continued employment of the employee. By allowing for subsidies covering part of these costs, the disability program may encourage firms to retain workers upon impairment.

- The costs of adjustments, net of subsidies, to make jobs and impaired workers match. Lowering these costs may reinforce a firm's inclination to retain impaired employees.

- The potential contribution of a replacement to the firm's proceeds. Other things equal, the higher the expected productivity of a replacement employee, the less inclined the firm will be to retain and accommodate the impaired worker.

- The cost of recruiting and training a replacement. Firms will be more inclined to retain employees after the occurrence of functional impairments if the individuals' skills are hard to find. If a replacement would need to go through a long period of job or firm-specific training to acquire the impaired employee's skills, replacement may be an unattractive alternative. Equally important, finding a suitable replacement in a tight labor market may involve considerable search costs. In this situation, external labor market conditions enter the cost-benefit calculus.

- The costs of enrolling an employee into the disability insurance program and the internal and external financial consequences of program enrollment. The higher these costs, the greater the firm's inclination to retain functionally impaired employees. Insurance devices, such as coinsurance and differentiation of contribution rates (experience rating), raise the cost-consciousness of firms with respect to these external expenses.

The countries reviewed have different approaches to the firm. Until recently, Swedish and Dutch firms did not incur any substantial cost if employees entered the disability rolls. Mandatory employment quotas still are absent, and contribution rates are uniform, although differentiation is under consideration. In both of these countries, program administrators have had a range of instruments at their disposal to help bridge the gap between impaired employees' productivity and market wages: fully subsidized training and rehabilitation, fully subsidized job accommodation provisions, and partial disability benefit entitlements. As mentioned, the effect has been very limited in these two nations.

Since 1987, both Sweden and the Netherlands have taken measures to remove adverse incentives and to introduce alternatives to benefit dependency. Between 1980 and 1987, benefit levels had already been cut. After that, the focus shifted from the employee to the employer, with measures affecting the cost to the firm of disability program enrollment and the benefit of retaining or hiring functionally impaired workers. In the Netherlands, a stick-and-carrot mechanism was introduced that puts a fine on every disability benefit award and provides a bonus for every newly hired functionally impaired employee. In the sickness benefit program, both in Sweden and the Netherlands, the employer has been made accountable for providing benefits during the first six (Holland) or eight weeks (Sweden). Additionally, in the Netherlands, legislation was put in place by which employers are obligated to make the accommodations necessary to employ functionally impaired employees. As these measures did not bring about the intended effects quickly enough, benefit levels were further reduced in 1993.

It would be unfair, however, to put all the blame on the employer. A provision enacted in 1986 empowering impaired workers in Holland with a legal instrument to enforce (subsidized) workplace accommodation did not have any impact on the claims for in-kind entitlements. Only a few cases were brought to court. This is indicative, not only of the apparent preference of Dutch disability benefit claimants for leaving the labor market, but also of the lax assessment procedures that allow claimants to act according to their preferences.

Germany and the United Kingdom have had a quota system for many years, although enforcement is weak, especially in Britain. Disabled employment is more substantial than in Sweden or the Netherlands, however. In Germany, the registered disabled account for over 4 percent of total employment. In the United Kingdom, this figure may be lower; but considering the huge difference in the sizes of the British and Dutch disabled populations relative to the labor force and the small differences, if any, in unemployment rates, it appears that many functionally impaired British citizens, who would have been entitled to disability benefits under the Dutch system, are gainfully employed.

The Administering Organizations

The extent to which individual preferences or firm-specific considerations have an impact on the number of disability beneficiaries depends on the behavior of the gatekeepers of disability insurance programs. Whether or not firms are successful in discharging impaired employees by making them apply for disability benefits depends on whether benefit dependency conforms with the preferences of the employee and the design and administration of the program. A leniently administered, and generous, disability insurance regime provides older workers with an early retirement option and offers firms ample opportunities to use disability insurance as an instrument for personnel management. Ideally, the adverse stimuli for employers and employees to "play the disability insurance system" should be counterbalanced by administrative regulations and routines that either reduce the discretionary powers of individual employers and employees or provide contrary incentives. To do this, administering organizations need adequate instrumentation, for example, standardized assessment and review protocols and the authority to enforce compliance with quotas and to prescribe and mandate rehabilitation. The administration also needs the motivation to apply the available instruments adequately.

While private insurance carriers get their incentive from a competitive market environment, public services require either bureaucratic control mechanisms or budget containment of some sort. In the four European countries, disability insurance is publicly administered, but there are significant differences in administrative design. In the United Kingdom, the government bears direct responsibility for administration. The Department of Social Security allocates the benefits, and the Department of Employment administers the job programs. Careful allocation of benefits is safeguarded by combining bureaucratic and budget controls. In the Netherlands, on the other hand, the government, until 1995, had only indirect administrative responsibilities since the actual administration and its supervision and control were delegated to semipublic organizations run by employers' and union representatives (the so-called social partners).[9] Bureaucratic controls were weak, and budget containment devices were virtually absent. The German and Swedish administrations are somewhere in between those of the Netherlands and the United Kingdom. Germany is closer to the Netherlands in its approach, as it allows some influence from labor and management, be it under strict government control. In Sweden, the system is closer to that of the United Kingdom; Swedish benefits are administered by government agencies, while the social partners only have a say in the provision of employment services. In both Germany and Sweden, the administrative system is closely monitored by the government.

Put in terms of a "principal agent scheme," with government as the principal and the administrative system as the agent, most European governments try to monitor the agents as closely as possible, so that social disability insurance is administered according to the public interest. In Holland, the agents, *in casu*, the social partners have had ample opportunities to serve their own interests, yielding to the preferences of their membership in times of economic recession and structural economic changes. As a consequence, nothing was done to counterbalance the adverse incentives of a lenient award policy on individual employers and employees. The result has been the two-decade-long sustained process of purging the labor force of marginally productive workers.

Lessons from Europe

In the 1980s, the need to cut back public expenditures led to the reevaluation of social insurance policies all over Europe. Initially, the focus was on the efficacy of social security programs. Measures were taken, for example, to improve the possibilities for timely intervention in order to reduce disability insurance dependency, to disentangle the unemployment and disability components in disability insurance, and to increase job opportunities by making workplace adjustment mandatory and by introducing quota legislation. In more recent years, when earlier policy adjustments appeared to be less effective than hoped for, the focus gradually shifted away from technical changes towards measures intended to restructure the incentives induced by social security systems. Especially in Sweden and the Netherlands, these incentive issues have been, and still are, heavily debated.

In Germany and the United Kingdom, the incentive structure is much less of a problem. In both of these countries, the private sector employment opportunities for people with disabilities are larger than in Sweden or Holland. These higher participation rates probably result from an administrative system that operates more efficiently and effectively and from benefit rates in Germany and, especially, Britain that, by their modesty, may spur preferences for work over transfer dependency. Under these stricter systems, the social costs of disability are likely to be lower and, to a larger extent, borne by private enterprises and households.

Currently, the operations of the third agent, the Social Security Administration, are the major object of policy reform in Holland. In 1993, a parliamentary commission officially concluded what an increasing number of observers already had suspected—that the administering organizations had grossly failed in achieving an efficient and effective allocation of social insurance resources. Now the debate on the social security system—on the concept of the welfare state, for that matter—is completely open. The proposals put forward range from total privatization of social insurance to full socialization under government control.

Similar developments can be observed in Sweden, the prototype of the welfare state. The general feeling is that government has reached the limits of what it can provide or even should want to provide. In contemporary societies, people are viewed as autonomous citizens, aware of their individual interests, and ready to act in response to these needs. In such an environment, where public authority is no longer obvious, workers, employers, and administrators have become less hesitant to respond to the incentives with which they are confronted.

Good social policy and practice, then, not only require able administrators, using appropriate policy tools, but an intelligent design of the incentive structures implied both by the programs and by their management. This may seem obvious, but it took about three decades before this insight finally broke through among European supporters of the welfare state.

Appendix Table. Disability Policies in Four European Countries

	Netherlands	Germany	Sweden	United Kingdom
I. Temporary disability (employees' sickness insurance)				
Benefit level	70% of earnings	80% of earnings	Day 2-3: 75% of earnings Day 4-14: 90% Day 15-365: 80% Day 366 on: 70%	Flat-rate benefit: £45.30 per week (low earnings) £52.50 per week (higher earnings plus dependents' supplements)
Qualifying conditions	Inability to perform current job	Inability to perform current job	Inability to perform current job (short term), other suitable job (longer term)	Inability to perform current job
Maximum duration	52 weeks	78 weeks	Unlimited	28 weeks
Funding: Contributors	Employer, employee	Employer, employee	Employer, employee, government	Employer, employee, government
Risk sharing	(Risk groups within) industry	Region, industry, or firm	National	National
Administration	Nongovernmental industry agencies run by employees' and employers' representatives; no direct government supervision	Nongovernmental agencies run by employees' and employers' representatives under direct government supervision	National agency under direct government supervision	National agency under direct government supervision

II. Permanent disability

Employees, Non-Work-Related Risks

Benefit level	70% of last earnings during 6-72 months depending on age at onset if older than 33; thereafter, or if younger than 33, 70% of minimum wage plus 1.4% of (earnings - minimum wage) for each year older than 15	General disability: 60% (plus 1.5% times age - 55) of assessed earnings	65% of assessed earnings	Flat-rate benefit: £57.75 - 65.70 per week plus dependents' supplements (e.g., £53.15: spouse + 2 children)
Partial benefits	Percentage of full pension, corresponding to loss of earning capacity (minimum 15%)	Occupational disability: 40% (plus 1% times age - 55) of assessed earnings	75%, 50%, or 25% of full pension corresponding to loss of earning capacity	Disability Working Allowance[a]
Waiting period	12 months	Flexible	Flexible	28 weeks
Maximum duration	Age 65	Age 65	Age 65	Age 65
Qualifying conditions	Incapacity for gainful activity	General: incapacity for gainful activity Occupational: 50% reduction of capacity in usual occupation	Inability to work in commensurate employment (above 60 years: previous work)	Inability to work
Funding:				
Contributors	Employer, employee	Employer, employee, government	Employer, employee, government	Employer, employee, government
Risk sharing	National	National	National	National

(continued)

Appendix Table. (continued)

Administration	Nongovernmental industry agencies run by employees' and employers' representatives; no direct government supervision	State agencies under direct government supervision	National agency under direct government supervision	National agency under direct government supervision
Employees. Work Injury				
Benefit level	No separate work injury scheme	66.7% of last earnings	70% of last earnings	Flat-rate benefit: up to £88.4 per week if 100% disabled plus dependents' supplements
Partial benefits		Percentage of full pension, corresponding to loss of earning capacity	Percentage of full pension, corresponding to loss of earning capacity	From £17.68 (14% disabled) to £79.56 (90% disabled); reduced earnings allowance up to £35.30 .
Waiting period		Flexible	Flexible	15 weeks
Maximum duration		Age 65	Age 65	Unlimited
Qualifying conditions		Loss of earning capacity due to work injury or occupational disease of at least 20%	Loss of earning capacity due to work injury or occupational disease of at least 6.7%	Loss of earning capacity due to work injury or occupational disease of at least 14%
Funding:				
Contributors		Employer	Employer	Employer, employee, government
Risk sharing		Risk group	National	National
Administration	Nongovernmental industry agencies run by employees' and employers' representatives; no direct government supervision	State agencies under direct government supervision	National agency under direct government supervision	National agency under direct government supervision

III. Vocational rehabilitation

Training/workplace adjustment	Programs available, limited significance	Programs available, very significant	Programs available, very significant	Programs available, moderately significant
Sheltered workshops	Available, substantial significance	Available, limited significance	Available, substantial significance	Available, limited significance
Public/private employment for disabled	Both of limited significance	Mainly private sector, very significant	Mainly public sector, very significant	Mainly private sector, moderately significant
Rehabilitation/ redeployment incentives for:				
Disabled employee	Trial work benefits[b]	Trial work benefits	Increased benefits[c]	Disability Working Allowance
Employers	Lump-sum bonus, wage subsidies	"Disabled worker" protection, enforced quota regulation	Wage subsidies	Not enforced quota regulation
DI administration	None	Some	None	None
Institutional links with disability insurance programs	Potentially strong, weak in practice	Strong	Strong	Moderate

SOURCE: Based on data published in Aarts, Burkhauser, and de Jong (1996) and U.S. Department of Health and Human Services, SSA (1994).

a. Means-tested benefits payable to disabled people with a job.

b. Continued benefit entitlements while at work on probation or participating in a rehabilitation program.

c. Rehabilitation program participants receive 90 percent of lost earnings.

NOTES

1. A practical consideration for choosing these four countries is that their disability policies are relatively well documented in the international literature, recently, for instance, in Bloch 1993.

2. For additional details, see U.S. Department of Health and Human Services, Social Security Administration (1994).

3. See National Academy of Social Insurance (1994), p. 38.

4. A similar early retirement option applies to employees who were unemployed for at least one year in the 18 months before age 60.

5. See, for instance, Lando et al. (1979) and Disney and Webb (1991).

6. Further legislation was enacted in 1986, through the Handicapped Workers' Employment Act (WAGW). The WAGW contains an additional budget to adapt job demands and working conditions to the functional limitations of impaired employees. Spending under WAGW is similarly low.

7. Quoted from "Social Security in Sweden: How to Reform the System," Report to the Expert Group on Public Finance, Ministry of Finance, Stockholm, 1994, p. 7.

8. For a fuller treatment of the determinants of disability benefit recipiency, see Aarts and de Jong (1992, chapter 3).

9. As of 1995, supervision of benefit administration is in the hands of an independent agency. The current government proposes privatization of both the sickness benefit and the disability insurance schemes.

References

Aarts, L.J.M., and P.R. de Jong. 1992. *Economic Aspects of Disability Behavior.* Amsterdam and New York: North-Holland.

Aarts, L.J.M., R.V. Burkhauser, and P.R. de Jong. 1992. "The Dutch Disease: Lessons for U.S. Disability Policy," *Regulation* (Spring): 75-86.

_____. Eds. 1996. *Curing the Dutch Disease: An International Perspective on Disability Policy Reform.* Aldershot, U.K.: Avebury. Forthcoming.

Aarts, L.J.M., W. Dercksen, and P.R. de Jong. 1993. "Arbeidsongeschiktheid, een internationale vergelijking," *Sociaal Maandblad Arbeid* 48: 755-769.

Aylward, M., and S. Lonsdale. 1996. "A U.K. Perspective on Dutch Disability Policy." In Curing the Dutch Disease: An *International Perspective on Disability Policy Reform,* L.J.M. Aarts, R.V. Burkhauser, and P.R. de Jong, eds. Aldershot, U.K.: Avebury. Forthcoming.

Berkowitz, M., and M.A. Hill, eds. 1986. *Disability and the Labor Market.* Ithaca, NY: ILR Press.

Bloch, F. 1993. *Comparative Study of Disability Claim Processing and Appeals.* Provisional draft, October.

Burkhauser, R.V., and Y.W. Kim. 1991. "The Importance of Employer Accommodation on the Job Duration of Disabled Workers: A Hazard Model Approach." Working Paper, Syracuse University.

De Jong, P.R. 1994. "Werk en Handicap: Where Are the Twain to Meet?" In *Arbeidsmarkt en sociale zekerheid,* H. Scholten and S.C. de Groot, eds. Tilburg: IVA.

Disney, R., and S. Webb. 1991. "Why Are There So Many Long Term Sick in Britain?" *Economic Journal* 101 (405): 252-262.

Employment Gazette. U.K. Department of Employment. London: Her Majesty's Stationary Office, several years.

Haveman, R.H., V. Halberstadt, and R.V. Burkhauser. 1984. *Public Policy Toward Disabled Workers.* Ithaca, NY: Cornell University Press.

Holmes, P., M. Lynch, and I. Molho. 1991. "An Econometric Analysis of the Growth in the Numbers Claiming Invalidity Benefit: An Overview," *Journal of Social Policy* 20: 87-105.

Lando, M.E., M.B. Coate, and R. Kraus. 1979. "Disability Benefit Applications and the Economy," *Social Security Bulletin* 42: 3-10.

Leonard, J.S. 1986. "Labor Supply Incentives and Disincentives for Disabled Persons." In *Disability and the Labor Market,* M. Berkowitz and M.A. Hill, eds. Ithaca, NY: ILR Press.

Lonsdale, S. 1993. *Invalidity Benefit: An International Comparison.* London: Department of Social Security, ASD-Publications.

Ministry of Finance. 1994. "Social Security in Sweden: How to Reform the System." Report to the Expert Group on Public Finance. Stockholm.

Ministerie van Sociale Zaken en Werk gelegenheid. 1994. *Sociale Nota*. Den Hague.

National Academy of Social Insurance. 1994. *Preliminary Status Report of the Disability Policy Panel*. Washington, DC: National Academy of Social Insurance.

Nijboer, I.D., R.W.M. Gründemann, and F. Andries. 1993. *Werkhervatting na arbeidsongeschiktheid*. Den Haag: Ministerie van Sociale Zaken en Werk gelegenheid.

Organization for Economic Cooperation and Development (OECD). 1992. *Employment Outlook*. Paris: OECD.

_____. 1993. *The Dutch Labour Market*. Paris: OECD.

_____. 1994. *Labour Force Statistics*. Paris: OECD.

Sadowski, D., and B. Frick. 1992. *Die Beschäftigung Schwerbehinderter: Betriebswirtschaftliche Analysen und politische Empfehlungen*. Schulz-Kirchner, Idstein.

U.K. Department of Employment. Several years. *Employment Gazette*. London: Her Majesty's Stationery Office. London.

U.S. Department of Health and Human Services. Social Security Administration. 1994. *Social Security Programs Throughout the World - 1993*. SSA Publication No. 13-11805, May.

U.S. Government Accounting Office. 1994. *Social Security: Disability Rolls Keep Growing, While Explanations Remain Elusive*. GAO/HEHS-94-34.

Return-to-Work Policy

169-87

USA
J28
I12
J15
J22

Patterns of Return to Work in a Cohort of Disabled-Worker Beneficiaries

Martynas A. Yčas
Social Security Administration

From the beginning of the Social Security Disability Insurance (DI) program, it has always been a priority to encourage and help as many beneficiaries as possible to return to the labor force and to leave the DI rolls. It is common knowledge that such transitions have proven to be rare; empirical evidence about these events is unusual as well. This paper reviews the actual post-entitlement experience of a cohort of disabled workers, a component of the New Beneficiary Data System (NBDS), in order to examine work efforts over the period from 1983 to 1991.

The New Beneficiary Disabled-Worker Sample

The New Beneficiary Survey (NBS) was originally designed as a free-standing, cross-sectional survey of persons coming onto the Social Security Administration (SSA) rolls. It was envisioned as a sequel to the 1968 Survey of Newly Entitled Beneficiaries, whose findings had become of doubtful relevance with the passing of time and with the accumulation of significant changes in the various programs. The NBS, therefore, drew and interviewed a nationally representative sample of persons who had begun receiving one of a number of specified types of Social Security benefits at the start of the 1980s (for further details, see Maxfield 1983).

The sample represented the universe of persons who started to receive benefits for a spell of disability (not necessarily their first) during the "window period" of July 1980 to June 1981. Some 242,257 of the 281,314 who came on the rolls in those months and who were not known to have died in March 1982 were eligible for sampling. Cases were randomly drawn, stratified only by sex, subject to a geographically constrained Primary Sampling Unit design intended to economize on field work. Target numbers were 3,450 completed interviews with disabled-worker men and 1,550 with disabled-worker women. On completion of field work at the beginning of 1983, 3,593 and 1,605 interviews had been obtained for men and women, respectively.

The NBS did not remain a static data base, however. During the following years, interview responses were periodically linked with SSA's Master Beneficiary, Summary Earnings, and Supplemental Security records, and to Medicare utilization records maintained by the Health Care Financing Administration. These made it possible to track changes in sample members' eligibility, covered earnings, and health status and essentially created a longitudinal data base. Because many important variables cannot be measured, or measured accurately, on the basis of data collected for other purposes, it was decided to conduct another round of interviews with surviving sample members (and to collect some further information from surviving spouses). Consequently, the New Beneficiary Followup (NBF) was in the field during the last months of 1991. Taken together, these three sets of data constitute a single complex data base sometimes referred to as the NBDS, the "New Beneficiary Data System" (Yčas 1992).

While some amount of labor force activity, at least at some point after coming on the disability rolls, is not uncommon, very few beneficiaries leave the rolls because their condition improves or because they find some way of offsetting or overcoming their limitations. The underlying aim of this paper is to focus on a relatively rare event, work among the disabled.   The present study, therefore, concentrates on those individuals in the NBDS disabled-worker sample who survived to complete interviews in 1991 and thus provide a full set of longitudinal data for comparative purposes.

Excluded Cases

This is by no means all of the information relevant to the experience of the disabled over time that can eventually be extracted from this data set, and, in fairness to the reader and to the large majority of the disabled, some of these issues should be briefly discussed. The common way to leave the rolls is to die.[1] It would be possible to obtain some material regarding decedents, for whom NBS, administrative, and, in some cases, surviving spouse information is available. Decedents are omitted from the analysis here because the comparability problems that they raise are not likely to be offset by a significant increase in program-relevant insight. Obviously, persons who die soon after coming on the rolls do not have much impact on program costs, and they are probably comparatively poor prospects for return to work while they are in benefit status.

These issues have been examined to some degree (McCoy, Iams, and Armstrong 1994). Mortality is concentrated among persons in their first years on the program; as noted, about 15 percent of the persons who had come on the rolls during the 1980-1981 "window period" had died by the time the sample was drawn, and others died before the interviewing was complete. Not a great deal is known about these individuals because of the limited machine-readable administrative data available for them. However, it is likely, *a priori*, that they differ considerably from other disabled workers. Some disabling health conditions can reasonably be called "killer" diseases; for example, by the time that neoplasms or AIDS results in work disability, life expectancy has become very short. Few of these persons will be observed over time on the rolls; in terms of program financing or return to work, they have correspondingly little impact. Other disabling "nonkiller" diseases, such as acute musculoskeletal problems, may have little effect on life expectancy, and it is these types of health problems that characterize the population on the rolls.

McCoy, Iams, and Armstrong did not have data for the short-lived disabled, but it is obvious that this disabled group has a very different mortality profile than the simple aging pattern associated with the retired population. Despite their considerably lower average ages, disabled-worker men and women were 14 times more likely than their retired counterparts to die during their first six months on the rolls, eight times more likely to die during their second six months, and four times more likely in the third six months. Subsequently, the disabled showed a generally stable death rate. This remained higher than that of retired workers for some years, but the latter rose steadily (no doubt reflecting the results of aging as this group proceeded into their 70s), and, by the end of the study period, retired workers were more likely to die than their disabled counterparts who had survived a similar duration on the rolls.

Another group excluded by this selection criterion comprises 2,939 disabled workers drawn from the same sample universe as the original NBS disability sample but interviewed only in the 1991 NBF. These cases were added for the specific purpose of increasing the number of observations of apparent return to work that could be studied (Hennessey and Muller 1994). They lack, of course, any of the data collected in the NBS and must be handled with care to maintain comparability. As the cases have recently been analyzed from a perspective similar to the one taken in this paper, they are not included in the numbers presented here; however, note is taken of results based on the work of Hennessey and Muller.

The Key Variables

When measuring recovery rates, it is useful to consider what the numerator and denominator ought to be. Rates are frequently discussed in terms of the percentage of the disabled who recover or otherwise leave the rolls, a seemingly commonsense definition, but one that can be rather misleading from a program perspective.

The disabled are by no means created equal. A majority are awarded benefits after the age of 50, and so the age distribution of current beneficiaries is markedly skewed when compared with the labor force at large. Discussions and tabulations of the disabled tend to be dominated by this relatively elderly numerical majority. From a simple cross-sectional perspective, this does indeed describe who is on the rolls at any given moment. However, from an over-time perspective, the point-in-time predominance of older beneficiaries severely distorts the dynamics of program financing and the experience of beneficiaries while they are on the program rolls.

Older disabled workers are not, by statutory definition, paid disability benefits for very long. If they survive until age 65 (and do not recover, as very few do), they are converted to retired-worker status.

From then on, ability to work, if any, is irrelevant to eligibility for benefits, and the "ex-disabled," like the retired, are subject to only marginal disincentives to work. Thus, mortality aside, a single worker disabled at 35 counts for three workers disabled at the more typical age of 55; a 25-year-old counts for four. This situation is rather comparable with patterns observed in the Aid to Families with Dependent Children (AFDC) program: most welfare clients will not remain in the program very long, but a core group, which remains dependent in the long run, accounts for a disproportionate share of program costs. In the case of disability, age enables us to target such a core group, the relatively small percentage of disabled workers who come onto the rolls in the earlier part of their working years. From a policy perspective, it is important to give less weight to the characteristics of the older majority and more to the particular characteristics of the younger group.

In a way, it is fortunate that these younger disabled workers are particularly important in their impact on program costs, because they would appear to be more promising prospects for return to work. For them, the financial incentives tend to be more compelling. Workers near the age of retirement appear to experience considerable difficulty in reentering the labor force, and the payoff for doing so is fairly minor. In most cases, the effort will yield only a few years of earnings and is not likely to make a major change in retirement income. Younger workers without life-threatening health problems, by contrast, face more sharply differentiated alternatives.

If they do not return to work, the younger disabled will spend the remainder of their lives, a matter of decades, receiving a fixed constant-dollar benefit. The formula used to calculate this benefit is the same fractional-replacement-of-past-earnings formula that is used to calculate retirement benefits (although it is based on fewer years and is thus somewhat more generous for workers under 30), but the early years of most persons' careers are characterized by comparatively low, entry-level earnings. Older disabled workers, by contrast, are likely to have approached their peak earnings years, and thus their benefit amounts approximate the expected retirement benefit had they not become disabled. Consequently, the DI benefits of younger disabled workers provide a considerably lower replacement rate when measured as a function of *what would have been earned* but for the onset of disability. On the other hand, a successful return to substantial work offers a prospect of many years of increased income, followed by an increased retirement benefit.

Similar considerations of economic incentives suggest the importance of differentiating the disabled according to another demographic variable, marital status. Married persons are parts of economic units, and the disability of one member of a couple does not necessarily diminish the earnings capacity of the partner. Indeed, through the pressure of economic need, it may often be an incentive for the partner to increase work effort. The incentive to return to work may be correspondingly reduced among the married disabled, a factor that should significantly differentiate them from their single counterparts.

However, responses may also reflect a third crucial variable, sex. A "disability insured" worker must have sufficient work activity (technically, quarters of coverage) to demonstrate recent and substantial attachment to the labor force. This is mediated by the longstanding differences between men's and women's patterns of labor force participation. The great majority of men work, such that a broad cross section of the male population has disability insurance. For women, the situation is more problematic. Labor force participation rates vary considerably among female subgroups and, particularly, according to the age and marital status variables of interest here.

Moreover, women's earnings tend to be lower than those of men, and this holds true for most married couples on the micro level. Accordingly, financial incentives to return to work are presumably lower on average for couples in which the wife, as compared with the husband, is disabled. It is not quite so clear how single persons would be affected, but given that the forgone wages of disabled single women are probably lower, their incentive may be less. Financial pressure aside, there are also normative differences. Working is a central component of the conventional adult male identity, but has a much less central role in the lives of women. Men, accordingly, may feel a greater pressure to resume work *ceteris paribus*.

Earlier Findings Based on the NBDS

The variables that have been highlighted can be singled out by little more than a commonsense understanding of the labor market. However, while this is a preliminary effort to take advantage of the full longitudinal potential of the New Beneficiary Survey data, it is grounded in earlier studies based on the 1982 data and on administrative records that suggest the correctness of this approach.

Packard (1987) found all three of the variables to have an obvious relationship with income. The Social Security system has conventionally been said to rest on the model of a "three-legged stool." This model (developed in 1935 to provide for retired workers, but extended unchanged in 1956 to disabled workers) assumes that Social Security benefits are not a fully adequate source of income by themselves but will normally be supplemented by two other sources, assets accumulated over the worker's career and pensions based on long-term employment. Obviously, the longer the working career, the more appropriate this model will be, and, conversely, the shorter the working career, the more severe the impact on total income.

As expected, Packard's results show that, in terms of both asset and pension income, the oldest disabled were markedly more similar to retirees than were the younger disabled. Thus, 53 percent of the married men and 17 percent of the unmarried men in Packard's oldest category (60-64) reported pension income, as compared to only 17 and 5 percent, respectively, for the men in his youngest group (18-44); the pattern for women was similar, and the increase in pension income with age was uniformly monotonic.

That this reflects differences in length of service, a frequent determinant of both eligibility and amount of pensions, is confirmed by Iams (1986). Examining characteristics of the longest predisability job, he found that in his youngest disabled-worker category (18-45), the large majority of both men and women (65.9 and 79.2 percent, respectively) had worked less than 10 years on this job, as compared to a modest 7.9 and 22.5 percent, respectively, in his oldest category (60-64). The distinction is significant because the Employee Retirement Income Security Act of 1974 (ERISA) had set maximum vesting requirements, usually 10 years of service, effective in 1976, several years before this group became eligible for disability.   The younger disabled were also less likely to have been covered by a pension plan than the oldest, 55.8 percent as compared to 35.3 percent for men and 63.6 percent as compared to 50.2 percent for women. Even those younger disabled who were covered were less likely to have received a lump sum or a currently paid or future pension.

The pattern was much the same for assets. Among the oldest group, Packard found rates of receipt of asset income of 73 percent for married men and 47 percent for single men, as compared to 47 and 21 percent, respectively, for their younger counterparts. The pattern of differences was similar among disabled women.   As might be expected, differences in average asset income reflect differences in average asset holdings (Yčas 1986). Ownership rates and median values were much lower for every type of asset than those reported by retired workers, and indeed, about one out of four of the disabled had no assets whatever. However, there were considerable variations within the disabled population. Older married men (the age range used here was 55-64) were the largest single subgroup in the disabled population. They were also comparatively well-off, although their median asset portfolios were worth only $3,600 when home equity was excluded. At the other extreme, younger single men (aged 18-54), the third largest subgroup, had negligible median assets regardless of how home equity was treated.

Throughout these results, the expected salience of marital status as well as of age is confirmed. Having a spouse who is (usually) able to work means that the career of the couple, the economic unit, is only partially impaired rather than brought to a halt. Thus, Packard found that 46 percent of married couples in which one spouse was disabled had earnings. This is considerably lower than the 96 percent observed for the population aged 18-64 at large, but it is far higher than the 6-7 percent observed for single disabled men and women.

Differences shown by sex have been generally as anticipated, but somewhat more complex. As expected, disabled wives were more likely to report earnings from their husbands than disabled husbands were from their spouses (Packard 1987). It is perhaps a little surprising under these circumstances that it was the disabled husbands who reported slightly larger median assets. Interpreting the differences among the groups lumped together as "single" is complicated by the fact that the less elderly unmarried men and women (under age 55) were quite different demographically from their older counterparts (Yčas 1986). The single men were some 10 years younger, on average, than the single women, but this difference largely disappears after controlling for specific marital status. Disabled-worker men were almost twice as likely never to have married, while the women were considerably more likely to be separated and, especially, widowed. Given the small sample sizes, it has unfortunately not been feasible to examine these differences in much depth; however, the area is worth pursuing as other data sets become available.

The hypothesis that being married affects the economic incentive to return to work is also suggested by differences observed in living arrangements (Packard 1987). The NBS showed that the majority of married disabled couples lived in households containing no other persons, and the majority of single disabled did not. Moreover, if other persons were in the households of the married disabled, they were generally children. Significant minorities of single men, and, to a lesser extent, women, lived with parents, siblings, or non-relatives, while virtually none of the married disabled did so. This may in part reflect different provisions for meeting a need for care, but it is plausible that it also reflects a greater need among the characteristically lower-income disabled to share living expenses or to have them paid by others.

In addition to financial incentives, return to work is, of course, greatly influenced by health problems. Packard (1993) examined reports from the NBS interviews of the disabled sample and found the individuals to be in notably poor health overall, with some important variations. His study, unfortunately, did not take account of marital status; age was again associated with substantial differences, while sex distinctions were comparatively minor. The health variables did not, however, vary monotonically with age. His youngest group (aged under 45) comprised only about a quarter of the disabled-worker sample but stood out in many respects. Fourteen percent had recovered from their disabilities, as compared with only 2 percent of those aged 45 or above. Twenty-nine percent were able to work at least part-time or occasionally, as compared with 9 percent of the older disabled workers, and 22 percent of the younger group expected their health to improve or thought that it might, as compared with 10 percent of the older group. Perhaps most significantly, 16 percent, twice the rate of the older group, were no longer receiving Social Security about two years after benefits had begun.

Muller (1992) took advantage of administrative data to examine work attempts after a considerably more extended period. These were explored in unusual depth. After any indications of work were found in automated files, the hard-copy claims folders were requested and examined in order to obtain more detailed information. Of the 1,495 claims folders requested, 1,150 were located. After reweighting the transcribed information to adjust for missing data (for example, folders were more often unobtainable for persons who were no longer on the rolls), work outcomes were examined. Just over 10 percent of the individuals in the sample were found to have worked, but less than 3 percent had been terminated for sustained substantial gainful activity, and, of these, almost a third had returned to the rolls. In the strict sense of returning persons with severe medical impairments to the workforce, then, the success rate was a meager 2 percent. It should be noted, however, that another 6 percent, who were not examined in this study, had been terminated due to medical recovery.

A number of factors were significantly associated with some work: among the variables that have been discussed, age was particularly salient, with almost a third of the disabled under 40 years old having worked, as compared with a scant 2.5 percent of those aged 60 or older. However, termination for substantial gainful activity was surprisingly difficult to predict. Of the variables examined, only race (whites were more likely) and the presence of mental conditions (less likely) were significantly related. It should be noted that this part of Muller's analysis was necessarily based on very small sample sizes.

More recently, Hennessey and Muller (1994) examined the work efforts not only of the NBDS disabled-worker sample but also of the parallel "add-on" sample from the same cohort, mentioned earlier, that was included in the 1991 NBF interviews for this purpose. After certain cases were excluded (e.g., those interviewed by proxy and those who denied ever receiving benefits), their combined sample comprised 4,405 cases. Four percent had been working at the time benefits began (presumably not at the level deemed to be substantial gainful activity), and 18 percent started work after benefits began. The majority of the latter cited "financial need" as their most important reason, and more than 80 percent gave it as a reason for working. The only other factor of considerable importance was "wanted to work," the primary motive of more than one-sixth of the sample.

An effort was made during the 1991 interviews to assess the effectiveness of the current measures intended to facilitate return to work, but the results are not encouraging. Only about 27 percent reported receiving any vocational rehabilitation services; for the most part, these took the form of physical therapy. In about three cases out of four, however, physical therapy did not help in returning to work. No more than a fifth to a tenth knew about the program features—trial work, extended eligibility, and extended Medicare—which are intended as incentives to reenter the labor force, and almost none said that they were influenced by these "incentives."

Additional Findings

This analysis is based on persons in the disabled-worker sample interviewed in both the 1982 NBS and the 1991 NBF—3,161 cases. The work status of these individuals was determined on the basis of both covered earnings in SSA's Summary Earnings Record for the years 1983-1991 and of self-reports of work activity during those same years.

As with many other issues, the results can be seen both as good news and as bad news. The good news here is that a larger-than-expected number of disabled persons surveyed had at least some tentative connection with the labor force after benefits began. Using the most generous criterion, a record of nonzero earnings in any year or any survey report of a job during the same interval, more than one out of four (27.6 percent) had worked after benefits began. In the following discussion, this group is described as experiencing some work. Less encouraging is the fact that, in the majority of these cases, the contact does indeed appear to have been marginal. Just over two out of five of this group, one-ninth of the total disabled workers, had covered earnings in excess of $3,600 (the annualized monthly substantial gainful activity threshold in force over most of the period) in more than one year.[2] This subset is referred to as substantial workers.

Even this number is not inconsequential, but its policy relevance is a little difficult to interpret. Slightly more than two-thirds of the substantial workers "had at some point been found to be medically recovered,"[3] and more than 90 percent of those who had ever recovered had also worked substantially. Taken at face value, this would seem to be somewhat discouraging from a policy perspective. While the disabled worker's condition may sometimes be improved by medical intervention, the possibilities for this appear quite limited and perhaps costly. If only a distinct minority of health-impaired individuals return to work, then the potential for increasing the rate of return in this unhealthy population would seem to be low.

However, there is some reason to question these findings. The period under study, beginning in 1983, came immediately after vigorous efforts were undertaken to remove disabled cases from the rolls via continuing disability reviews (CDRs). This move sparked considerable criticism in many quarters, and, in response, CDRs were cut back to a relatively low level beginning in 1983. Moreover, even in later years, the pressure to allocate administrative resources in other directions has prevented any resumption of large-scale CDRs. It is highly likely that such reviews will still take place when the record shows substantial gainful activity. The implication is that recovery significantly affecting work capacity may have taken place among a certain proportion of marginal workers and nonworkers, but never been reflected in the administrative records. In other words, the pool of potential labor force returnees may be larger, perhaps much larger, than the record now shows.

In any event, without trying to control consistently for apparent medical recovery (which would result in precariously small cell sizes in some instances), the pattern of differences is somewhat as expected when sex and, especially, age are taken into account; however, the importance of marital status emerges only when the interactions of these variables are considered. Thus, as shown in table 1, only about 11 percent of both married and single disabled workers are likely to have had substantial work, although the single group is a little more likely to have worked only marginally. With respect to sex, the difference is quite small (12 and 10 percent for men and women, respectively), but with respect to age, it is obvious. Thirty-two percent of the younger

Table 1. Age and Marital Status in 1982 of Disabled-Worker Beneficiaries by Return-to-Work Status

	Total (percent)	Substantial workers (percent)	Marginal Workers (percent)	Nonworkers (percent)
All disabled	100.0	11.3	16.4	72.4
Sex				
Men	100.0	11.9	16.6	71.5
Women	100.0	9.9	15.9	74.2
Marital status				
Married	100.0	11.3	15.0	73.7
Single	100.0	11.2	18.4	70.4
Age				
Under 35	100.0	31.8	27.6	40.6
35 - 50	100.0	14.0	17.2	68.9
50 or older	100.0	4.9	13.2	81.9
Under age 35				
Married men	100.0	49.3	21.9	28.9
Married women	100.0	32.6	18.3	49.1
Single men	100.0	21.4	30.5	48.1
Single women	100.0	28.9	34.9	36.2
Age 35-49				
Married men	100.0	13.7	16.0	70.3
Married women	100.0	12.2	13.1	74.6
Single men	100.0	14.9	19.2	65.9
Single women	100.0	15.1	21.4	63.5
Age 50 and older				
Married men	100.0	5.5	14.0	80.5
Married women	100.0	4.2	13.5	82.4
Single men	100.0	4.8	12.2	83.1
Single women	100.0	4.1	11.8	84.1

SOURCE: New Beneficiary Data System, persons newly entitled to disabled-worker benefits in 1980-1981 who were interviewed in both 1982 and 1991.

NOTE: Substantial workers had covered earnings in excess of $3,600 (the annualized substantial gainful activity threshold) in more than one year between 1983 and 1990. Nonworkers had no indication of work. Marginal workers fell in between these limits. Percentages may not sum precisely to 100 due to rounding..

disabled had worked substantially, compared to 14 percent of the middle-aged and only 5 percent of the older group.

When the three factors are taken together, a more complex pattern emerges. As might be expected, younger men are the most likely to have worked substantially, or for that matter at all. Within this group, the impact of marital status is quite striking: virtually half of the married subgroup consisted of substantial workers, compared to only a little more than a fifth of this segment's single counterparts. Conversely, nearly half of the single men had no indication of work, far more than the two out of seven married. The pattern for younger women was also distinctive, but quite different. The proportion of married versus single women with substantial work was similar, a little under a third for both groups, but single women were almost twice as likely to have had some marginal contact with the labor force (35 compared to 18 percent).

Absolute levels of work activity were lower among the middle-aged disabled than in the younger group. Curiously, women showed the same pattern of differences by marital status, while, for men, marital status was almost irrelevant. Contrasts by both marital status and sex virtually disappeared in the older group, which made up nearly three-fifths of the disabled and reported very modest levels of work activity, utterly different from those of their younger counterparts.

The health information collected in 1991 is not necessarily rigorously supported by clinical or medical evidence, nor does it speak directly to changes as they affect the timing of return to work, but it does lend support to the thesis that work and health are positively related. As table 2 indicates, the majority (56 percent) of those who never worked reported their health to be "poor," compared with only a quarter of the substantial workers. Nearly a quarter of the latter rated their health as "excellent" or "very good," compared to a desultory 4 percent of the nonworkers. Marginal workers are, appropriately, in the intermediate range of these percentages.

The distribution of health status is, perhaps unsurprisingly, quite similar to the distribution of levels of work when marital status, age, and sex are taken into account. It is easy to generate an unwieldy amount of cells with unacceptably small numbers of observations if too many variables are controlled for in the process of tabulation, so table 2 does not attempt to break the subgroups out by work status. Nonetheless, it is obvious that the groups with the greatest propensity for labor force activity are also those in which health was rated the most positively. It is notable that, after controlling for age, the other two variables are associated with only minor differences. The age-health relationship, again, is far from monotonic: those under 35 were uniformly much more positive in their self-assessment, while the middle-aged and older disabled differed very little.

Table 2. Reported Health Status in 1991 by Return-to-Work Status

	Substantial workers (percent)	Marginal workers (percent)	Nonworkers (percent)
Total	100.0	100.0	100.0
Good-to-excellent health	49.8	26.9	15.5
Fair health	24.5	36.7	28.7
Poor health	25.7	36.4	55.8
Health limits the amount or kind of work	65.5	90.0	93.8

SOURCE: New Beneficiary Data System, persons newly entitled to disabled-worker benefits in 1980-1981 who were interviewed in both 1982 and 1991.

Somewhat similar patterns appeared when health status was asked in terms of "other people your age," but recovery appears far from complete in this population. Even among the substantial workers, only 17 percent thought it to be better, and more than two-fifths thought it to be worse. Similarly, two-thirds of the substantial workers (and nearly all of the nonworkers) reported some work limitation in 1991.

Although substantial workers felt that they were healthier, they were not a great deal happier. It is true that nearly a third of them were "delighted" or "pleased" with their lives in general, compared with only a fifth of the nonworkers, but they were nearly as likely to have negative feelings (16 percent compared to 20 percent). As far as being satisfied with the family standard of living, there was virtually no difference, and the substantial workers worried considerably more often about their financial situations. This argues that their greater work effort, while it may be enabled by better (perceived) health, also is apparently driven to some extent by a greater sense of financial need.

Conclusion

The NBDS is a rich data base that can, given due attention, tell us considerably more about the dynamics of disability and work among the population already on the assistance rolls. This paper is, obviously, by no means the last word on what can be found in the NBDS. However, the limitations of the data base should also be recognized. It represents a cohort of persons who came onto the program at a particular point in time. These individuals experienced a number of changes in the economy and in the administrative climate that may be quite different from those in the years to come. Given the volatile nature of the disability program growth, the characteristics of this group may differ to an uncertain degree from those of more recent cohorts of entrants who will drive the program's future.

This paper has attempted to focus on the more striking or clearly defined differences among subgroups that are least likely to be susceptible to such changes, but generalizations should always be made with caution. It is for this reason that a methodologically simple tabular approach has been taken to these data. The temptation to resort to standard, more sophisticated multivariate techniques is natural, but probably one to be resisted until the data are better understood. Despite the relatively large overall size of the disabled-worker component of the sample, the subgroups of particular interest are often quite small, many observations are left- or right-censored, there is substantial multicollinearity among key variables, and distributions are frequently truncated and far from normal. The painstaking, almost case-by-case approach taken by Hennessey and Muller is probably the key to minimizing these problems and to maximizing the degree of understanding that can be derived from the NBDS.

However, the outlines of some basic conclusions are already clear. The older majority of disabled workers are very different from the comparatively small younger group in many key respects relevant to return to work. The older group offers minimal prospects for return to work on any scale and ensures that observed recovery rates for the total disabled population will never be high. While incentives can be offered and recovery is a realistic possibility for a limited number of cases, disability policy would do well to treat older disabled workers in general as another class of retirees. Older workers already are awarded benefits on a less restrictive basis, as the disability definition is relaxed at ages 50 and 55, so this point is tacitly accepted in current law. Perhaps it ought to be revised and extended further in the context of equitably raising the retirement age.

The small subgroup of younger disabled workers is quite different, although none of the research presented here can tell us exactly how different. It is notable that various studies of the same sample have found it convenient to define "younger" using age ceilings ranging from the mid-30s to the mid-50s according to sample size and analytic convenience. However, no effort has yet been made to estimate precisely which age breaks best discriminate between different patterns of relevant variables. Still, the age 35 cutoff employed here indicates that, below this age, return to work, to at least some extent, is quite common already. It is likely that development and refinement of a "work-prone profile," of which age would be a major component, could be of considerable use both in identifying and notifying disability beneficiaries who might be helped by available services or respond to targeted incentives. For that matter, such a profile might also be used more proactively for identifying beneficiaries not much interested in employment who might be urged more vigorously to make work attempts.

The potential of the NBDS to support such studies has not yet been fully exploited. It may be, of course, that the experience of this cohort is a less-than-perfect guide to the new cohorts of individuals coming onto the benefit rolls. In this context, however, it is encouraging (if any silver lining can be found in the cloud of unexplained program growth) that increases in disability awards reflect more and more grants to comparatively young beneficiaries. Perhaps the improved understanding of return to work that we are now deriving will be all the more useful as we address emerging challenges in program administration and policy formulation.

NOTES

NOTE: The views expressed here are those of the author and do not necessarily reflect those of the Social Security Administration.

1. In the case of Social Security Disability Insurance, as opposed to Supplemental Security Income (SSI), the disabled are converted to retired-worker status at age 65. This has some minor

effect on how they are treated by the program, but, in practice, very few individuals in conversion cases return to work or otherwise leave the rolls at more advanced ages.

2. The numbers reported here differ, and in general indicate more return to work, from those reported earlier by Muller. This reflects both differences in the definition of what constitutes "work" and a longer time period under review, which gave the disabled additional opportunity to return to the labor force.

3. More specifically, they had been coded "no longer disabled" in the Ledger Account File records that were pulled for each year in December. Thus, a few cases in which an individual's recovery lasted less than a year may have been excluded (although such a brief recovery would seem to be of little policy relevance). On the other hand, the timing of recorded work and periods of recorded recovery were not disentangled, and, in some instances, work may have taken place during periods of medical disability in these "recovered" cases.

References

Hennessey, John, and Scott Muller. 1994. "Work Efforts of Disabled-Worker Beneficiaries: Preliminary Findings from the New Beneficiary Followup Survey," *Social Security Bulletin* 57, 3 (Fall): 42-51.

Iams, Howard M. 1986. "Characteristics of the Longest Job for New Disabled Workers: Findings from the New Beneficiary Survey," *Social Security Bulletin* 49, 12 (December): 13-18.

Maxfield, Linda Drazga. 1983. "The 1982 New Beneficiary Survey: An Introduction," *Social Security Bulletin* 46, 11 (November): 3-11.

McCoy, John, Howard Iams, and Timothy Armstrong. 1994. "The Hazard Of Mortality of Aged and Disabled Men: A Comparative Sociodemographic and Health Status Analysis," *Social Security Bulletin* 57, 3 (Fall): 76-87.

Muller, L. Scott. 1992. "Disability Beneficiaries Who Work and Their Experience Under Program Work Incentives," *Social Security Bulletin* 55, 2 (Summer): 2-19.

Packard, Michael D. 1987. "Income of New Disabled-Worker Beneficiaries and Their Families: Findings from the New Beneficiary Survey," *Social Security Bulletin* 50, 3 (March): 5-23.

_____. 1993. "Health Status of New Disabled-Worker Beneficiaries: Findings from the New Beneficiary Survey." In *SSA's 1982 New Beneficiary Survey: Compilation of Reports*, September.

Yčas, Martynas A. 1986. "Asset Holdings of the Newly Disabled: Findings from the New Beneficiary Survey," *Social Security Bulletin* 49, 12 (December): 5-12.

_____. 1992. "The New Beneficiary Data System: The First Phase," *Social Security Bulletin* 55, 2 (Summer): 20-35.

The Effectiveness of Financial Work Incentives in Social Security Disability Insurance and Supplemental Security Income

Lessons from Other Transfer Programs

Hilary Williamson Hoynes
University of California, Berkeley
Robert Moffitt
Johns Hopkins University

USA

J28   I38

I12

H55   J15

The major programs for the disabled in the United States, Social Security Disability Insurance (DI) and Supplemental Security Income (SSI), are each intended to provide financial support to individuals who have an impairment that prevents them from engaging fully in productive labor force activity. As originally enacted, these programs based eligibility not only on evidence of a disabling condition but also on low earnings. Over the last several years, however, it has been increasingly recognized that the disabled are capable of at least some productive labor force activity and that basing eligibility on low earnings may provide work disincentives to existing recipients or even discourage some of the genuinely disabled from applying for benefits in the first place. In both programs, this development has led to changes in the rules governing earnings receipt, which are designed to encourage work. Additional programmatic changes to increase work incentives even more have also been proposed.

In this paper, we assess the implications of existing research on work incentives in programs for the nondisabled for the likely effectiveness of the current and proposed work-incentive provisions in disability programs. While there has been relatively little study of work effects in DI and SSI, there has been a tremendous amount of research on the work incentives of transfer programs for the low-income population, such as Aid to Families with Dependent Children (AFDC) and the Food Stamp program, and there has even been a small amount of research on the work-incentive effects of Medicaid. The relevance of this literature comes not so much from its rather large body of empirical evidence on the responsiveness of the low-income population to work-incentive provisions, since the responsiveness of the disabled may be quite different, as from the lessons that have been learned about the way in which work-incentive provisions operate and what their effects, both intended and unintended, might be. We shall argue that there are a number of important insights from this research literature that have implications for existing work-incentives and for proposed work-incentive reforms in DI and SSI.

In the next section, we discuss the major U.S. transfer programs for the low-income population, what their work-incentive effects are generally presumed to be, and what the empirical evidence suggests on the impact of current work-incentive rules and of past and proposed changes in those rules. Subsequently, we provide a parallel discussion of DI and SSI and draw lessons for those programs from the literature on nondisability programs. We discuss the probable effects of both existing and proposed work-incentive provisions. In the final section of the paper, we draw policy conclusions.

Transfer Programs for the Nondisabled

In our discussion of nondisability transfer programs, we will focus on income-conditioned programs for the nonaged and therefore exclude both Social Security and unemployment insurance from our survey. Instead, we will concentrate on the AFDC program, the Food Stamp program, and Medicaid.

Description of Program Rules

The AFDC program currently provides cash benefits to families with dependent children, where a "dependent" child is defined as a child living in a family with only one parent or with an unemployed parent.[1] Most AFDC families are headed by women with no adult male present, although the AFDC Unemployed Parent (AFDC-UP) provision permits some families to receive benefits where both parents are present. In families where income and asset conditions for eligibility are met, an adult's earnings, if any, are taken into account in calculating the amount of the benefit (which also varies by family size). First, earnings that cover work-related expenses are allowed, up to a certain maximum, without any reduction in benefits, as are earnings that cover child care expenses up to a maximum. In addition, for the first four months of earnings after joining the program, a deduction from income of one-third of earnings above work-related expenses plus $30 is allowed. The marginal tax rate (MTR) on earnings is thus 67 percent for earnings beyond deductions. The one-third disregard is eliminated after four months of earnings, leading to a 100 percent MTR on earnings above deductions.[2] The AFDC program also imposes a maximum on the gross income a family can receive from all sources, earned and unearned; if income exceeds these amounts, eligibility ends. An increase in earnings that pushes family income above these maximums thus results in an MTR exceeding 100 percent. An MTR exceeding 100 percent occurs when an increase of earnings of $1 leads to a decrease in benefits of more than $1. This can occur when eligibility ends.

The AFDC program provides extended, or "transitional," child care support to families who have been made ineligible for benefits because of increased earnings. Child care subsidies are provided for up to 12 months following the date of exit from the rolls. These provisions can be thought of as lowering the effective MTR on earnings.

The Food Stamp program provides food coupons to all families with income and assets below defined amounts, with or without children and regardless of individuals' marital status. In computing benefits for families with earnings, a standard deduction is allowed, as well as a deduction of 20 percent of earnings and deductions for child care and shelter expenses up to certain maximums. Earnings above these deductible amounts reduce benefits by 30 cents per dollar, leading to a 30 percent MTR. However, as in the AFDC program, families are made ineligible if income rises above certain limits.[3] This leads to an MTR of over 100 percent at the point at which earnings push a family above one of the maximums.[4]

The Medicaid program has historically provided subsidized or free medical care mainly to families receiving AFDC (or SSI) benefits. The types and amount of medical care for which an AFDC family is eligible are independent of its income or benefit amount, and thus the tax rate on Medicaid benefits is implicitly zero as long as the family is on the AFDC rolls. Until recently, eligibility for Medicaid was lost in its entirety when a family left AFDC, generating an MTR of over 100 percent on increased earnings at that point. However, Medicaid eligibility is currently not as closely tied to AFDC receipt as it once was. Many states have a Medically Needy program, for example, which provides Medicaid benefits to families who are below somewhat higher income and assets limits than those for AFDC or who experience heavy medical expenses that push their net incomes below those limits. In addition, recent federal legislation has extended Medicaid eligibility to some children and pregnant women in families who are not on AFDC but whose income is below 133 percent of the federal poverty line. Finally, transitional Medicaid benefits are available for up to 12 months following exit from the rolls to families leaving the AFDC rolls because of increased earnings. These provisions, taken together, can once again be thought of as effectively lowering the MTR faced by individuals leaving AFDC.

Cumulative MTRs for families receiving multiple programs can be quite high (Keane and Moffitt 1994; Giannarelli and Steurle 1994). In many states, recipients who work part-time at the minimum wage rate have lower disposable incomes than they would have if they were not to work at all, implying an average tax rate of over 100 percent. Average tax rates between no work and full-time work at the minimum wage for program recipients are between 70 and 80 percent nationwide and exceed 100 percent in some states.[5] Aside from the Medicaid notch, which can cause high tax rates alone, separate notches are created for AFDC and the Food Stamp program. In addition, payroll and income taxes generally raise the cumulative tax rate, since they are only partially (i.e., not fully) deductible in the programs.

Since the 1980s, most of the policy interest in these programs has centered on employment and training for welfare recipients instead of on financial inducements to work (the major current project of this type is the Job Opportunities and Basic Skills (JOBS) training program in AFDC). Such programs can be mandatory or voluntary. Mandatory employment programs necessarily increase work effort among those recipients whose participation is required, while voluntary work and training programs provide incentives through the prospect of increased future earnings or employability. If future wages and job prospects are increased by participation in such a program, the effective MTR (taking into account projected earnings) is lowered even if the current, nominal MTR is 100 percent.

Our paper is mainly concerned with the effectiveness of financial incentives rather than with the efficacy of work, employment, and training programs. However, we will discuss the policy merits of both approaches in our concluding section.

Expected Effects of Work-Incentive Provisions

The conventional labor-leisure model provides the framework within which work incentives of welfare program tax rates are generally analyzed. This model uses the assumption of utility maximization to justify the commonsense presumption that individuals trade off the amount of take-home income they would have for different levels of hours of employment with the desire to work and difficulty involved in that employment. As an empirical matter, the model implies that the choice of how much to work is based partially upon how much take-home income is gained by working various amounts, or by how much is gained by working less, in the case of some transfer programs.

The model is illustrated in figure 1, which shows the budget constraints for welfare programs with different tax rates. In this figure, segment $ACDE$, with slope equal to the hourly wage rate, w, applies to individuals off welfare. Segment BC applies to welfare recipients if the tax rate is 100 percent. Segment BD applies to welfare recipients if the tax rate takes on a value t that is less than 1. The theory implies that an individual will work less on welfare than off welfare, whether segment BC or BD applies.

A major focus of attention in the research literature has concerned the effects of a reduction in the tax rate on work effort. Perhaps surprisingly, the literature does not yield a clear verdict on whether work effort would go up or down as a result. The arrows in the figure illustrate the types of responses that might occur from a shift from segment BC to BD. For individuals initially on welfare and not working (i.e., initially at point B), the reduction in the tax rate may encourage the type of movement shown by arrow 1, reflecting an increase in work effort. At the same time, a reduction in t expands the range of incomes eligible for the benefits. Unfortunately, some individuals who were initially ineligible for welfare and were hence initially off the welfare rolls are made eligible by the reduction in t; some of these people will go onto welfare and reduce their work effort, as illustrated by arrow 2 in the figure. In addition, some individuals who are ineligible for benefits even at the new, lower tax rate may take advantage of the financial inducement to combine welfare and work by reducing their work effort enough to become eligible for benefits, as illustrated by arrow 3.[6]

Figure 1. AFDC Budget Constraints with Different MTRs
(BC:MTR = 100, BD: MTR = $t > 0$)

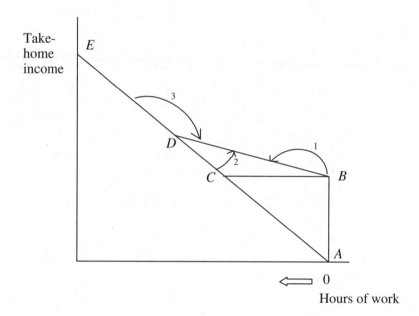

The net effect of the reduction in the tax rate is thus ambiguous and could be positive or negative on the overall level of work effort. It is even theoretically possible that 100 percent tax rates result in the *greatest* amount of overall work effort in the low-income, eligible population. This would occur if any reduction in t below this level induced large numbers of individuals to come onto the rolls and to work less than they had been working off the rolls.

The possibility that large numbers of eligibles would rush onto the welfare rolls if the tax rate were lowered seems implausible in many circumstances. However, the same end result would occur even if entry rates onto welfare were completely unaffected by the level of the tax rate, but if exits from the rolls were. Assuming that individuals joined the rolls only because of unforeseen job losses, adverse health events, or other unplanned changes in household structure (e.g., divorce), the increased generosity of the program brought on by a low tax rate would decrease the likelihood that they would leave the rolls. There may be many welfare recipients who would, for example, ordinarily leave the rolls to take a full-time low-wage job if the tax rate were 100 percent, but who would choose to stay on the rolls and work part-time if the tax rate were lower. After a period of time, some recipients would end up working while on the rolls who would have otherwise been off the rolls working longer hours.[7]

Whether this possibility has any relevance to actual situations will be discussed in the context of the available empirical evidence. However, even if it is relevant to actual situations, it does not imply that reductions in tax rates below 100 percent are undesirable, only that they must be justified on some grounds other than as a means to increase average work effort. For example, it may be desirable *per se* to have welfare recipients work, even if this can only be achieved by broadening the recipient population to include individuals who would have otherwise been off the rolls (they are likely to be low-wage individuals as well, of course). Alternatively, it may be desirable to avoid a division of the low-income eligible population into those who are on welfare and not working and those who are off welfare and working long hours. A reduction in the tax rate that increases the work effort of the former group but reduces it for the latter group may serve to equalize the distribution of earnings and income in the eligible population and lessen polarization. In addition, a program that offers income supplements to individuals who work part-time but are still poor (assuming that such work is covered by a low t) may be considered worthwhile simply because such persons are believed to be deserving of assistance, even if by doing so some recipients may reduce work effort from full-time to part-time. Finally, low tax rates may be a means to prevent underreporting of income and fraudulent work by individuals while receiving benefits.[8]

Another possibility is that employment provides a welfare recipient with work experience and increased skills, thereby raising earnings ability (i.e., the wage rate) and encouraging exit from the rolls in the future. Whether the types of jobs that welfare recipients are likely to have while on the rolls provide a stepping-stone to permanent self-sufficiency, or whether such jobs are likely to be high-turnover, dead-end positions that lead nowhere but back onto the rolls, is an empirical question. However, if progress towards permanent employment is the goal of the reduction in the MTR, it could be fairly asked whether job training programs are not a superior method of increasing skills.

Finally, the literature in this area has shown that the same work-incentive difficulties that arise with tax rate reductions occur when transitional child care and Medicaid benefits are provided (Moffitt and Wolfe 1990). In this situation, such benefits provide an incentive for individuals who leave the rolls to work less than they would have otherwise during the transition period. Also, for those who are on the borderline between applying or not applying for benefits in the first place, there is an incentive to apply because they know that transitional benefits will be available should they go off the rolls. Consequently, transitional child care and Medicaid benefits may have the undesirable effect of actually increasing the caseload and reducing average levels of work effort.

Empirical Evidence

Empirical evidence on the effects of welfare program tax rates on work effort comes from three sources: (1) econometric estimates of tax rate effects from cross-sectional survey data, (2) estimates from controlled experiments testing a negative income tax, and (3) historical information from actual tax rate changes in recent decades in particular programs such as AFDC. We will not discuss any evidence on the effect of transitional child care and Medicaid benefits on work effort and the caseload, since those provisions have not been studied. Also, we will not look at the earnings and caseload impacts of welfare employment and training programs, since our focus is on financial inducements to work.

Cross-sectional econometric estimates of the effect of welfare programs on work effort generally relate differences in hours of work to differences in benefit levels and MTRs among welfare-eligible individuals living in states with varying benefit schedules (Danziger, Haveman, and Plotnick 1981; Moffitt 1992). Most of these studies have examined the effect of welfare on the level of work effort *per se* and have found that welfare programs provide some disincentive and therefore that work effort would be higher in the absence of the programs. However, only a minority of the studies examined the issue of whether the net effects of a change in the MTR on work effort would be positive or negative; instead, most studies estimated the "marginal" effects of changing the MTR conditional on program participation, that is, the effect of a change in the MTR on hours of work for those on AFDC before and after the change.[9] On this issue, the research showed nonzero, but moderately sized, responses to benefit levels and MTRs: both higher benefits and higher MTRs are correlated with less work effort, assuming AFDC participation by the individual before and after the change.[10] Thus, arrow 1 in figure 1 was found to be significantly positive: when faced with a lower MTR, many AFDC recipients enter the labor force and work.

Three studies reviewed by Danziger, Haveman, and Plotnick did estimate net effects of changes in MTRs, however. The research (Masters and Garfinkel 1977; Levy 1979; Barr and Hall 1981) found either no net effect of tax rates on work or a "perverse" effect, i.e., higher tax rates increase work levels. The explanation given for these findings was that the positive effects on the work effort of initial recipients are canceled out by the negative effects from new entrants and from a decline in the exit rate. Thus, the theoretical possibility of significant offsetting effects to the work incentives of lower tax rates is, unfortunately, supported by the evidence.

There have been only a few additional studies of the AFDC program since the review by Danziger, Haveman, and Plotnick, and these provide further evidence supporting the weak effects of changes in the MTR. Moffitt (1983) applied more advanced econometric methods to the problem but found, again, essentially no net effect on work effort due to changes in the tax rate. Keane and Moffitt (1994) incorporated the housing program into a model of AFDC and Food Stamps and found that changes in cumulative MTRs had very little net impact on work effort. Hoynes (1996), in the first work-incentive study of the AFDC-UP program, found that reductions in the MTR on earnings had essentially zero net effect on the work effort of husbands and wives.[11]

Only a few studies have been conducted on other programs. Fraker and Moffitt (1988) estimated the effects of the Food Stamp program on the work effort of female heads of household and found, again, that the net effect of MTR reductions was zero. Estimates of the effect of the Medicaid program on work effort have been conducted by Blank (1989), Moffitt and Wolfe (1992), and Winkler (1991). Two of the studies showed rather weak effects of the Medicaid program on work effort, while the third showed quite strong effects. However, none of these studies specifically examined the effect of the notch imposed by Medicaid.[12]

The negative income tax (NIT) experiments conducted in the 1970s provided additional evidence on the responsiveness of welfare recipients to welfare programs (Burtless 1987; Moffitt and Kehrer 1981; SRI International 1983). In these experiments, a sample of the low-income population in several cities was selected, and its members were randomly assigned either to an experimental group, which received a welfare program (NIT) with varying benefit levels and MTRs, or to a control group, which was eligible only for the existing welfare system. Estimates were obtained by comparing work effort levels of the control group to those of the different experimental groups. The results of the experiments showed that an NIT with higher benefit levels than those in the existing AFDC system would reduce the work effort of female heads of household, and that an NIT of any type would lower the work effort of men and women for whom no existing program was available. The experiments also provided estimates of the responsiveness of welfare recipients to changes in benefit levels and MTRs, assuming individuals to be on AFDC before and after the change. The estimates were found to be nonzero, but slightly lower in magnitude than those derived from cross-sectional survey data.[13] Unfortunately, the experiments provided little evidence on the net effect of changes in welfare program tax rates. In part, this is because the experiments were not designed for such estimates: the studies excluded families with income very much above the break-even level and hence could not capture the effects of tax rate changes that might arise from that group.[14]

Finally, some studies have been conducted on the effects of two historical changes in the AFDC tax rate: its reduction from 100 percent to 67 percent in 1969, as a result of the 1967 Social Security Amendments, and its increase from 67 percent to 100 percent in 1981, due to the 1981 Omnibus Budget Reconciliation Act (OBRA). Early studies of the 1967 Social Security Amendments examined the changes in employment and earnings among recipients remaining on the AFDC rolls; once again, the studies excluded responses from entry and exit and did not estimate net effects (Appel 1972; Bell and Bushe 1975; Smith 1974). The research suggested that work effort rose among women initially on the AFDC rolls. However, aggregate data on the AFDC participation rates and work effort levels of female heads of household in the United States in the early 1970s, just following the reduction in the tax rate, showed increases in participation rates and decreases in work effort (Moffitt 1992). Thus, net effects appeared to be zero, and, consequently, there was no evidence of increased work following the legislation.

The 1981 OBRA legislation has been evaluated more formally. The best study, conducted by the Research Triangle Institute (1981), examined the exit rates and work effort levels of women initially on the AFDC rolls at the time of the legislation, some of whom were made ineligible by the increase in the MTR. The results of the evaluation indicated that the increase in the tax rate to 100 percent had no discernible work-discouraging effects on those who were initially on the rolls and working, in the sense that there was no evidence of their having reduced work effort to zero to retain eligibility for benefits. The study did find that the exit rate from AFDC increased, which is consistent with the expected effects discussed previously. Unfortunately, the study failed to gather information on the work effort levels of those who left the rolls following the change or on the work effort levels of those who failed to apply for benefits following the tax rate increase. Hence, the total (i.e., net) effect of the change could not be ascertained. However, once again, subsequent time series evidence on the work effort levels of female heads of household showed very little impact of the legislation (Moffitt 1986).

In summary, the empirical evidence from the welfare program literature reveals a consistent pattern of inelastic (i.e., weak) responsiveness of work effort to changes in MTRs. Despite MTRs of or in excess of

100 percent, there is very little indication that reductions in those MTRs would induce any statistically detectable increase in overall hours of work or in employment among the low-income population. This realization by analysts and policy makers explains, in part, why efforts in the 1980s to change work patterns among AFDC recipients shifted so strongly toward employment and training programs and away from the use of financial incentives.

Transfer Programs for the Disabled

The primary cash transfer systems for the disabled consist of the Social Security DI and SSI programs.[15] DI is a major part of the Old-Age, Survivors, and Disability Insurance (OASDI) program. It was added to the program in 1957 and is designed to provide partial earnings replacement to all workers under age 65 who sustain severe, long-term (typically career-ending) disabilities. All workers covered under Social Security (about 95 percent of the U.S. workforce) are also covered for DI benefits, and financing for the program comes out of employer- and employee-paid Federal Insurance Contributions Act (FICA) taxes. In 1993, the DI program provided benefits for about 5 million disabled, nonaged individuals, for a total cost of $34.5 billion (U.S. House of Representatives 1994).

The SSI program provides benefits to the aged, blind, and disabled. The goal of SSI is to provide an income floor, and receipt is not tied to previous work experience. The program, enacted in 1972 and implemented in 1974, is funded from general revenues, and benefits are standardized across the states. However, most states supplement the federal SSI benefits through their own SSI programs. On average, 4 million disabled workers and their dependents received monthly federal SSI benefits in 1993, for a total annual cost of about $35 billion. The disabled represent about 75 percent of the total SSI caseload. DI recipients with low benefits can use SSI to supplement their income; about 16 percent of DI recipients also receive SSI (U.S. Department of Health and Human Services (HHS), Social Security Administration (SSA) 1994).

Description of Program Rules

Both programs define disability as "the inability to engage in any substantial gainful activity by reason of medically determinable physical or mental impairment which can be expected to result in death or which has lasted or can be expected to last for a continuous period of not less than twelve months" (HHS, SSA 1992). Therefore, the medical definition of disability is not sufficient for benefit receipt. Instead, initial and continuing eligibility for both programs is tied to the ability to work. Substantial gainful activity (SGA) is defined as a threshold level of earnings, which is currently set at $500 per month.[16]

Social Security Disability Income Program (DI)

Eligibility for DI requires meeting the definition of disability (as previously stated), having sufficient work history in Social Security covered jobs, [17] and not working, or working and earning less than the SGA threshold. When determining if earnings exceed SGA (both for initial as well as continuing eligibility), deductions are allowed for impairment-related work expenses (IRWE). The DI benefit is equal to 100 percent of the worker's primary insurance amount (PIA), which is a function of the individual's earnings history in Social Security covered employment.[18] This benefit can be significant and is typically equal to the full value of the worker's potential Social Security retirement benefit. In 1993, DI benefits for disabled workers averaged $642 per month. The PIA calculation is based on a progressive structure under which high-wage workers obtain lower earnings replacement rates than lower-wage workers. The replacement rate in 1994 ranged from 78 percent for workers with low average monthly earnings ($500) to 29 percent among workers with high monthly earnings ($4,500) (U.S. House of Representatives 1994).[19]

To analyze the work-incentive provisions of DI, we must examine the five possible phases of the program that working recipients can experience. First, there is a five-month waiting period after disability begins before benefits can be received (although there is no waiting period if the individual returns to the rolls within five years of leaving). Second, a trial work period (TWP) allows for nine months of employment over a 60-month period. If the individual earns over $200 in a month, it is counted as a trial month. Third, individuals who accumulate nine months of work have their cases reviewed; if the work in which they have been engaged is "SGA" (generally meaning that it reflects an ability to earn more than the SGA monthly threshold), benefits are extended for three more months (the grace period) and then stop. During the TWP, benefits are provided in full regardless of the level of earned or unearned income and are intended to let recipients test their ability to work, without danger of losing benefits. Fourth, recipients who have reached this point enter the extended period of eligibility (EPE), which lasts 36 months. After the three-month grace period during the EPE, benefits are provided in full if earnings (net of allowed deductions) are less than SGA, but benefits are reduced to zero if earnings are over SGA. After the EPE is exhausted, individuals are dropped from the rolls if they have achieved SGA (or they must file a new application if they are still disabled).[20]

The marginal tax rates (MTRs) on earnings in the DI program are generally much lower than those found in programs for the nondisabled. During the TWP, for example, the MTR is zero. Further, the MTR is also zero during the EPE if earnings are below SGA. However, by eliminating benefits for workers over SGA, an MTR of more than 100 percent is created on earnings that push the individual just over SGA. This creates a "notch" that resembles the MTR of over 100 percent created by the loss of Medicaid benefits in the nondisabled programs discussed previously. Hoynes and Moffitt (1996) find that, overall, DI recipients considering entering the labor force on a part-time basis face average tax rates in the range of 60 to 91 percent, depending on their earnings capacity. Those considering entry at full-time levels face average tax rates of about 40 percent.

Supplemental Security Income Program (SSI)

While DI is an earnings replacement program, SSI is a means-tested transfer program that is not tied to previous work experience. The eligibility and benefit formulas are consequently similar to those in the means-tested programs for the nondisabled. In order to be eligible for SSI, the individual must meet the definition of disability, have income and assets below the eligibility requirements, and not work, or work and earn less than the SGA threshold. The income test, asset test, and benefit level vary by living arrangement. The asset limit is $2,000 for single persons and $3,000 for couples, excluding home and automobile, while the income test requires that countable income, which includes both earned and unearned income, not exceed $446 for single persons and $669 for couples in 1994. The main deductions used in calculating countable income include the full deduction of IRWE, $20 of monthly income, $65 of earned income, and one-half of the remaining earnings. This creates an MTR of 50 percent for earnings above deductions. Benefits are equal to the program guarantee ($446 for single persons and $669 for couples) less countable income.[21] These benefit levels are adjusted annually for changes in the cost of living. All SSI recipients are also eligible for health benefits through the Medicaid program.

Work effort is observed to be quite low in both the DI and SSI programs. In a study of a sample of new entrants to DI in the early 1980s, only 10 percent of all participants had any work experience over a 10-year period following initial benefit receipt (Muller 1992). Three percent left the rolls because of increased earnings, and 5 percent attempted trial work, but this did not result in SGA termination. Those who worked were more likely to be younger, white, female, single, with higher education levels, lower DI benefits, and less severe disabilities. SSI workers have represented about 6 percent of the total SSI caseload since the mid-1980s (HHS, SSA 1993).

Expected Effects of Work Incentive Provisions

The DI and SSI programs are designed to replace (or supplement) earnings for workers who are unable to engage in "substantial gainful activity." There is, of course, a potential moral hazard problem associated with these programs inasmuch as disability is not a purely medical condition but may respond to economic and other factors. High benefits or lenient application procedures may lure those in poor health, but with employment possibilities, out of the labor market. Furthermore, a high MTR may lead to low work effort among the recipient population.

To begin, consider how the existence of the DI program affects work effort among the disabled. First, eligibility requires that recipients earn less than SGA during the application and waiting periods. This will act to lower employment effort. The time spent out of the labor force while establishing eligibility may be quite costly, especially since many recipients are initially denied and since acceptance may follow only after a lengthy appeals process. Bound (1991) estimates that DI recipients are jobless for an average of 8.5 months before receiving benefits.

Figure 2. DI Budget Constraint during TWP

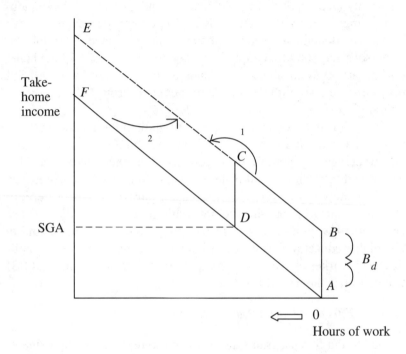

Second, the level of work effort is affected by the TWP. Figure 2 shows the one-period budget constraint that operates for the TWP as well as for the grace period. Without DI, the relevant budget segment is *ADF*. During the TWP, benefits are received in full regardless of earnings (MTR equals zero), thus shifting out the budget constraint by the amount of the benefit and resulting in the DI budget segment of *ABCE*. In this case, the DI program operates through a pure income effect, causing work effort to fall, for example. High benefits may induce some workers to accept DI and to reduce labor supply, possibly even leaving the labor force altogether.

Third, a different effect of the DI program on work effort is created during the EPE. The income opportunities during the EPE are shown by budget segment *ABCD* in figure 3. If earnings are less than SGA, benefits are provided in full. Above H_{BE}, the break-even level of hours, the benefit is cut off completely, and the MTR is over 100 percent. In this case, the worker would have to increase hours of work to H_1 to make up for lost DI income. The EPE, like the TWP, provides a negative income effect that reduces work, as illustrated by arrow 1. In addition, the notch provides a strong incentive to work at levels below SGA. In this situation, shown by arrow 2, some individuals who might otherwise have had high employment effort are induced by the DI benefits to work less in order to remain below SGA. Overall, providing benefits to the disabled through the DI program will reduce labor supply among the disabled.

Figure 3. DI Budget Constraint during EPE

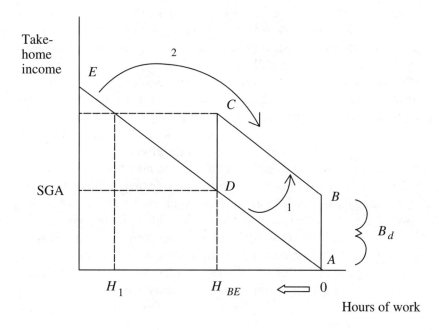

These effects are not necessarily of greatest policy interest, because they concern the impact of the DI program relative to having no program at all. Of more note are the expected effects of the DI provisions that are intended to provide work incentives, mainly the TWP and the EPE, relative to a DI program without such provisions. To examine the outcomes of these incentives, or of any proposed modifications in existing incentives, we need to consider not only differences in work effort among current recipients but any changes in entry and exit rates that (also) contribute to changes in the overall level of work effort among the disabled.

First, consider the effects of adding a TWP to a "strict SGA" program in which benefits are unaffected if work is below SGA but are eliminated entirely for work above SGA.[22] The impact of the TWP on the budget constraint is illustrated in figure 2. Without any DI program at all, the budget constraint is *ADF*, while the budget constraint is *ABCDE* under the strict SGA DI program. The addition of the TWP prolongs benefits regardless of earnings, extending the DI budget constraint to *ABCE*. As intended, this change provides an incentive for those recipients who were initially at or a bit below SGA to work more than SGA, as shown by arrow 1. However, by making the program more generous for those who can and wish to work above SGA, exit rates from the program will fall in the longer term: some recipients who would have left in order to work above SGA will stay on the program.[23] Thus, while work effort among current participants may increase in the short run, it may fall in the long run. Those who would have exited the program will ultimately work less than they would have otherwise, as illustrated by arrow 2 (income effects induce a reduction in hours of work). In addition, benefits can now be received above SGA, which was not possible before, and this may affect entry rates, by creating incentives for eligible nonparticipants to apply for benefits, should they think that work above SGA is likely if they go onto DI. This would also increase the caseload and result in reduced work effort. Overall, the introduction of the TWP has ambiguous net effects on the employment effort of DI recipients and the eligible population, for the increased work among initial recipients may be outweighed by the likely future reductions in work among those who delay exit and those who enter.

The effects of the EPE, which was introduced in 1980, are, at least at first inspection, more clear-cut: the benefit schedule reverts to its strict SGA form of loss of benefits for work above SGA (aside from the retention of Medicare benefits, whose effects are similar to the TWP and are provided above SGA). Once a worker is in the EPE, the incentives to work above and below SGA are the same in each month as they were in the strict SGA program. However, the main impact of the EPE is in its provision of insurance for 36 months against a drop in earnings. In the strict SGA program, a recipient might have hesitated to work above SGA because of the danger of not being able to sustain such high earnings and having to reapply for benefits. Avoiding this concern is part of the intention of the EPE program and presumably increases work effort during the EPE period.

Even with the EPE there is the possibility of increased entry. The greater generosity created by the EPE may make the DI program more attractive to eligibles who are on the margin of applying for benefits and may tip them in the direction of applying. Actually applying will depend on the extent of information about the DI program, whether eligibles have reasonably good expectations of attempting to work when on the program, and on the costs associated with application. If any entry occurs, this will raise the DI caseload and reduce work effort, since those who enter will work less, on average, while on the DI program than they would have if they had stayed off DI. Thus, in principle, the direction of the net effect of the EPE is ambiguous and can only be determined by empirical research.[24]

This discussion shows that there is a basic similarity between the TWP and EPE work provisions of the DI program, on the one hand, and the MTR reductions in nondisability programs, which are also aimed at increasing work effort, on the other. Both have ambiguous net impacts on the recipient and eligible populations: while they have positive employment incentives for some, they also reduce exit rates and possibly increase entry rates, both of which lower long-run work effort (and raise the caseload). Each type of financial incentive operates by making the program more generous, and therefore more attractive, to working individuals as compared to their prospective situations off the program.[25]

The work incentives of SSI differ considerably from those of DI, while they are similar to those in the AFDC or Food Stamp programs.

The work incentives of SSI can be analyzed by referring to the welfare budget constraint for the nondisabled in figure 1, substituting the SSI implicit tax rate on earnings of 50 percent for t ($t = 0.5$ in figure 1). The 50 percent MTR implies that if earnings are increased by \$1, total income increases by only 50 cents. Benefits are phased out as earnings increase and reach zero at the break-even level (point D). As before, the static labor supply model implies unambiguously that the existence of SSI will reduce work effort among the disabled relative to having no program at all. There is an income effect associated with the guarantee (as with the DI program), but the 50 percent MTR induces a substitution effect that is not present in the DI program. The income and substitution effects work in the same direction, and hours of work must fall. If the MTR is reduced, the net impact on work effort is ambiguous in direction, however. As discussed for nondisability programs, such a reduction lowers work effort because of a delay in exit and an increase in entry.[26]

Empirical Results

The scope of the empirical literature on work incentives of disability income programs is somewhat limited compared to the literature for the nondisabled. The main body of empirical studies examines the effect of the level of DI benefits on program participation (or caseload size).[27] Participation in DI is typically estimated as a function of the potential DI benefit, which is imputed for those not on the program, individual attributes such as age and education, and locational characteristics.[28] The principal parameter of interest, the elasticity of DI participation (or nonparticipation in the labor market), with respect to the DI benefit, varies widely in the literature. The results based on samples of older men (aged 45-62) provide elasticities ranging from 0.06-1.80. The highest elasticities in the literature are found by Parsons and range from 0.63 (Parsons 1980a) to 1.80 (Parsons 1980b). Slade (1984) estimates an elasticity of 0.81. The magnitude of these elasticities is sufficient to explain all of the observed decline in labor force participation rates by older men in the 1970s. Haveman and Wolfe (1984a) claim that Parsons' estimates are flawed and instead estimate an elasticity between 0.06 and 0.21 (Haveman and Wolfe 1984b; Haveman, de Jong, and Wolfe 1991). The other main estimates fall in the range of

0.10 to 0.20 (Halpern and Hausman 1986; Leonard 1979). Older workers, those in poor health and with greater disabilities, and individuals with lower earnings have been found to be more responsive to changes in benefits (Haveman and Wolfe 1984b; Slade 1984). de Jong, Haveman, and Wolfe (1988) find evidence that women are more sensitive to benefits, with estimated elasticities of 0.97 for female heads of household and 0.23 for married women.[29]

Variation in the leniency of determining eligibility has been used to examine the sensitivity of DI participation to the uncertainty of benefits. Parsons (1991a) and Gruber and Kubik (1994) use over-time and across-state variation in DI denial rates to estimate how DI applications and nonparticipation in the labor market are affected by such uncertainty. Parsons finds the elasticity of applications with respect to the denial rate to be –0.18. Gruber and Kubik find the elasticity of nonparticipation with respect to the denial rate to be 0.27.

While much of the empirical work in this literature is of great interest, the results fall significantly short of what is needed to estimate the effect of the TWP, the EPE, or other work-incentive provisions. In the absence of direct evaluations of the TWP, for example, inferences about its effects can be made only by estimating the number of individuals who would prefer to work above SGA but still receive benefits; wage elasticities as well as income elasticities are needed for this prediction. The marked absence of attempts at estimated wage elasticities is, in fact, the literature's major defect for assessing the effectiveness of work-incentive provisions.[30] Furthermore, in these studies, participation in DI is considered equivalent to nonparticipation in the labor market, which rules out examining the sort of responses shown by the arrows in figures 2 and 3.

As noted, the empirical evidence for nondisability programs should generate skepticism that there are any significant positive net effects of financial inducements for recipients to work while on the rolls. While the TWP and EPE are quite different in form from a simple MTR, the same types of effects are involved; therefore, the results from the nondisability programs should generate concern about the effectiveness of the TWP and EPE. In an assessment of whether the nondisability results are applicable to DI programs, one issue that would presumably be very important is whether the responsiveness of the disabled to changes in benefits and tax rates (i.e., their income and substitution elasticities) are similar to those of female heads of household and other low-income groups that commonly receive nondisability benefits. Whether the responsiveness is higher or lower seems unclear from the literature. Nonetheless, it is important to point out that the populations and programs are distinctive in many ways, which may contribute to different responsiveness levels.[31]

Expected Effects of Reforms to DI Work Incentives

The passage of the Americans with Disabilities Act (ADA) reflects a desire to encourage labor force participation among the disabled. As is often noted, the existence of the DI program runs counter to this goal, by encouraging reductions in work effort among the disabled. Compared to a program with a strict SGA limitation, however, the TWP and EPE features of DI do produce work incentives for current recipients, even though the direction of these features' overall impact is ambiguous. Several changes to the work incentives of the DI program are under consideration, including increasing the SGA, extending the length of the TWP, and imposing a 50 percent MTR on earnings after the end of the TWP.[32]

Raising the SGA increases the DI caseload but has ambiguous impacts on work effort among the disabled.[33] The change affects employment effort, program exit, and program entry in two ways. First, the costs of application are reduced because higher work effort can be sustained without exceeding SGA (as required for initial application). Second, as shown in figure 4, increasing the SGA shifts up the notch in the budget constraint during the EPE. Increasing the SGA level from SGA_0 to SGA_1 shifts out the DI budget constraint from *ABCD* to *ABCEF*. This will lead to increases in hours of work among some current recipients, as shown by arrow 1 in the figure. However, by allowing for higher levels of work with full benefits, the more generous program lowers the exit rate from the rolls for some recipients, who ultimately work less than they would have otherwise. In addition, the change attracts new applicants, who, if accepted into the program, will take advantage of the SGA to work while on the rolls; however, they will work fewer hours than they would have had they been off the rolls, as shown by arrows 2 and 3. Some of these new entrants are eligible under the expanded program (arrow 2), and others may take advantage of the increased benefits and reduce their work effort to become eligible (arrow 3). This leads to a rise in the caseload, through increases in the entry rate as well as decreases in the exit rate.

Figure 4. Effect of Increasing SGA on EPE Budget Constraint

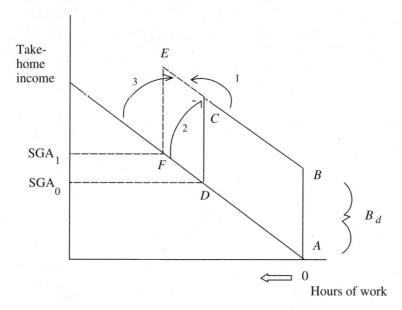

Similarly, adding a partial benefit or MTR on earnings during the EPE will tend to increase work levels among current DI recipients, but the impact on overall work effort among all disabled persons is indeterminate in direction (the caseload will unambiguously rise). Figure 5 shows the budget constraint for the EPE before and after the introduction of the partial offset, where the MTR is imposed only on earnings over the SGA. Under current law and with this expansion, the slope of the budget constraint below the SGA (*ABC*) is *w*, reflecting an MTR of zero. With the expansion, above the SGA there is an MTR of 50 percent, which operates until benefits are reduced to zero. As before, arrow 1 shows the likely movement in work levels among current recipients. This increase in work effort is the intended effect of the expansion. However, a positive income effect and negative substitution effect suggest that work levels will fall for others, as shown by arrows 2 and 3, both from reduced exit and increased entry. The potential growth in the caseload is quite large under this expansion. Using the average benefit in 1993 of $642, the break-even earnings level increases from SGA to about $1,800 per month or about $22,000 per year.[34]

Figure 5. Partial Benefit Offset (50 percent) over SGA

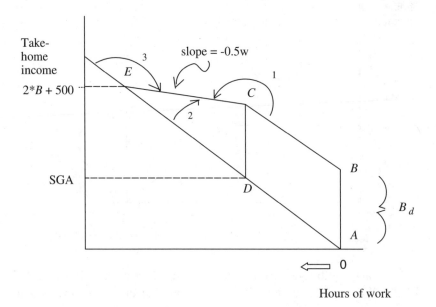

Extending the length of the TWP also has ambiguous effects on work incentives. By allowing recipients to work for more months before being taxed (e.g., before entering the EPE), the effective MTR in the program decreases. This will probably increase work levels and the length of time on the program for current participants. In addition, it may reduce exit rates for current participants and attract new participants, with both of these groups working fewer hours during the additional 12 months than they would have otherwise. This would augment the caseload as well.

The empirical literature, as described, provides limited insight into the likely results of these proposed reforms to DI work incentives. In general, the impact on overall work effort depends critically on the relative sizes of the income and substitution effects for current recipients and potential entrants. Existing research provides very little reliable information on these parameters. The total effect also depends on the size of the increase in break-even income and on the density of the eligible population in these areas of the earnings distribution, that is, on the relative numbers of disabled individuals who can and prefer to work just above the SGA.

Conclusions and Policy Implications

As the issue of increasing work incentives in the DI and SSI programs becomes of greater policy interest, the lessons from similar provisions in plans for the nondisabled should be studied. Our review of the nondisability program literature demonstrates that simple financial inducements or changes in benefit formulas are unlikely to be as effective as they first appear. The empirical research on such reforms in nondisability programs is quite uniform in its failure to find strong responses to financial incentives and decreased MTRs. A set of possible explanations includes new entry into the programs as well as decreased exit. Our review of the empirical research on DI and SSI does not allow us to reach any conclusions about whether the *magnitude* of the responses in DI programs is likely to be greater than that in nondisability programs. However, the different types of responses to financial considerations, both the intended increases in work effort and the unintended reductions, should be present in DI and SSI, at least to some degree. This leads us to urge caution in using financial inducements as a means of work-incentive reform in those programs without further, concrete evidence of their effectiveness.

Policy for AFDC recipients has evolved away from financial incentives in recent years and has shifted toward the use of education and training programs to directly encourage, and sometimes require, work. This transition began in the 1970s and occurred in part because of the perceived failure of financial inducements, such as provided by the

1967 Social Security Amendments, to increase AFDC recipient employment levels and to reduce caseloads. In addition, the move reflected a society-wide change in attitudes toward work by women with children, as it became increasingly the norm for such women to be employed rather than to stay at home. A similar change in attitudes toward the disabled appears to have occurred, with many arguing that all recipients should work to the degree they can. However, the use of financial inducements is still more favorably viewed in policy discussions of SSI and DI than of AFDC and other welfare programs. As we have stressed, this perspective is not necessarily justified by the evidence.

Finally, a recent policy direction taken for AFDC and related programs is to provide financial incentives to *leave* the welfare rolls via earnings and wage supplements for private sector work. The most prominent of these programs is the Earned Income Tax Credit (EITC), which provides supplements to low-income families and which has been greatly increased in generosity. The attractiveness of the EITC is that it has the potential to increase work and earnings and to reduce the welfare caseload at the same time. The philosophy behind the EITC and similar private sector wage subsidy programs is diametrically opposite to that behind the use of financial inducements to work more while on welfare; the latter has the potentially deleterious consequences of increasing the caseload and reducing some individuals' work effort, which we have discussed at length. These undesirable results would not occur if financial incentives were offered only for off-welfare (or both on- and off-welfare) work. Policy discussions of disability assistance might fruitfully turn to wage subsidies, perhaps by investigating special private sector earnings subsidies for the disabled or modifications in the EITC to make more disabled individuals eligible for its benefits.

NOTES

NOTE: The authors would like to thank Gary Painter for excellent research assistance and John Bound, Richard Burkhauser, David Stapleton, and Finis Welch for comments.

1. The rules described in this section can be found in the 1994 "Green Book" (U.S. House of Representatives 1994).

2. The $30 flat deduction is eliminated after 12 months of earnings. Both the twelve months of a $30 deduction and the four months of the one-third deduction can be reestablished after one year, provided that the recipient has gone off AFDC and not returned in the interim. We should

also note that some states use a payment method called "fill-the-gap," which permits a total disregard of earnings up to a certain maximum, after which the tax rates noted in the text are applied.

3. Unlike the AFDC program, the FSP has two maximums, one on gross income and one on net income (i.e., income after deductions). A family loses eligibility if either maximum is exceeded.

4. We should note that the AFDC benefit is included in countable income for those FSP recipients who are also on AFDC. This inclusion tends to lower the cumulative MTR for those who are on both programs, since an increase in earnings generally reduces the AFDC benefit, which, therefore, increases the FSP benefit. In simple cases, the cancellation is complete: a $1 increase in earnings lowers the AFDC benefit by $1, so countable income in the FSP is unchanged, and hence the FSP benefit is unchanged.

5. We have not discussed the MTR arising from participation in public and subsidized housing programs because there has been too little research on their effects. Keane and Moffitt (1994) provide estimates of these MTRs.

6. Another possible response can occur if there are initially individuals along segment AC who are eligible for benefits but do not receive them, either because of a stigma associated with AFDC receipt or because the "hassle" and other costs of applying for and receiving assistance outweigh the benefits of the potential payment. A reduction in t, which increases potential payments, may induce some of these individuals to go onto welfare after all, with an associated reduction in work effort.

It should be noted that the welfare program caseload unambiguously rises. Providing work incentives by lowering the tax rate increases the caseload.

7. In this discussion, we have to a degree shifted to a model of exit and entry, unlike the static model of our diagrams. In truth, even in the presence of "fixed" budget constraints, there are continual flows onto and off the rolls, in response both to unforeseen and uncontrollable events (layoffs, health events, etc.) and to conscious decision and purposeful behavior (e.g., leaving the rolls to take a job offer). Purposeful behavior that takes relative income and work incentives into account will result in a long-run equilibrium similar to that portrayed in the static model, as a larger proportion of the population ends up with higher income.

8. Although very little is known of underreporting among AFDC recipients, many suspect it to be common, based on anecdotal evidence. One study of 50 AFDC families in Chicago found that all 50 were receiving some form of unreported income (Edin 1991). The general presumption in the literature is that the frequency and magnitude of income underreporting are positively associated with the level of the tax rate.

9. Technically, these studies estimated the substitution and income elasticities assuming that the budget constraint segment upon which individuals were located did not change.

10. That is, income elasticities are estimated to be negative, and substitution elasticities are positive.

11. Another approach taken to estimating the net impacts of tax rates has been to simulate those effects from a microsimulation model, applying estimated elasticities from the econometric literature to representative household data bases (Moffitt 1992; Fortin, Truchon, and Beausejour 1993). These studies confirm that lowering tax rates in welfare programs may reduce work effort, depending upon the size of the estimated responses but also upon the relative numbers of eligible individuals in different portions of the income distribution.

12. A recent study by Yelowitz (1995) did examine the impact of the Medicaid notch, however, and found that it had negative effects on the probability of working.

13. See Moffitt and Kehrer (1981) for details.

14. The experiments further excluded eligible nonrecipients, whose responses would also affect the net result in real-world welfare programs.

15. Other public programs that provide cash benefits for the disabled include several veterans' compensation programs, workers' compensation, and (optional) state-provided temporary disability benefits. The discussion in this paper will be limited to the DI and SSI programs.

16. The SGA is not indexed for price changes and has been increased nine times in the program's 35 years. The SGA started in 1957 at $100 and was set at $300 from 1980 to 1990 before the latest increase to $500.

17. To qualify for DI, applicants must have worked 20 of the last 40 quarters preceding the quarter of application, although the rules differ somewhat for younger workers. The work history required for DI is virtually the same as that required for Social Security retirement benefits.

18. The benefit can be as large as 150 percent of PIA for disabled workers with families.

19. The earnings figures refer to the worker's average indexed monthly earnings (AIME) in Social Security employment. The DI benefit, equal to the worker's PIA, is a function of the AIME. Benefits are adjusted for changes in the cost of living. The PIA and AIME are calculated in roughly the same way as they are for Social Security retirement benefits.

20. If a person has *never* achieved SGA, the EPE is extended indefinitely. However, benefits will be discontinued the first time that SGA is achieved.

Medicare benefits are available after 24 months of DI benefit receipt. Once the individual enters the EPE, Medicare benefits are obtainable for the next 39 months. Thus, Medicare is provided for three months past the end of EPE. Once a worker reaches age 65, the DI case is automatically transferred to the Social Security retirement system.

21. All figures refer to 1994 levels.

22. The original DI program did not have the TWP or EPE features. The TWP was introduced in 1960 and the EPE in 1980.

23. Once again, such exit rates can only be understood if it is realized that a dynamic model involving normal flows onto and off the rolls underlies the static diagrams we have drawn. Normal exits from the rolls occur, for example, due to job opportunities, even though the budget constraint does not change in the ordinary sense of the word. Whether an individual takes advantage of such opportunities will no doubt be based in part on the relative income gain or loss associated with leaving versus staying on the rolls. These are the same considerations that underlie the arrows in our static diagrams, although in a dynamic context.

24. The EPE may also reduce exit rates from DI when averaged over the 36-month period. For example, recipients may try out a job with possibly short duration, knowing that they will probably return within a few months to collect benefits. While this encourages employment among those who would not have worked at all, it discourages work effort by those who would have otherwise chosen to go off the rolls altogether at a job with greater prospects of stability and longevity.

25. Some important dynamic considerations of the DI program have been left out of this discussion. For example, even though benefits are not reduced during the TWP, potential benefit cutoffs begin after nine months of work if the recipient enters EPE. Consequently, taking advantage of the TWP will increase income at the time but decrease prospective income, effectively raising the MTR and reducing work effort. Similarly, individuals who consistently work above SGA during the EPE will eventually be dropped from the system altogether after 36 months, thus losing Medicare benefits as well as the insurance of DI benefits if wages fall below SGA. This also operates to increase the effective MTR. Lastly, Medicare benefits will be lost three months after the end of the EPE when leaving the DI rolls. There is anecdotal evidence that losing health benefits may be a larger work disincentive for the disabled than the prospect of losing cash benefits (National Academy of Social Insurance 1994).

26. This discussion shows that the main difference between SSI and DI is in the treatment of earnings. In SSI, SGA is only used when determining initial eligibility, and benefits are reduced

with increases in earned income. The notch in the DI budget constraint during the EPE does not exist in SSI. However, this difference is only a result of recent legislative changes in the SSI program. Provisions referred to as 1619(a) and 1619(b) started in 1980 and were made permanent in 1986. These provisions dramatically changed the earnings opportunities for disabled workers. Previously, SSI recipients had a trial work period, and Medicaid and cash benefits were lost when a worker had countable earnings that exceeded SGA. In that case, there was an MTR of 50 percent below SGA, at which point the remaining benefits (and Medicaid coverage) were lost in entirety. Provision 1619(a) allows SSI (and Medicaid) benefits to be continued even at earnings exceeding SGA (until sufficiently high earnings move a person off the rolls completely). To ease the transition back to work, provision 1619(b) extends Medicaid coverage when workers' earnings render them ineligible for SSI benefits.

27. This literature is critically reviewed in Leonard (1986) and in the exchanges between Parsons (1984) and Haveman and Wolfe (1984a) and Parsons (1991b) and Bound (1991).

The empirical studies of the work disincentive effects of the SSI and workers' compensation program are much less developed. McGarry (1993) considers the impact of potential benefits on the take-up of SSI benefits among the low-income elderly.

28. The majority of the literature defines the dependent variable to be labor force participation or nonparticipation (de Jong, Haveman, and Wolfe 1988; Gruber and Kubik 1994; Haveman and Wolfe 1984b; Parsons 1980a, 1980b; Slade 1984). Leonard (1979) specifies the dependent variable as DI participant or nonparticipant. Operationally, there is little difference between these approaches. Halpern and Hausman (1986) consider three states: DI recipient, DI-rejected applicant, and nonapplicant. Haveman, Wolfe, and Warlick (1988) consider the DI recipient, Social Security early retirement, and labor force participant choices.

29. The elasticities cited are from the econometric studies that utilized cross-sectional data. The time series studies are summarized by Leonard (1986).

30. Some of the studies (e.g., Parsons 1980a and 1980b) do include wages, but only their predisability level, and only in the form of a replacement rate, which results in neither an income nor a wage elasticity. There are many difficulties in estimating the work-incentive effects of the DI program that are not encountered in the literature for the nondisabled. Such problems include the endogenous nature of DI benefits, due to the relationship with previous work experiences, the uncertainty of DI receipt, and the difficulty in imputing DI benefits for nonrecipients. These issues and their relevance for the empirical literature are discussed in Leonard (1986), Haveman and Wolfe (1984a), Bound (1991), and Hoynes and Moffitt (1996).

31. It is clear that DI recipients confront different obstacles to labor market success than do female heads of household. Disabled individuals may face difficulties in labor supply (due to the physical or emotional conditions impacting the ability to work) and labor demand (due to the availability of jobs for persons with disabilities). Furthermore, contrasted with AFDC, receipt of DI benefits is uncertain and subject to long waiting periods because of difficulties in evaluating the medical definition of disability. Lastly, the availability of public health insurance may be quite important for disabled workers, especially due to preexisting condition clauses in private insurance.

32. Specifically, the National Academy of Social Insurance report (1994) outlines five possible reforms: indexing the SGA amount to keep pace with wage growth; raising the SGA to the level for the blind ($930 in 1993) and indexing to keep pace with wage growth; providing a partial offset (MTR) of 50 percent to be imposed after the TWP on earnings above the monthly SGA; providing a partial offset (MTR) of 50 percent to be imposed after the TWP on earnings above $85 a month; and extending the TWP by 12 months. With the partial offset, the work-incentive effects of the DI program are made more similar to those in the SSI program.

33. Increasing the SGA would also expand eligibility for SSI. The impacts are likely to be larger for the DI program since the SGA only affects initial (but not continuing) eligibility for the SSI program.

34. This is calculated by setting benefits $[B-0.5*(wH-500)]$ equal to zero, where w is the hourly wage and H is hours worked, and solving for the earnings level where benefits are just exhausted.

Imposing a 50 percent MTR on earnings over an $85 exclusion during the EPE would result in closer parity between the SSI and DI work incentives. This change differs from those considered in the text: since the $85 exclusion is below the SGA level of $500, benefits would be lower than they are under current law for some ranges of earnings. By increasing the tax rate (from 0 to 50 percent), we may see a reduction in work effort for current recipients. However, eliminating the notch (and its high MTR) and extending benefits past the SGA may result in an increase in work levels among some recipients. For this program change, the caseload as well as the net work effects are ambiguous. The direction of the change in entry and exit rates is not predictable since for some ranges for hours worked the program has been expanded while, for others, the program is less generous.

References

Appel, Gary Louis. 1972. "Effects of a Financial Incentive on AFDC Employment: Michigan's Experience Between July 1969 and 1970." Minneapolis:
Institute for Interdisciplinary Studies.

Barr, Nicholas, and Robert Hall. 1981. "The Probability of Dependence on
Public Assistance," *Economica* 48 (May): 109-124.

Bell, Winifred, and Dennis Bushe. 1975. *Neglecting the Many, Helping the
Few: The Impact of the 1967 AFDC Work Incentives*. New York: Center for
Studies in Income Maintenance Policy.

Blank, Rebecca. 1989. "The Effect of Medical Need and Medicaid on AFDC
Participation," *Journal of Human Resources* 24 (Winter): 54-87.

Bound, John. 1989. "The Health and Earnings of Rejected Disability Insurance Applicants," *American Economic Review* 79, 3 (June): 482-503.

_____. 1991. "The Health and Earnings of Rejected Disability Insurance
Applicants: Reply," *American Economic Review* 81, 5 (December): 1427-
1434.

Burtless, Gary. 1986. "Social Security, Unanticipated Benefit Increases, and
the Timing of Retirement," *Review of Economic Studies* 53, 5 (October):
781-805.

_____. 1987. "The Work Response to a Guaranteed Income: A Survey of
Experimental Evidence." In *Lessons from the Income Maintenance Experi-
ments*, Alicia Munnell, ed. Boston: Federal Reserve Bank of Boston and
Brookings Institution.

Danziger, Sheldon, Robert Haveman, and Robert Plotnick. 1981. "How
Income Transfers Affect Work, Savings, and the Income Distribution: A
Critical Review," *Journal of Economic Literature* 19 (September): 975-
1028.

de Jong, Philip, Robert Haveman, and Barbara Wolfe. 1988. "Labor and
Transfer Incomes and Older Women's Work." NBER Working Paper No.
2728, October.

Edin, Kathryn. 1991. "Surviving the Welfare System: How AFDC Recipients
Make Ends Meet in Chicago," *Social Problems* 38 (November): 462-474.

Fortin, Bernard, Michel Truchon, and Louis Beausejour. 1993. "On Reforming the Welfare System: Workfare Meets the Negative Income Tax," *Journal of Public Economics* 51, 2 (June): 119-151.

Fraker, Thomas, and Robert Moffitt. 1988. "The Effect of Food Stamps on
Labor Supply: A Bivariate Selection Model," *Journal of Public Economics*
35, 1 (February): 25-56.

Giannarelli, Linda, and Eugene Steurle. 1994. "It's Not What You Make, It's What You Keep: Tax Rates Faced by AFDC Recipients." Paper presented at the Meetings of the Association for Public Policy and Management, Chicago, October.

Gruber, John, and Jeffrey Kubik. 1994. "Disability Insurance Rejection Rates and the Labor Supply of Older Workers." Mimeographed, Massachusetts Institute of Technology, August.

Halpern, Janice, and Jerry Hausman. 1986. "Choice Under Uncertainty: A Model of Applications for the SSDI Program," *Journal of Public Economics* 31, 2 (November): 131-161.

Haveman, Robert, and Barbara Wolfe. 1984a. "The Decline in Male Labor Force Participation: Comment," *Journal of Political Economy* 92, 3 (June): 532-541.

_____. 1984b. "Disability Transfers and Early Retirement, A Causal Relationship?" *Journal of Public Economics* 24, 1 (June): 47-66.

Haveman, Robert, Barbara Wolfe, and Jennifer Warlick. 1988. "Labor Market Behavior of Older Men: Estimates from a Trichotomous Choice Model," *Journal of Public Economics* 36, 2 (July): 153-175.

Haveman, Robert, Philip de Jong, and Barbara Wolfe. 1991. "Disability Transfers and the Work Decision of Older Men," *Quarterly Journal of Economics* 106, 3 (August): 939-949.

Heckman, James. 1979. "Sample Selection Bias As a Specification Error," *Econometrica* 47, 1 (January): 153-161.

Hoynes, Hilary. 1996. "Welfare Transfers in Two-Parent Families: Labor Supply and Welfare Participation Under AFDC-UP," *Econometrica* 64, 2 (March): 295-332.

Hoynes, Hilary, and Robert Moffitt. 1996. "Tax Rates and Work Incentives in the Social Security Disability Program: Current Law and Alternative Reforms." University of California, Berkeley, January.

Keane, Michael, and Robert Moffitt. 1994. "A Structural Model of Multiple Welfare Program Participation." Mimeographed, Brown University.

Leonard, Jonathan. 1979. "The Social Security Disability Program and Labor Force Participation." NBER Working Paper No. 392, August.

_____. 1986. "Labor Supply Incentives and Disincentives for Disabled Persons." In *Disability and the Labor Market*, Monroe Berkowitz and Anne Hill, eds. Utica, NY: Industrial and Labor Relations Press.

Levy, Frank. 1979. "The Labor Supply of Female Heads, or AFDC Work Incentives Don't Work Too Well," *Journal of Human Resources* 14, 1 (Winter): 76-97.

Marvel, Howard. 1982. "An Economic Analysis of the Operation of SSDI," *Journal of Human Resources* 17, 3 (Summer): 393-412.

Masters, Stanley H., and Irwin Garfinkel. 1977. *Estimating the Labor Supply Effects of Income Maintenance Alternatives.* New York: Academic Press.

McGarry, Kathleen. 1993. "Factors Determining Participation of the Elderly in SSI." Mimeographed, University of California, Los Angeles.

Moffitt, Robert. 1983. "An Economic Model of Welfare Stigma," *American Economic Review* 73, 5 (December): 1023-1035.

_____. 1986. "Work Incentives in the AFDC System: An Analysis of the 1981 Reforms," *American Economic Review* 76, 2 (May): 219-223.

_____. 1992. "Incentive Effects of the U.S. Welfare System: A Review," *Journal of Economic Literature* 30, 1 (March): 1-61.

Moffitt, Robert, and Kenneth Kehrer. 1981. "The Effect of Tax and Transfer Programs on Labor Supply: The Evidence from the Income Maintenance Experiments." In *Research in Labor Economics*, Vol. 4, Ronald Ehrenberg, ed. Greenwich, CT: JAI Press.

Moffitt, Robert, and Barbara Wolfe. 1990. "The Effects of Medicaid on Welfare Dependency and Work." Special Report No. 49. Madison: Institute for Research on Poverty.

_____. 1992. "The Effect of the Medicaid Program on Welfare Participation and Labor Supply," *Review of Economics and Statistics* 74, 4 (November): 615-626.

Muller, Scott. 1992. "Disability Beneficiaries Who Work and Their Experience Under Program Work Incentives," *Social Security Bulletin* 52, 5 (Summer): 2-19.

National Academy of Social Insurance. 1994. "Preliminary Status Report of the Disability Policy Panel." March, Washington, DC.

Parsons, Donald. 1980a. "The Decline in Male Labor Force Participation," *Journal of Political Economy* 88, 1 (February): 117-134.

_____. 1980b. "Racial Trends in Male Labor Force Participation," *American Economic Review* 70, 5 (December): 911-920.

_____. 1984. "Disability Insurance and Male Labor Force Participation: A Response to Haveman and Wolfe," *Journal of Political Economy* 92, 3 (June): 542-549.

_____. 1991a. "Self-Screening Targeted Public Transfer Programs," *Journal of Political Economy* 99, 4 (August): 859-876.

_____. 1991b. "The Health and Earnings of Rejected Disability Insurance Applicants: Comment," *American Economic Review* 81, 5 (December): 1419-1426.

Research Triangle Institute. 1981. "Final Report: Evaluation of the 1981 AFDC Amendments." Research Triangle Park, NC.

Slade, Frederic. 1984. "Older Men: Disability Insurance and the Incentive to Work," *Industrial Relations*, 23, 2 (Spring): 260-269.

Smith, Vernon. 1974. "Welfare Work Incentives: The Earnings Exemption and Its Impact Upon AFDC Employment, Earnings, and Program Cost." Lansing: Michigan Department of Social Services.

SRI International. 1983. *Final Report of the Seattle-Denver Income Maintenance Experiment: Design and Results*. Vol I. Menlo Park, CA: SRI International.

U.S. Department of Health and Human Services. Social Security Administration. 1992. *Annual Statistical Supplement to the Social Security Bulletin.* Washington, DC: Government Printing Office.

_____. 1993. "Quarterly Report on SSI Disabled Workers and Work Incentive Provisions." June.

_____. 1994. *Social Security Bulletin* (Summer).

U.S. House of Representatives. 1994. Committee on Ways and Means. *Background Material and Data on Programs within the Jurisdiction of the Committee on Ways and Means*. Washington, DC: Government Printing Office, various issues.

Winkler, Anne. 1991. "The Incentive Effects of Medicaid on Women's Labor Supply," *Journal of Human Resources* 26, 2 (Spring): 308-337.

Yelowitz, Aaron. 1995. "The Medicaid Notch, Labor Supply and Welfare Participation: Evidence from Eligibility Expansions," *Quarterly Journal of Economics* 110, 4: 909-940.

Lessons from the Vocational Rehabilitation/Social Security Administration Experience

Edward Berkowitz
George Washington University
David Dean
University of Richmond

In the long history of efforts to link the vocational rehabilitation (VR) program and the income maintenance programs for persons with disabilities run by the Social Security Administration (SSA), three distinct eras emerge. Even before the passage of Social Security Disability Insurance (DI) in 1956, there were discussions of how to use rehabilitation as an alternative to income maintenance benefits. The period between 1957 and 1981 featured the rise and fall of the Beneficiary Rehabilitation Program (BRP). Since 1982, Congress has legislated a new system for rehabilitating DI beneficiaries that includes stricter reimbursement mechanisms.

The inability to rehabilitate persons after they have been declared eligible for DI retirement pensions, a common feature of all three of the eras, marks a major failure of modern disability policy. The barriers between vocational rehabilitation, which attempts to facilitate the labor force participation of people with disabilities, and DI, which grants tickets out of the labor force, remain high. The only way to lower the barriers is to change the entire disability system.

As an exercise in analytical description, this paper examines the history of VR-DI linkage efforts. The first section recounts the early plans to rehabilitate disability beneficiaries. The second section chronicles the arrival of the BRP program, describes its operation, and cites some of the reasons for its demise. The results of the revised "retrospective" payment schema are examined in the third section.

The Linkage in the Planning Stage, 1935-1956

The idea of building a link between disability insurance and vocational rehabilitation preceded the formal establishment of DI in 1956. Indeed, during the period between 1935 and 1956, SSA planners experimented with different ways to match applicants for disability benefits with rehabilitation services. Their counterparts in the Office of Vocational Rehabilitation developed techniques for rehabilitating people on the public assistance caseload. In this same period, advocates of both programs engaged in complex political negotiations that left a permanent mark on the nation's response to disability.

Social Security administrators included provisions for rehabilitation services in their earliest blueprints for a disability insurance program. Late in 1938, for example, I.S. Falk, the director of research and statistics for the Social Security Board, noted that a program of social insurance against disability should include occupational retraining for persons with chronic impairments and cited vocational rehabilitation as an example of a program that provided such services (Falk 1938, pp. 9-10).

Vocational rehabilitation had existed since 1920 as a modestly funded federal grant-in-aid program that, in a typical year during the 1930s, placed fewer than 40,000 people with disabilities in the labor market. The program, run differently in each of the states, relied heavily on the counseling of people with disabilities. In addition, the program had the authority to purchase a wide array of services, such as training courses, that might help persons overcome their handicaps and enter the labor market (MacDonald 1944).

The Social Security Board planners proceeded to fit rehabilitation into their designs. When individuals' disability claims were being validated, their suitability for rehabilitation could also be tested. The initial estimates called for 10,000 referrals in 1940 and 25,000 referrals in 1945, indicating the modest expectations that officials had of the vocational rehabilitation program (Falk 1938, pp. 19, 29). In 1940, however, the Board expanded the estimates and refined the rehabilitation part of the program. Draft legislation for permanent disability insurance included a $400,000 appropriation for the Board to administer a program of "medical, surgical, rehabilitation, and other services to disability beneficiaries"; in the future, the appropriation was not to exceed 2 percent of estimated expenditures for disability insurance. "Rehabilitation," Board officials claimed in one internal planning document, "is in the interest not only of the worker but also of the insurance system" (Social Security Board 1940).

The 1940s proved to be inauspicious for the passage of a disability insurance program, and, for the moment, the idea of a VR-DI linkage faded. During this decade, Congress repeatedly rejected proposals to expand Social Security by initiating health and disability insurance. Congress paid far more attention to old age assistance than to old age insurance, and the number of people on welfare exceeded the number of people on Social Security (Achenbaum 1986). The vocational rehabilitation program also seemed to be at a low ebb. The pioneering generation that had launched the program in the 1920s was retiring, and, in its place, came a series of uninspired administrators who failed to make a strong case for the plan in Congress. Although the program benefited from the strong wartime economy, in which it was easy to achieve mass rehabilitations simply by assembling a group of people with disabilities and matching them with employers eager for workers, vocational rehabilitation faltered after the war. In 1944, the program rehabilitated 44,000 people, and in 1946, only 36,106 (E. Berkowitz 1988, pp. 17-18).

With the revival of both programs in the late 1940s and early 1950s, the idea of a linkage between the two once again gained currency. In May of 1948, an advisory council submitted a report to Congress that, for the first time, endorsed the establishment of a disability insurance program. After President Truman's surprising victory in the 1948 elections, Congress gave serious consideration to creating such a program. In so doing, Congress confronted the question of the relationship between DI and VR. In planning documents, SSA officials noted that encouraging rehabilitation was "almost as important as the payment of cash benefits."

To provide such encouragement, draft legislation in 1949 included a provision that authorized the Federal Security Administrator (the forerunner of the Secretary of the Department of Health and Human Services to use money from the disability insurance trust fund to furnish rehabilitation services. If individuals should refuse rehabilitation services, they would lose their cash benefits. According to the SSA's plans, the two agencies would share medical information and expertise. Improvements would accrue to both programs. By rehabilitating beneficiaries, the Social Security program would save money; by receiving increased federal funds from the disability insurance trust fund, VR would be able to take on the tough cases that met the demanding Social Security standards for permanent and total disability (U.S. Congress 1949).

Although the House of Representatives passed a disability insurance program in 1949, the measure ran into serious opposition in the Senate and died in 1950. Even before the House passed the measure, however, it deleted the section that allowed the Federal Security Administrator to purchase rehabilitation services for the severely disabled. Wilbur Cohen, at the time the Social Security program's chief congressional liaison, later noted that Representative Robert Doughton, the chairman of the House Ways and Means Committee, could not reconcile a program designed to aid permanently disabled people with a rehabilitation program. Congressman Doughton told Cohen that his agency would have to choose between one or the other. Arthur Altmeyer, Cohen's boss, chose permanent disability insurance over rehabilitation (E. Berkowitz, forthcoming). Members of the Senate made the opposite choice. Rehabilitation, according to the Senate Committee on Finance, held "at least equal significance as providing income for disabled people" (U.S. Congress 1974, p. 109).

While Congress did not pass permanent disability insurance in 1950, it did create a compromise measure in the form of a new public assistance category for the permanently and totally disabled. This category eventually became the most important component of Supplemental Security Income (SSI). Mary Switzer, a seasoned bureaucrat appointed to head the vocational rehabilitation program in 1950, chose to make the rehabilitation of public assistance recipients, particularly those on Aid to the Permanently and Totally Disabled (APTD), a priority of her agency. She wanted to revive the program, and she seized on the nation's concern over growing welfare costs. Using rhetoric that had guided the program almost from its beginnings, Switzer noted the need to substitute the positive ideal of rehabilitation for the negative type of social welfare represented by public assistance. She reminded rehabilitation workers that the Bureau of Public Assistance recommended that states use a team approach to disability determination and suggested that a vocational rehabilitation caseworker be placed on the team. In this way, the two programs could share clients. To facilitate this sort of dynamic interaction, Congress had left room in the new public assistance category to admit clients who were not quite permanently disabled and who could benefit from rehabilitation (Dabelstein 1951).

With Mary Switzer's active intervention, the rehabilitation program responded to this opportunity. Between October 1950 and December 1952, the number of APTD recipients grew from 58,000 to 222,000. In this same period, the percentage of those on public assistance (primarily APTD) at the time of acceptance for VR service provision among those rehabilitated increased from about 9.8 to 12.5. The increase meant that in 1952, the vocational rehabilitation program successfully rehabilitated 7,800 individuals who had previously been on public assistance (U.S. Congress 1952). This provided the nation's first bit of hard evidence that a link could be forged between rehabilitation and income maintenance programs for people with disabilities.

It was a natural extension to forge a linkage between VR and Old-Age and Survivors Insurance (OASI) beneficiaries who became disabled. On October 23, 1953, Secretary Oveta Culp Hobby of the newly created Department of Health, Education, and Welfare suggested to the president that the "OASI system be permitted to underwrite the cost of providing rehabilitation services, through the Vocational Rehabilitation agencies of the States, to insured persons who become disabled." She argued that this provision would cost only a modest amount "but no accountant can estimate the physical rewards, the sense of independence, pride and usefulness and the relief from family strains, which accrue to one of the disabled when he returns to his old job" (Hobby 1953). Despite this eloquent plea, probably drafted by Mary Switzer, the Eisenhower administration decided against the use of trust funds for rehabilitation.

Congress finally passed disability insurance in 1956. Despite determined SSA opposition, Mary Switzer continued to insist that there be a link between vocational rehabilitation and disability insurance. She never realized her vision. The rehabilitation agencies, in the absence of increased funds for this purpose, lacked the time to see all or even most of the applicants for disability insurance. Between 1957 and 1960, all of these applicants were 50 years or older and nearly all had dropped

out of the labor force. Such people made very poor candidates for rehabilitation. The state VR agencies, concerned that their program statistics demonstrate a high success rate, sought a means of screening out
disability insurance applicants. In concert with the SSA, they worked
out a procedure in which they would not interview people who were
over the age of 55, bedridden, institutionalized, mentally ill with negative prognosis, or who had impairments that were worsening (E.
Berkowitz 1987, p. 161).

Arrival of the Beneficiary Rehabilitation Program

Not surprisingly, few disability applicants, perhaps one thousand out
of 1.5 million, were rehabilitated between 1956 and 1959. These early
years set the pattern for the program, even after the elimination of the
age 50 restriction in 1960. In fiscal year 1963, the vocational rehabilitation program interviewed 456,000 DI applicants for possible rehabilitation. Only 48,800 were accepted. That same year, the vocational
rehabilitation agencies terminated 10,200 cases referred from the
Social Security program, of which they managed to rehabilitate successfully only 5,600 (E. Berkowitz 1987, pp. 161-162).

Between 1955 and 1965, more than 2 million severely disabled persons received DI benefits, and only about 19,000 were rehabilitated by
the state vocational rehabilitation agencies. Less than 2 percent of the
successful rehabilitations in the federal-state program were beneficiaries of the DI program at the time of acceptance for VR services (M.
Berkowitz et al. 1982, p. 4). In other words, the rehabilitation program
did less well with the DI program than it had done with APTD referrals
a few years earlier.

The failure to establish an effective link could, at least in theory, be
attributed to a lack of a specific appropriation for this purpose.
Although the SSA recommended that trust fund money be used for
rehabilitation, Mary Switzer resisted the suggestion. She wanted
increased funds for her program that she could control. She realized
that, if the SSA used trust fund money to finance rehabilitation, it
would insist on close supervision of the process and might ultimately

absorb her agency. In 1965, the SSA managed to overcome her objections, and Congress approved the BRP.

This breakthrough occurred in 1965 due to a change in the definition of disability in the Social Security program. After 1965, a disability no longer needed to be of "long-continued and indefinite duration" to qualify an applicant for benefits; the disability could instead be expected to end in death or to last for 12 months. This change somewhat softened the definition and allowed for a greater possibility that a disability applicant might be accepted for benefits but within a few months become a candidate for rehabilitation.

Beyond this obvious motivation, the BRP stemmed from optimism that an investment of trust fund monies in the rehabilitation process would result in savings for the program. Social Security was extremely popular, as the passage of Medicare in the same legislation as the BRP indicated. Indeed, despite the momentous changes in the disability program in 1965, disability was an incidental concern in the legislation; Congress devoted nearly all of its attention to Medicare. Vocational rehabilitation also retained its popularity from the previous decade, as demonstrated by the fact that in the early 1960s the program obtained increased responsibilities to serve new populations, such as the mentally retarded. Further, Mary Switzer, as part of a major departmental reorganization in 1963, acquired new prestige within the federal bureaucracy. She worried less that Social Security would somehow absorb her agency.

She need not have worried; the terms of the BRP were in fact quite generous. For one thing, the BRP provided money to VR on more favorable terms than those on the contributions the program usually received from the federal government. Most of the federal funds that the VR program obtained required at least some state matching. For every $10 the federal government contributed, the states contributed about $4. Money from the BRP, in contrast, came entirely from the federal government, with no need for any sort of state matching. Further, the money was paid prospectively by means of a formula that matched allocations to the states with the percentage of the total DI caseload living in that state. The overall allocation was set at 1 percent of total disability insurance payments.

Understanding what happened to the BRP requires some general background. Table 1 provides an overview of the growth of the DI pro-

Table 1. DI Cash Benefits Paid, Total Beneficiaries, New Awards, and Terminations from DI Rolls, by Reason, 1969-1992

Fiscal year	DI cash benefits ($millions)	Total beneficiaries on DI rolls at start of year (000)	Total number of new awards during year (000)	New awards as a percent of total beneficiaries	Number of terminations during year (000)	Number of terminations due to death of beneficiary (000)	Number of terminations for retirement of beneficiary (000)	Number of terminations for other reasons[a] (000)	Terminations as a percent of total beneficiaries	Number of beneficiaries terminated from DI rolls
1969	2,542	1,295.3	NA	NA	251.3	108.8	93.5	49.0	19.4	2,799
1970	3,067	1,394.3	350.4	25.1	260.4	105.8	102.9	51.7	18.7	3,978
1971	3,758	1,492.9	415.9	27.9	266.5	109.9	107.0	49.6	17.9	2,325
1972	4,473	1,647.7	455.4	27.6	261.7	NA	NA	NA	15.9	2,468
1973	5,718	1,832.9	491.6	26.8	304.8	NA	NA	NA	16.6	2,597
1974	6,903	2,016.6	536.0	26.6	321.0	NA	NA	NA	15.9	2,721
1975	8,414	2,236.9	592.0	26.5	329.5	NA	NA	NA	14.7	3,595
1976	9,966	2,488.8	551.5	22.2	351.5	NA	NA	NA	14.1	4,822
1977	11,463	2,670.2	568.9	21.3	358.9	140.3	151.9	66.7	13.4	4,760
1978	12,513	2,837.4	464.4	16.4	413.6	144.9	192.7	76.0	14.6	6,363
1979	13,708	2,879.8	416.7	14.5	422.5	141.9	205.3	75.3	14.7	7,841
1980	15,437	2,870.6	396.6	13.8	408.1	143.2	199.7	65.2	14.2	NA
1981	17,199	2,858.7	345.3	121	NA	NA	NA	NA	NA	NA
1982	17,338	2,776.5	298.5	10.8	NA	NA	NA	NA	NA	NA
1983	17,530	2,603.6	311.5	12.0	453.6	134.3	193.7	125.6	17.4	NA

231

Year										
1984	17,900	2,569.0	357.1	13.9	371.9	133.9	185.8	52.3	14.5	NA
1985	18.836	2,596.5	377.4	14.5	340.0	136.7	186.2	17.0	13.1	NA
1986	19,847	2,656.6	416.9	15.7	NA	NA	NA	NA	NA	NA
1987	20,512	2,728.5	415.8	15.2	331.5	135.4	185.4	10.7	12.1	NA
1988	21,692	2,785.9	409.5	14.7	346.3	151.3	181.5	13.5	12.4	NA
1989	22,873	2,830.3	425.6	15.0	360.2	155.9	193.5	10.8	12.7	NA
1990	24,803	2,895.4	468.0	16.2	327.8	138.0	179.6	10.2	11.3	NA
1991	27,662	2,011.3	536.4	17.8	320.3	144.4	174.6	1.3	10.6	NA
1992	31,091	3,194.9	636.6	19.9	345.9	154.4	180.3	11.2	10.8	NA

SOURCE: McManus (1981), table 1, p. 20; *Social Security Bulletin*, Annual Statistical Supplement 1993, table 6.F2, p. 279, and table 4.A.4, p. 164.
NOTE: NA indicates that data are not available.
a. These data do not include disabled beneficiaries whose monthly benefits have been suspended because of their ability to engage in SGA. These persons continue to be eligible for Medicare for a three-year period.

grams and of DI terminations. One notes the steady growth in cash benefit payments (in nominal dollars) throughout the period. The number of persons on the DI rolls also rose from the inception of the BRP program reporting in 1969 through 1979. There was a decline through 1984 and a subsequent rise through 1992. Two "flow" factors have contributed to the recent growth in beneficiaries. One reflects an explosion (more than a 50% percent increase from 1988 through 1992) in new awards. The other centers on the fact that the number of terminations from the rolls has leveled off. As a percentage of total beneficiaries, the termination rate stands at an all-time low of about 11 percent.

From the beginning, the BRP contained a number of perverse incentives. The greater the DI caseload, the more money was spent on the BRP program. The object of the BRP was at least in part to restrain the growth of the disability rolls, yet its fiscal health depended on the growth of those rolls. The better job that the BRP did, the less need there would be for its services and the less money that would be spent on it.

Not only did the BRP program grow as a result of the rise in the DI rolls, it increased through pressures generated by the political process. Like any federal grant program, the BRP became subject to appeals for its incremental expansion. In this manner, the proportion of DI payments devoted to the BRP increased to 1.25 percent in 1973 and to 1.50 percent in 1974. Combined with the explosive growth in the DI caseload and in program expenditures, the BRP grew into a significant subsidy to the VR program. In 1972, for example, the allotment was $30.5 million, and it rose to $102.6 million four years later. By 1976, BRP money accounted for 9.2 percent of VR expenditures (M. Berkowitz et al. 1982, p. 10).

Beyond these features that related to the financing formula, the BRP contained a vital flaw that inhibited its value as a link between the disability determination and vocational rehabilitation processes: the BRP program benefited only those who were already on the rolls. Recall that service provision for VR clients who were merely applicants for DI had to be partially funded, at least initially, from state coffers. VR services for DI beneficiaries were 100 percent federally financed. Because of this difference in the state matching requirements, it cost the program more to serve DI applicants before they entered the rolls than it did afterwards. Once on the rolls, however, a person made a very poor candidate for rehabilitation. It was an axiom of rehabilitation theory that the sooner the program intervened, the better would be the outcome. By using the BRP to serve only those on the rolls, policy makers lost the most significant part of the huge VR recruiting scheme envisioned in 1954.

The failure of the BRP to stem the rise in the DI rolls did not deter its expansion. Congress moved under the comfortable cover of precedent to extend the BRP to SSI recipients, after the SSI program began in 1974. This move made sense since SSI and DI used the same disability definition and determination process.

It was much harder to rationalize the expenditure of funds for disability applicants rather than for disability beneficiaries. The BRP was created to save trust fund money, not to reform the nation's approach to disability. Congress therefore insisted that BRP money be spent only on clients of the Social Security disability programs. Other expansions of the rehabilitation process would have to be handled through the vocational rehabilitation program itself.

For these and other reasons, the BRP did not transform the relationship between VR and DI. The numbers for 1978, are only a little more encouraging than in 1963. In fiscal year 1978, the state vocational rehabilitation agencies served 154,541 Social Security and federal welfare beneficiaries. They rehabilitated 12,268 people at an average cost of $7,904 (see table 2). However, someone who was rehabilitated did not necessarily leave the rolls. States counted someone as rehabilitated who worked in suitable employment, paid or unpaid, for 60 days. Unpaid work would not count as "substantial gainful activity" under the rules developed by the Social Security programs and would not cause someone to leave either the SSI or DI rolls. If a person worked for 60 days at a well-paying job and then left the labor force, the individual would also not have to leave the DI rolls. Hence, although more than 12 thousand people were rehabilitated in 1978, only 6,346 people were removed from the rolls, despite the fact that SSA reimbursements were nearly $97 million.

Such performance casts doubt on the entire exercise, and in time a pervasive critique of the BRP developed. The intellectual sources of this critique were varied. First, economists began to devote serious attention to the effect of disability benefits on labor force participation rates. This research and the very real fact of DI's growth caused policy-

Table 2. BRP Experience, 1967-1981: Expenditures by SSA, Rehabilititations, Terminations, and Costs per Rehabilitation

Fiscal year	SSA trust funds expended	Number of DI recipients rehabilitated under the BRP	Number of beneficiaries in the BRP	Number terminated from DI rolls	Percent terminated	Average cost per rehabilitation
1967	$9,846,158	1,815	NA	170	9.4	$5,425
1968	15,440,712	5,934	26,455	1,068	18.0	2,602
1969	17,557,281	8,036	32,911	2,799	34.8	2,185
1970	20,983,873	9,307	35,275	3,978	42.7	2,255
1971	24,375,764	9,799	40,711	2,325	23.7	2,488
1972	30,390,442	9,983	45,111	2,468	24.7	3,044
1973	42,934,953	11,580	52,011	2,597	22.4	3,708
1974	56,461,818	13,358	60,651	2,721	20.4	4,227
1975	81,022,057	12,585	69,653	3,595	28.6	6,438
1976	96,190,226	12,826	78,063	4,822	37.6	7,500
1977	89,243,374	11,760	80,037	4,760	40.5	7,589
1978	96,963,162	12,268	94,979	6,363	51.9	7,904
1979	102,070,666	13,302	94,936	7,841	58.9	7,673
1980	NA	NA	NA	NA	NA	NA
1981	85,771,908	13,197	NA	NA	NA	6,499

SOURCE: McManus (1981).
NOTE: NA indicates that data are not available.

makers to explore means of limiting disability expenditures. Second, a series of cost-benefit studies, launched by independent investigators in the General Accounting Office (GAO) and in universities, brought into question the efficacy of the BRP. This development occurred simultaneously with a critical reevaluation of the VR program itself. The reappraisal took the form of cost-benefit studies and of criticisms that the program did not serve the population of severely disabled individuals who, arguably, needed its services the most.

On May 13, 1976, the GAO released a study of the BRP that found a benefit-cost ratio of only 1.15. By way of contrast, an earlier analysis done by SSA's Office of the Actuary showed a benefit-cost ratio of 2.50. A subsequent report by SSA calculated a range of $1.39 to $2.49 returned for each dollar invested in the BRP (M. Berkowitz et al. 1982, p. 17).

The 1976 GAO study examined 350 DI beneficiaries who had been reported as rehabilitated through public sector VR and whose DI benefits were subsequently terminated. The research found that most of the terminations, perhaps five out of eight, were not due to VR services. In slightly more than half (51 percent) of the cases, the individual's DI benefits were stopped because of medical recovery, not VR's intervention. Indeed, SSA officials maintained that these individuals did not meet the BRP selection criteria and should not have been accepted as BRP candidates in the first place. Another 11 percent of the people in the GAO sample returned to work through their own efforts and had received no VR services. In fact, several of these cases had been discontinued from the DI rolls prior to acceptance for services by a state VR agency.

The GAO study also focused on the discrepancy between the relatively large number of rehabilitations claimed by the state VR agencies and the relatively small number of DI beneficiaries who left the rolls. Beginning in 1967, the number of successful rehabilitations in the BRP grew steadily. Table 2 shows that rehabilitations increased more than sixfold between 1967 and 1973, to reach 11,580. Yet, over the same period, the number of beneficiaries removed from the rolls stabilized at roughly 2,500 in 1973, after peaking at 3,978 in 1970.

The GAO attributed this divergence to the misinterpretation of BRP program eligibility criteria by state VR agencies. Instead of striving for benefit terminations, the state agencies were using the less restrictive "rehabilitation" mandate of the basic VR program. Some 40 percent of a sample of 400 randomly selected DI beneficiaries classified as rehabilitated were placed in noncompetitive employment such as homemaker, sheltered work, or unpaid family member. Another one of six cases in this sample had worked at competitive employment for 60 days (i.e., with successful rehabilitation as a Status 26 closure) but had not been terminated from the DI rolls because the individual was not able to continue working.

Ironically, as the GAO and Rutgers studies were released, there was a dramatic increase in the number and percentage of BRP candidates terminated from the DI rolls. The fourth through sixth data columns of table 2 demonstrate this trend. From a low of 2,325 cases in 1971, DI terminations through the BRP more than doubled (to 4,822) by 1976. By the end of the decade, terminations had more than tripled (to 7,841) the 1971 figure. The number of persons rehabilitated under the BRP increased by a much smaller percentage, from 9,799 to only 13,302 over the same period. Thus, in the first half of the decade, one out of four or five rehabilitants was terminated from the DI rolls, but by the end of the decade the ratio exceeded one-half.

Despite this irony, the general impact of the GAO and other studies was to dispute the effectiveness of the BRP. The tradition in the VR program had been to portray returns on investments on the order of 10 to 1. Mary Switzer had long argued that for every dollar of tax money spent on vocational rehabilitation, the program returned 10 dollars in tax payments by the rehabilitants. The analysis of the BRP showed nothing like that. In a climate in which disability insurance was viewed as an uncontrollable entitlement program, the BRP came to be seen as a source of expenditures, rather than of revenues.

In the critical atmosphere of the late 1970s, pressures grew to reform the BRP program. Staff members on the Social Security Subcommittee of the House Committee on Ways and Means sought to make the BRP an accountable program of unambiguous benefit to the DI trust fund instead of a general subsidy to the VR program. To accomplish this result, they proposed to substitute retrospective for prospective payment and to reimburse the states only for successfully removing someone from the DI rolls. After lengthy consideration, Congress took this step in 1981, the same year in which the Reagan administration launched an ambitious campaign to remove from the rolls those people thought to have medically recovered. Under the new arrangements, VR agencies received subsidies only for people who, as a result of VR services, engaged in substantial gainful activity for nine continuous months. Unlike the rest of the Social Security program, DI was regarded by the Reagan administration as a source of current savings. Cutting the costs of the BRP would add to those savings.

The Post-BRP Experience of Retrospective Service Payments

The new program differed radically from the old. In 1981, as table 2 reveals, SSA reimbursements to VR totaled about $86 million. In the next year, the reimbursements fell to about $3 million. In effect, the reform of the BRP wiped out the SSA subsidy to vocational rehabilitation. Over the course of the decade, as the states adjusted to the situation, the BRP enjoyed a recovery, although the subsidy never returned to the level of the 1970s. In part, the tremendous resurgence of the DI and SSI rolls in the late 1980s accounted for this trend as did the fact that the states learned how to submit claims to SSA so that more of them would be accepted.

The experience of the post-BRP era is presented in table 3. In the first part of the 1980s, state VR agencies attempted to adapt to the new retrospective payment regime stipulated by SSA (GAO 1987, p. 14). Still, in 1985, VR agencies submitted fewer than 5,000 claims for reimbursement by SSA for rehabilitation services for DI beneficiaries. SSA allowed a little more than half of these claims (2,645/4,912, or 55.2 percent) for a total reimbursement of slightly less than $10 million. During the 1990s, the annual number of claims submitted by state VR agencies has increased to more than 10,000. The approval rates in the 1990s have ranged from 57.3 percent to 71.7 percent. That means that SSA has allowed an average of some 6,450 claims on an annualized basis, at an average cost of roughly $10,000 per approved claim.

A comparison of tables 2 and 3 reveals three unequivocal impacts of the BRP reforms. First, SSA's aggregate reimbursement has fallen considerably to state VR agencies for DI beneficiaries receiving rehabilitation services. The nominal expenditures in the 1990s represent less than two-thirds of the amounts in the latter part of the 1970s. In real terms (1987 dollars), the 1992 total outlay was only one-third of the 1979 level.

Table 3. Post-BRP Experience: Expenditures by SSA, VR Claims, Allowances, and Average Costs per Allowance

Fiscal year	SSA trust funds expended	VR claims received by SSA	VR claims processed	Number of VR claims allowed	Percent of processed VR claims allowed	Average cost per allowed VR claim
1983	$ 216,000	3,626	1,813	110	3.0	$1,964
1984	4,094,000	7,739	4,990	2,202	28.5	1,859
1985	9,850,000	4,912	5,019	2,645	53.8	3,724
1986	20,195,374	6,649	6,482	3,693	55.5	5,469
1987	28,087,992	8,092	7,414	4,469	55.2	6,285
1988	36,456,373	11,032	9,361	5,092	46.2	7,160
1989	48,740,569	11,267	9,762	5,828	51.7	8,363
1990	60,245,993	10,222	12,539	7,330	71.7	8,219
1991	66,593,433	12,300	11,004	6,032	49.0	9,382
1992	63,692,775	10,567	11,510	6,269	59.3	10,160
1993	64,467,533	10,744	10,818	6,155	57.3	10,474

SOURCE: "SSA Reimbursement Program: Making Rehabilitation and Employment Services Available to Disability Beneficiaries," Social Security Administration, 1994.

Second, this reduction does not necessarily imply fewer VR services per eligible DI beneficiary. Rather, SSA has reduced the number of rehabilitations that it reimburses. The number of claims allowed annually in 1991 through 1993 was less than half the number that SSA reimbursed through the BRP in the latter part of the 1970s.

Third, the number of rehabilitations submitted for reimbursement by state VR agencies in the retrospective payment era has dropped from the totals in the BRP period. Clearly, the reform of the prospective payment scheme has caused state VR agencies to be more circumspect in choosing claims for reimbursement. Specifically, the number of claims submitted in the period from 1988 through 1993 averaged some 11,000 cases annually. For the comparable six-year period of 1974 through 1979, the average annual number of rehabilitations exceeded 12,500 cases. Over the two periods, a one-eighth reduction in the number of claims submitted for reimbursement has occurred.

What do these trends imply for the state VR agencies? Somewhat fewer claims submitted and dramatically fewer claims allowed for reimbursement suggest that the state agency must fund the denied claims from the basic VR program. As table 3 shows, SSA annually denies some 4,000-6,000 claims for reimbursement. In fiscal year 1993, SSA denied most of the cases (2,546 of 4,567 or 55.7 percent of all denials) because the rehabilitant had not demonstrated the sustained capacity to work or had accumulated earnings below the level defined as substantial gainful activity (National VR Denial Report 1993). These denials highlight the distinction between a VR successful rehabilitation and an SSA reimbursement.

Because it so much harder to rehabilitate DI cases, VR counselors tend to shy away from them. The SSA population is older and more severely disabled than the rest of the VR caseload (GAO 1987). Because not all DI beneficiaries get rehabilitated and even fewer meet the SSA's stringent requirements for reimbursement, DI beneficiaries compete with other rehabilitation clients in the basic state VR programs. In such a competition, DI beneficiaries most often lose.

Unfortunately, little data exist to permit a comparison of the post-1981 reforms with the BRP era of 1967-1981. Here one must delve into the problems of data reporting. SSA measured success in the BRP by the number of terminations from the DI rolls, but these data have not been published for the 1981-1991 period. The number of allowances by SSA for reimbursement is not an adequate proxy.

A second shortcoming in reporting also makes comparisons difficult. The average service cost figure reported in table 2 is provided on a
per-rehabilitant basis. In table 3, the cost figure is on a per-allowed-
claim basis. Ideally, the cost reporting should be across comparable
cohorts. Without tabulating such figures on an individual claimant
basis, cross-period cost comparisons lack validity.

One last data issue complicates comparison across the two periods.
Changes in the standard Rehabilitation Services Administration (RSA)
closure report form in 1985 (from the RSA300 to the RSA911) have
eliminated most of the extensive information about a client's DI status
while in the VR system. For example, on the R300 report, VR clients
were asked about their DI status (beneficiary, denied, pending, not an
applicant, unknown) at both application and closure from the program.
The RSA911 form only requires that a client report whether he or she
was receiving DI (a yes/no binary) upon termination from the program.

Conclusion

The bulk of the empirical evidence reinforces the maxim that, once
on the rolls, people tend to stay on them. The GAO has stated flatly that
"Rehabilitation contributes little to terminations" (GAO 1994, p. 19).
The link between VR and DI continues to resemble a long funnel into
which the Disability Determination Services pour cases, to have only a
few trickle out the other end. The disparities between the ends of the
funnel are staggering. The Disability Determination Services made
over a million favorable decisions in fiscal year 1993 and recorded
6,154 successful rehabilitations. The revamped BRP undoubtedly
saved the SSA money, an estimated $321.9 million in fiscal year 1993,
but this was nearly irrelevant to either the DI or SSI programs ("Developing a World-Class Employment Strategy" 1994, charts 10 and 11).

This raises the more fundamental question of where the relationship
between rehabilitation and Social Security went wrong. To be sure, it
did not help that bureaucratic rivalry inhibited cooperation in the 1950s
and 1960s, but the problems were more fundamental. Social Security
advocates pressed for a disability program that they regarded as an
extension of the old-age retirement system; disability to them was a

cause for early retirement. Vocational rehabilitation advocates campaigned for an extension of the basic counseling and service program; disability to them was a source of adjustment in one's labor force status that, with the right sort of intervention, could be remedied. To a large extent, the two programs worked with completely different target populations. Efforts to force the DI and, later, the SSI population onto the VR program largely failed.

Furthermore, most of the history recorded here occurred without recourse to serious analysis. Congress simply mandated a relationship between vocational rehabilitation and the disability programs without investigating the feasibility of maintaining such a bond. The efforts at analysis of the BRP had ambiguous findings and hence were not of much use to policy makers. Over time, however, the cost-benefit analyses of both the BRP and vocational rehabilitation did add to the policy environment and provided at least one reason for altering the BRP.

There is also a greater irony. While the conventional wisdom now holds that linkages between VR and DI are destined to end in failure, many claim to favor labor force participation over retirement benefits as a response to disability. Fiscal conservatives, who currently occupy a wide range of the political spectrum, are joined by members of the disability rights movement in this sentiment. If we wish to achieve their objective, the only avenue appears to be fundamental reform of the system, with the attendant high political costs and possibilities for unintended, damaging effects. To put it plainly, the present system of providing DI benefits does not allow beneficiaries to return to work, even though policy makers continue to advocate return to work as a policy goal. At the same time politicians do not appear to have the stomach for changing the system. Almost invariably, reform centers on tightening eligibility rules, not on rehabilitating people with disabilities.

Although the potential remains to make the disability determination process a recruiting station for rehabilitation, the promise of such an approach has never been realized. Despite an initial success with welfare beneficiaries in the early 1950s, the link between rehabilitation and income maintenance has never been forged. Historical circumstance and political maneuvering account for the current situation as much as anything else.

References

Achenbaum, W. Andrew. 1986. *Social Security: Visions and Revisions*. New York: Cambridge University Press.

Altmeyer, Arthur J. 1956. Letter to Wilbur Cohen. October 8. Cohen Papers. Wisconsin State Historical Society, Madison.

Berkowitz, Edward. 1987. *Disabled Policy: America's Programs for the Handicapped*. New York: Cambridge University Press.

_____. 1988. "The Cost-Benefit Tradition in Vocational Rehabilitation." In *Measuring the Efficiency of Public Programs: Costs and Benefits in Vocational Rehabilitation*, Monroe Berkowitz, ed. Philadelphia: Temple University Press.

_____. Forthcoming. *Mr. Social Security: The Life of Wilbur J. Cohen*. Lawrence: University Press of Kansas.

Berkowitz, Monroe, Martin Horning, Stephen McConnell, Jeffrey Rubin, and John Worrall. 1982. "An Economic Evaluation of the Beneficiary Rehabilitation Program." In *Alternatives in Rehabilitating the Handicapped: A Policy Analysis,* Jeffrey Rubin, ed. New York: Human Sciences Press.

Calkin, Hugh. 1960. Memorandum for the Welfare File. March 14. Records of the President's Commission on National Goals. Box 9. Dwight D. Eisenhower Library, Abilene, KS.

Cohen, Wilbur J. 1956a. "The Situation in Social Security." February 15. Box 70. Wilbur J. Cohen Papers. Wisconsin State Historical Society, Madison.

_____. 1956b. Letter to Elizabeth Wickenden. March 4. Elizabeth Wickenden Papers. Wisconsin State Historical Society, Madison.

_____. 1985. Interview with Blanche Coll. Copy available in Lyndon Baines Johnson Library, Austin, TX.

Dabelstein, Donald. 1951. Letter to Regional Directors. July 20. Record Group 290. Accession 62A-190. Container 4. Washington National Records Center, Suitland, MD.

"Developing a World-Class Employment Strategy for People with Disabilities." 1994. *A Briefing for Commissioner Chater and Principal Deputy Commissioner Thompson, Social Security Administration*, August 5.

"Disability Planning." 1952. Oasis News (An employee publication of the Social Security Administration) 12 (August: 1-2.

Falk, I.S. 1938. "Permanent Total Disability (Invalidity) Insurance: A Memorandum Prepared for the Consideration of the Advisory Council on Social Insurance." Written with Marianne Sakman, B.S. Sanders, and Louis Reed. December 9. Copy available at Department of Health and Human Services Library, Washington, DC.

Hobby, O.C. 1953. Memo to President Eisenhower. October 15. Volume 43, Nelson Rockefeller Papers. Rockefeller Archives, Pocantico, NY.

MacDonald, Mary E. 1944. *Federal Grants for Vocational Rehabilitation.* Chicago: University of Chicago Press.

McManus, Leo. 1981. "Evaluation of Disability Insurance Savings due to Beneficiary Rehabilitation," *Social Security Bulletin* 44, 2 (February): 20.

"National VT Denial Report for FY 93." 1993. Rehabilitation Programs Branch, Social Security Administration, November.

"Our New Arrival." 1955. *Oasis News* (An employee publication of the Social Security Administration) (January): 3-4.

Perkins, Roswell B. 1968. Interview with Peter Corning. Columbia Oral History Collection, New York.

President's Commission on National Goals. 1960. Panel Discussion on Rehabilitation. Records of the President's Commission on National Goals. Box 7. Dwight D. Eisenhower Library.

Social Security Board. 1940. "Permanent Disability Insurance—The Wagner Bill and a Critical Review of Its Provisions." 1940. May 21. In Record Group 47, Office of the Commissioner, Chairman's File 1935-1942, 056.11-056.12. National Archives, Washington, DC.

Switzer, Mary. 1942. Letter to Elizabeth Brandeis. Mary Switzer Papers. Schlesinger Library. Cambridge, MA.

_____. 1944. Letter to Tracy Copp. Mary Switzer Papers. Schlesinger Library, Cambridge, MA.

_____. 1953. Memo to Russell R. Larmon. November 19. Record Group 235, File 450, Box 215. National Archives, Washington, DC.

U.S. Congress, House of Representatives. 1949. "Background Material on HR 2893." Record Group 235, Accession 56A-533. Container 2. Washington National Records Center, Suitland, Maryland.

U.S. Congress, House of Representatives. Committee on Ways and Means. 1974. *Staff Report on the Disability Insurance Program.* Washington, DC: Government Printing Office.

U.S. Congress, House of Representatives. 1952. "Major Source of Support at Acceptance." In "Special Study: Public Assistance and Critical Occupations," September 30. Record Group 290, Accession 62A-190. Container 5. Washington National Records Center, Suitland, MD.

U.S. General Accounting Office. 1976. "Improvements Needed in Rehabilitating Social Security Disability Insurance Beneficiaries." Washington, DC: Government Printing Office.

_____. 1987. "Social Security—Little Success Achieved in Rehabilitating Disabled Beneficiaries." Washington, DC: Government Printing Office.

———. 1993. "Vocational Rehabilitation: Evidence for Federal Program's Effectiveness is Mixed." Report 93-19. Washington, DC: Government Printing Office.

———. 1994. "Social Security Disability Rolls Keep Growing, While Explanations Remain Elusive." HEHS 94-34. Washington, DC: Government Printing Office.

"The Vocational Rehabilitation of Disabled OASI Beneficiaries." 1953. December 10. Record Group 290, Accession 62A-90. Box 7. Washington National Records Center, Suitland, MD.

Disability and Work
Lessons from the Private Sector

H. Allan Hunt
W.E. Upjohn Institute for Employment Research
Rochelle V. Habeck
Michigan State University
Patricia Owens
UNUM Insurance Company
David Vandergoot
Center for Essential Management Services

The Problem

The human and social costs of disability are well known, and increases in the number of beneficiaries and in expenditures are both causes of concern. The real economic cost of disability, namely, the lost production from individuals not at work, has been growing rapidly in recent years. Nominal, or budget, outlays have also been increasing as private and public payments for disability benefits have soared in the last 20 years. Using a nonrandom sample, a recent study estimated that employers were paying 8 percent of payroll for disability-related expenses, including both direct and indirect costs of disability (Chelius, Galvin, and Owens 1992).

At the same time, a very specific issue has arisen in the Social Security Disability Insurance (DI) and Supplemental Security Income (SSI) programs. The return-to-work rate has declined precipitously since the 1970s. According to the Disability Policy Panel of the National Academy of Social Insurance:

> The proportion of beneficiaries who leave the disabled-worker benefit rolls because of recovery has never been large. During the 1970s, it generally ranged between 1.5 and 2.5 percent of the benefit rolls. Terminations due to recovery peaked in the early 1980s, when SSA pursued an aggressive policy of reviewing the rolls and terminating benefits. In the 1990s, terminations for recovery are at

an all time low, in 1991-1993 they are below 0.5 percent (National
Academy of Social Insurance 1994, p. 82).

We take this "recovery" or return-to-work issue as the impetus for
our paper.[1] Are private sector actors more successful in returning persons with disabilities to work? How do they do it? Are there lessons
that can be learned about return to work from the private sector that
could be transferred to public sector programs? What problems would
have to be overcome to translate private solutions to the public sector?

Equity and efficiency considerations are key in evaluating policy.
Economic efficiency requires that we obtain the maximum amount of
goods, services, and leisure time from the human and other resources
in society. Thus, any human resource that is unemployed or underem-
ployed reduces the total production available for all to consume and
thereby decreases the economic well-being of all citizens. Economic
equity is harder to define, but ultimately it deals with the distribution of
those goods, services, and leisure time that a society can produce.
Some use a standard of equity that specifies "to each according to his
or her contributions"; others prefer "to each according to his or her
needs." In either event, the issue is who gets to consume what share of
total production (Okun 1975).

There is also another sense of equity, and that is the equity of participation. For the last three decades or more, we as a society, have been
concerned about the full and equal participation of racial minorities,
females, older Americans, and persons with disabilities in the economic life of the country. We have enacted statutes attempting to promote the opportunity for such participation by outlawing
discrimination against these groups. In some cases, we have even
required "affirmative action" to try and involve disadvantaged groups,
especially where their participation has been prevented or hindered by
past discrimination. The Americans with Disabilities Act of 1990
(ADA) seeks to remove barriers to employment for persons with functional limitations by requiring employers to reasonably accommodate
these individuals' disabilities. The clear goal of ADA is to facilitate the
greater participation of persons with disabilities in the world of work
by removing the environmental and societal barriers to participation
and integration.

However, if individuals are being encouraged to "maximize" their *dis*ability rather than their ability in order to receive cash or in-kind benefits, we will have a loss of both efficiency and equity. We will lose efficiency in the sense that society will produce less than it could if all resources were fully employed. We will lose equity if some individuals are not participating, thereby not contributing their share to producing the goods, services, and leisure time that we are all consuming. In this sense, equity and efficiency both mandate the optimum participation of persons with disabilities in economic life.

Reframing the Return-to-Work Issue

Traditional Approach

Before the disability management movement, attention to return-to-work or stay-at-work goals for people with functional impairments was rare in the private as well as in the public sector. A medical model of treatment and recovery was dominant, with the emphasis on benefit administration, not return to work. That is, the process moved in a linear sequence from diagnosis of impairment to independent provision of medical treatment, passive recovery at home, and claim monitoring at eligibility points by the carrier. Only when it became clear that the injured employee was failing to return to work was recourse to the vocational rehabilitation system considered.

Over the past decade, there has been growing disenchantment with the medical or clinical model of disability and with the outcomes of the traditional approach to vocational rehabilitation. Meanwhile, an ecological model of disability has gained acceptance. That is, a given individual with an impairment functions in interaction with an environment that has certain attitudinal, physical, economic, and policy characteristics, which, in large part, determine whether the consequences of an impairment will result in a work disability. Increasingly, disability has become recognized as an interactive phenomenon, not simply deriving from the medical or even the functional aspects of the impairing condition (Berkowitz 1985).

From a public policy perspective, this changing viewpoint has led to additions to the state-federal program of vocational rehabilitation, with the inclusion of such approaches as independent living services and supported employment. We have also seen the de-emphasis of the clinical model of vocational rehabilitation services in the 1992 amendments to the Rehabilitation Act (which governs the federal-state vocational rehabilitation system), particularly in regard to determination of eligibility. More fundamentally, the ecological or sociopolitical view of disability fueled the development and adoption of the ADA, explicitly changing the focus to the capabilities of persons with disabilities and requiring the larger environment to provide reasonable accommodation to allow for the participation of this "minority" group of citizens.

Further, subsequent evaluations of the modest employment outcomes achieved by the state-federal system (General Accounting Office [GAO] 1993) have recently motivated the Council of State Administrators of Vocational Rehabilitation (CSAVR 1993) to launch an initiative that calls for significant linkage with the employer community, including disability management efforts, and emphasizes employment as the desirable outcome. In summary, the service model that ignores the labor market until the end of a lengthy process has been identified by virtually all constituents as a flawed approach to employment for people with disabilities (CSAVR 1993; Stubbins 1982; Vandergoot 1994; GAO 1993).

The Disability Management Approach

During the late 1970s and early 1980s, a confluence of economic and policy factors led to heightened awareness of disability costs in the business community. Reduced profitability in the face of rapidly escalating health care and disability benefit costs led to an examination of workers' compensation and other disability programs as significant management concerns. No longer could these issues be ignored as simply a cost of doing business.

Simultaneously, many leading companies, as part of their human resource commitment, became actively involved in national and international efforts to promote the employment and full participation of people with disabilities. The Independent Living movement led to increased leadership and expectations of the disability community in policy efforts. The field of vocational rehabilitation discovered employers as necessary partners to achieving further goals. From many directions, the economic and social forces converged to set the stage for the emergence of the disability management model. This history has been adequately summarized by other authors (e.g., Galvin 1986; Tate, Habeck, and Galvin 1986; Akabas, Gates, and Galvin 1992; Habeck et al. 1994).

In their comprehensive book on the subject, Akabas, Gates, and Galvin (1992) define disability management as

> a workplace prevention and remediation strategy that seeks to prevent disability from occurring or, lacking that, to intervene early following the onset of disability, using coordinated, cost-conscious, quality rehabilitation service that reflects an organizational commitment to continued employment of those experiencing functional work limitations. *The remediation goal of disability management is successful job maintenance, or optimum timing for return-to-work...* (p.2, emphasis added).

Disability management, effectively implemented, is intended to achieve a win-win situation that addresses the reciprocal economic and humanistic needs of the true stakeholders in disability management, namely, employers and employees. Common interests that can be achieved through an effective program include reducing the risks of injury and illness, retaining productivity, effectively using human resources and health care services, improving financial security, avoiding adversarial relationships, and achieving the requirements of disability legislation.

The interest of the business community in disability management has been astounding. Since early reports of significant cost savings began to circulate a decade ago, there has been an explosion of programs. Employers by the thousands have embraced disability management techniques as a way to combat the upward spiraling of disability costs and, often, to demonstrate commitment to the well-being of their employees. Disability management conferences abound, and virtually every insurance carrier has developed a disability management product in response to this interest. In 1993, a survey of 1,050 companies revealed that more than 84 percent were actively attempting to control their workers' compensation costs through various disability management techniques (Towers Perrin 1993).

During the last few years, a growing number of organizational case studies and empirical efforts have documented the dramatic cost reductions achieved in these initiatives. Every company is unique in the specific constellation of job risks, human resources, and business factors that must be taken into account in tailoring a disability management program to meet its needs. Nevertheless, the literature indicates several traits that successful disability management programs share. The essential components, adapted from reviews by Schwartz et al. (1989) and Habeck (1991), are as follows:

1. Companywide commitment to reduce disability costs and provide needed assistance to encourage return to work

2. Analysis and modification of related benefits and policies to support disability management objectives

3. Comprehensive assessment of corporate needs, experiences, and responses to injury and illness incidents

4. Organization of the disability management initiative across levels and locations, with clearly assigned responsibilities and accountability among all necessary people and operating units

5. Creation of an integrated, usable, and effective information system to document, analyze, manage, and evaluate relevant data about incidence, employees, costs, services, and impact

6. Educational efforts directed toward managers, supervisors, and line workers to create understanding and involvement in disability management efforts

7. Active use of safety and prevention strategies to avoid disability occurrence

8. Early intervention and ongoing monitoring for health risks and disability cases

9. Contact with the injured/ill employee and the treating physician within 24 hours of impairment onset

10. Facilitating early return to work of disabled workers through an organized process that provides modifications in assignments, hours, and/or duties

11. Systematic procedures for effective use of health care and rehabilitation services

12. Writing an individual plan of service and return to work by the responsible case manager with the participation of the employee

13. Using professional expertise to design accommodations that permit workers with disabilities to perform work in a satisfactory manner

14. Collaboration with public and private agencies to provide necessary mental health and rehabilitation services

15. Use of incentives in benefit design, cost accounting, and performance evaluation to encourage participation of employees, supervisors, and managers

One can presume that, if there is this much interest by the private sector in a specific set of techniques, there must be a substantial payoff.

Empirical Evidence on the Impact of Disability Management

Although very limited research evidence is available to document and quantify the impacts of these practices, there are a few studies that provide clear support for the significant effect of the organization's behavior on the disability experience of the company and its employees. For example, Rousmaniere (1989) and his colleagues found the most important cause of variation in disability impact among 24 hospitals in New England to be the hospital's internal system of risk management and post-injury response. Rousmaniere (1990) has further asserted that how a company responds to and manages injuries determines roughly 50 percent of the costs. Similarly, according to the National Rehabilitation Planners organization (1993), companies can reasonably expect to reduce workers' compensation costs by 25 to 30 percent after the first year of implementing a disability management program, with nearly twice those savings realizable when long-term, inactive cases are more effectively resolved.

Lewin and Schecter surveyed 77 companies in 1989 and found that human resource policies were significantly related to disability incidence. Use of employee involvement programs, conflict resolution procedures, workforce stabilization measures, and disability management policies were each inversely associated with levels of lost work days due to occupational and nonoccupational illnesses and injuries (Lewin and Schecter 1991).

Two recent studies of disability prevention and management in Michigan demonstrate the impact of employer practices on the frequency of disability. The first study, based on a nonrandom survey of 124 firms, explored the hypothesis that a significant portion of the variability between workers' compensation experience in different companies was due to internal actions that were within the employer's control (Habeck et al. 1991). The following findings and conclusions were reached:

1. Great variability, at least tenfold differences, could be found between the workers' compensation claim rates of the firms with the highest and lowest claims within each of 29 industries studied.

2. Only part (25 percent) of this variability in claim rate could be explained by industry, size, and location of the firms.

3. Firms with high claims incidence had twice as many injuries but had four times as many workers' compensation claims, supporting conjecture that there are two distinct processes involved in disability management. The first portion involves strategies that prevent potentially disabling incidents from occurring, and the second involves managing the incident after it occurs, with each process contributing substantially to eventual outcomes.

4. Organizational characteristics, such as unionization and tenure of the workforce, are also related to the claim rate.

5. Favorable claims experience (i.e., a low claim rate) is significantly related to the managerial philosophy and the particular policies and practices adopted by the firm, including an open

managerial style, a positive human resource orientation, more rigorous pursuit of safety and preventive interventions, and specific procedures to manage disabilities. In regard to the latter, firms that had lower claims rates reported significantly more frequent use of employee assistance resources, light duty and modified work to help restricted individuals resume employment, and procedures to promote supervisors' efforts to assist in the return to work of injured employees in their departments.

The second study was conducted to quantify the impacts of specific workplace policies and practices on the incidence and outcomes of work-related disability within firms (Hunt et al. 1993). The impacts of disability prevention and management behaviors were estimated in a multivariate analysis that controlled for a wide range of organizational factors, using a random, cross-sectional survey of 220 firms in seven industries. The results demonstrate that companies engaging more frequently in behaviors defined as "Safety Diligence" and "Proactive Return-to-Work" experienced significantly fewer cases with lost workdays, fewer total lost workdays, and less frequent workers' compensation claims; in sum, they experienced less work-related disability.

Specifically, firms that reported 10 percent more frequent achievement of Safety Diligence (disability prevention) experienced 17 percent fewer lost workdays per 100 employees. Safety Diligence is interpreted as the rigorous behaviors of companies that act on their stated safety goals and put their safety measures into continuous practice. These behaviors have been accepted by managers, supervisors, and employees as an integral part of their regular functions.

Firms that reported 10 percent more frequent achievement of Proactive Return-to-Work (disability management) experienced approximately 7 percent fewer lost workdays per 100 workers. Proactive Return-to-Work is interpreted as supportive, company-based interventions for personally assisting those involved in an injury or disability, from the beginning of the incident to its positive resolution. The actions and responsibilities of individuals within the company and external providers are spelled out and related to the ultimate goal of resumption of employment.

Further, these results appear to be enabled and perhaps multiplied by the managerial commitment and corporate culture of the organization.

One observation is that firms that demonstrate their concern and commitment for injured workers receive, in turn, greater trust and cooperation from their employees. This is also manifest in the finding that "Disability Case Monitoring," defined as a reactive approach to cost containment and claims control, actually was associated with a greater incidence of lost workday cases (Hunt et al. 1993).

In addition to the survey, on-site plant visits were made to a subsample of 32 firms in order to verify the quantitative findings and to gain operational understanding of the company behaviors that contributed to low disability rates. The initiatives of successful firms are summarized as follows:

1. Extensive use of data to measure performance and identify problems

2. Analysis of problems to identify the root causes of injury and work disability and to target interventions accordingly

3. Receipt or development of the active support of top management for the goals, policies, and procedures undertaken

4. Education of labor to understand the relevance of safety and disability performance to the well-being of the company and to themselves

5. Immediate response to identified problems, which convinces labor and supervisors of the genuineness of management's concern and determination

6. Realization that their actions and performance in safety are related to their disability performance and to workers' compensation costs

7. Movement upstream in prevention through ergonomic initiatives in design

8. Development of effective working relationships with designated, knowledgeable, and responsive health care providers

9. Maintenance of an active role in case management, even when professional services are used, in order to keep the company in control of the process

10.Implementation of the return-to-work process in a systematic way throughout the organization, yet tailoring the process to meet the needs of the individual situation and maintaining a transitional perspective in accommodations made

These findings support a causal connection between the disability prevention and management policies and practices of a firm and disability performance results. The strategies of prevention and management have both been shown to be effective in reducing workplace disability in those firms that have implemented them rigorously. As expected, prevention strategies have a higher payoff, but management techniques have also been effective at reducing the total incidence and severity of work-related disability.

Case management is one of the techniques included under the broader disability management umbrella. One example of its application to Social Security claimants will be reported. An experimental design was used to test an independent case manager model with persons who had applied for Social Security disability benefits (Hester et al. 1990). Over 3,850 applicants were referred to the project. After rigorous screening for probable success, a final selection of 753 persons (20 percent) was made of those felt to be eligible for return to work.

These individuals were assigned to one of three groups. The first was an early referral group, comprised of individuals who were offered case management services to promote return to work within two weeks of their application for benefits. The second was a late referral group, in which participants were offered the same case management but not until after they had been approved for benefits. The third group was a control. Case management services included physician contact; an assessment of vocational skills, with a work evaluation if indicated; job development with former employers, if possible; referral to state vocational rehabilitation agencies for skill training; and direct placement services. Among the relevant findings were the following:

- only 6 percent in the late referral group accepted services, as opposed to 22 percent in the early referral group;

- 46 percent of those who accepted services were employed at the end of the project, as opposed to 13 percent of those in the control group; and

• 21 percent in the early referral group returned to work, as opposed to 3 percent in the late referral group.

These observations indicate that a case management approach using early intervention (even though six months or more after onset of disability) may be particularly useful before disability benefits are awarded for encouraging return to work for those still in the applicant stage. While these empirical research findings are very limited, they do strongly suggest that disability prevention and management techniques work for reducing the incidence and consequences of work-related injuries in the private sector. Some of the techniques may even work with DI claimants.

Private Sector Examples

In an attempt to determine how particular elements are implemented in private sector disability management programs, and how they might impact Social Security Administration (SSA) program concerns, we conducted a set of nine case studies. They were meant to represent a broad range of private sector experience, but not necessarily "best practice," since much more systematic survey work would be required to determine just what best practice really is. We talked with some self-insured employers from widely divergent sectors of the economy, insurance carriers with very different books of business, and varied types of service providers. Due to the limitations of space, just three of these examples are presented here: one self-insured employer, one insurance carrier, and one service provider.[2] A summary of the lessons learned is provided at the end of the section.

Owens-Corning Fiberglas

Owens-Corning Fiberglas is a global manufacturer of fiberglass products. The firm has 50 U.S. plants with about 12,000 employees.

Approach to Disability Management and Return to Work

Owens-Corning characterizes its approach as an "aggressive stance" toward disability management and return to work. Owens-Corning has taken corporate responsibility for all of its claims, including work-related and nonwork-related disabilities. The company has brought the process in-house and no longer relies solely on third parties. This approach was adopted in response to significant rises in costs in all disability areas and to anticipated changes due to national health care reform. The goal is to reduce disability costs as a means of increasing company profit, but to do so in a way that is consistent with corporate principles of (1) customer satisfaction, (2) individual dignity, and (3) shareholder value.

Specific Interventions

The major features in the administration of the Owens-Corning approach include the following:

1. A site disability case manager is used to coordinate all activities and provide case management services;

2. Case management begins on day one of the occurrence;

3. Benefit checks are cut in-house to assure prompt payment;

4. Performance standards have been tightened for third-party administrators of the company's plans;

5. The company has changed vendors for its long-term disability insurance to one that has a progressive disability management philosophy and shares the firm's vision;

6. Corporate oversight is used to address responsibility for overall disability outcomes;

7. Human resource managers and supervisors at all plants were brought in for education regarding program goals and operation; and

8. Provisions for disability management and return to work have been incorporated into contract negotiations with the company's represented groups.

Expected Outcomes

Owens-Corning stipulated the outcomes that should be accomplished by the end of the first three years of the program, which was implemented in 1992. These outcomes included a 10 percent reduction in total disability costs, including indemnity benefits and medical costs; a 10 percent reduction in lost workdays; and a 10 percent increase in the use of modified, restricted workdays. In less than two years, each of these three goals had already been achieved. In 1992, the firm's disability cost total was estimated at $25 million; the current goal is to reduce these costs to $15 million by 1998 (a 40 percent reduction).

Relationship to the Social Security System

Owens-Corning sees Social Security as an added benefit. Owens-Corning recognizes that it cannot provide for all needs and that Social Security represents an important resource to the corporation. The firm provides assistance to its employees in applying for DI, including provision of information for the applicant to carry to the SSA if needed.

UNUM Insurance Company

UNUM Corporation is a specialty insurance holding company whose affiliates include UNUM Insurance Company of America, a leading provider of disability insurance and of employee benefits, long-term care, and retirement products.

Approach to Disability Management and Return to Work

Disability management and return to work at UNUM are best pictured as a continuum. The preferred disability management activity at the beginning of the continuum is disability prevention and stay at work. To that end, UNUM works with high-risk employers at an organizational level to identify trends in claim causes that suggest prevention activity, such as job restructuring, ergonomic engineering, or training in how to work more safely.[3] The Long-term disability (LTD) product offers an Employee Assistance Program (EAP) for help with personal issues that can contribute to disability.

Further along the continuum, if a person does have an impairment and a functional limitation that prevents work, early intervention is important. Under short-term disability (STD) policies, that can happen much sooner than in LTD where there is a 90-to-180 day waiting period. Where UNUM provides both STD and LTD, an STD objective is early intervention and management to prevent or minimize an LTD claim. UNUM also provides stay at work services for employees. Stay at work services include functional assessment of the person and the job, along with identifying and paying for job modifications within certain limits.

Specific Interventions

From the insurance carrier perspective, a plan design that sets waiting periods and replacement rates that provide significant incentives to return to work is an important management tool. Collection of complete impairment and work information is also key to making a fair decision regarding the person's functional ability in relationship to clearly stated job demands. These facts determine if the definition of disability is operable and if the individual is entitled to benefits.

For STD, the major tool is duration management according to guidelines that indicate how long individuals may not be able to perform the functions of their jobs or occupations, considering their age and impairment-related functional restrictions and limitations. Using these guidelines, expectations of recovery and return to work are set when the claim is approved, causing people to think of return to work from the beginning. For LTD, a case plan is set and return-to-work expectations are conveyed, but with less formal duration guides. For both STD and LTD, if expected recovery does not occur, claims managers work with treating physicians to review the medical aspects of claims and the individual's job functions, in order to facilitate return to transitional or modified employment.

Specific management protocols are developed for the more problematic impairment categories such as psychiatric, cardiac, maternity (STD primarily), and chronic back pain cases with no objective medical findings. These protocols involve specific physician questionnaires and physical/functional evaluation. Regular follow-up is used to track progress and to communicate with employee, employer, and the treating physician in pursuit of the case plan.

UNUM has developed a copyrighted return-to-work prediction scale, which claims specialists use as a guide for identifying rehabilitation candidates with return-to-work potential. For persons who have both STD and LTD eligibility, rehabilitation potential is assessed during the STD claims management for those likely to go on to long-term disability. In some circumstances, case managers will use outside vendors for rehabilitation services, where there is likelihood that such services can return the claimant to work. A cost-benefit formula is applied based on the cost of the services, the cost of providing present and future benefits, and employer and employee motivation. For long-term disability, about 18-20 percent of new claimants are reviewed and accepted for rehabilitation.

Expected Outcomes

Success is measured by company profits as well as by customer (both employer and employee) satisfaction. Outcomes for long-term disability claimants are tracked based on the relationship between the cost of the intervention that UNUM will cover and the projected savings in future benefits that would have been paid if the person had continued on claim status (the industry calls this reserve release). By this calculation, there has been a return in the range of $5.00 to $7.00 for every $1.00 expended over the last three years. Outcomes are also measured in terms of client satisfaction and recoveries, and, of course, in increased sales and renewals of insurance policies.

Relationship to the Social Security System

There is a formal Social Security referral program in the LTD claim process. Social Security is a consideration in setting up a case plan for a claimant. However, return to work is the first goal, and Social Security referrals are made based on the severity and duration of the impairment and when other efforts to achieve return to work are not successful. UNUM's benefits are in addition to those of Social Security and the LTD insurance price reflects this potential offset.

United Health Care

United Health Care (UHC) is one of the largest health maintenance organizations (HMOs) in the country, with over 2.7 million enrollees. UHC has purchased a workers' compensation preferred provider network (FOCUS) to augment integrated disability management services, starting with the medical event. The organization's disability management services are discussed from the perspective of a vendor that markets integrated disability management to insurance companies and large employers.

Approach to Disability Management and Return to Work

UHC provides a "managed care" approach, assisting clients in integrating their occupational and nonoccupational medical and disability management programs. From the onset of a claim, employees and their families have a specific primary care nurse as their contact for health care education, utilization review, and disability management services. This nurse communicates with the attending physician, the employer, and the claims payor(s) to negotiate an effective treatment plan that includes early return to appropriate transitional/modified work as part of the recovery process.

Specific Interventions

Depending on clients' utilization of services, key features could include the following:

- centralized disability application processing for STD/LTD claims;

- early intervention by a primary care nurse (or masters-prepared social worker), who contacts the employee, employer, and provider within two business days of notification;

- health care utilization management, including preferred providers and second opinion/independent medical examination services;

- telephonic return-to-work coordination with the employer, utilizing on-site resources as needed for job accommodation, ergonomic evaluation, etc.;

- comprehensive measurement and reporting to evaluate trends, demonstrate impact, and continuously improve the efficiency and effectiveness of the program;

- employer program development support to clarify internal roles and responsibilities, identify transitional work opportunities, and influence attitudes and cultural expectations within the organization;

- rehabilitation vendor selection and management;

- specialized injury prevention programs for cumulative repetitive trauma and back conditions;

- maternity education and high-risk pregnancy programs;

- chronic disease management programs based on client-specific trends.

Expected Outcomes

Outcome indicators include the average length of disability, total wage replacement benefits paid, and total medical costs by diagnosis/ procedure and by work location. In a voluntary referral program, a recent employer client report indicated that 67 percent of referred claims experienced an average 31 percent reduction in the total number of weeks of disability, as compared to the attending provider's initial plan. However, only a small percentage of the client's total claims were managed. In a mandatory referral program, 41 percent of claims were positively impacted with a 15 percent average reduction in the total weeks of disability. The program objective is a minimum five-to-one return on investment. While these results probably represent outstanding examples, it seems clear that disability outcomes are amenable to influence.

Summary

Each of these examples illustrates different aspects of the disability management continuum. Owens-Corning takes a stance typical of progressive self-insured employers that are trying to manage their disability costs aggressively. The company uses a case manager model with obvious corporate commitment to communicate among the players, solve problems, and coordinate services for a positive outcome. UNUM emphasizes prevention, early intervention, and incentives in addition to case management services for difficult categories of disability. The insurer also makes an explicit judgment about the costs and benefits of intervening in specific cases in particular ways. United Health Care uses a traditional managed care model with a strong return-to-work focus. All seem to promise substantial returns in the form of lower costs of disability, either through reduced duration, lower incidence, and/or savings from better process management.

Clearly, not all of the disability management tools developed in the private sector are completely relevant for the DI or SSI programs. For example, while prevention of disability is critically important in the private sector, it is hard to imagine how SSA could directly affect the incidence of disabling conditions. Early intervention has been shown to be crucial in private sector experience, and many believe the first 24 hours is critical to the eventual outcome. However, with a five-month waiting period, it is difficult to see how SSA could achieve early intervention in this same sense. Another consideration is that there is no private parallel to SSA concerns about children with disabilities.

In addition, in a very real sense, SSA must deal with the failures of private sector disability management treatments, i.e., the cases of those people who still have not returned to work despite private efforts. So the scope for action at SSA may be very different than in the private sector. One obvious observation is that the lessons from the private side of the economy are likely to be more relevant for the population with recent work experience. Nevertheless, there are some well-established disability management principles that might transfer to public programs, such as rationalization of incentives, a proactive return-to-work philosophy, and case management techniques.

Policy Implications

We will begin with a description of the SSA disability determination and return-to-work procedures of the past.[4] Then, we will recount the lessons from private sector disability management efforts and examine their applicability to Social Security programs.

Critique of DI Process

For adults, the current approach to determining eligibility for DI benefits basically works to convince individuals that they belong to one of two categories. Either they have relatively few limitations and can manage on their own, or they have limitations so severe that they can never again be productive members of society on a competitive basis. Further, the system provides little support or encouragement for either group to obtain employment. Only a select few in the second group are referred to the state/federal system of vocational rehabilitation, and this occurs only after considerable time has elapsed since their previous labor market experience. These individuals are then supposed to make an immediate reversal in their self-concepts. Suddenly, they have become potential workers, without the benefit of any intervention, other than the passage of time, to bring about this considerable change.

This approach to disability is counter to conventional wisdom and available research, which suggests that a focus on ability and early intervention is required to prevent persons from losing touch with their identification as workers. It is not surprising that only a small percentage of those referred to vocational rehabilitation are rehabilitated. The public resources available through the Social Security system are simply not designed to help adults with disabilities achieve employment. In fact, the system may actually encourage disability through factors such as excessive delays in processing claims, over-reliance on medical evidence in determining disability, and insufficient or nonexistent disability management tools.

First, the time that elapses between the onset of disability and the determination of eligibility for benefits can be months, if not years. Some of this cannot be avoided if there must be a statutory waiting period of five months, but SSA reports that the subsequent delays in processing are prodigious. According to an internal study by the SSA Office of Workforce Analysis, an initial determination of beneficiary status from SSA may take up to 155 days from first contact with the agency, with from 16 to 26 employees involved, but requires only about 13 hours of actual "task time." If the decision is negative and the individual appeals, a further 400 days may pass before a final decision is received by the claimant, of which only 32 hours is actual task time (U.S. Department of Health and Human Services, SSA, 1994, pp. 8-9). During all this time, the individual claimant is concentrating on his/her disability, rather than on the ability that could be used in an employment situation.[5] This approach discourages motivation to return to work and minimizes personal investment in productivity-restoring activities.

Second, the primary data used to assess eligibility for benefits are medical in nature, hence input from physicians often is the deciding factor. Although medical information is certainly critical to the decision process, almost exclusive reliance on it obscures the reality that disability results from a complex array of factors. The preeminence of medical diagnostic criteria perpetuates a model that focuses on disability rather than ability. It also deflects attention from the variety of interventions or environmental changes known to be able to remove or ameliorate many of the functional limitations producing disability, as called for in more contemporary public and private policy.

Third, there is no real case management built into the system. There seems to be an assumption that the only factor to consider is the impairment that led to eligibility in the first place. If medically verifiable improvement occurs, then there is the chance for a later review of a person's condition. However, the review is only for the purposes of establishing the severity and duration of the disability and whether these remain substantial enough to warrant continued benefits. Again, the pressure is to demonstrate disability and limitations, not ability and potential participation. Nevertheless, the examples cited earlier in this paper suggest significant results are available from case management techniques alone.[6]

Although the employment incentive provisions in the 1980 disability policy reforms can support return-to-work activities, practically speaking, these are really only useful when people are ready, on their own, to make a work attempt.[7] There is no systematic case management system to guide a person through effective utilization of these incentives, or in obtaining appropriate health care services, or in pursuing education that could qualify an individual for alternative jobs more suitable to existing limitations. There is no system to assist treating physicians in understanding the functional requirements of specific jobs for which the individual might be qualified. Finally, no one works with employers to develop appropriate accommodations that can open job opportunities by minimizing the impact of limitations, even though the employer has this obligation under the ADA. Persons receiving disability benefits are virtually left to their own devices, and to the resources of family members, to overcome the variety of limiting features that contribute to their disability.

Lessons Learned

Some of the problems that have been described are familiar to private employers and insurers. However, in recent years the private sector has improved its experience with disabled workers through prevention, early intervention, disability case management, and proactive return-to-work policies of accommodation and rehabilitation. The disability management movement in the private sector has been driven by the stimulus of unacceptably high workers' compensation and other disability costs and has produced a practical, sequential, problem-solving approach. The public programs can and must follow this same path, with the advantage of the past decade of private sector experience to draw from in redesigning a comprehensive disability policy. Let us review what we have learned from the private sector evidence presented earlier, recognizing that these lessons are most applicable to those disabled individuals who have recently been in the labor force.

Return-to-Work Focus

The first lesson is that return to work should be the ultimate goal.[8] While it is clear that not all persons with disabilities can be expected to work, failing to adequately assist individuals with functional impairments to develop the opportunity to be employed, to participate, and to contribute is inequitable and inefficient. We must realize that disability is a continuum, and a benefit structure that maintains a bifurcated view of the world (either disabled or not) is no longer relevant. Our evidence shows that return to work is not a disconnected function that occurs at some specific point in the treatment process. Rather, it is a commitment that evolves out of early intervention and case management activities with the individual, the physician, the employer, and others. The return-to-work "treatment" does not follow medical treatment and maximum medical improvement, as has frequently been the case with the tertiary vocational rehabilitation model. It should be part of a comprehensive disability management process from day one.

From the company examples reviewed earlier, it is obvious that one key to disability management success is the immediate creation, or maintenance, of the expectation that the individual has the potential to work and will return to work. This requires personal contact and support, which must be maintained on a regular basis, either in person or by telephone. As indicated by the SSA Disability Process Reengineering Team, current SSA procedures are far from this ideal (SSA, Plans for a New Disability Claim Process, 1994). The proposals of the SSA Reengineering Team for a more efficient and inclusive process are certainly a step in the right direction, but much more could and should be done. SSA needs to design ways to partner with private sector employers, insurance carriers, medical practitioners, and other service providers to ensure that the return-to-work goal is addressed from the beginning of an emerging disability.

Positive Incentives

It may be contentious to talk about financial incentives, but a system that encourages people with functional limitations to think of themselves as disabled is immoral. A system that effectively limits earnings to $500 per month and then threatens to take away all supports if earnings exceed that level does not fit with an ecological model of disability. Disability is a continuum, and our support systems should mirror that reality. Partial benefits and carefully crafted implicit tax rates are needed to maintain incentives for all persons with disabilities to work as much as they can.

There are also perverse incentives for other actors in the system—employers, insurers, and service providers. Our case studies show that many private sector disability claims end with a "pass-off" to Social Security. There is no motivation for the employer or insurer to stay involved beyond that point. Further, there is no real incentive to try to prevent this outcome, since it can be regarded as a "success" from the narrow point of view. Perhaps it is time to consider experience rating of the Social Security taxes that employers pay, in order to encourage prevention of disabilities. SSA needs to consider establishing policies that encourage private sector players to serve the public interest.

We need to be sure that all incentives reinforce the social policy objective of maximizing the contribution of each individual, of achieving optimum equity and efficiency, in bringing persons with disabilities into the labor force to the extent feasible. Return to work is not appropriate for everyone, but we need to make sure that we adequately support those for whom this is a realistic goal.

Early Intervention

Early intervention is another lesson from the private sector that cannot be overemphasized. Private sector insurance carriers and third-party administrators have discovered that this is not a question of months, but of days. It would not be an exaggeration to say that the earlier the intervention begins the better for the ultimate goal of recovery or maintenance of employment. Even after six months, however, there is evidence that additional delays are harmful, particularly as compared to a system that focuses on return to work and maintains positive incentives to promote this goal.

SSA must find a way to reach forward (even into the five-month waiting period) to address the needs of individuals with functional impairments as soon as possible. Thought might be given to some innovative sort of technical assistance, consultative service, and financial incentives that could assist employers and treatment providers in preventing disability and in meeting employers' accommodation obligations under the ADA. An appropriate partnership with SSA could be made attractive to all interested parties, bearing in mind that persons with disabilities must be the major beneficiaries.

Case Management

The evidence is clear from the private sector that case management services save money for both insurance carriers and self-insured employers and reduce unnecessary disability outcomes. The marketing effort that is currently going into third-party case management services indicates that many private sector players understand this relationship. The hypothesis that the effect extends to public programs is being formally tested in the ongoing Project Network experiments for SSA clients (Rupp, Bell, and McManus 1994). Without prejudging the results of the research, it should not come as a surprise that investing time and energy in managing any process will lead to better outcomes. Evidence available from the private sector suggests that efficiency savings of from 10 to 20 percent are readily achievable through case management techniques alone. When combined with the return-to-work orientation and early intervention perspectives that we have suggested, considerably larger gains should be available.

Final Reflections

Disability management offers a critically important mechanism for stemming the tide of individuals who leave employment unnecessarily and enter disability systems, while simultaneously addressing the economic survival needs of American business and the security of the jobs it provides. In a comprehensive view of national disability policy, disability prevention and management should be seen as the keys to promoting the maximum contribution of all disabled individuals and to reducing the public burden of preventable disability.

About 10 years ago, private sector employers began to realize that nobody was going to solve the problem for them and that they had to do it themselves. It is amazing what has been accomplished in the intervening decade at "best practice" companies. Reductions of 50 percent, or more, in work-related disability incidence are possible where the company is willing to make the commitment to an integrated disability prevention and management strategy. Many of these cases have now been documented in the literature.

It is certain that public sector programs will show more limited gains, because the severity of disabilities encountered is greater, because the claimant's connection to the world of work is more tenuous, and because entitlement to public sector benefits is a matter of right (Galvin, Dean, and Kirchner 1991). However, it is our obligation to make sure that every individual has been given the opportunity and the needed support to participate. The private sector has pointed the way in developing specific disability prevention and management programs; it is up to all of us to make sure that the public sector does not ignore the lessons that are there to be learned.

NOTES

1. We specifically include stay-at-work efforts under this topic as well.

2. The full content of the interviews is available upon request from the W.E. Upjohn Institute for Employment Research. The subjects include Owens-Corning Fiberglas, Rohr, Digital Corporation, Union Pacific Railroad, UNUM Insurance, Wausau Insurance, United Health Care, University of Cincinnati Medical Center, and S. Yangouyian & Associates.

3. While UNUM is not a workers' compensation carrier, short-term and long-term disability benefits are paid during workers' compensation waiting periods and above maximum workers' compensation benefit levels.

4. However, see the *Plan for a New Disability Claim Process* (U.S. Department of Health and Human Services, SSA 1994). Clearly, SSA has become aware of these shortcomings.

5. See Bound (1989) for evidence that under 50 percent of rejected male applicants actually return to work. We are not suggesting that these people are not disabled, but simply that the longer the eligibility determination process requires, the higher the proportion of individuals that will be disabled, other things equal.

6. These gains are being examined experimentally in Project Network. See Rupp, Bell, and McManus (1994) for details of the design.

7. See *Rethinking Disability Policy* (National Academy of Social Insurance 1994), chapter 5, for a brief history of DI and SSI policy.

8. Of course, this could be restated as securing and retaining gainful employment for those who have never held a job.

References

Akabas, S.H., L.B. Gates, and D.E. Galvin. 1992. *Disability Management: A Complete System to Reduce Costs, Increase Productivity, Meet Employee Needs, and Ensure Legal Compliance.* New York: AMACOM.

Berkowitz, M. 1985. "Forestalling Disincentives to Return to Work," *Business and Health* 2, 4: 30-32.

Bound, J. 1989. "The Health and Earnings of Rejected Disability Insurance Applicants," *American Economic Review* 79,3: 482-503.

Chelius, J., D. Galvin, and P. Owens. 1992. "Disability: It's More Expensive than You Think," *Business and Health* 11, 4: 78-84.

Council of State Administrators of Vocational Rehabilitation. 1993. "Recommendations for a Model Service Delivery System for Public Vocational Rehabilitation." Washington, DC: Council of State Administrators of Vocational Rehabilitation.

Galvin, D.E. 1986. "Employer-Based Disability Management and Rehabilitation Programs." In *Annual Review of Rehabilitation*, E.L. Pan, S.S. Newman, T.E. Backer, and C.L. Vash eds. New York: Springer.

Galvin, D.E., D. Dean, and K.A. Kirchner. 1991. *Applying State-of-the-Art Disability Management to Social Security Beneficiaries.* Washington, DC: Washington Business Group on Health, September.

Habeck, R.V. 1991. "Managing Disability in Industry," *NARPPS Journal & News* 6, 4: 141-146.

Habeck, R.V., M. Kress, S.M. Scully, and K. Kirchner. 1994. "Determining the Significance of the Disability Management Movement for Rehabilitation Counselor Education," *Rehabilitation Education* 8, 3: 195-240.

Habeck, R.V., M.J. Leahy, H.A. Hunt, F. Chan, and E.M. Welch. 1991. "Employer Factors Related to Workers' Compensation Claims and Disability Management," *Rehabilitation Counseling Bulletin* 34, 3: 210-226.

Hennessey, J.C., and J.M. Dykacz. 1993. "A Comparison of the Recovery Termination Rates of Disabled-Worker Beneficiaries Entitled in 1972 and 1985," *Social Security Bulletin* 56, 2 (Summer): 58-69.

Hester, E.J., E.L. Gaddis, P.G. Decelles, and V.E. Webb. 1990. *Project Return: Rehabilitation of SSDI Applicants.* Topeka, KS: Menninger Foundation.

Hunt, H.A., R.V. Habeck, B. VanTol, and S.M. Scully. 1993. "Disability Prevention among Michigan Employers." Technical Report #93-004. Kalamazoo, MI: W.E. Upjohn Institute for Employment Research.

Levitan, S., and R. Taggart. 1977. *Jobs for the Disabled.* Baltimore: Johns Hopkins University Press.

Lewin, D., and S. Schecter. 1991. "Four Factors Lower Disability Rates," *Personnel Journal* 70, 5: 99-103.

National Academy of Social Insurance. 1994. *Rethinking Disability Policy: The Role of Income, Health Care, Rehabilitation and Related Services in Fostering Independence.* Washington, DC: National Academy of Social Insurance, March.

National Rehabilitation Planners. 1993. *Hospitals and Work Disability: A Summary Fact Sheet.* Columbus, OH: National Rehabilitation Planners.

Okun, A.M. 1975. *Equality and Efficiency: The Big Tradeoff.* Washington, DC: Brookings Institution.

Rousmaniere, P. 1989. "Too Many Cooks, No Chef," *Health Management Quarterly* 11, 2: 1-3.

Rousmaniere, P. 1990. "Stop Workers Comp from Shooting Holes in Corporate Profits," *Corporate Cashflow* 11, 3 (March): 24-28.

Rupp, K., S.H. Bell, and L.A. McManus. 1994. "Design of the Project Network Return-to-Work Experiment for Persons with Disabilities," *Social Security Bulletin* 57, 2 (Summer): 3-20.

Schwartz, G.E., S.D. Watson, D.E. Galvin, and E. Lipoff. 1989. *The Disability Management Sourcebook.* Washington, DC: Washington Business Group on Health.

Stubbins, J. 1982. *The Clinical Attitude in Rehabilitation: A Cross Cultural View.* Rehabilitation Monograph No. 6. New York: World Rehabilitation Fund.

Tate, D.G., R.V. Habeck, and D.E. Galvin. 1986. "Disability Management: Origins, Concepts, and Principles of Practice," *Journal of Applied Rehabilitation Counseling* 17, 3: 5-11.

Towers Perrin. 1993. *Regaining Control of Workers' Compensation Costs: The Second Biennial Towers Perrin Survey Report.* New York: Towers Perrin.

U.S. Department of Health and Human Services. Social Security Administration. 1994. *Plan for a New Disability Claim Process.* SSA No. 01-005. Washington, DC: Government Printing Office, September.

U.S. General Accounting Office. 1993. *Vocational Rehabilitation: Evidence for Federal Program's Effectiveness is Mixed.* GAO/PEMD-93-19. Washington, DC: General Accounting Office.

Vandergoot, D. 1994. "Reactions to 'Current Models of Job Placement and Employer Development: Research, Competencies and Educational Considerations,'" *Rehabilitation Education* 7, 4: 269-271.

Quantitative Outcomes of the Transitional Employment Training Demonstration

Summary of Net Impacts

Aaron J. Prero
Social Security Administration

USA
J28
J15
I12

J24

In the period from 1985 through 1987, the Transitional Employment Training Demonstration offered job placement and special training to 375 recipients of Supplemental Security Income (SSI) with mental retardation. The demonstration was organized and largely funded by the Social Security Administration (SSA). A six-year retrospective view of the demonstration, presented here, reveals a mix of results regarding the effectiveness of SSA's providing these services. On average, the trainees' employment rate and earnings increased because of their participation. SSI payments declined only slightly, however, not nearly enough for SSA to recoup the costs.

The demonstration outcomes, therefore, do not yield simple policy implications in favor of SSA's support of transitional employment. Rather, the value of a transitional employment program will depend on the nature of the population being served, the features of the plan, and the weight policy makers attach to its various objectives. For example, a program targeted to groups for which the benefits are expected to be large can be more effective than a program offered, as in this demonstration, to a less select group. A program that substitutes for other expensive, government-funded services (like sheltered work) would incur lower net costs. A program cosponsored by several agencies, whose missions include increasing participants' income and employment, will more likely be economical than one whose goal is simply to save money for the SSI program.

This paper summarizes the findings of a comprehensive evaluation of the demonstration (Thornton, Dunstan, and Schore 1988, Decker and Thornton 1994) and extends that research by examining some subgroup impacts in greater detail. A more extensive discussion of the implementation of the demonstration, nonquantitative findings, and transitional employment, in general, can be found in Prero and Thornton (1991).

Description of the Demonstration

The objective of the demonstration was to determine the results of SSA's offering transitional employment training to a specific population, as described in the next section. The effect of main interest was savings to the SSI program. That is, could SSA justify paying the cost of services on the expectation that the costs would be exceeded by the resulting reductions in SSI payments?

Population and Experimental Design

The participants in the demonstration were 745 SSI recipients aged 18 to approximately 40 with mental retardation. Job placement and training were provided by eight nonprofit agencies in various localities around the country, whose operations under the demonstration were funded mostly by grants from SSA. (These organizations are referred to here as the sites.)

SSA has a particular interest in the habilitation of persons with mental retardation, since retardation is a leading cause of disability among SSI recipients. SSI statistics suggest that roughly 1.2 million children and adults under age 65 receive SSI payments on the basis of a primary diagnosis of mental retardation, some 29 percent of all SSI recipients under 65.[1] Based on the average monthly SSI disability payment of $402.47 in December 1994, payments to recipients with mental retardation approximate $5.8 billion per year. In addition to these individuals, an unknown number of recipients whose primary diagnosis is some other condition are also mentally retarded.

Eighty-five percent of the people in the demonstration were drawn from a pool of some 12,000 SSI recipients whom SSA invited by letter to inquire about participation. The invitees were persons for whom mental retardation was listed as the primary or secondary diagnosis on their SSI records and who lived in the localities of the sites. To participate, the recipient had to volunteer and had to be accepted by the local site. The remaining 15 percent were SSI recipients who were recruited by the sites, generally through referrals from vocational and social service agencies. The referred participants also had mental retardation.

The demonstration was designed as a formal experiment, in order to assure the rigor of the analysis of outcomes. Half of the participants, designated as the treatment group, were offered the demonstration's services, and half, the control group, were not. Individuals were assigned by random number to one of the groups after they agreed to participate, were accepted by the site, and had completed the participant questionnaire. (All participants and/or their guardians understood at the time of enrollment that the probability of being assigned to the control group was 50 percent.)

Members of the control group were free to obtain vocational and additional services from sources other than the demonstration. Thus, the test was not of the effect of the demonstration's services as compared with no vocational services, but the effect of the demonstration's services compared with the services that were then otherwise available or that have since become available.

Some of the post-demonstration changes experienced by the treatment group in employment, earnings, SSI, and other measures would have been realized even without demonstration services and should not be attributed to the demonstration. The extent to which change would have taken place regardless is measured by the experiences of the control group. Indeed, the average control group member, who earned $615 during the year following enrollment in the demonstration, earned about twice that in each of the third through sixth years (Decker and Thornton 1994, p. 23).

Random assignment assured that the treatment and control groups were alike at the time of enrollment with respect to characteristics that were or were not measured or may not even be measurable. Comparison of known characteristics of the participants confirms that the two groups, in fact, resembled each other closely (Thornton, Dunstan, and Schore 1988, pp. 58-60, or Prero and Thornton 1991, pp. 12-13). The two groups were alike in terms of their distributions by age, race, gender, IQ scores, sources of income, receipt of benefits from assistance programs besides SSI, types of work experience, and other personal characteristics.

Characteristics of the Sample

The results of the demonstration can be generalized to a population described by the selection criteria of the sample: SSI recipients 18 to 40 years old with mental retardation who would volunteer for and be accepted by this sort of program. The results cannot be generalized to a population that consists of volunteers and nonvolunteers.

Table 1 compares characteristics of the sample with those of the 11,430 persons who were invited by letter to participate and did not volunteer or were not accepted. These invitees comprise the large majority of SSI recipients in the sites' local areas who had a primary or secondary diagnosis of mental retardation and were in the 18-to-40 age range. (We might have preferred to compare the participants with recipients nationally of the same diagnosis and age, but we cannot readily identify all recipients by diagnosis.)

On average, the participants were somewhat younger than the invitees. The proportions of males and blacks among the participants were somewhat higher than among the invitees. Mean earnings in the year prior to the demonstration were low for both groups but were twice as high for the participants as for the invitees.

Services and Providers

Key services of the transitional employment model for training are

- training by a job coach on a real job, that is, on a paid job consisting of tasks that another worker would otherwise perform for the employer and in which the worker has an opportunity to interact with nondisabled coworkers or the public;

- placement in a potentially permanent real job, either the job on which the training was received or, after the training, in a similar position.

If the permanent placement is in a job that was not the training position, additional instruction by the coach is available as needed. Subse-

Table 1. Characteristics of Participants and Nonparticipant Invitees, Transitional Employment Training Demonstration

Characteristics	Participants	Nonparticipant invitees
Number	745	11,430
Age (percentages)		
Under 22	22.3	20.5
22-30	55.6	40.0
31 or older	22.2	39.5
Mean age (in years)	26.5	27.9
Gender (percentages)		
Male	59.2	54.6
Female	40.8	45.4
Race (percentages)		
White and other	69.7	73.4
Black	30.3	26.6
Income		
Mean annual SSI payment	$3,638	$3,390
Mean annual earnings	$450	$225
Mean years of SSI receipt	6.5	7.0
Concurrently receiving SSI and social security benefits (percentage)	31.0	32.5

SOURCE: Decker and Thornton (1994, pp. 54 and 81-83), based on SSA administrative data of the SSI program and the Demonstration Intake Data Collection forms.
NOTE: Items may not total precisely 100 due to rounding.

quent to training, job-retention support is provided when necessary to resolve occasional difficulties that may arise on the job.

A job coach is a specialist in training persons with disabilities and is usually employed by a service agency rather than by the trainee's employer. The scope of training by the coach includes appropriate behavior on the job, relationships to supervisors, communication, transportation to the job, and other nonwork, as well as work, skills.

Training and intensive support are transitional in the sense that they are expected to be of limited duration, generally between 6 and 18 months. Transitional employment is intended as a bridge to working independently of vocational services except for occasional job-retention help. When the need for intensive support services is expected to be ongoing, the service model is usually referred to as *supported employment*. In the Transitional Employment Training Demonstration, job coaching and other intensive services were provided for a maximum of a year.

The demonstration sites provided the services. Of the eight sites, three were universities or university affiliated. They were:

- Children's Hospital, Boston, Massachusetts

- University of Washington, Seattle, Washington serving Portland, Oregon in cooperation with Portland Community College

- University of Wisconsin-Stout, Menomonie, Wisconsin, serving a rural area in west central Wisconsin

Three of the sites were units of the Association for Retarded Citizens (ARC) or Goodwill Industries:

- Association for Retarded Citizens, Monmouth Unit, Monmouth County, New Jersey

- Exceptional Children's Foundation, Los Angeles, California (a unit of ARC)

- Goodwill Industries, Milwaukee Area, Milwaukee, Wisconsin

Two were independent rehabilitation agencies:

- AHEDD, Inc., Lemoyne, Pennsylvania, serving Harrisburg, Lancaster, Philadelphia, Pittsburgh, and York, Pennsylvania, and Dover, Delaware

- Center for Rehabilitation and Training of the Disabled, Chicago (also known as the CENTER)

Besides offering training and employment services, the sites provided or arranged for case management and other indirectly related services.

SSA granted waivers to the trainees that protected their SSI status while in training. Subsequent amendments to the SSI statute now provide similar protection to all SSI recipients. The waivers did not change the way income reduces SSI payments to recipients and did not protect social security insurance benefits.

Data Collection

The main source of data on outcomes is the SSI administrative computer files. SSA verifies and records the monthly earnings and other income of SSI recipients to determine the amount of the monthly payment. Historic records of earnings and income are retained by computer, in order to refigure the payment amount retroactively for any month for which SSA receives new information relevant to the payment.

The record generally remains available even for SSI recipients whose earnings rise to a level at which no cash payment is made. Such recipients usually remain on the SSI rolls, and continue to report their incomes, for purposes of Medicaid eligibility. By the end of the sixth year following enrollment, 87 of the 745 participants had left the SSI rolls entirely. Their earnings and income data are, therefore, missing for one or more years (but their SSI payments are known to be zero).

Attrition was approximately the same from the treatment and control groups, at 11.7 percent of the former and 11.6 percent of the latter. The single most common reason for losing SSI eligibility was new entitlement to social security benefits. Decker and Thornton (1994, pp. 12-14 and 25-28) analyze the possibility of a differential impact of attrition on the treatment and control groups' average outcomes and show that it is unlikely that there is any substantial bias.

Data on personal characteristics of the participants come from three major sources: a uniform intake questionnaire that was administered by the sites to all participants (and/or their care givers) before randomization, IQ scores obtained from SSA medical documentation of disability or released by the participants from other sources, and the computerized SSI records.

Data on hours of direct staff services provided to a subsample of clients were kept by all sites in a uniform manner. These data, collected in the demonstration's client service record, and records of program expenditures are the basis of the cost estimates.

Outcomes of the Demonstration

Measures of the Difference Made by the Demonstration

The *net impact* of the services on the treatment group is the difference between the outcomes the treatment group experienced and the outcomes that would have been realized without the demonstration services, as measured by the experience of the control group. Most of the net impacts as reported here are adjusted using regression techniques to account for preexisting differences in characteristics between the treatment and control group members and for attrition of participants from the data file. However, as described, the preexisting treatment-control differences are quite small, and, therefore, so are the consequent econometric adjustments.

The control group's outcomes, as tabulated in this section, serve as the reference points for the net impacts. That is, an impact expressed in dollars plus the mean for the corresponding control group equals the outcome for the treatment group (with small econometric adjustments). For each impact, the table also lists the ratio of the impact to the control group outcome, expressed as the percentage change that is attributed to the training.

The impacts are labeled "estimated" because they estimate the consequences of transitional employment training for an entire population, based on the experience of the demonstration's 745-member sample. (The population consists of all recipients of the same age and diagnosis who would volunteer for this type of training.)

Participants enrolled between May 1985 and June 1986. Each treatment group member was eligible for demonstration-funded services for one year from the date of enrollment. Outcomes are reported for that year and for the five subsequent years, beginning each year at the month of the participant's enrollment, rather than at the same time for all participants. All dollar measures are adjusted for inflation to 1986 dollars. This facilitates comparison with the costs of the demonstration services, which were incurred from mid-1985 to mid-1987.

Summary of Outcomes

The impacts are presented as averages of all 375 members of the treatment group, despite the fact that 121 members of the group, 32 percent, were never placed in a training or permanent job. Some of those 121 refused the placements they were offered, some dropped out of the program, and some were not offered placement because the sites found it too difficult to serve them. (This is not a surprising result, since SSA encouraged the sites to accept participants with less than the usual level of screening for suitability.) It is necessary to include all members of the treatment group in the mean outcomes to preserve comparability with the control group. Also, the costs of the demonstration are averaged over all members of the treatment group.

Of the remaining 254 treatment group members, 127 were holding permanent jobs when their participation was completed. This is 34 percent of the treatment group. Another 57 trainees (15 percent of the group) were placed in one or more permanent jobs but failed to retain those jobs. An additional 70 trainees (19 percent) were placed in training jobs but could not be subsequently placed in potentially permanent jobs (Thornton, Dunstan, and Schore 1988, p. 107).

Demonstration services cost about $7,650 per treatment group member, of which somewhat more than $2,000 is attributable to the resources used to start up and terminate the demonstration (Thornton, Dunstan, and Schore 1988, pp. 117-130). The service provided in the demonstration would thus cost an average of about $5,600 (1986 dollars) in a program operating in a steady state over the long run. This amount includes expenditures for job coaching, job development, client recruitment, and other activities performed directly for clients, as well as program administration and an allocated portion of agency overhead. Average cost at the individual demonstration sites is shown in table 2.

Table 2. Estimates of Costs, by Site, Transitional Employment Training Demonstration

	AHEDD	ARC Monmouth	The CENTER	Children's Hospital	Exceptional Children's	Goodwill	Univ. of Wash./PCC[a]	Univ. of Wisconsin	Total
Total operational expenditure[b]	$308,647	$381,483	$379,556	$161,731	$630,812	$328,112	$454,456	$221,153	$2,865,950
Average operational expenditure per client	$3,810	$9,782	$14,058	$5,577	$8,192	$9,114	$10,099	$5,394	$7,643
Estimated average operational expenditure for an ongoing program per client[c]	$2,800	$5,500	$7,200	$4,700	$7,300	$6,200	$8,100	$4,400	$5,600
Estimated average direct labor cost per client[d]	$266	$1,038	$631	$1,630	$2,101	$698	$1,742	$1,061	$1,159
Ratio of total labor cost to direct labor cost	5.7	3.7	7.0	1.8	2.0	6.0	2.4	1.9	3.7
Ratio of total cost to total labor cost for 1986	1.8	1.5	1.6	1.6	1.7	1.5	2.0	2.2	1.8
Number of treatment group members	81	39	27	29	77	36	45	41	375

SOURCE: Thornton, Dunstan, and Schore (1988, p. 120) based on the Client Service Record and site financial records.

a. Costs to Portland Community College. Because the University of Washington primarily provided technical assistance to start this project, the university's costs have been excluded from the operational cost. The University of Washington costs totaled approximately $160,000.

b. These costs exclude payments for clients' wage subsidies and project costs incurred prior to the start of enrollment.

c. These costs are estimated as the product of average direct labor cost per client, the ratio of total labor cost to direct labor cost, and the ratio of total cost to total labor cost.

d. These estimates include the wages and fringe benefits of staff time devoted directly to serving specific clients. The estimates are derived from Client Service Record data and project expenditures during 1986.

During the six-year observation period, the average trainee earned a total of $4,282 more due to the training. Earnings were approximately $10,256, which is 72 percent more than control group mean earnings (table 3). Some or all of a participant's earnings during the first year may be thought of as being derived directly from participation in the demonstration. Earnings excluding that year are a measure of post-demonstration outcomes. The net impact on earnings for the total of years two through six is an increase of $3,736, which is 69 percent over the control group mean of $5,391 (Decker and Thornton 1994, p. 23).

Table 3. Estimated Impacts of the Demonstration on Postenrollment Earnings

Year after enrollment	Estimated impact (standard error in parentheses)	Control group mean	Estimated percentage impact
1	$ 678* (96)	$ 615	110
2	835* (137)	921	91
3	737* (160)	1,167	63
4	574* (172)	1,336	43
5	869* (184)	1,206	72
6	637* (182)	1,131	56
Total, years 1 to 6	4,282* (761)	5,974	72
Total, years 2 to 6	3,736* (714)	5,391	69

SOURCE: Decker and Thornton (1994 p. 23), based on SSA administrative data of the SSI program and the Demonstration Intake Data Collection forms.
NOTE: Estimates are based on multiple regression models that control for individual preenrollment characteristics and site. The sample includes between 650 and 745 individuals assigned to either the treatment group or the control group. The exact size of the sample depends primarily on attrition from the SSI program. Statistical tests indicate that attrition does not bias the estimated impacts. Estimates are expressed in 1986 dollars.
*Significantly greater than zero at the 1 percent level of significance using a one-tail test.

The effect on SSI payments is small by any standard. The estimated six-year impact is a decrease of $870 per participant (table 4). For the second through sixth years, the estimated impact is a $731 decrease. This is a reduction of 5 percent from the means of $18,956 and $15,325 that the control group received over the six- and five-year periods, respectively (Decker and Thornton 1994, p. 31). It amounts to about $12 per month.

Table 4. Estimated Impacts of the Demonstration on Postenrollment SSI Receipt

Year after enrollment	Estimated impact (standard error in parentheses)	Control group mean	Estimated percentage impact
1	$-138* (65)	$ 3,630	-4
2	-104 (87)	3,443	-3
3	-156 (97)	3,264	-5
4	-121 (102)	3,037	-4
5	-183 (112)	2,876	-6
6	-167 (113)	2,705	-6
Total, years 1 to 6	-870* (471)	18,956	-5
Total, years 2 to 6	-731* (439)	15,325	-5

SOURCE: Decker and Thornton (1994 p. 31), based on SSA administrative data of the SSI program and the Demonstration Intake Data Collection forms.
NOTE: Estimates are based on multiple regression models that control for individual preenrollment characteristics and site. The sample consists of 745 individuals assigned to either the treatment group or the control group. Estimates are expressed in 1986 dollars.
* Significantly less than zero at the 5 percent level of significance using a one-tail test.

A mean reduction in SSI of $870 can be consistent with mean additional earnings of $4,282, depending on the operation of the SSI exclusions. That is, income of recipients reduces their SSI payments dollar for dollar, but certain amounts of income are excluded from being counted against the SSI payment. If an SSI recipient has no income other than earnings, $85 of monthly earnings plus half the remaining earnings are excluded.

According to the preceding figures, a mean of only $870 was counted against SSI, of the mean $4,282 that was earned. The remaining $3,412 of the earnings impact must have been excluded. On a monthly basis, these amounts correspond to $59 ($4,282/72 months) in mean additional earnings of which $47 ($3,412/72 months) was excluded, for six years. At least some treatment group members had income besides the income that the demonstration generated; their $85 exclusion may not have been available to apply to the additional demonstration-based earnings. Thus, the extent to which the additional earnings could be excluded depends on the *distribution* of earnings among participants, not just on the means.

One reason for the exclusion of so large a proportion of earnings was that the participants' jobs were often part-time. Workers' total earnings are typically low when they work part-time, and the initial exclusion of $85 comprises a larger fraction of lower than of higher earnings. The 127 members of the treatment group who were in permanent jobs when they exited the demonstration (see preceding discussion) worked an average of 27 hours per week in those jobs.

The Younger Participants

Just over half of the participants were of age 25 or less. The outcomes in this age range are informative with regard to transition from school to work, since students with disabilities can be entitled to public education until they are 22 years old. The SSI and earnings outcomes for this group (not regression adjusted) are presented in table 5.

Mean total SSI payments for the six years following enrollment in the demonstration fell by $1,376, from $20,402 for the controls to $19,026 for the treatment group. For the second through sixth years, the difference is $1,105, representing about the same proportionate relationship between treatment and control, -7 percent, as for the first through sixth years.

Table 5. Estimated Impacts of the Demonstration on Postenrollment and SSI Receipt, for Persons Aged 25 and Younger

Variable	Estimated impact (standard error in parentheses)	Control group mean	Estimated percentage impact
SSI receipt Total, years 1 to 6	$-1,376 (1,073)	$20,402	-7
Total, years 2 to 6	-1,105 (925)	16,441	-7
Earnings Total, years 1 to 6	3,383* (987)	6,266	54
Total, years 2 to 6	2,836* (920)	5,776	49

SOURCE: SSA administrative data of the SSI program.
NOTE: Estimates are based on observed means, not on multiple regression models. The sample for the SSI estimates consists of 383 individuals assigned to either the treatment group or the control group. The sample for the earnings estimates is the same, except for the exclusion of 20 members of the treatment group and 23 members of the control group for whom earnings data are missing in one or more years. Estimates are expressed in 1986 dollars.
*Significantly greater than zero at the 1 percent level of significance using a one-tail test.

These differences are larger, both absolutely and by percentage, than those reported for the entire age range (table 4). However, based on a sample of the 383 participants aged 18 to 25 rather than on 745 participants of all ages, the differences for the younger group are not statistically significant.[2]

The differences in earnings are larger than the SSI differences and are statistically significant. The six-year and five-year differences are, respectively, $3,383 and $2,836. That is, the treatment group did 54 percent and 49 percent better in the respective time intervals. (Twenty members of the treatment group and 23 members of the control group are omitted from the earnings comparisons because their earnings data are missing in at least one year. The issue of attrition from the sample has been discussed.)

Although not shown in table 5, it is noteworthy that the control group's mean earnings rose from $490 in the year following enrollment to $791 and $1,136 in the next two years, before reaching a plateau. Mean earnings of the treatment group rose from $1,038 in the first year to $1,519 in the second year, fluctuating mildly after that to a mean of $1,773 in year six. Thus, the sharper rise in control group earnings accounts for the reduced difference between treatment and control groups, from 54 to 49 percent, when the first year's earnings are disregarded.

Costs and Benefits

Based on the preceding information, the costs of the demonstration far exceeded the reductions in SSI payments that SSA realized. This conclusion addresses the main question that the demonstration was intended to answer, but it is not a benefit-cost judgment in the standard sense. A full treatment of benefits must consider those to the federal government as a whole, to other levels of government, and to private organizations and individuals.[3] A full treatment of costs must consider that, during training and subsequent employment, other services the client would have received may not be necessary.

Economic benefits that have not been considered here include, for example, the additional goods and services produced as a result of the employment of program participants. The counterpart of this production is the workers' earnings and the income and payroll taxes paid by workers and employers. A comprehensive benefit-cost analysis would also account for personal and social benefits to the participants resulting from their greater role in the social mainstream.

Examples of services that might be rendered unnecessary by transitional employment include sheltered work and other day activities. The costs of these services, which can amount to several thousand dollars per year, would have been borne by the federal or local governments or others. The observed cost of transitional employment should be adjusted to reflect the savings for these services (or the savings should be treated as another benefit). A transitional employment program that might be proposed for funding by a government agency with a broader mission than SSA's, or jointly by SSA and other agencies, would be more appropriately evaluated by a comprehensive benefit-cost analysis.

Qualifications of the Analysis

The conclusions of this report regarding the costs and benefits to SSA are subject to several qualifications. First, members of the control group may have received employment services from sources other than the demonstration. That is, the demonstration tested the effect of SSA's adding its services to existing opportunities. The test was not of the difference between service or no service.

The second qualification is that the conclusions of this experiment should be corroborated by additional research. Methods of providing transitional employment training can differ grossly or subtly among providers. An approach that focuses more on the effectiveness of specific training practices than did this demonstration could lead to other cost and benefit outcomes. Even in the present demonstration, in which the sites' services were organized according to certain unifying specifications (Prero and Thornton 1991, pp. 8-11), the variation among sites' styles of operation and outcomes was sufficient to warrant analysis of cross-site differences. (Decker and Thornton's analysis of the site earnings impacts "show a considerable level of variation across sites," although the samples were not large enough to support a statistically significant difference in these impacts across the eight sites [1994, pp. 65-77].)

Third, the costs per participant can vary greatly, depending on the treatment mode and operating efficiency. Within this demonstration, the estimated cost per participant for replication on an ongoing basis is $2,800 at the lowest cost site and over $8,000 at the highest cost site (table 2). Administrative costs and organizational overhead, which are included, also varied widely.

Fourth, the rules of the demonstration severely limited the extent to which sites could screen applicants for the program. More comprehensive screening could have led to more effective service. The main reason for the policy was to limit the personal involvement of members of the control group. In this way, the intake process would be as neutral as practical with regard to the control group's desire to seek training and employment. Limited contact prior to randomization also reduced the possible disappointment to participants who were subsequently assigned to control status. Abbreviated screening incidentally promoted the demonstration's goal of testing transitional employment on a wide variety of participants.

Screening and Targeting

One way to increase the ratio of benefits to costs in a project of this nature is to target services to groups for whom net impacts are expected to be high. Then, depending on the criteria for targeting, screening methods may have to be developed to assure that the group that was targeted is the one that is served.

Targeting does not necessarily mean "creaming," or serving the clients with the mildest disabilities. Although those who are least disabled might be expected to accomplish the most after training, they are also the ones who would accomplish the most without training. Thus, the net impact of the training might not be large.

Analysis of subgroups of the demonstration sample suggests, but does not lead conclusively to, some possible targeting criteria. For example, table 6 shows that, classifying age in three subgroups, the greatest impact was experienced by participants 22-to-29 years old and that this impact is statistically significant. The differences in impacts among the age subgroups, however, are not statistically significant. Participants with IQ scores greater than 55[4] show the highest impacts among the subgroups based on IQ score.

Another subgrouping that shows differing impacts is based on a subjective rating of the participant's high, medium, or low probability of success, as judged by the interviewer during the intake process. Again, the impact of the high-probability subgroup is not dissimilar enough from that of the combined medium- and low-probability subgroup for the difference to be statistically significant. The observed impacts, nevertheless, suggest that program staff have some ability to forecast outcomes even beyond the predictions based on client characteristics incorporated in the regression model (Decker and Thornton 1994, pp. 47-48). One interpretation of staff workers' insight is that they consciously or unconsciously consider client characteristics that were not measured and may be difficult to measure. These factors might include motivation and family support, both of which are anecdotally thought to be important.

290

Table 6. Estimated Impacts of the Demonstration on Cumulative Postenrollment Earnings and SSI Receipt, Years One to Six

Characteristics	Estimated impact on earnings	Control group mean earnings	Estimated percentage earnings impact	Estimated impact on SSI	Control group mean SSI	Estimated percentage SSI impact
Age						
Under 22	$2,548	$6,818	37	$435	$21,027	2
22-30	5,474**	6,478	85	-1,639*	19,313	-9
31 or older	3,637*	4,795	76	-353	16,252	-2
IQ score						
Greater than 70	9,697***[a]	4,482	216	-3,154*	18,175	-17
55 to 70	5,011***[a]	5,826	86	-677	18,562	-4
40 to 54	2,254[a]	7,194	31	-770	19,711	-4
Less than 40	2,611[a]	4,245	62	953	17,416	6
Intake worker's opinion of probability of success on a competitive job						
High	5,491**	8,018	69	-1,026	15,607	-7
Medium or low	3,744**	5,175	72	-756	20,573	-4

SOURCE: Decker and Thornton (1994, pp. 40-41 and 44-45), based on SSA administrative data of the SSI program and the Demonstration Intake Data Collection forms.

NOTE: Estimated are based on multiple regression models that control for individual preenrollment characteristics and site. The sample includes between 650 and 745 individuals assigned to either the treatment group or the control group. The exact size of the sample depends primarily on attrition from the SSI program. Statistical tests indicate that attrition does not bias the estimated impacts. Estimates are expressed in 1986 dollars.

* Significantly at the 5 percent level, earnings are greater than zero by a one-tail test and SSI is greater or less than zero by a two-tail test.
** Significantly at the 1 percent level, earnings are greater than zero by a one-tail test and SSI is greater or less than zero by a two-tail test.
a. The hypothesis that the impacts for all subgroups in the category are equal can be rejected at the 10 percent level of significance.

It should be noted that, in the analysis of subgroups, the regression model holds all other characteristics constant when analyzing the impact with respect to a particular characteristic. Also, the present subgroup analysis is limited to benefits. Costs cannot be compared with benefits within subgroups because the costs are not known at that level of detail.

Moving beyond the overall mean impacts, analysis of the *distribution* of earnings provides another perspective on the potential for targeting. A distribution of earnings can be constructed by summing the earnings of each participant over the six postenrollment years. The sums of earnings of the treatment group are ordered from lowest to highest, as are the sums of earnings of the control group. (Earnings of 39 members of the treatment group and 37 members of the control group are omitted from the distributions because data are missing in at least one year.)

We then compare, for example, the highest third of the treatment group's distribution with the highest third of the control distribution. This comparison does not assume that the selected portion of the control group is the counterpart of the selected portion of the treatment group. Rather, the highest third of the control group yields an upper bound for the sums of earnings of any third of the control group, no matter how selected.

Mean earnings of the highest third of the treatment group are $23,645 over the six-year period, as compared with $14,479 in mean earnings for the highest third of the control group (table 7). Since the control group mean is an upper bound, this implies that the net impact for these members of the treatment group is at least the difference of $9,166. (Statistical significance has not been calculated.)

Excluding earnings in the year of demonstration services, mean earnings of the highest third of the treatment group are $21,596 over years two through six. Mean earnings for the highest third of the control group are $13,243 for the second through sixth years, yielding an impact of at least $8,353.

Table 7. Mean Earnings of the Highest One-Third and Two-Thirds of the Distribution of Total Earnings and Minimum Net Impacts for All Participants in the Transitional Employment Training Demonstration and for Participants 25 and Under

Fraction of earnings distribution	Mean treatment group earnings	Mean control group earnings	Minimum net impact	Percentage minimum impact
All ages , years 1 to 6				
Highest 1/3	$23,645	$14,479	$9,166	63
Highest 2/3	15,103	9,071	6,032	66
All ages, years 2 to 6				
Highest 1/3	$21,596	$13,243	$8,353	63
Highest 2/3	13,583	8,224	5,358	65
Ages 25 and under, years 1 to 6				
Highest 1/3	$21,418	$14,431	$6,987	48
Highest 2/3	14,078	9,323	4,756	51
Ages 25 and under, years 2 to 6				
Highest 1/3	$19,657	$13,436	$6,221	46
Highest 2/3	12,680	8,609	4,071	47

SOURCE: SSA administrative data of the SSI program and the Demonstration Intake Data Collection forms.
NOTE: Estimates are based on observed means, not on multiple regression models. Participants for whom earnings data are missing in one or more years are omitted from the sample. The highest one-third of the sample for all ages consists of 223 individuals, and the highest two-thirds consists of 446 individuals, assigned to either the treatment group or the control group. For participants 25 and under, the highest one-third consists of 114 individuals, and the highest two-thirds consists of 227 individuals. Percentage minimum impact is the minimum net impact as a percentage of the mean control group earnings. Estimates are expressed in 1986 dollars.

Similar calculations for the highest two-thirds of each group's distribution yield a treatment mean of $15,103, a control mean of $9,071, and a difference of $6,032 for the six-year observation period. Over years two through six, the treatment mean is $13,583, the control mean is $8,224, and the difference is $5,358.

Among participants in the 25 years and younger segment, one-third of the sample consists of 59 treatment group members and 55 control group members, after excluding cases with missing earnings data. The mean earnings of the highest-earning one-third, totaled over six years, are calculated to be $21,418 and $14,431, respectively, or a minimum difference of $6,987. Over the second through sixth years, mean total earnings are $19,657 for the treatment group and $13,436 for the controls, a minimum difference of $6,221. This suggests some potential for targeting in the years of transition to adulthood, as well.

These analyses of the distributions of earnings give us no hint of the targeting or screening criteria that might be necessary to obtain desired results in a population. However, we can infer that, if research on the characteristics of clients produces appropriate criteria, transitional employment could be found to be cost-effective for a portion of the population, even on the basis of a narrow set of benefits.

Effective Practices

Another way to increase the ratio of benefits to costs is to modify the provision of services so that benefits are increased. For example, placement in part-time rather than in full-time jobs was cited as a reason why the decline in SSI benefits is so much less than the rise in earnings. A focus on full-time placement might be more cost-effective. On the other hand, development of part-time jobs is easier and, thus, probably less expensive. Also, an emphasis on full-time jobs might draw a different mix of clients into the program, which could alter the impacts.

Decker and Thornton (1994, pp. 65-76) infer certain suggestions for effective practices based in part on apparent differences in impacts across sites. The sites with the largest impacts were more flexible in offering a wide array of job placements, so that the circumstances and interests of clients could be better matched to jobs. The more successful sites were also willing to work with clients for longer periods of time and did not require that clients be employed in jobs reserved for training before being placed in a potentially permanent job.

Prero and Thornton (1991, pp. 17-22) base additional suggestions on their observation of the demonstration. One is that training organizations should recognize that convenient transportation is important to success in every phase of training and employment. However, since these suggestions are not based on the experimental design of the demonstration, they generally fall outside the scope of the present paper.

In summary, the outcomes do not support the hypothesis that savings in SSI payments cover the cost for SSA to offer transitional employment services as provided in this demonstration. However, it appears that outcomes can be enhanced by more narrow targeting and by services that are better designed in light of ongoing research.

Further, cost effectiveness might be achieved in a program that had a broader set of economic objectives and, therefore, accounted for more kinds of benefits. Such gains would include the productivity of otherwise unemployed workers and reduced costs for other social services. The calculation of benefits would also value the greater community regard and self-respect that individuals would have from participating in the producing mainstream of society.

NOTES

NOTE: This paper represents the opinions of the author, not necessarily those of the Social Security Administration. Thanks are due Craig Thornton and his associates at Mathematica Policy Research, Inc., and to Kalman Rupp, Lewis Frain, and Salvatore Gallicchio for their assistance.

1. Kochhar estimates that 28.7 percent of SSI recipients under age 65 have a primary diagnosis of mental retardation, based on 1988 data (1991, table 12). A total of 4,176,729 persons under age 65 received SSI payments in December 1994.

2. Not being statistically significant means that, even in a situation where training would have no effect whatsoever on the mean SSI of a *population*, there would be a reasonable probability of observing a decline of $1,376 in the mean SSI payment of a *sample* of that population. A small decline is attributable to a sample's not being representative of the population from which it was selected. The smaller the sample, the greater the risk that it is not representative.

3. For a discussion of comprehensive benefit-cost analyses of rehabilitation programs, see Burkhauser and Haveman (1982, pp. 68 ff.).

4. This observation relative to IQ level does not correspond to a finding in another transitional employment demonstration that some impacts were greater on the employment of persons with moderate as opposed to mild retardation. See Kerachsky et al. (1985, p. 82 and elsewhere).

References

Burkhauser, Richard V., and Robert H. Haveman. 1982. *Disability and Work.* Baltimore: Johns Hopkins University Press.

Decker, Paul, and Craig Thornton. 1994. "The Long-Term Effects of the Transitional Employment Training Demonstration." Princeton, NJ: Mathematica Policy Research.

Kerachsky, Stuart, Craig Thornton, Anne Blumenthal, Rebecca Maynard, and Susan Stephens. 1985. "Impacts of Transitional Employment for Mentally Retarded Young Adults: Results of the STETS Demonstration." New York: Manpower Demonstration Research Corporation.

Kochhar, Satya. 1991. "Development of Diagnostic Data in the 10-Percent Sample of Disabled SSI Recipients," *Social Security Bulletin* 54 (July): 10-21.

Prero, Aaron J., and Craig Thornton. 1991. "Transitional Employment Training for SSI Recipients with Mental Retardation," *Social Security Bulletin* 54 (November): 2-25.

Thornton, Craig, Shari Miller Dunstan, and Jennifer Schore. 1988. "The Transitional Employment Training Demonstration: Analysis of Program Operations." Princeton, NJ: Mathematica Policy Research

Policies for People with Disabilities in U.S. Employment and Training Programs

Burt S. Barnow
Johns Hopkins University

This paper discusses the federal government's employment and training policies and programs for individuals with disabilities. For each program considered, a brief description is provided, followed by a discussion of any policies and provisions especially applicable for persons with disabilities, a summary of available evidence on services provided to this population, and an assessment of potential programmatic and policy improvements that could be made.

There are several important issues that, for various reasons, are not covered in the paper. First, programs whose main purpose is to deal with discrimination in the labor market are not included. Thus, government antidiscrimination programs administered by the U.S. Equal Employment Opportunity Commission (EEOC) and the Department of Labor's Office of Federal Contract Compliance Programs (OFCCP) are not discussed. With the important exceptions of vocational rehabilitation and vocational education, which are joint federal-state undertakings, the paper excludes programs administered by the states or by other federal agencies.[1]

Another important limitation is that the paper does not address the issue of whether the level of services to people with disabilities is adequate or even if people with disabilities are served in proportion to their share of the eligible population. Although it would be desirable to include such information, there has been a variety of definitions used over time and by various sources at a given time. Additionally, some sources use self-identification, while others rely on observations by the individuals compiling the information or on administrative data. Indeed, it is the lack of coordination in defining the population in need and in establishing roles for various programs that makes it difficult to determine how well the nation is doing in serving people with disabilities who need training.

Vocational Rehabilitation

The vocational rehabilitation program, authorized under Title I of the Rehabilitation Act of 1973, provides grants to states to provide comprehensive vocational rehabilitation that meets the "needs of individuals with handicaps so that such individuals may prepare for and engage in gainful employment to the extent of their capabilities." Disabled individuals must satisfy a number of requirements to be eligible to participate in the program. Participants must have a physical or mental disability that can be medically described, they must have a substantial handicap to employment, and they must be capable of achieving employability (i.e., they have rehabilitation potential). All vocational rehabilitation activities are conducted at the state level, but they are reviewed and monitored by the Rehabilitation Services Administration of the U.S. Department of Education. Currently, there are over 80 "state" agencies administering vocational rehabilitation in the 50 states, the District of Columbia, the territories, and other government units (U.S. General Accounting Office 1993, U.S. Department of Education 1992). About half the states have two agencies, one for the blind and one for people with other disabilities. In the remaining states, a single agency is responsible for all vocational rehabilitation services. In fiscal year 1992, total federal funding available for state grants was approximately $1.78 billion. These funds are allocated on a formula basis (depending on state population, per capita income, etc.), and there is a state matching fund requirement (80 percent federal and 20 percent state except for construction of facilities).

Approximately 1 million individuals are served by state vocational rehabilitation agencies annually, and approximately 200,000 are "successfully rehabilitated."[2] The number of cases rehabilitated dropped slightly below 200,000 in 1992 (to 191,000 cases) for the first time in 25 years. Data on the characteristics of clients who were rehabilitated in fiscal year 1991 (the most recent year for which these data are available) are shown in table 1.[3] About half of all clients were between the

Table 1. Characteristics of Persons Rehabilitated in Vocational Rehabilitation, Fiscal Year 1991)

Characteristics	Total rehabilitations	
	Number	Percent
Total	202,831	100.0
Age at referral		
Number reporting	202,170	100.0
Under 18	15,214	7.5
18-24	44,137	21.8
25-44	100.982	49.9
45-64	34,612	17.1
65 and over	7,225	3.6
Sex		
Number reporting	202,640	100.0
Male	112,452	55.5
Female	90,188	44.5
Race		
Number reporting	2.2,580	100.0
White	162,602	80.3
Black	35,973	17.8
American Indian/Alaskan Natives	1,313	0.6
Asian and Pacific Islander	2,692	1.3
Hispanic origin		
Number reporting	202,591	100.0
Hispanic origin	17,057	8.4
Not of Hispanic origin	185,534	91.6
Education		
Number reporting	201,507	100.0
No grades completed	897	0.4
1-7 grades completed	7,926	3.9

(continued)

Table 1. (continued)

Characteristics	Total rehabilitations	
	Number	Percent
8-11 grades completed	45,067	22.4
12 grades completed	78,225	38.8
13 grades and over completed	37,528	18.6
Special education	31,870	15.8
Marital status		
Number reporting	201,923	100.0
Married	56,018	27.7
Widowed	7,848	3.9
Divorced	28,955	14.3
Separated	11,506	5.7
Never married	97,596	48.3
Severity of disability		
Number reporting	202,831	100.0
Severely disabled	139,794	68.9
Nonseverely disabled	63,037	31.1
Veteran status		
Number reporting	202,623	100.0
Veteran	9,445	4.7
Nonveteran	193,178	95.3
Weekly earnings at application		
Number reporting	201,887	100.0
No earnings	158,059	78.3
Less than $100	14,866	7.4
$100-$199	14,136	7.0
$200 and over	14,826	7.3

SOURCE: U.S. Department of Education (1992).
NOTE: Items may not total precisely 100 due to rounding.

ages of 25 and 44. Participants were more likely to be never-married, male, and white. In addition, the average participant was more likely to be severely disabled and to be a nonveteran. A recent analysis of the vocational rehabilitation program (U.S. General Accounting Office 1993) found that the demographic characteristics of accepted applicants are very similar to those of individuals not accepted. The study found applicants and participants more likely to be men and under the age of 45 than the eligible population as a whole.

A significant majority, about 78 percent, of rehabilitated clients had no earnings at application to the program. The program is supposed to focus on individuals with severe disabilities, and 65 percent of the individuals accepted were classified as severely disabled, as compared to 35 percent of those not accepted. The most common disabling conditions among those accepted were mental and emotional (43 percent) and orthopedic (24 percent).[4]

Table 2 shows data on the various services received during the course of their rehabilitation by clients whose cases were closed in 1988. Although the majority of participants served received diagnosis and evaluation (87 percent) and counseling and guidance (73 percent), slightly less than half (47 percent) received training of any sort. Training is broadly defined in this program and includes education; program participants are classified as receiving training if they are given academic, business, vocational, or personal and vocational adjustment training from any source as arranged for by the state agency. Some participants received more than one type of training. Services provided in 1988 did not vary by severity of the disability. The average cost of services in 1988 per participant was $1,573 (U.S. General Accounting Office 1993). In 1991, the average cost per client rehabilitated was $2,518 (U.S. Department of Education 1992).

There have been few evaluations of the impact of vocational rehabilitation on earnings and employment because it is difficult to identify an appropriate group of untreated individuals to use as a comparison group. One study (U.S. General Accounting Office 1993) found that rehabilitants with physical disabilities, emotional disabilities, and mental retardation were likely to earn $2,000, $1,600, and $1,000 more, respectively, than would dropouts from the program. In interpreting this result, it is important to keep in mind that the definition of rehabilitation includes placement in a job, so the comparison being made is not between those who receive services and those who do not receive such services. Another recent study, which was limited to Virginia, included all closed cases in the treatment group and used dropouts as the comparison group (Dean and Dolan 1991). This research found statistically significant one-year impacts for men ($910) and women ($1,632) with physical disabilities. For mental and emotionally disabled participants, the impacts were also positive but smaller in magnitude and statistically significant only for women with mental disabilities.[5]

Table 2. Percentage of 1988 Vocational Rehabilitation Clients Who Received Various Types of Services

Category of service	All VR clients	Severely disabled clients
Diagnosis and evalution	87	88
Counseling and guidance	73	75
Restoration	33	35
Transportation	27	28
Placement	22	23
Referral	21	22
Income maintenance	20	20
Adjustment training	19	23
Business or vocational training	12	12
Miscellaneous training	12	14
College or university training	11	10
On-the-job training	8	9
Other services	22	23

SOURCE: U.S. General Accounting Office (1993).
NOTE: These figures are based on cases closed in 1988.

As the General Accounting Office has pointed out, the vocational rehabilitation program clearly deserves more study. Better data are needed to determine who receives services and what the impacts of the program are on employment and earnings. Recent efforts to develop and analyze longitudinal data have improved matters somewhat, but good evaluations of the program are still few in number.

The Job Training Partnership Act Title II Programs

The Job Training Partnership Act (JTPA) authorizes the nation's major employment and training programs for individuals with specific labor market needs. JTPA was passed in 1982 to replace the Comprehensive Employment and Training Act (CETA), and the programs began operation in 1983. The specific programs established by JTPA are authorized in Titles II, III, and IV of the Act. Major provisions include training services for economically disadvantaged adults (Title II-A) and youth (Title II-C), the summer youth employment and training program (Title II-B), employment and training services for dislocated workers (Title III), employment and training programs for Native Americans and migrant and seasonal farm workers (Title IV-A), the Job Corps (Title IV-B), and veterans' employment and training programs (Title IV-C). Each of the JTPA programs has specific eligibility requirements, although an individual may qualify for more than one program. The Economic Dislocation and Worker Adjustment Assistance Act (EDWAA) of 1988 modified the JTPA Title III program substantially, and major amendments to JTPA were enacted in December 1992.[6]

The JTPA Title II program for economically disadvantaged adults and youth is operated through a partnership of federal, state, and local government with the private sector. The program is financed by the federal government, with funds distributed by formula to over 600 state and local governmental units, called service delivery areas (SDAs). Each SDA must form a private industry council (PIC) comprised of representatives of the private sector and of other governmental and nonprofit organizations. PICs may choose to run the program or to serve more as a board of directors, providing guidance. Private sector members of the PIC must constitute a majority of the membership. Major activities for participants enrolled in JTPA include the following:

- *Basic skills and remedial education.* These programs provide participants with classroom instruction in reading, arithmetic, and other academic skills. The programs are often intended to lead to a general equivalency diploma (GED) or high school diploma.

- *On-the-job training (OJT)*. Work opportunities with individual employers are offered in OJT programs. The employer typically receives a reimbursement of 50 percent of wages paid to the participant for up to six months to cover the cost of formal and informal training.
- *Work experience.* Work experience programs provide paid employment for participants with government or nonprofit agencies and organizations. Participants are generally paid the minimum wage. The intent of the program is for the individuals to gain experience that will help them qualify for an unsubsidized job.
- *Job search assistance*. Participants are helped to improve their job search methods and skills.

The amount of work experience that can be provided is limited by provisions governing the use of funds, and the 1992 amendments to JTPA restricted the use of job search assistance provided without training and placed constraints on the use of OJT, particularly for youth. In program year 1993, the most common activities for adults were classroom training (46 percent), job search assistance (19 percent), and on-the-job training (18 percent), as reported by Stanley (1995). In 1993, the average length of stay for adults was about four months, and the average cost per terminated participant was about $3,300.

JTPA programs have several features that encourage the state and local governmental units that receive funding to serve people with disabilities, but the programs are generally targeted to needy groups, and people with disabilities must often compete with other disadvantaged individuals for scarce program resources. The original legislation defines a handicapped individual as "any individual who has a physical or mental disability which for such individual constitutes or results in a substantial handicap to employment." The December 1992 amendments replaced the term "handicapped individual" with the term "individual with a disability" but otherwise left the definition unchanged. Beginning in program year 1992 (the 12-month period beginning July 1, 1992), however, programs were required to report individuals with a disability using the following definition based on the Americans with Disabilities Act (ADA).

Any individual who has a physical (motion, vision, hearing) or mental (learning or developmental) impairment which substantially limits one or more of such person's life activities and has a record of such an impairment, or is regarded as having such an impairment. Record the code as follows:

1 – Yes, individual has such an impairment that *does* result in a substantial barrier to employment;

2 – Yes, individual has such an impairment that *does not* result in a substantial barrier to employment;

3 – No, individual has no disability (U.S. Department of Labor 1994).

The reporting instructions state that a response of 1 to the revised definition is the same as the definition used in prior years, although these do not appear to be equivalent. While the revised version is to be used for reporting characteristics, this definition differs from the statutory definition, which is to be used for determining eligibility.

The JTPA Title II programs have enrolled a significant number of people with disabilities. Comparisons over time are difficult because of the change in the definition for reporting purposes as of program year 1992. Between program years 1989 and 1991, the total number of individuals terminated from Title II-A programs dropped substantially, from 613,200 to 481,600, and although the proportion of these individuals with disabilities increased from 12.9 percent to 14.2 percent, their absolute numbers declined from 79,000 in program year 1989 to 68,200 in program year 1991 (U.S. Department of Labor 1992 and 1993a). Data for program year 1993 indicate that 10.6 percent of adults terminated and 19.8 percent of the youth terminated had disabilities.

Table 3 shows the characteristics and outcomes for individuals terminated from Title II-A programs. The information is for program year 1991, the latest for which data are currently available. There are some notable differences between the characteristics of disabled and nondisabled persons, but the outcomes are only slightly worse for those with disabilities. Relative to nondisabled Title II-A participants, those with disabilities were more likely to be men (58 percent compared to 42 percent), white non-Hispanic (70 percent compared to 47 percent), young (42 percent under age 19 compared to 26 percent), not on Aid to Families with Dependent Children (AFDC) or other welfare (9 percent on AFDC compared to 30 percent), and a high school student (41 percent compared to 18 percent). Individuals with disabilities were just as likely to be economically disadvantaged as those without disabilities (92 percent compared to 93 percent).

Table 3. Comparison of Characteristics of Participants Terminated with and without Disabilities in JTPA Title II Programs during Program Year 1991 (July 1991-June 1992)

Selected characteristics and outcomes	People with disabilities (percent)	People without disabilities (percent)
Sex		
Male	58	42
Female	42	58
Minority status		
White excluding Hispanic	70	47
Black excluding Hispanic	20	36
Hispanic	7	13
Other	3	4
Age at enrollment		
Younger than 19	42	26
19-21	12	16
22-54	43	54
55 and older	4	5
Economically disadvantaged	92	93
Receiving AFDC	9	30
Receiving any public assistance	30	53
Unemployment compensation claimant	4	7
Education status		
School dropout	17	30
Student (high school or less)	41	18
High school graduate	42	53

Table 3. (continued)

Selected characteristics and outcomes	People with disabilities (percent)	People without disabilities (percent)
Program activity		
Classroom training	39	45
On-the-job training	9	15
Job search assistance	15	15
Work experience	7	6
Other services	29	19
Median length of stay (days)	150.4	136.5
Average entered employment rate by type of service received		
Overall	49	50
Classroom training	36	43
On-the-job training	78	73
Job search assistance	72	65
Work experience	43	41
Other services	46	41
Average hourly wage at termination by type of service received		
Overall	$5.44	$5.82
Classroom training	$5.98	$6.08
On-the-job training	$5.32	$5.76
Job search assistance	$5.52	$5.78
Work experience	$4.96	$5.07
Other services	$4.99	$5.55

SOURCE: U.S. Department of Labor (1993a).

Participants with disabilities received a slightly different mix of services than did other participants. The proportions acquiring classroom training and on-the-job training were lower (39 percent compared to 45 percent and 9 percent compared to 15 percent, respectively), and more participants with disabilities received "other services" (29 percent compared to 19 percent). Participants with disabilities remained in the program about two weeks longer than other participants (150.4 days compared to 136.5 days). In terms of outcomes, the proportions entering employment at termination were virtually identical (49 percent for participants with disabilities compared to 50 percent for those without disabilities), and the hourly wage rate for those obtaining employment was somewhat lower for participants with disabilities ($5.44 per hour compared to $5.82).

Thus, in spite of the potential problems with the performance standards system (described below), JTPA Title II programs have been able to attract a reasonable number of participants with disabilities, and the outcomes have been close to those achieved for participants without disabilities. This relative success does not mean that improvements could not be made. It is possible that the favorable results ensue from creaming among the population with disabilities. Thus, additional incentives in the performance standards system may still be warranted, and SDAs should consider negotiating with the governor to obtain lower standards if enrolling severely disabled individuals is being considered.

The Department of Labor recently funded a controlled experiment to determine the effectiveness of JTPA Title II-A programs (Orr et al. 1994). The evaluation took place in 16 sites throughout the country, and the treatment and control groups were followed for 30 months after random assignment. In-school youth were excluded from the experiment. Major findings, as reported by Orr et al. (1994) and Stanley (1995) are as follows:

- For youth, the evaluation found no significant impact on earnings during the 30 months after random assignment. Estimates of the impact on earnings were positive but not statistically significant for young women and were negative and not significant for young men.

- The program increased earnings for both adult men and adult women participants. During the second post-program year, both men and women experienced gains of about $900 in 1993 dollars over the control groups. These gains represented a 15 percent differential for women and a 10 percent differential for men.

- The earnings gap between the experimental and control groups widened over the post-program period, especially for men. Subsequent analyses may lead to larger impacts of the program.

- The impacts were generally greatest for participants assigned to receive OJT and/or job search assistance, and the impact for vocational classroom training was always positive (but not always statistically significant for subgroups).

At this time, the future of JTPA is very uncertain. A number of proposals have been made to modify the nation's employment and training system. Options being considered include abolishing the programs entirely and providing the eligible population with vouchers, and providing employment and training block grants to states.

There are several special features of JTPA that either encourage local SDAs to enroll people with disabilities or make it easier for people with disabilities to meet the entry requirements. While these features are likely to have increased enrollment of people with disabilities in the programs, it is impossible to gauge how large the impact has been.

Special Definition of Family for People with Disabilities

The Title II JTPA programs have strict targeting requirements. At least 90 percent of the participants must be economically disadvantaged, and a maximum of 10 percent may have some other barrier to employment.[7] Individuals with disabilities are permitted to have only their personal income considered in determining eligibility rather than having the entire family's income counted. This provision permits an individual with disabilities to qualify even if his or her parents or spouse earns enough to exceed the income limits. Estimates are not available on the number of additional individuals with disabilities who are eligible because of this provision.

Requirement for Enrollment of the Hard to Serve

The December 1992 amendments to JTPA added requirements that at least 65 percent of both Title II-A adult and Title II-C youth participants fall into a category of "hard to serve." In addition, the Secretary of Labor is required to establish performance standards and a reward structure for SDAs that exceed the 65 percent requirement. Section 203 defines the term hard to serve for adults to include the following categories:

- individuals who are basic skills deficient,
- individuals who are school dropouts,
- recipients of cash welfare programs, including AFDC), Supplemental Security Income (SSI), and general assistance,
- offenders,
- individuals with disabilities,
- homeless individuals, and
- individuals in another category approved by the governor but not to include "poor work history" or "unemployed."

For youth, the disabilities category is expanded to include learning disabilities, and the welfare recipient category is omitted; categories added are pregnant or parenting individuals, runaways, and persons with educational attainment at least one grade level below what is appropriate.

Although the hard-to-serve requirements could, in theory, increase enrollments of individuals with disabilities, it is unlikely that these provisions will have much impact. The Department of Labor has chosen to implement the performance standards by making achievement of the required enrollment of hard-to-serve individuals a "gate" that must be passed to receive any other incentive funds; however, no incentive funds are received simply for meeting or exceeding the hard-to-serve participation requirements. A series of group discussions was held at three regional conferences in the spring of 1994 for an evaluation of the impact of the 1992 amendments. At the meetings, representatives of most SDAs indicated that they were already fulfilling the hard-to-serve requirements, and so they would not have to change their enrollment behavior as a result of the amendments. Representatives of some SDAs stated that they have selected food stamp recipients as their additional target group, and because the eligibility requirements are relatively broad for the food stamp program, such SDAs would have little trouble satisfying the 65 percent requirement. Thus, the hard-to-serve stipulations are likely to have little, if any, impact on enrollment of people with disabilities (or of other hard-to-serve groups, for that matter): most SDAs already meet the requirement and the additional category provides SDAs with sufficient flexibility to satisfy the rules without serving other groups.

Performance Standards Adjustments

The JTPA Title II programs include a performance management system in which SDAs are held accountable for meeting goals. The basic parameters of the system are established at the national level, but governors have a significant amount of latitude to change the level of expected performance to meet their own criteria, to add additional evaluation measures, and to decide how the various standards will be aggregated to assess total outcomes. SDAs that exceed expected results receive additional funding; SDAs that fall short receive technical assistance, and, if performance remains poor for two consecutive years, they are reorganized.

There are currently four core performance standards for adults served under Title II-A of JTPA and two standards for youth served under Title II-C:

- the adult follow-up employment rate, defined as the total number of adult terminees who were employed at least 20 hours per week during the 13th week after termination, divided by the total number of adult terminees;
- adult follow-up weekly earnings, defined as total weekly earnings for all adults who were employed for at least 20 hours per week during the 13th week after termination, divided by the total number of adults employed at follow-up;
- the welfare adult follow-up employment rate, defined for adult welfare recipients in the same manner as for all adults;
- welfare follow-up weekly earnings defined for adult welfare recipients in the same manner as for all adults;
- the youth entered employment rate, defined as the total number of youth who, at termination entered employment with at least 20 hours per week, divided by the total number of youth who terminated (other than potential dropouts who remained in school); and

- the youth employability enhancement rate, defined as the total number of youth terminating from the program who obtained one of the employability enhancements at termination, divided by the total number of youth who terminated.[8]

Satisfactory performance on each of the measures is adjusted to take account of the characteristics of participants served and local economic conditions. The adjustments are determined through regression analysis based on data submitted by SDAs in previous years. Linear regression models are used to determine which participant and local economic variables have a statistically significant impact on the performance measures.[9] Variables with insignificant coefficients or coefficients with what appears to be the "wrong" sign are omitted from the adjustment equation. Note, for example, that percentage Hispanic does not appear as an adjustment for the adult follow-up employment rate, so SDAs receive no adjustment in expected performance for serving more Hispanics. The constants in the equations are set so that approximately 75 percent of all SDAs will exceed the standards, but governors may vary the constant to take account of conditions in their states.

Adjustment models for program year 1994 (July 1, 1994 through June 30, 1995) have recently been released. Table 4 shows the adjustments in program year 1994 for the percentage of participants with disabilities and for three other characteristics that apply to the six core performance measures. The two measures with adjustments of zero (the two welfare measures) make no modification in expected performance for serving individuals with disabilities, i.e., SDAs are expected to achieve as well on these measures for people with disabilities as they do for other participants. To interpret the adjustments, consider the following example for the adult follow-up employment rate. The percentage of participants with a disability coefficient of −.090 means that, if the share of participants who have a disability is increased by one percentage point (such as from 10 percent to 11 percent), then the acceptable level of performance on the measure is decreased by.09 percentage points. The adjustments in the standards for the adult follow-up employment rate and adult follow-up weekly earnings are greater for serving people with disabilities than are the adjustments for dropouts, blacks, and females; however, the adjustments for welfare adults with disabilities on follow-up employment and earnings are zero and are, therefore, smaller than the adjustments for the other three categories.

Table 4. Performance Standards Adjustments in Program Year 1994 (July 1994-June 1995) for Title II-A Core Standards for Persons with Disabilities and Selected Other Groups

Performance measure	Population characteristics			
	Disability	Dropout	Black	Female
		(percent)		
Adult follow-up employment rate	-.090	-.084	-.086	-.056
Adult follow-up weekly earnings	-.558	-.276	-.325	-.443
Adult welfare follow-up employment rate	0	-.062	-.048	-.144
Adult welfare follow-up weekly earnings	0	-.274	-.340	-.642
Youth entered employment rate	-.047	-.162	-.090	-.061
Youth employability enhancement rate	-.047	0	-.059	0

SOURCE: Social Policy Research Associates (1994).

Although the adjustment procedures provide some stimuli to serve people with disabilities, the incentives do not appear especially strong and suffer from several shortcomings. To see the size of the incentives, consider an SDA that initially has all factors in the adjustment model at the national average and has the option of doubling the percentage of people with disabilities it serves, from 10.6 percent to 21.2 percent. For an SDA with average values of all factors in the adjustment model, the standard for the follow-up employment rate would be 59.0 percent (based on the Department of Labor worksheet). If the SDA doubled its proportion of people with disabilities to 21.2 percent, the follow-up employment rate standard would drop by .95 percentage points (10.6 x .09 = .95) to 58.05 percent. Thus, although an SDA receives a reduction in its level of required performance for serving additional people with disabilities, the magnitude of the incentive is probably too small to have much impact. The result is also quite small when the same exercise is performed for follow-up weekly earnings: the standard for follow-up weekly earnings for an SDA with average factor values would drop from \$245 to \$236 if the proportion of participants with disabilities doubled from 10.6 percent to 21.2 percent. In the case of adult welfare recipients, an increase in the proportion of participants with disabilities would have *no* impact on minimum acceptable performance.

Another shortcoming of the adjustment procedure is that it treats all disabilities alike. An SDA receives the same adjustment for serving a person with a minor or a major disability. SDAs who wish to maximize measured performance avoid serving people with major disabilities and concentrate on people with minor disabilities.[10] Under the current performance management structure, it is impossible to overcome this problem because there are too few participants with disabilities to be disaggregated into finer categories for the regression analysis used to determine the adjustments.

Note that even if the adjustment procedure worked as intended, it would provide no incentive to serve people with disabilities. As explained in the latest technical assistance guide (Social Policy Research Associates 1994, p. III-1), "Performance standards are adjusted to 'level the playing field' by making the standards neutral with respect to who is served and to local economic conditions." Thus the current system is not intended to provide net incentives to serve people with disabilities; if the Department of Labor wished to provide such motivation, the adjustments would have to do more than level the playing field.

Another problem with the current approach to adjusting performance is that, because the percentage of participants with disabilities is relatively small, the regression coefficients are probably unstable, particularly for the adult welfare group, which is likely to include very few people. The small proportion of welfare recipients with disabilities probably results in a failure to find an appropriate adjustment for adults on welfare. Unfortunately, under the current approach, SDAs receive no modification in their expected performance for adults on welfare for serving recipients with disabilities. Although the program year 1994 adjustment models for youth included a factor for the proportion of participants with disabilities, the 1993 models included no such adjustment. It is unlikely that the reason for the change in the status of the variable is in any way related to changes in the efficacy of the programs for people with disabilities; instead the change probably stems from the instability of the regression coefficients estimated.

Finally, by estimating the adjustment models on participant data rather than on the unserved eligible population, the current approach may create several problems. First, if the SDAs do tend to cream among the disabled, the adjustments produced by the regressions will apply to the "more advantaged" population already served and may not provide enough incentive for those with more severe disabilities to be served. In addition, by estimating the relationships on the basis of participant data, the coefficients derived combine training impacts with labor market differences that would have resulted in the absence of the program.[11]

In sum, the performance management system in JTPA has mixed effects in its incentives to serve people with disabilities. If there were no performance management system, SDA administrators would not consider creaming as a means of assuring that they have high measured performance. The performance management system includes adjustments for serving groups with various outcomes, but the adjustments for serving people with disabilities do not take account of the degree of disability; the effects are sometimes impossible to measure, resulting in no adjustment; and the adjustments are based on the population currently served rather than on the population interested in participating. Although the current regression-based system has an objectivity that has helped make it credible with the SDA administrators, it may not provide them with strong enough incentives to enroll people with disabilities in adequate numbers. The Department of Labor should seriously consider the possibility of modifying the adjustments to achieve greater enrollment of groups of interest.[12] Although regression modeling provides a useful starting point for adjustments and was very helpful in getting SDAs to accept the performance management system, the Department of Labor should now determine whether the current procedures do an adequate job of promoting its policies. In situations where the regression model for the current year produces coefficients that are judged inappropriate for inclusion, the Department of Labor could use estimates from previous years, pool data from several years, or use results obtained from another group. This would avoid having no adjustment for adult welfare follow-up employment and earnings in program year 1994. In addition, the Department of Labor should reconsider whether it wants simply to "level the playing field" or to provide actual incentives to serve people with disabilities and other groups with high needs.

Vocational Education

Vocational education programs provide students at the secondary and postsecondary levels with training that will enable them to pursue employment in a broad range of occupations. Federal support for vocational education is authorized under the Perkins Act, which defines vocational education as follows:

> Vocational education means organized educational programs which are directly related to the preparation of individuals for paid or unpaid employment, in such fields as agriculture, business occupations, home economics, health occupations, marketing and distributive occupations, technical and emerging occupations, modern industrial and agricultural arts, and trades and industrial occupations, or for additional preparation for a career in those fields, and in other occupations requiring other than a baccalaureate or advanced degree (P.L. 98-527).

There is little, if any, distinction between vocational education and training provided under JTPA and other programs, so it is appropriate to treat vocational education as a training program for this study.

Vocational education is primarily funded by the states rather than by the federal government, but federal support is currently $1.178 billion annually (Apling and Irwin 1994).[13] Most of that money is distributed to states by a formula based on population and per-capita income. States are required to distribute 75 percent of their federal funds to local areas using a formula based on proxy measures of poverty. States have discretion to allocate the funds between the secondary and postsecondary levels. Most states spend a majority of the funds on secondary education; in fiscal year 1993, with 44 states reporting, 62.2 percent of federal funds were used at the secondary level, with the percentage varying from 8.6 percent up to 91.9 percent (U.S. Department of Education 1994). In the discussion that follows, attention is restricted to postsecondary vocational education.[14]

About two-thirds (65.7 percent) of individuals enrolled in postsecondary vocational programs in the 1989-1990 school year were in public community colleges, and 22.5 percent were in proprietary schools (Tuma 1993). The remaining students were enrolled in public vocational-technical schools (3.7 percent), private junior colleges (2.9 percent), public four-year colleges (3.2 percent), and private four-year colleges (1.9 percent).

Analysis of the National Postsecondary Student Aid Survey (NPSAS) indicates that many people with disabilities participate in postsecondary vocational education. Of the 5.76 million students enrolled in vocational programs in the 1989-1990 school year, about 12.7 percent, or 732,000, had a physical or learning disability,[15] The proportion of students with disabilities was greater in vocational curricula than in academic two-year programs (11.9 percent) and four-year degree programs (7.6 percent).

The literature concerning the impact of postsecondary vocational education on earnings is somewhat inconsistent. One review of the literature concludes that each additional year of education beyond high school, academic or vocational, increases earnings by 5 to 10 percent even if a degree or other credential is not obtained (Stanley 1995). Another survey of the literature is much more cautious and concludes that analysis of the returns to higher education is hampered by a lack of recent, high-quality data and by methodological problems (U.S. Department of Education 1994).

Several approaches have been included in the Perkins legislation to encourage states and local school districts to adequately enroll and serve individuals with disabilities. Prior to 1990, 10 percent of the federal funds were earmarked for services to participants with disabilities. The 1990 legislation eliminated the set-aside but gave states and local districts increased responsibilities such as

- obtaining input from state personnel responsible for programs for students with disabilities,

- adjusting performance standards and measures "to encourage service to targeted groups or special populations,"

- assuring that the state will monitor the degree to which the needs of special students are met, and

• assuring that the state will guarantee equal access to quality vocational education programs for special population students and establish procedures for community input at the state and local levels (U.S. Department of Education 1994).

The National Assessment of Vocational Education conducted a survey to determine if the elimination of the set-aside resulted in reduced services for disabled students and concluded that "elimination of the set-aside funds did not lead to a reduction in services [to students with disabilities] among postsecondary institutions" (U.S. Department of Education 1994). The use of adjustments to performance standards to reflect the proportion of students with disabilities was completed or in process in 45 percent of the states by the 1992-1993 school year (U.S. Department of Education 1994). It is likely that states are moving slowly in this area because they are reluctant to express a willingness to accept lower performance for special populations than for the regular population.

Postsecondary vocational education is a major source of training for people with disabilities. The recent National Assessment of Vocational Education has indicated that alternatives to set-asides can result in maintaining the enrollment level of individuals with disabilities. An important issue for further exploration is what is and should be the respective roles of vocational rehabilitation and vocational education. Is there a need for separate programs, and if so, what should the responsibilities of each program be? In addition, estimates should be made of the impact of vocational education on the employment and earnings of the population with disabilities.

The Employment Service

The U.S. Employment Service (or job service, as it is sometimes known) is a federal-state partnership providing labor exchange and related services and activities to U.S. workers and firms. The employment service is one of the nation's oldest employment and training programs, dating back to the Wagner-Peyser Act of 1933. The program is funded through the federal unemployment insurance tax on employers, with the money channeled back to state employment service agencies.

In this section, the provision of basic labor exchange activities for persons with disabilities is discussed, along with the targeted jobs tax credit (TJTC), which was administered by the employment service. The treatment of disabilities in the testing program is also briefly reviewed.

Although the employment service is intended to assist to all segments of the labor force, special provisions apply to individuals with disabilities.[16] When the Job Training Partnership Act of 1982 amended the Wagner-Peyser Act, people with disabilities were the only population group for whom states were required to include provisions in their annual plans. Section 8(d) of the Wagner-Peyser Act indicates the following:

> Such (annual state) plans shall include provision for the promotion and development of employment opportunities for handicapped persons and for job counseling and placement of such persons, and for the designation of at least one person in each State or Federal Employment office, whose duties shall include the effectuation of such purposes.

Each October, the Employment Service observes National Disability Employment Awareness Month. During October, special promotional kits prepared by the President's Committee on Employment of People with Disabilities are distributed to state employment service agencies. The kits are intended to assist the state agencies in observing the program and in advancing opportunities for people with disabilities.

The most recent data on characteristics of applicants and the services provided to them are for program year 1992 (July 1992 through June 1993), and highlights are presented in table 5. People with disabilities made up a very small proportion of all applicants: only 529,000 out of 21.346 million applicants, or 2.5 percent, as of program year 1992. This is somewhat less than one would expect based on their share of the labor force.[17] Relative to all applicants, those with disabilities were more likely to have been males (72.4 percent compared to 58.3 percent), over age 44 (31.1 percent compared to 19.1 percent), and economically disadvantaged (25.7 percent compared to 15.8 percent). Surprisingly, the percentage on welfare was about the same for the two groups (5.9 percent for applicants with disabilities and 5.6 percent for those without disabilities).

Table 5. Characteristics and Activities of Employment Service Applicants, Program Year 1992 (July 1992-June 1993)

Characteristics and activities	All applicants	People with disabilities
Total active applicants	21,346,000	529,000
	(Percent)	
Male	58.3	72.4
Female	41.7	27.6
Age		
Under 22	15.5	7.8
22-44	65.3	61.2
45-54	12.0	19.8
55 and over	7.1	11.3
Economically disadvantaaged	15.8	25.7
Welfare recipient	5.6	5.9
Services received		
Assessment	8.8	17.2
Testing	2.4	3.6
Job search activities	15.2	23.8
Referral to employment	37.3	42.5
Placement	12.6	14.4

SOURCE: Data provided by the U.S. Department of Labor, United States Employment Service, October 1994.

Employment service applicants with disabilities were more likely to have received services and obtained a job than other applicants. Assessment was provided to 17.2 percent of applicants with disabilities but to only 8.8 percent of all applicants. A slightly higher percentage of applicants with disabilities were tested (3.6 percent of applicants with disabilities and 2.4 percent of all applicants), but this result must be interpreted with caution as testing is inappropriate for some people with disabilities. Individuals with disabilities were also more likely to have had job search activities (23.8 percent compared to 15.2 percent for all applicants) and to have been referred for a job (42.5 percent compared to 37.3 percent). Finally, and perhaps most importantly, applicants with disabilities were slightly more likely to have been placed in a job (14.4 percent compared to 12.6 percent). Thus, individuals with disabilities have done quite well relative to people with no disabilities in terms of the labor services provided to them and the results achieved. The only area that may be of concern is that the proportion of people with disabilities using the employment service has been lower than one would anticipate.

TJTC was enacted in 1978 to provide incentives for firms to hire workers with selected characteristics. The program has been controversial throughout its life, and it has been scheduled for termination numerous times. The program expired December 31, 1994, but some parties have expressed interest in reviving the program. Many of the provisions that have generated disputes about TJTC were either corrected or did not apply to workers with disabilities. In previous years, for example, firms were able to receive retroactive certifications for hiring members of the target groups, and young workers with no special barriers to employment were eligible if they were in a cooperative education program.

Evaluations of the program indicate that it may have had a small positive effect on employment of economically disadvantaged youth, but the results are not robust, and research on the impact of the program on people with disabilities has not been conducted.[18] In addition, one study found that advising employers of one's eligibility through participation in a welfare program actually hurt job prospects; because disabilities are more difficult to conceal, it is unlikely that this effect would pertain to people with disabilities (Burtless 1985).

Eligible individuals could obtain vouchers from the employment service indicating that they qualified for the credit. An employer was required to request certification when or before the employee began work. If the job applicant had a voucher, the employer had five days to request certification. For individuals without vouchers, the employer was required to certify to the employment service that a good faith effort was made to determine eligibility.

The tax credit for most groups was 40 percent of the first $6,000 in qualified wages, with a maximum credit of $2,400. Employers claiming the credit reduced their tax deduction for wages by the amount of the credit. The Committee on Ways and Means (U.S. Congress 1994, p. 709) notes that the effective subsidy was about 18 percent for a full-time employee hired at the minimum wage by an employer in the 35 percent tax bracket.

In its final form, TJTC applied to nine groups:

- people with disabilities who have been referred to an employer from the vocational rehabilitation program of either a state or the U.S. Department of Veterans Affairs;

- recipients of federal SSI, the welfare program for poor individuals and couples who are aged, blind, or disabled;

- youth aged 16 to 19 who are from economically disadvantaged families and who participate in a qualified cooperative education program;

- economically disadvantaged Vietnam-era veterans;

- recipients of state or local general assistance payments for at least 30 days;

- youth aged 18 to 22 from economically disadvantaged families;

- economically disadvantaged ex-convicts who are hired no later than five years after the earlier of release from prison or the date of conviction;

- recipients of AFDC who have received assistance for at least 90 days prior to being hired; and

- economically disadvantaged youth aged 16-17 when hired for a summer job, if they have not previously worked for the same employer.

Although people with disabilities could have been in any of the nine categories, they were most likely to be in the first two. In program year 1991, 500,000 certifications were issued (Landini 1995). The most recent year for which the distribution of certifications by eligibility category is available is calendar year 1989. In that year, 9.0 percent of the certifications were for vocational rehabilitation referrals and 1.6 percent were for supplemental security income recipients. If those proportions remained the same, slightly over 50,000 certifications were issued per year for people with disabilities. (Of all certifications, economically disadvantaged youth 18 to 22 years old and AFDC recipients were the two largest groups, constituting about three-quarters of the total.) Although TJTC may have certified a significant number of individuals with disabilities, the lack of any evidence showing that the program increased employment or earnings for those certified makes it likely that the program's expiration has not produced much harm for the U.S. population with disabilities.

As part of its procedure of matching job applicants and employers, the Employment Service has long used aptitude tests, particularly the General Aptitude Test Battery (GATB). In the 1970s and 1980s, the testing program became increasingly controversial, primarily for reasons unrelated to disabilities. Issues of importance included the question of whether test scores could be generalized and applied to most or all occupations (validity generalization or VG) and how differences in mean scores across demographic groups should be handled in scoring the GATB and reporting results to employers (group norming). In addition, the test was nearly 45 years old, and there was concern about how well it was holding up in predicting job success.

To deal with these and other concerns, including the applicability of tests such as the GATB for people with disabilities, the Department of Labor provided funds to the National Research Council to investigate matters related to fairness in employment testing. Although most of the resulting report deals with other topics, the National Research Council Committee has several recommendations regarding employment testing for people with disabilities:

- For applicants with handicapping conditions, we recommend the continued use of job counselors to make referrals.

- Measures should be taken to ensure that no job order is filled automatically and solely through the VG-GATB system. Job counselors who serve handicapped applicants, disabled veterans, or other populations with special needs must have regular access to the daily flow of job orders.

- To ensure that handicapped applicants who can compete with tested applicants are given that opportunity, the GATB should be

used when feasible to assess the abilities of handicapped applicants. But the test should be used to supplement decision making,
not to take the place of counseling services.

• Because special expertise in assessing the capabilities of people
  with handicaps is necessary and available, we recommend that the
  Department of Labor encourage closer coordination between state
  rehabilitation agencies and State Employment Service Agencies.
  States should consider placing their rehabilitation counselors in
  local employment service offices that serve a sizable population of
  handicapped people (Hartigan and Wigdor 1989).

As a result of the National Research Council study, the employment
service has undertaken a major psychometric research agenda to adapt
its testing procedures to meet the needs of employers and applicants
without discriminating against particular groups. Results of these studies are now becoming available. The interim policy is to recognize that
tests can be useful, but no referral can rest solely on test scores. As
noted, testing currently involves only a small proportion of applicants,
but the percentage is slightly higher for those with disabilities.

Employment of Workers with Disabilities under Special Certificates

Since 1938, the Fair Labor Standards Act (Section 14[c]) has permitted employers meeting certain requirements and obtaining special
certificates to pay workers with disabilities less than the minimum
wage.[19] The term "worker with a disability" is defined for this law as
"an individual whose earning or productive capacity is impaired by a
physical or mental disability, including those related to age or injury,
for the work to be performed." Employers who wish to make use of
this provision must obtain a certificate from the Wage and Hour Division of the Department of Labor's Employment Standards Administration.

The covered employee is to be paid a "commensurate wage," which
is defined as the prevailing wage for the work adjusted for the productivity of the person with the disability relative to the typical worker in

the area. Thus, if the prevailing wage for a given job is $5.00 per hour and a disabled worker is 80 percent as productive as a typical worker, the disabled individual could be paid .80 x $5.00 = $4.00 per hour, which is less than the regular minimum wage, provided that the employer obtains the certificate.

An employer who wishes to operate such a program must calculate both the prevailing wage rate and the relative productivity of the workers. Because worker productivity varies, employers are responsible for measuring the productivity of each person employed under the program to assure that the individual is not paid less than the commensurate wage. Workers must be reviewed at least once every six months to reassess their commensurate wage. Because of the computations that must be conducted and employer fear of violating discrimination law, particularly the ADA, most affected individuals are employed by sheltered workshops that exclusively hire workers with disabilities, and few such workers are hired by regular firms. A Department of Labor official has estimated that approximately 7,000 employers have certificates and that about 200,000 workers are employed under the program. It is believed that the majority of those working under the program have mental retardation as their disability. In carrying out investigations, the Wage and Hour Division has found that employers sometimes underestimate the productivity of their workers with disabilities.

Although the special certificate program affects a large number of people with disabilities, the Department of Labor has not evaluated the program in over 20 years, due to a shortage of resources. The net impact of the program on job creation and whether the program could or should be expanded are of particular interest. Especially worth exploring is the potential for expanding the use of the program by regular employers.

Conclusions

A number of federal employment and training programs are available for people with disabilities. In reviewing the variety of programs that serve this population, is that there does not appear to be a comprehensive plan for assessing these individuals' employment and training needs or for developing a comprehensive service strategy. Many of the programs use different definitions of disabilities, and programs often appear disconnected from others in the same cabinet department and linked even less with programs and agencies in other departments. A comprehensive review of all the major employment and training programs for people with disabilities is overdue. Among the questions that need to be answered are the following:

- What are the unique responsibilities of each program in serving individuals with disabilities?

- When (if ever) is it appropriate to serve individuals with disabilities in special programs such as vocational rehabilitation, and when is it better to serve them in general programs such as vocational education and JTPA?

- How can the coordination of programs be encouraged, so that duplication of effort is avoided and so that people with disabilities are served most effectively?

- What are appropriate levels of service to individuals with disabilities in each of the programs? What is the appropriate level of service overall?

- If some programs are not serving appropriate numbers of people with disabilities, what incentives or requirements should there be for them to meet these goals?

It is apparent that all of the major employment and training programs have an interest in serving individuals with disabilities. Unfortunately, the lack of a single lead agency has led to decentralized, uncoordinated efforts with inconsistent and incomplete data, and one cannot judge whether the resources provided are adequate or if the mix of programs and services is appropriate.

NOTES

1. The paper also does not cover the Dictionary of Occupational Titles (DOT) program. To the extent that the DOT (or its successor) indicates essential functions of occupations, the DOT may be important in interpreting provisions of the Americans with Disabilities Act. The DOT is in the midst of a major revision, and Department of Labor staff have indicated that they are aware of the issues, but the DOT revision project is at too early a stage for any findings to have been reported.

2. Closures from the active caseload are classified as rehabilitated if the individuals have (1) been declared eligible for services, (2) received appropriate diagnostic and related services, (3)

had a program for vocational rehabilitation services formulated, (4) completed the program, (5) been provided counseling, and (6) been determined to be suitably employed for a minimum of 60 days.

3. Note that since these data only apply to cases that were closed with rehabilitation during fiscal year 1991, they may not exactly reflect the total population of individuals being served by the program.

4. Figures in this paragraph are for individuals accepted into the program in 1988 (U.S. General Accounting Office 1993). Data on cases rehabilitated in 1991 (U.S. Department of Education 1992) provide similar but not identical findings.

5. Dean and Dolan note that the use of dropouts as a comparison group is not ideal, but they argue that dropouts are the best available group for the analysis.

6. The Title III program for dislocated workers serves very few people with disabilities and is not discussed further in this paper. In program year 1990, for example, only 2 to 3 percent of individuals terminated, depending on the source, were reported as having disabilities.

7. Economically disadvantaged is defined in Section 4 of JTPA as an individual who is a member of a family that receives cash welfare payments under a federal, state, or local welfare program, is a member of a family receiving total family income for the six months prior to application that is less than either the poverty level or 70 percent of the lower living standard income level, is receiving or is eligible to receive food stamps, qualifies as a homeless individual under the McKinney Act, or is a foster child on whose behalf state or local payments are made.

8. Youth employability enhancements include attaining two or more PIC-recognized youth employment competencies, completing a major level of education following participation of at least 90 days or 200 hours in the program, and entering and remaining at least 90 days or 200 hours in non-Title II training or receiving a certificate of occupational skill attainment.

9. Governors are not required to use the Department of Labor's adjustment models, but virtually all states now do. In the early years of the program, many states used the Secretary's standards without adjusting for participant characteristics and local economic conditions.

10. This "creaming" problem is not unique to people with disabilities, and, as noted, Congress amended JTPA in 1992 to require SDAs to assure that at least 65 percent of participants fall into a category of "hard to serve."

11. See Barnow 1994. Barnow demonstrates that, if the goal of the performance management system is to maximize total impact on the performance measures, then the current system leads to disincentives to serve members of groups for whom the program is most effective.

12. This point applies to any hard-to-serve group. See Barnow and Constantine (1980).

13. It is widely believed that federal monies account for 8 to 10 percent of funding for vocational education, but accurate estimates are unavailable.

14. The Perkins Act also supports several "special" and "national" programs. In fiscal year 1995, funded programs include vocational education provided by community-based organizations, tech-prep education, consumer and homemaking education, and tribally controlled postsecondary vocational institutions (Apling and Irwin 1994).

15. Figures in this section were estimated by the author based on data from NPSAS (Tuma 1993).

16. The Disabled Veterans' Outreach Program (DVOP) is administered through the Office of the Assistant Secretary for Veterans' Employment and Training. DVOP funds about 1,880 specialists who provide outreach, job development, and placement services to veterans with disabilities. About three-quarters of the DVOP staff are located in local employment service offices.

17. One must be cautious in making comparisons because of variation in the definitions used, but people with disabilities comprise about 4.2 percent of the labor force. In 1993, there were 5.4 million people with disabilities out of a total of 128 million people in the adult labor force.

Because the unemployment rate for individuals with disabilities is about twice as high as for those without work disabilities, one would expect the former to show greater use of the employment service. See LaPlante, et al. 1996).

18. For a brief review of some of the literature on TJTC, see Ehrenberg and Smith (1994).

19. This section is based on a telephone interview with Mr. Howard B. Ostmann of the Employment Standards Administration and on Title 29, Part 25, of the Code of Federal Regulations.

References

Apling, Richard N., and Paul M. Irwin, 1994. "Carl D. Perkins Vocational and Applied Technology Act: Reauthorization and Overview." Washington, DC: Congressional Research Service, May 17.

Barnow, Burt S. 1994. "Design Report for Analysis of Performance Management and Program Impact." Unpublished manuscript, November 4.

Barnow, Burt S., and Jill Constantine, 1989. "Performance Management and Services to Hard-to-Serve Individuals in JTPA: The Issues Involved and Some Suggested Approaches." National Commission for Employment Policy Research Report.

Burtless, Gary, 1985, "Are Targeted Wage Subsidies Harmful? Evidence from a Wage Voucher Experiment," *Industrial and Labor Relations Review* (October): 105-114.

Dean, David H., and Robert C. Dolan. 1991. "Fixed Effects Estimates of Earnings Impacts for the Vocational Rehabilitation Program," *Journal of Human Resources* (Spring): 381-391.

Ehrenberg, Ronald G., and Robert S. Smith. 1994. *Modern Labor Economics.* Fifth edition. New York: Harper Collins.

Hartigan, John A., and Alexandra Wigdor, eds. 1989. *Fairness in Employment Testing: Validity Generalization, Minority Issues, and the General Aptitude Test Battery.* Washington, DC: National Academy Press.

Landini, Michael J. 1995. *Understanding Federal Training and Employment Programs.* Washington, DC: National Commission for Employment Policy, January.

LaPlante, Mitchell, Jae Kennedy, H. Stephen Kaye, and Barbara L. Wenger. 1996. *Disability and Employment,* Disability Statistics Abstract Series No. 11, Disability Statistics Rehabilitation Research and Training Center, University of California, San Francisco.

Orr, Larry L., Howard S. Bloom, Stephen H. Bell, Winston Lin, George Cave, and Fred Doolittle. 1994. *The National JTPA Study: Impacts, Benefits, and Costs of Title II-A.* Draft Report, Abt Associates, March.

Social Policy Research Associates. 1994. *Guide to JTPA Performance Standards for Program Years 1994 and 1995.* Menlo Park, CA: Social Policy Research Associates, July.

Stanley, Marcus. 1995. *What's Working (and What's Not): A Summary of Research on the Economic Impacts of Employment and Training Programs.* Office of the Chief Economist, U.S. Department of Labor, January.

Tuma, John. 1993. "Patterns of Enrollment in Postsecondary Vocational and Academic Education." Draft paper prepared for the National Assessment of Vocational Education. Berkeley, CA: MPR Associates, April.

U.S. Congress. House of Representatives. Committee on Ways and Means. 1994. *Overview of Entitlement Programs: 1994 Green Book.* Washington, DC: Government Printing Office, July.

U.S. Department of Education. Office of Research. Office of Educational Research and Improvement. 1994. *National Assessment of Vocational Education: Final Report to Congress.* Washington, DC: Government Printing Office, July.

U.S. Department of Education. Rehabilitation Services Administration. 1992. *Annual Report to the President and to the Congress: Fiscal Year 1992 on Federal Activities Related to the Rehabilitation Act of 1973, as Amended.* Washington, DC: U.S. Department of Education.

U.S. Department of Labor. Employment and Training Administration. Office of Strategic Planning and Policy Development. Division of Performance Management and Evaluation. 1992. *Job Training Quarterly Survey: JTPA Title IIA and III Enrollments and Terminations During Program Year 1990 (July 1990-June 1991).* Washington, DC: U.S. Department of Labor.

_____. 1993a. *Job Training Quarterly Survey: JTPA Title IIA and III Enrollments and Terminations During Program Year 1991 (July 1991-June 1992).* Washington, DC: U.S. Department of Labor.

U.S. Department of Labor. Employment and Training Administration. Unemployment Insurance Service. 1993b. *Comparison of State Unemployment Insurance Laws.* Washington, DC: U.S. Department of Labor, August.

_____. 1994. "JTPA Standardized Program Information Report Instructions." Training and Employment Information Notice No. 5-93, change 1, June 23.

U.S. General Accounting Office. 1993. *Vocational Rehabilitation: Evidence for Federal Program's Effectiveness.* GAO/PEMD-93-19. Washington, DC: U.S. General Accounting Office, August.

Improving the Return to Work of Social Security Disability Beneficiaries

Monroe Berkowitz
Rutgers University

This paper explores alternatives to the present system of rehabilitating or returning to work persons who are applicants for or beneficiaries of the disability programs of the Social Security Administration (SSA). The proposals are presented in two parts. Part I pertains to beneficiaries and is based on the benefit system as it currently exists. Part II proposes changes in how the SSA determines eligibility for benefits.

The following assumptions and beliefs underlie the recommendations:

1. The current Return to Work (RTW) system in social security is functioning poorly, as evidenced by the low number of persons who leave the rolls for reasons other than death or transfer to the retirement system.

2. The SSA's role in the RTW process should be minimized in favor of allowing market forces to operate.

3. Private sector providers should be encouraged to enter the market and to bear the associated risks, and they should be rewarded based on performance rather than on the costs of services provided.

The Existing Return-to-Work Program

Under the current arrangements, SSA is supposed to advise applicants about rehabilitation possibilities. Using SSA guidelines that may be adapted to state conditions, the state Disability Determination Service (DDS) refers beneficiaries to the state vocational rehabilitation

(VR) agency. The exact substance of this referral is not at all clear. The applicant may be informed of the existence of the VR program or may be given literature about it.[1] Apparently, in most SSA field offices, there is no concerted effort to inform applicants about what the program might do for them or about the relationship between these services and eligibility for the SSA benefits program.[2]

The individual interested in rehabilitation must submit a formal application to the state VR agency with evidence of his/her physical or mental condition. The VR counselor will interview the applicant, perhaps order further psychological or physical examinations, and decide whether the person should be accepted for services. If accepted, the client works out an individual written rehabilitation plan (IWRP) with the counselor that sets forth the intended services and the objective of the program.[3]

Under the usual VR rules, a client is considered rehabilitated if placed in a job or homemaker status for a period of two months. In order for the VR agency to be reimbursed by SSA for the costs of the services, it must meet a sterner test of rehabilitation. The beneficiary must be back at work earning more than the "substantial gainful activity" (SGA) level (currently $500 per month) for a period of at least nine months. If return to work for that period comes about, the VR agency is reimbursed for all reasonable expenses it incurred, subject to a maximum payment equivalent to the estimated savings to the SSA trust fund.

Using the traditional VR test, 40,155 beneficiaries were rehabilitated during fiscal year 1991, in the sense that they returned to work and remained at work for at least 60 days.[4] The average cost for their rehabilitation was about $3,600, more than $1,000 greater than the average cost for the nonbeneficiaries who were rehabilitated. The cost data are from the VR program and essentially represent purchased services. VR overhead and staff salaries, including the cost of the VR counselors, are not included in the averages.[5]

If the test is the one that SSA imposes before reimbursements are made, the number of rehabilitants decreases to a little more than 6,000 per year. In fiscal year 1993, nearly 300,000 persons were referred to VR, and 6,154 were rehabilitated in the sense of having earned SGA or more for nine months. The rehabilitation total is a relatively small number, some one-half of 1 percent of the persons on the rolls.

The appropriate comparison, however, is not with the number of persons on the rolls at a given time. It would be more meaningful to take a cohort of persons on the rolls and to follow this group through time to determine the number of individuals that return to work. Preliminary data from the New Beneficiary Survey show that most persons who leave the SSA rolls do so because they attain the age of 65 and transfer to the old age program or because they die. Some small number of persons return to work. We have no information about the number who return to work after receiving RTW services and the number that return without them. It seems safe to say that 3 percent, not all of whom have received any RTW services return to work, which is hardly a large number (Hennessey and Dykacz 1992 and 1993). The objective of a RTW program should be to improve that percentage.

Overall, nearly $64.5 million was paid to VR in reimbursements in fiscal year 1993. However, it appears that the program was cost beneficial from the point of view of the trust fund. The projected savings for fiscal year 1993 of $321.9 million was five times the amounts reimbursed.

Up until now, SSA's arrangements to reimburse providers have been with the joint federal-state VR program exclusively. In March 1994, SSA revised its regulations so as to allow the private sector to compete for the business. If the VR agency does not take on the case after a period of four months, the new policy will allow referral to alternative providers, including those from the private sector. This program is not yet in effect and awaits the issuance of detailed rules and regulations by SSA.

Allowing Market Forces to Operate

The limited effectiveness of the public VR system in taking persons off the rolls is not surprising. The VR programs have found other clientele, as Congress has asked them to concentrate on the disadvantaged, the mentally ill, persons with mental retardation, and persons with severe disabilities (Jenkins, Patterson and Szymanski 1992). Persons receiving benefits may be considered as difficult to rehabilitate since return to work means the loss of benefits. The issue of the disincentives facing beneficiaries has to be faced squarely since it plays such an important role in return-to-work efforts.

We can consider a person who has recently been granted benefits. Obviously, that individual chose to apply for benefits and, with the award in hand, is now in an "equilibrium" position with no great incentive to change by starting an RTW program. Yet, the whole rationale for the RTW programs is that, somehow, the person will be better off by using RTW services, getting a job, and giving up the benefits. There may be a bit of a contradiction in this situation: having "chosen" to be on the benefit rolls, how could a person be better off by using RTW services and eventually leaving the rolls?

Before dealing with that issue, it is important to recognize that the interests of the benefits-paying agency and the interests of the individual beneficiary may be different. SSA is providing benefits, and it would be worthwhile for the agency to spend an amount on RTW services equal to what would be saved if the person left the rolls. The test for determining the amount is different, but would not the beneficiary be well advised to invest in RTW services so long as the cost is less than the net gain the person would enjoy by returning to work?

There are, however, two obvious sets of problems facing both the individual and the agency. One involves information. There simply is a great deal of uncertainty surrounding the efficacy of rehabilitation technology, the future labor market, and the success of RTW services in getting a person back to work at a wage that will be attractive to the individual and that will allow the agency to sever benefits. Obviously, since there are uncertainties, there are risks. Investments must be made today, but the return will not be forthcoming until some time in the future when and if the person returns to work. There is no guarantee of success, and the expenditures might be ineffective in putting the individual back to work.

The other problem has to do with the financing of RTW services. Even if the beneficiary is convinced that the timing is right and that a particular set of services that can be purchased from a provider is just the ticket to get back to work, the person may lack the necessary financing. The proposals in part II suggest some ways to deal with the capital markets problem. SSA would not have the same financial difficulties as the beneficiary since trust funds may be tapped to support these services. Although SSA has the advantage in the financing, the agency probably faces more severe informational hurdles than does the individual. SSA has the problems of selecting beneficiaries for whom RTW services may be effective and of deciding the type of services, the provider, the timing of the services, and a host of other issues. The individual beneficiaries may be in a far better position than SSA to assess personal motivation and the type of services and providers with which they will be comfortable.

However, the individual beneficiary's evaluation of future prospects may be distorted. Beneficiaries may overestimate the value of leisure or they may underestimate the labor market value of their residual functioning capacities. A more realistic notion of the jobs for which they might be eligible, after a period of counseling, guidance, and perhaps even retraining, might emerge from a joint decision of the beneficiary and a provider of RTW services. The recommendations in this paper are based on the assumption that competition among providers in offering plans, together with the freedom that the beneficiary has in choosing a plan will result in an optimal solution to the information problem.

The alternative, of course, would be for SSA to pick out the candidates for RTW services or to offer these services to all. Offering and paying for rehabilitation services on an universal basis can be an expensive course of action, as demonstrated by the experience in workers' compensation. The large increase in the number of private sector rehabilitation providers came about after California amended its workers' compensation law to cover what might be termed mandatory rehabilitation. Although nothing in the law compelled employees to accept rehabilitation, employers and insurers were required to offer such services upon application of employees. Rehabilitation services were accompanied by a continuation of benefits, and the appropriateness of rehabilitation became an issue in the legal struggles over the rights to compensation benefits. Originally forecast to range from 3 to 5 percent of benefit costs, the program outlays reached as high as 15 percent (Monroe Berkowitz 1990; California Workers' Compensation Institute 1983). Variations of the mandatory rehabilitation provisions were enacted by several other states, including Colorado, Washington, Florida, and Maine. When the costs of the programs began to soar, each of these states abandoned the notion of compulsory rehabilitation.

The problems with compulsory rehabilitation were not difficult to identify. Rehabilitation services became a matter of right and were viewed as an attractive additional form of aid and a way to prolong periods of compensation benefits. Providers were paid for services rendered, be they evaluation services, counseling, training, or other types. Payment to the providers was not linked to results in the sense of return to work.

SSA's situation differs from that in workers' compensation, however. In the SSA programs, benefits are not a given for a finite period, and hence there would be less of a temptation for individuals to accept vocational rehabilitation just to prolong the period of benefits. On the other hand, the problems are similar, in that there are no obvious ways for the administrators to select persons for rehabilitation services. To make such services available to all brings with it expenses that may be out of proportion with the eventual benefits to the system.

Although states have abandoned mandatory rehabilitation or even mandatory evaluation for rehabilitation in workers' compensation, one legacy of that experience has been a thriving business of private sector rehabilitation providers. These individuals and firms are retained by employers and insurers to give services on demand. Since the employers are footing the bill, obviously these providers are called upon only when the employer or insurer makes a decision that the marginal dollar spent on services will yield a savings of that amount. It is doubtful that a public program such as SSA would be allowed to exercise these types of benefit-cost judgments in individual cases. Equity considerations would probably require uniform treatment of broad classes of beneficiaries. The following scheme proposed for beneficiaries of the system takes advantage of the growing number of private sector rehabilitation providers and minimizes the discretion exercised by SSA in the selection of clients to be offered services.

Part I: An Incentive-Based Reimbursement Scheme for SSA Disability Insurance Beneficiaries

The recommendations center around an incentive-based reimbursement scheme that assumes no change in the current test for benefits eligibility. It has two central features:

1. Payments to providers are conditioned on outcomes, with no necessary relationship to the costs of services.

2. All risks are borne by providers.

The scheme can be outlined briefly. SSA certifies a broad range of providers from the public and private sectors. VR becomes one of the players but would compete with providers from the private sector and possibly other providers from the public sector, including employment services. The watchword here is diversity, and hopefully providers would cover a wide scope of philosophies and methodologies.

1. SSA would screen new beneficiaries and eliminate those persons with no reasonable chance of returning to work--the terminally ill or those with only a few remaining years of eligibility on the disability insurance (DI) rolls, and also those persons who are expected to recover and to leave the rolls without any RTW services. All other beneficiaries would receive what can be termed a "ticket" or, to employ a term advocated by Steve Lavery from New Zealand, a "job card"[6] that can be used to receive services at any of the providers.

2. The ticket would have no predetermined value. Once deposited by the beneficiary at a provider, the ticket would become a contract between SSA and the provider to pay the latter a portion of the savings to the trust fund *during the period of time that the beneficiary is off the rolls and at work*.

3. The provider would not receive any compensation for services provided until the beneficiary completed the nine-month trial work period and was back at work for a period of time earning more than SGA. At that point, the provider would be paid a predetermined percentage of the amount that would have been paid

in benefits had the beneficiary remained on the rolls.

4. Providers would be paid each year that the beneficiary remained off the rolls for all or a portion of the year, according to the amount of savings to the trust fund.

Rationale for a New Scheme

The basic justification for a new scheme is that the current system is "broke and needs fixing." In a world where private sector providers are playing an increasing role in other benefit programs, it seems unwise either to exclude them or to have them play a secondary role in this market. There does not appear to be any reason for allowing the private sector in only after the public sector rejects or ignores the case.[7]

Beyond that, however, are the matters of monitoring and of provider incentives. Under the current system, providers bear the risk and are compensated only after the person leaves the rolls, and then solely for actual expenses incurred. Once the system begins to apply to private sector providers, SSA will have the unenviable task of auditing records and deciding issues of legitimacy of costs. Can fee schedules and utilization protocols be far behind? All this may not be too much of a problem in the VR program since the expenses of the agency are met from general appropriations, and, in a sense, the SSA reimbursements are found money for the VR agency.

Under the proposed scheme, there will be no auditing or monitoring problems since payment is according to results and not according to the cost of services provided. This should be a plus for the proposed system since, as is abundantly clear from the reengineering studies, SSA has difficulties in accomplishing its main tasks in the DI program without the challenge of monitoring a rehabilitation program (U.S. Department of Health and Human Services [HHS], SSA, September 1994a and November 1994b).

The prime virtue of the proposed system is that it seeks to replicate as many of the features of the private market as is possible. The tickets are held by the beneficiaries, who have the option of depositing them with a wide variety of providers. The providers are assumed to range along a spectrum, from job developers to those oriented more to the professional goals of rehabilitation counselors.

This scheme would appear to have many of the advantages of privatization that Weaver (1991, 1994) has stressed. Beneficiaries would have a choice among many competing providers, with different ideas about how to restore the person to a job. Providers would have few of the present constraints on the freedom of the VR program to devise return-to-work plans. The VR program understandably is obliged to follow the current priorities established by Congress and to follow prescribed procedures and processes. Adherence to the correct process may take precedence over outcomes.

Under the proposed scheme, the beneficiary is given a great deal of discretion. There is no obligation to deposit the ticket with any provider. The individual may choose to hold onto the ticket, preferring benefits to undergoing any regimen of rehabilitation. No mandatory compliance is contemplated. If, however, providers know that a particular person has a ticket, they will do all they can to persuade or cajole the person to deposit the ticket with them, and such competition for the custom of the beneficiary is all to the good.

The opposite situation may also prevail: no provider may agree to accept the ticket of a particular beneficiary. There may not be any provider who believes that the risk is worthwhile, that the person can be made job ready within the constraints of the reimbursement formula. Again, this would be an acceptable outcome. It would be a market judgment that the case cannot be handled at a profit to the provider.

Some Problem Areas

Who Should Be Issued Tickets?

One solution is simply to issue tickets to all beneficiaries. Persons who are terminally ill would not be in a position to deposit the tickets, and they probably would not be accepted once their condition was known. Older persons within a few years of age 65 might also have little motivation to deposit the tickets, and providers would be reluctant to accept them in light of the limited number of years remaining in which payments could be collected. The problem may solve itself, and there may be no good reason for SSA to try to sort out these groups. However, it would always be possible for SSA to write the rules so as to deny tickets to those over a particular age or with diagnoses where death is expected within a short period of time. An alternative would be to issue tickets to persons in this group only on request.

A thornier problem is posed by those individuals who are expected to recover and leave the rolls without any services. Allowing these persons to have tickets will lead to accusations of "creaming" on the part of providers: the latter would only have to secure the tickets and retain them until the person went to work—and then claim the rewards. On the other hand, this is a difficult group to identify with any degree of certainty. Rather than expending the time and energy on identification, the strategy would be to issue tickets and to let the providers gain the benefits that might counterbalance some of the extraordinary costs involved in the more difficult cases. In all instances, the most that SSA would be paying would be a portion of the amounts spent had the person remained on the rolls.

In spite of the argument that no monetary losses accrue to SSA, perceptions are important in these matters. Therefore, SSA should try to identify a group that is likely to exit the rolls without services. Eliminating that contingent would allow the providers to prioritize services to those who have tickets and would keep them from "creaming" in the primal sense of giving assistance to persons who otherwise would have reached the same result.

What Happens if There Is a Change of Providers?

Two situations might be distinguished. One is where the beneficiary is dissatisfied with the provider, and the other is where the provider is unhappy with the beneficiary. The latter situation would seem to pose few problems. The provider can simply return the ticket to the beneficiary, or, if possible, sell it to another provider. There should be no objection to a market developing in these tickets.

The more difficult situation is where the beneficiary refuses to have anything more to do with the provider. In that case, the provider might still be able to sell the ticket to another provider. The ticket would be worth little to the former if the beneficiary has announced that no return to work is feasible until the original provider is off the case. An alternative to writing detailed rules and regulations and deciding subsequent disputes, would be to leave such matters to the negotiations between all of the parties, including more than one provider.

Inevitably some conflicts will arise, and it would seem to be reasonable to write legislation authorizing another mechanism to resolve such matters. One possibility would be final and binding arbitration with provisions for an expedited hearing.

What Is the Size of the Market?

An estimated 200,000 persons per year would realistically be in the market for RTW services. This number is based on the fact that 629,700 awards were made in 1993 (HHS, SSA 1994a, table 6.C1). If we eliminate all those over 50 years of age (316,669 persons) and those who are terminally ill (93,953 persons), we have 219,078 individuals remaining. Possibly 12 percent of the last number might be expected to recover and exit the rolls without assistance, which would leave 192,789 or roughly 200,000 persons to be issued tickets. Obviously, the number would be three times as great if everyone coming on the rolls were issued the tickets, but it is likely that there would be some reluctance on the part of SSA to issue tickets to those persons who were expected to leave the rolls without services. In addition, the older and sicker group would not be very attractive to providers.

How Will Providers Be Reimbursed?

The essence of the proposal is that providers are to be paid based on results as they become known. It is contemplated that the providers would expend the funds for services or find some other agency or body to finance them. The providers would not be reimbursed until such time as the person left the rolls, after which the provider would be paid a percentage of the benefit amount for the period the person was off the rolls. Such a calculation would be done yearly, and the provider compensated accordingly. Thus, the provider would have the incentive not only to return the person to work but to keep the person at work.[8]

A question can be raised as to whether the provider should be paid in the event the beneficiary medically recovers but does not return to work. In my view, payment should be conditioned not only on removal from the rolls, but on return to work. The provider can be seen as an advocate for the beneficiary, and it would seem problematic to have providers striving to prove to SSA that a medical recovery has occurred, without having the burden of placing and keeping the person in a job that paid more than the SGA level. Thus, the proposed scheme would reimburse the provider only in the event of a return to work.

Table 1 illustrates how this reimbursement might work. The monthly benefit shown is the average amount awarded to a person of that age with a single dependent. The provider is assumed to be paid 30 percent of the annual savings. This is an arbitrary percentage that could vary and eventually would have to be set in negotiations between SSA and the providers.

Table 1. Incentive-Based Payments to Providers

Age	Annual benefit[a]	30 percent payable to provider annually	Potential number of years on DI rolls[b]	Present value of payments to providers[c]
25	$7,317	$2,195.10	39	$32,814.71
35	$9,853	$2,955.90	29	$40,173.63
45	$11,711	$3,513.30	19	$39,201.14
50	$11,936	$3,580.80	14	$33,282.92

SOURCE: HHS, SSA (1993a) and author's calculations.

a. Annual benefit amount is based on the average benefit to a person of the age indicated, as shown in the *Annual Statistical Supplement to the Social Security Bulletin* (HHS, SSA 1993a, p. 178), plus one-half of that amount for one dependent.

b. The recipient may be on the DI rolls until age 65. One year is subtracted to account for the nine-month trial work period plus three months.

c. Present value of payments to providers was calculated assuming a 6 percent discount rate and annual compounding.

The reimbursement to the providers would be on a year-to-year basis. However, it is useful to calculate the present value of these payments so that providers can have some criterion for deciding how much should be spent in an individual case.[9] In making these present value calculations, the assumption is that the person remains on the rolls until age 65, unless death occurs previously. The calculations, in addition to taking mortality into account, make an adjustment for inflation and the fact that, under the most optimistic of assumptions, it would take at least a year before the person would leave the rolls. That amount of time is due to the nine-month trial work period plus the three-month period before a person is taken off the rolls. The present value figure is a maximum amount that could be paid under the 30 percent sharing assumption. It is difficult to estimate the cost to the providers of the services necessary to remove the person from the rolls. Under the VR program, the average cost per case has been running about $10,000. A return of three to four times that amount is probably not excessive, considering that the payment is available only for successes. The provider would be paid nothing if the person never left the rolls.[10]

Part II: An Incentive Based Proposal for SSA Disability Insurance Applicants and Beneficiaries

There are obvious advantages in providing RTW services before the benefits eligibility decision is made. One advantage is timing (Gardner 1988). The sooner the person is reached, the better the chances that services will be effective. The question is whether the whole spirit and ethos of the decision-making process in SSA might be changed so that rehabilitation or return to work takes precedence over benefits.

The SSA DI program bears the stamp of its origins. Unlike the situation in some countries, DI did not begin as an offshoot of the health program but as an addition to the retirement program. The concern was for persons whose income had stopped due to a disability. They were forced to "retire" due to a medical condition, and the feeling was that they should have somewhat the same benefits as people who retired due to old age.

The emphasis of SSA has been on the increasingly difficult task of determining who is and who is not eligible for benefits, in spite of the location of the determination process in the state agencies linked to the VR program, and in spite of the cooperative efforts through the years of the Beneficiary Rehabilitation Program (Monroe Berkowitz et al. 1982) and the current VR program. Rehabilitation has not come before benefits. It has been the other way around.

A policy such as the German one of placing "rehabilitation before pensions" (Aarts and de Jong, this volume) is not easy to bring about. New Zealand, for example, has changed the name of its basic accident statute from the Accident Compensation Act to the Accident Rehabilitation and Compensation Insurance Act, but there is no real evidence that the new name has been accompanied by different priorities. Changing from an agency whose primary task is to determine which applicants should be paid cash disability benefits to one whose first interest is the return to work of applicants is not only difficult but probably requires modifications in support systems and other legislation.

One possible approach would be to charge the Disability Determination Services (DDS) with the responsibility of making a rehabilitation decision before making the basic one dealing with eligibility for benefits. The initial decision would be whether the applicant should or should not receive a "ticket," "job card," or simply a "voucher" for rehabilitation services. After that choice is made, the DDS would proceed to considering the matter of eligibility for benefits. Some applications would be allowed and others denied, without regard to whether the individuals were issued vouchers.

The test for the voucher could be essentially that now specified for acceptance into the general state-federal VR program. First, it must be established that the person has a physical or mental condition that constitutes a substantial handicap to employment for this individual; second, there must be a reasonable expectation that vocational rehabilitation services will benefit the individual's employability.

Just as the DDS may now call on testimony from medical experts in deciding whether to allow benefits, it may also call upon expert evaluators for advice regarding the benefits of vocational rehabilitation services for the individual's employment chances.[11] There are many different ways that the DDS might classify an individual's vocational rehabilitation potential. The simplest approach would probably be to place all applicants into three categories.

The first category would be those persons who are deemed not to have a physical or mental condition that would interfere with their employment. These people would be expected to return to the labor market without any VR services. Although the determination of vouchers and the determination of benefits would be done separately, presumably all of the persons in this category would end up in the group denied benefits.

The persons in the second category would be those who meet the eligibility requirements and who would be issued vouchers. SSA benefits would later be allowed for some of these individuals and would be denied for others.

In the third category would be those persons with a sufficiently disabling physical or mental condition but who are so severely impaired that the judgment is made that they would not benefit from receiving VR services. The presumption is that most of these individuals would be allowed disability insurance payments, but some may not be able to meet the rigorous disability tests in the DI law.

In a second stage, the DDS would move to consider the applications on their merits. Persons in the first category presumably end up without vouchers and without benefits. It is anticipated that benefits would be allowed to persons in the third category who were denied vouchers based on the severity of their conditions and the poor outlook for employment. It is people in the middle category who pose the interesting issues. Some of these individuals might be denied outright, due to not meeting the existing SSA eligibility tests; however, they would still have their vouchers. This presents two problems. One is that, if we still wish to keep an incentive-based system for providers, we no longer have any obvious yardsticks with which to measure the compensation due providers who successfully find jobs for people in this group. The second problem is that there is no obvious source of financing for the RTW expenses. It is doubtful that there is any rationale for tapping trust funds on behalf of persons who have been denied benefits.

Financing Vouchers from a Loan Fund

One possible solution to the financing problem is to have Congress establish a loan fund from general revenues. The risks would be limited by the finite amount of the fund, which would be replenished by the repayment of the loans. Loans would be available at minimal rates of interest, and the obligation to repay would begin only when and if the person returned to gainful employment. Obviously, "failures" would result in a rapid depletion of the fund.

The fund could be used for two purposes. One would be to provide, where necessary, a modest living allowance for the person who might be without necessary support, having been denied SSA benefits. The other would be to reimburse the provider of RTW services. In order to adhere to the incentive- or performance-based philosophy, the provider would not be paid unless and until the person returned to work and remained at work for a period of time. A minimum period of six months would be advisable.

Another issue has to do with the value of the voucher. Obviously, the higher the value, the more attractive it will be to providers, who are being asked to bear the risks of the RTW program. On the other hand, the value of the voucher will have to depend on the size of the fund. Since this proposal is not for an open-ended entitlement system, the fund will have a finite amount of money available to finance RTW programs. The generosity of the voucher might well fluctuate in accordance with fund balances.

There appears to be no ideal way to set the value of the voucher, but solutions might come from some experimentation over time. One approach would be to determine if the fund administrator, the DDS, or another appropriate body could make distinctions among applicants, based on the probability of their returning to work or on the forecast of the necessary services that would enable them to get back to work. Another experiment would focus less on the diagnosis of the individual and more on simulations, which would take into account fund balances and the attractiveness to providers of vouchers with values differing for persons in different disability categories.

Time-Limited Benefits

The other contingent of those persons issued vouchers would be individuals who qualified for benefits under the present definitions of disability. This group could be treated in the same way as proposed earlier for beneficiaries who would be issued tickets. However, in order to emphasize the philosophy of rehabilitation first and benefits second, the concept of time-limited benefits should be introduced. In a sense, any case that is recorded for a continuing disability review (CDR) is time limited. However, due to the press of other business, CDRs have not been conducted on a regular basis. A time-limited benefit would be different: recipients would be alerted to the fact that they are expected to return to the labor market and that their benefits are given to them for a finite period of time.

At the outset, a period of two years should be sufficiently long to determine whether RTW services were effective in getting the person back to work. After the two-year period, benefits would automatically cease. If the person were not at work, a new application could be filed, with the understanding that, in addition to the usual tests of disability, SSA would take into account the record of cooperation of the applicant with the RTW services. In all other respects, the incentive-based scheme for beneficiaries that has been proposed would apply.

An Incentive-Based Proposal for Supplemental Security Income

It might be misleading to label this an RTW process since some of the Supplemental Security Income (SSI) clients may not have had any work experience. However, the problems are essentially the same, and an incentive-based proposal, as in part I would seem to be as applicable to SSI as to DI.

Certainly, there are also differences that need to be considered. First, in the case of DI, the test is the inability to work, whereas, in SSI, there is not only this criterion, but a test based on assets and income. Second, the conditions for entering the SSI rolls are not the same as the conditions for exiting from the rolls. Although there is talk about additional employment incentive provisions for DI, in the form of allowing the recipient to retain a portion of benefits while working, these rules are not yet in effect. Such incentives, plus a host of others, are in place for SSI recipients (HHS, SSA 1992, *Red Book on Work Incentives*). These provisions pose no real problems, although their existence does diminish the savings to government when a recipient goes to work. Of course, SSI is financed on a different basis than is DI. There is no trust fund for SSI, and payments are from general revenues.

In principle, the issues and procedures applicable to DI can be transferred to SSI. As in the case of DI, decisions would have to be made as to whether tickets would be issued to all SSI recipients at the time they are put on the benefit rolls, or whether tickets ought to be withheld from those too disabled, too old, and those expected to recover without the need for services.

It would be necessary to estimate the savings to the taxpayer if the person who has qualified for SSI is removed from the rolls. Such a calculation is currently made in order to evaluate the maximum amounts

that could be paid to VR in the case of rehabilitation of an SSI beneficiary. These estimates would be used, and a percentage of the savings
would determine the value of the ticket.

Successful providers might have to be paid a different percentage of
savings than would be true in the case of DI beneficiaries. Thirty percent may not be sufficient in the situation where the recipient is
allowed to retain one dollar of benefits for every two dollars of earnings. The exact percentage should be set after a more thorough examination of the projected savings.

Conclusions

The current system designed to return disabled beneficiaries to work
desperately needs to be changed. SSA is assumed to have its hands full
trying to make the disability determination process work in an equitable and efficient manner and to have neither the expertise nor the
financing to engage in the day-to-day management of the rehabilitation
of its beneficiaries. At the same time, the return to work of persons on
the rolls is assumed to be a responsibility of SSA.

Another important assumption is that no one formula, modality, or
type of rehabilitation service is obviously superior to another when it
comes to returning beneficiaries to work. Problems of what service to
be used, when it should be used, and who should provide the service
are best left to the market, where the individual preferences of beneficiaries can be matched with the different approaches of providers.

This paper advances several proposals for reform of the RTW system. In part I, the proposal pertains only to beneficiaries and requires
no change in the present definitions of disability. The beneficiary
would be provided with a ticket that could be used to obtain services
from a wide variety of providers. Coming up with a set of services and
the conditions for the administration of these services would be left to
the interaction of the beneficiaries and the providers. In the absence of
a market, the proposed system would have some of the advantages of a
market.

Payments to providers would be based on results. If the beneficiary
does not return to work, no payments would be due. The risk would be

borne entirely by the provider, whose incentive to get into this business would be based on the generosity of the amounts received if the beneficiary resumes employment. The experience of the DI program is that persons move off and on the rolls. The system of compensation proposed here, where providers are paid on a yearly basis only so long as the person is off the rolls, guarantees that the providers will have continued interest in monitoring the employment of persons returned to work.

SSA has nothing to lose from this system, in the sense that the agency can never pay providers more than a fraction of the savings accruing to the trust fund, and this would occur only after evidence is received that the savings have been realized. In this sense, the new system should not cost the agency any additional money. However, it is necessary to take into account any induced demand for benefits brought about by the increased payments to providers. The benefits package may now be more attractive to some persons who now would file for benefits. These costs are difficult to estimate but it is wise to assume that some additional costs would occur because of the induced demand.

For the system to work, providers have to be attracted to it and be willing to finance back-to-work programs on this contingency basis. Congress has to be convinced that providers should be paid amounts that have no necessary relationship to the cost of services provided.

Part II proposals are based on changes in the way that SSA administers the disability programs. Although the difficulties in bringing about fundamental change are not underestimated, the success of the part II proposals depends on SSA placing rehabilitation first and benefit awards second. Persons should be evaluated initially for suitability for RTW services, and those found suitable should be issued vouchers that are essentially claims on a loan fund. For those persons who are denied benefits, the value of the voucher would be determined by experiments. It is proposed that the funds be used for income support as well as for RTW services.

The incentive-based aspects of the RTW proposals for beneficiaries are maintained in part II, albeit in a modified form. For persons with vouchers who are allowed benefits, the proposed system should operate in much the same manner as in part I for beneficiaries, except that the benefits should be awarded on a two-year, time-limited basis.

The SSI program poses its own problems, stemming from the lack of an identifiable trust fund and the SSI incentive provisions that allow persons who are working to retain a portion of their earnings. The incentive-based scheme for beneficiaries (part I) should be applied to the SSI program, with appropriate modifications in the reimbursement formula for providers.

Change never comes easily to an established governmental program, nor should it. Each innovation ought to bear the burden of proving that it will bring benefits commensurate with its costs. Yet the RTW record cries out for reform. In keeping with the philosophy of the 1990s, this change ought to be one that does not create new open-ended entitlement programs or call upon the bureaucracy to accomplish tasks for which it is ill suited. In each of the schemes proposed in this paper, risk is transferred to the providers, payments are made only when results are evident, and a positive marginal benefit-cost ratio is guaranteed.

NOTES

1. The state Disability Determination Service (DDS) sends a list of beneficiaries and denied applicants who are considered to have rehabilitation potential to the state VR agencies. These agencies may or may not contact the individual, who may or may not apply for services (Reno and staff 1994).

2. If asked by the applicant, personnel at the SSA district offices are instructed to tell claimants about the VR program and to give them a brochure with the address and phone number of the local VR agency. A brochure giving an overview of state VR services was last printed by SSA in 1981 and has been out of print for many years (Reno and staff 1994).

3. A more complete explanation of how the process works in the joint federal-state vocational rehabilitation program can be found in Mandeville and Brabham 1992. The VR program is based on legislation that began in the 1920s. A summary look at the chronology of this legislation can be found in Jenkins, Patterson, and Szymanski 1992, table 1.2. For a broader historical examination of the VR program, see Edward Berkowitz 1987.

4. Our discussion is narrowly focused on VR activity. A study by Hennessey and Dykacz (1993) of a 1972 cohort of beneficiaries projected that 11 percent of the individuals would have either a medical or a work recovery, 36 percent would die, and 53 percent would have their benefits converted to retired-worker status at age 65. Of course, all beneficiaries will die eventually; the reference here is to the first event of interest after entitlement.

5. These data are from unpublished tabulations from the Rehabilitation Services Administration, May 1994, and are cited in Reno and staff 1994.

6. Lavery 1994. The advantage of the job card is that it can be encoded with information that might be used to differentiate potential rehabilitants, or, as Lavery would refer to such persons, "customers," in terms of the reimbursement formulas or other characteristics.

7. The preferential status granted the VR program is embodied in the law. However, section 222(d)(2) of the Social Security Act allows the Commissioner of Social Security to contract with other public or private agencies where a state is unwilling to participate or where it does not have

a suitable plan. By reason of these provisions, SSA will be contracting with private providers where the state VR chooses not to serve the person if and when detailed regulations are issued.

8. Keeping persons at work or off the rolls is a problem. In their examination of a 1972 cohort of beneficiaries, Hennessey and Dykacz (1993, p. 59) show that about 43 percent of those beneficiaries who recovered ended their post-recovery period by becoming reentitled to disabled worker benefits.

9. Present value calculations are obviously sensitive to assumptions about trends in benefit amounts, termination rates, rates of discount, and a number of other factors. For purposes of compensating VR where reimbursement cannot exceed savings to the trust fund, the SSA actuaries compute these present values. The following table presents the application of their formula to persons with the assumed benefits as shown. These sums are a good bit lower than the present-value sums in table 1. Unlike the VR arrangements, the reimbursements under the proposed scheme would be on a year-to-year basis. Since it is contemplated that these reimbursements would always be merely a fraction of the yearly savings and would be paid only after these savings accrue, there would be no possibility of a payment to the providers greater than the savings to the trust fund.

SSA Computation of Present Value of Program Savings from Successful Rehabilitation

Age	Monthly benefit[a]	Computation of savings[b]
25	$407	$47,118.02
35	$547	$66,610.27
45	$651	$68,985378
50	$663	$61,887.88

a. Monthly benefit amount is based on the average benefit to a person of the age without dependents as mandated in the *Annual Statistical Supplement to the Social Security Bulletin* (HHS, SSA 1993a, p. 178).
b. The formula for total savings to the SSA is as follows: "A-Factor" +[(PIA-WC+SSI)* "B-Factor"], where the "A-Factor" represents savings resulting from administrative costs, and the "B-Factor" represents savings resulting from the expected eventual termination of benefit payments. PIA = Title II Primary Insurance Amount, WC = Workers' Compensation payment, and SSI = Supplemental Security Income payments. Tables of A and B factors are based on the alternative IIB set of disability, economic, and health utilization assumptions found in the 1988 SSA Trustees' Reports.

10. In a meeting of private providers held on June 26, 1994, the basic outlines of the proposal were covered. Some providers expressed doubts that the program would be a viable one and were concerned about having to finance the services over what might be long periods of time before any returns would be received. Other providers thought the program offered opportunities and felt that it could be financed by recourse to bank loans or to the equities market. Before such a program is put into effect, it would be desirable to review concrete business plans from some of the providers who feel that the proposal would be attractive to them.

11. Evaluation for vocational rehabilitation feasibility is a difficult matter. If the DDS offices use a cadre of evaluators to decide who is and who is not a suitable candidate, it would be desirable to separate this function from the provision of RTW services in order to avoid any conflict of interests.

References

Berkowitz, Edward. 1987. *Disabled Policy* (A Twentieth Century Fund Report). New York: Cambridge University Press.

Berkowitz, Monroe. 1990. "Should Rehabilitation be Mandatory in Workers' Compensation Programs?" *Journal of Disability Policy Studies* (Spring).

Berkowitz, Monroe, Martin Horning, Stephen McConnell, Jeffrey Rubin, and John D. Worrall. 1982. "An Economic Evaluation of the Beneficiary Rehabilitation Program." In *Alternatives in Rehabilitating the Handicapped - A Policy Analysis,* Jeffrey Rubin and Valerie LaPorte, eds. New York: Human Sciences Press.

California Workers' Compensation Institute. 1983. *A Report to the Industry - Vocational Rehabilitation.* San Francisco.

Gardner, John A. 1988. "Improving Vocational Rehabilitation Outcomes: Opportunities For Earlier Intervention." Cambridge, MA: Workers' Compensation Research Institute.

Hennessey, John C., and Janice M. Dykacz. 1992. "Comparison of Individual Characteristics and Death Rates of Disabled-Worker Beneficiaries Entitled in 1972 and 1985," *Social Security Bulletin* 55, 3 (Fall): 24-40.

_____. 1993. "A Comparison of the Recovery Termination Rates of Disabled-Worker Beneficiaries Entitled in 1972 and 1985," *Social Security Bulletin* 56, 2 (Summer): 58-69.

Jenkins, William M., Jeanne Boland Patterson, and Edna Mora Szymanski. 1992. "Philosophical, Historical, and Legislative Aspects of the Rehabilitation Counseling Profession." In *Rehabilitation Counseling: Basics and Beyond* (2nd edition), Randall M. Parker and Edna Mora Szymanski, eds. Austin, TX: Pro-Ed.

Lavery, Steve. 1994. "Disability and Employment: The Move to Market Power." Churchill Fellowship Paper, prepared for Workbridge, Inc., New Zealand.

Mandeville, Kerry A., and Robert Brabham. 1992. "The State-Federal Vocational Rehabilitation Program." In *Rehabilitation Counseling: Basics and Beyond* (2nd edition), Randall M. Parker and Edna Mora Szymanski, eds. Austin, TX: Pro-Ed.

Reno, Virginia, and staff. 1994. "Linking Return to Work Services to the DI Disability Assessment: Alternative Approaches." Paper Prepared for the Disability Panel of the National Academy of Social Insurance.

Szymanski, Edna Mora, and Michael J. Leahy. 1993. "Rehabilitation Counseling Credentialing: Research and Practice," *Rehabilitation Counseling Bulletin* 37, 2 (December): 67-70.

U.S. Department of Health and Human Services. Social Security Administration. 1989. Memo from William B. Kelley, Office of the Actuary, to William Ermatigner, Office of Disability, on Revised Table for Computing the Present Value of Program Savings from Successful Vocational Rehabilitation. June 15.

_____. 1992a. *Red Book on Work Incentives: A Summary Guide to Social Security and Supplemental Security Income Work Incentives for People with Disabilities*. SSA Pub. No. 64-030. Washington, DC: Government Printing Office.

_____. 1992b. *Social Security Bulletin*. 55, 3 (Fall).

_____. 1993a. *Annual Statistical Supplement to the Social Security Bulletin*.

_____. 1993b. *Social Security Bulletin*. 56, 2 (Summer).

_____. 1994a. *Annual Statistical Supplement to the Social Security Bulletin*.

_____. 1994b. *Disability Process Redesign: Next Steps in Implementation*. Pub. No. 01-006.

_____. 1994c. *Plan For A New Disability Claim Process*. Pub. No. 01-005, September.

Weaver, Carolyn L. 1991. "Incentives Versus Controls in Federal Disability Policy." In *Disability and Work - Incentives, Rights, and Opportunities*, Carolyn L. Weaver ed. Washington, DC: AEI Press.

Weaver, Carolyn L. 1994. "Privatizing Vocational Rehabilitation: Options for Increasing Individual Choice and Enhancing Competition," *Journal of Disability Policy Studies* 5, 1: 53-76.

The Role of Health Care and In-Kind Benefits in Promoting Work

People with Disabilities

Access to Health Care and Related Benefits

Robert B. Friedland
Alison Evans
National Academy on Aging

Having health care coverage, whether through private insurance or through public programs, is a major determinant in obtaining health care. Whether one has access to specific services often will depend on the source of one's coverage—generally an employer or a public program, such as Medicare or Medicaid. For people with existing medical, physical, or cognitive conditions who need ongoing, specialized, or medically related services, obtaining coverage is uncertain. They are less likely to be able to obtain private insurance and may not meet the specific rules for public programs. Even when obtained, the scope and depth of that coverage are likely to be restricted, with respect to a particular individual's health care needs.

The linkages between employment-based coverage and public programs often create negative incentives. Some people may be trapped in a job for fear of losing health care insurance. Others face real and perceived disincentives for leaving public programs and seeking employment, since having a job may mean losing needed coverage. This disincentive arises because the employer might not offer any health insurance or because the coverage is different. For example, private insurance is less likely to provide for chronic, long-term, or health-related needs.

Health care reform proposals, such as those debated by President Clinton and Congress in 1994, would have eliminated many, but not all, impediments in the labor market related to health coverage. For most people with disabilities, these changes would have meant considerable improvement. In the absence of comprehensive health care reform, the efforts of public and private payers to contain their health care expenditures will dominate the situation. Private insurers will continue to avoid those at higher risk of using services and will seek ways to reduce coverage.

This paper undertakes two tasks. First, it provides an overview of the health care needs of people with disabilities and outlines sources of and gaps in their health care coverage. Second, it addresses the challenges from resorting to incremental steps rather than comprehensive reform to close these gaps.

The Connection between Disability and Health Care

On average, people with disabilities tend to use more health care services than people without disabilities, but many of the health care needs of persons with disabilities are shared with the general population. Individuals with disabilities are not necessarily in poor health. An analysis of data from the National Health Interview Survey found that nearly half of all persons with a limitation in activity due to a chronic condition reported that they were in fair or poor health (Ries 1991, p.2). Nonetheless, even when in good to excellent health, people with disabilities reported more than twice as many physician contacts and more than five times as many hospital days as others in good health. The small portion (6.1 percent) of the population that reported limitations in activity and fair or poor health accounted for nearly 20 percent of all physician contacts and 41 percent of all hospital days in the United States.

Physical Impairments

Approximately 40.2 million individuals had a condition (not including mental or emotional disorders) that caused a physical limitation, a limitation in activities of daily living (ADLs), or a limitation in instrumental activities of daily living (IADLs), based on data from the 1991-92 Survey of Income and Program Participation (U.S. Chamber of Commerce 1993, p. 16).[1] Less than half of all disabilities identified in the Survey of Income and Program Participation (SIPP), however, were classified as severe.[2]

Generally, people with chronic conditions require physician and hospital care, as would others, but they also may need very specialized attention from providers or multidisciplinary teams. Health care utilization varies considerably, depending on the type and severity of the disabling condition. Persons with multiple conditions (e.g., mental illness and chronic physical health conditions) must have providers who understand these interactions. Some people may have a greater need for prescription drugs, long-term occupational, physical, or speech therapy, or home care services. Others may require assistance with activities of daily living (e.g., personal care such as bathing or eating), adaptive equipment, interpreter services, transportation, adapted clothing, or even institutional care. Additional needs may include help with instrumental activities of daily living (e.g., shopping or managing money) or employment. Families and caregivers may also need support groups, stress management, training and counseling, time off, or help in coordinating and managing services.

People with severe chronic illnesses or disabling conditions also are at risk for secondary health problems like pressure sores or nutritional problems (U.S. Department of Health and Human Services [HHS] 1991, p. 39). Limited physical activity or immobility can increase the risk of circulatory, respiratory, and musculoskeletal problems. In order to reduce the chance of secondary problems, people with disabilities may need special equipment, rehabilitation or habilitation (i.e., maintenance) therapies, including audiology, occupational therapy, physical therapy, psychosocial services, respiratory therapy, speech-language pathology services, cognitive, vision, and behavioral therapies, or therapeutic recreation (National Council on Disability 1994, p. 27). Thus, for persons with disabilities, prevention takes on a broader meaning.

Among people with disabilities, some may be economically disadvantaged, elderly, homeless, or severely mentally ill, and, therefore, may need other types of services. For example, they might need case management, care coordination, assistance with obtaining housing or disability benefits, supervision of daily activities, community living supports, transportation, or psychosocial rehabilitation (Schlesinger and Mechanic 1993, p.125). Others may need oversight because their disability makes them vulnerable to neglect or abuse.

Mental Impairments

The National Institute of Mental Health estimates that there are between 4 and 5 million adults with "serious mental illness" (not including substance abuse disorders or mental retardation) who are either living in institutions or in the community (Barker, et al. 1992, p. 1). Based on the 1989 National Health Interview Survey, approximately 1.4 million adults between the ages of 18 and 69 were unable to work or were limited in their work because of mental illness. Over 82 percent of these individuals had had this work limitation for a year or longer. Furthermore, approximately 48 percent of adults with severe mental illness indicated that they were in fair or poor health, compared to 12 percent for the adult household population overall.

Persons with severe mental illness have many health and health-related needs. The nature of this condition is such that it requires periodic, intensive use of services and varying levels of ongoing support. Persons with severe mental illness may require hospitalization, outpatient care, institutional care, prescription drugs, crisis intervention, care in group homes, or home-based services. At various times, they may also need assistance with daily activities, such as personal hygiene, self-care, learning, social transactions, and relationships. In fact, 36 percent of adults aged 18 to 69 with severe mental illness reported not having a work limitation. However, 58 percent of these adults had other limitations such as coping with day-to-day stress (53 percent); social functioning, i.e., forming and keeping friendships (27 percent); concentrating long enough to complete tasks (21 percent); or instrumental activities of daily living, i.e., managing money, household chores, shopping, or getting around outside the home (5 percent). In addition, family members may need assistance to enhance their coping skills.

Persons with less severe mental illness or those suffering significant upsets in their everyday lives may need assistance from a range of mental health providers, such as family or marriage counselors, social workers, psychologists, or primary care physicians. Concern about the potential overuse of such services when people have third party coverage is part of the reason that provision for mental illness is so limited in many proposals. It has been difficult to design broad coverage targeted to just the most severely mentally ill.

Two groups are not included in the preceding national data: persons with substance abuse disorders and persons with mental retardation. The 1991-92 SIPP indicated that 300,000 people, aged 15 and older, had an alcohol or drug problem disorder that caused a physical, ADL, or IADL limitation (U.S. Department of Commerce 1993, p. 71). In addition to the needs that have been listed, individuals with these problems may require care in residential treatment or detoxification centers. Of the approximately 500,000 working-age people with mental retardation, 75 percent had a work limitation, 53 percent were unable to work, and 37 percent needed assistance with ADLs or IADLs (National Institute on Disability and Rehabilitation Research [NIDRR] 1991, p. 27).* Depending on the cause of the mental retardation, for example, fetal alcohol syndrome, traumatic brain injury, or Down's syndrome, individuals may require a wide range of medical services or assistance with basic life activities (HHS 1991, p. 455). Other related needs might include prevocational training or supported employment.

Children and Disability

Children need comprehensive primary and preventive health care. All children must have their physical and mental development monitored, be immunized, and receive dental and vision care. As children reach adolescence, they increasingly need psychosocial support, mental health services, education, family planning, and health guidance. Thus, a large proportion of care for children is provided on an outpatient basis.

Developmental, learning, and emotional problems are among the most common chronic conditions for both children and adolescents, yet children are less likely to be chronically ill or disabled than adults. Approximately 5 percent of children under age 15 experience a limitation in activity caused by chronic conditions, as compared to 9 percent for people aged 15-44 and 22 percent for those aged 45-64 (National Center for Health Statistics [NCHS] 1992). Other studies indicate that, while approximately 5 percent of children have special needs, about 1 to 2 percent have severe impairments (Taylor, Epstein, and Crocker 1990, p. 28). Still, the array of conditions among this relatively small number of children is vast. In contrast, adults generally have a more limited and predictable range of disorders (Durch 1994, p. 5). Thus, children with these rare conditions require specialized care that may be difficult to access. In addition, any chronic condition in children has broader implications for overall development and schooling. Children who are chronically ill, independent of how severe, are at risk for behavioral or psychiatric problems and, therefore, may need special pediatric counseling and support services (Perrin, Guyer, and Lawrence 1992, p. 71). Special services may be necessary to compensate for frequent absences from school. Moreover, family members, foster care parents, and siblings may need special training, guidance, and time off.

Coverage Today

Today's health care system has many gaps. Some people do not have coverage. Among those who do, coverage is not uniform. Private insurance and Medicare tend to have restricted scope and depth of protection, whereas Medicaid and veterans' coverage is broader but is fraught with other limitations.

Of the approximately 8 million adults aged 18 to 64 who were unable to work because of a disability in 1989, 17.3 percent had neither private nor public coverage, 34.3 percent had private insurance, 34.3 percent had public coverage, and 13.2 percent had both private and public coverage (NIDRR 1993, p.18).[3] Individuals without work limitations had much higher rates of private health insurance coverage (78 percent), lower rates of public coverage (4 percent), and somewhat lower uninsured rates. National data also show clearly that not having health coverage means not getting timely or continuous care. Disabled or not, people who do not have health coverage have fewer physician contacts and hospitalizations than people who do (NIDRR 1993, p. 37).

Gaps in health care coverage lead to perverse work incentives. Because private insurance is largely linked to employment, this protection can be jeopardized with each job change.[4] Public coverage is usually linked to receipt of public cash benefits. Some cash benefit programs are not available to those who are able to work or to those who have too much income, thus creating disincentives for beneficiaries to resume employment. As a result, the need for health coverage, or coverage of a certain type, may influence decisions concerning whether or not to work and where to work.

Private Health Care Coverage

Private insurance varies considerably, depending on the employer, the location, and the plan chosen. Persons with limitations, whether in work or in basic life activities, are less likely than persons without limitations to have private coverage. The extent of this coverage varies with the ability to work as well as with the need for assistance (see table 1). In 1989, of individuals unable to work, 48 percent had private coverage through a former employer or a spouse's employer or had purchased it individually. However, among those unable to work *and* needing assistance with basic life activities (activities of daily living or instrumental activities of daily living), a smaller proportion relied solely on private coverage because this group had high rates of public coverage also.

Employer-provided coverage is the most common form of private insurance for disabled and nondisabled people. However, it is not evenly accessible across industries or size of firm (Employee Benefit Research Institute [EBRI] 1994, p. 10). Differences also exist across educational levels. Thirty-one percent of high school graduates have direct employer coverage, as compared to 39 percent of people with a college level education or more. Overall, disabled workers who have low labor market skills are disadvantaged in terms of employment opportunities (National Academy of Social Insurance 1994, p. 10) and in gaining access to private health coverage.

Even when private health insurance is available, several features make it difficult for persons with disabilities. Often the definition of covered services is too narrow, providing too little protection outside of acute episodes of hospital and physician care. Additionally, there may be restrictions on a given service (i.e., the amount, duration, or scope), limits on total coverage or "lifetime caps," and high out-of-pocket costs (e.g., copayments or deductibles). As a consequence, families that include a member with chronic care needs are exposed to tremendous costs.

Table 1. Type of Health Coverage among Adults Aged 18-64, by Disability, 1989

Type of disability (work activity and self-care)	Private	Private only	Medicare	Medicare only	Medicaid	Medicaid only	Military	Not insured
			Source of health insurance coverage (percentage)					
Unable to work	**47.5**	**34.3**	**23.9**	**7.3**	**26.8**	**17.3**	**6.2**	**17.3**
and								
Needs assistance, ADL	44.8	18.4	38.7	10.3	38.1	20.4	5.8	12.4
Needs assistance, IADL	44.6	28.8	30.7	9.0	34.3	20.6	5.5	13.3
Does not need assistance	48.6	37.8	20.2	6.4	23.2	16.0	6.4	19.1
Limited in amount or kind of work	**71.2**	**66.3**	**2.8**	**0.8**	**6.7**	**4.8**	**5.0**	**19.8**
and								
Needs assistance, ADL	57.3	40.3[a]	15.8[a]	[b]	28.3[a]	21.8[a]	4.5[a]	10.6
Needs assistance, IADL	65.5	57.8	10.1	4.6[a]	17.3	11.3	3.6[a]	15.4
Does not need assistance	72.2	67.0	2.3[a]	0.6	5.9	4.3	5.1	20.2
Limited in nonwork activity only	**75.5**	**71.5**	**3.2**	**1.2**	**6.6**	**5.1**	**3.8**	**15.8**
and								
Needs assistance, ADL	45.1	36.6[a]	18.2[a]	9.7[a]	30.1[a]	25.1[a]	5.4[a]	9.5[a]
Needs assistance, IADL	60.8	52.2	10.7[a]	7.2[a]	24.1	17.9	2.1[a]	11.1[a]
Does not need assistance	76.3	72.6	2.7	0.9	5.7	4.3	3.8	16.0

365

No work limitation	79.3	77.7	0.4	0.1	2.8	2.5	2.1	16.6
and								
Needs assistance, ADL	b	b	b	b	b	b	b	b
Needs assistance, IADL	24.5[a]	24.5[a]	31.9[a]	10.6[a]	39.8[a]	18.5[a]	b	25.2[a]
Does not need assistance	79.3	77.7	0.4	0.1	2.8	2.5	2.1	16.6

SOURCE: 1989 National Health Interview Survey data published in NIDRR 1993.

NOTE: The percentages reflect the proportion of individuals in each disability category who have various types of insurance coverage. For example, 48.6 percent of individuals who are unable to work and do not need assistance have private coverage.

1. Low statistical reliability.

b. Standard error indeterminate, estimate=0.

Large versus Small Groups

Competition in the employer market has moved private insurance from pooling risk across groups to managing the risk exposure for specific, smaller groups. Not all employer groups can get health insurance, even if they want it, and not all insurance policies are the same. Most private insurance covers small groups. The same coverage is more expensive for small than for large groups, primarily because of relatively higher administrative costs, additional risk premiums, and the cost of medical underwriting. In the small group health insurance market, insurers compete based on their ability to sell to low-risk groups and to avoid relatively high-risk groups. In smaller groups, employers are encouraged to switch policies as a means of saving money.[5] During such changes, employees lose coverage for "preexisting" conditions. Consequently, people with disabilities are more likely to be denied full insurance, especially if they are covered through a relatively small firm.

In larger groups (firms with more than 200 employees), the possibility is greater that employers will self-fund the cost of workers' health care. In other words, these employers take on the risk directly and avoid state taxes on health insurance premiums. Even if the large group is not self-funded, the cost of its health insurance is basically the expected cost of that group. Large firms usually pay less than small firms for the same amount of coverage. Large firms traditionally offer more choices of health plans, have more comprehensive benefits, and generally pay a larger portion of the cost of family coverage.

The Americans with Disabilities Act and Health Care

The Americans with Disabilities Act (ADA) applies to employer-provided health insurance, whether it is self-funded or purchased from an insurance company (U.S. Equal Employment Opportunity Commission [EEOC] 1993, p.1). Under the ADA, employees with disabilities must be accorded equal access to whatever health insurance the employer provides to employees without disabilities. Furthermore, specific insurance terms or conditions, covered treatments, or procedures may not single out a particular disability or group of disabilities.

However, not all health-related distinctions of such plans would violate the ADA; thus, the impact of the ADA on employer-provided health coverage is limited. The EEOC gives examples of permissible distinctions: benefits provided for the treatment of physical conditions may be different from those provided for the treatment of mental or nervous conditions. Although this approach has a differential impact for people with mental illness, the plan conditions must apply equally to people with and without disabilities. Employers may have preexisting condition clauses or dollar caps, or they may place limits for all enrollees, such as on the number of covered blood transfusions or x-rays, without violating the ADA. Plans may not, however, exclude coverage of specific conditions, like deafness, schizophrenia, or kidney diseases.

Private Long-Term Care Coverage

Today, virtually no one has private insurance for long-term care services. Although most health insurance plans now provide for nursing home and home health care, this coverage is usually defined as an alternative to hospital care or for post-acute recuperation. It is not available for chronic, long-term situations. Separate private long-term care insurance is available, but relatively few people—at most 5 percent of the elderly and a negligible percentage of the nonelderly—have purchased it (Wiener, Illston, and Hanley 1994). Private long-term care insurance is primarily sold to seniors and is not marketed to people with disabilities or to children. Most of this insurance does not cover specific services. Instead, it pays a fixed dollar amount if the beneficiary qualifies for services. However, the cash amount may not be sufficient to cover the cost of care. Private insurers claim that sales are low because of uncertainty surrounding taxation; unlike health insurance, long-term care is not explicitly addressed in the tax code. Thus, it is not clear, for example, whether premiums can be paid on a pretax basis through employer flexible benefit plans.[6]

Medicaid

Medicaid is a federal- and state-funded program, which provides coverage for medical care and related services for some, but not all, low-income persons. Covered groups, defined by federal requirements with a great deal of state discretion, include pregnant women, children, and elderly or disabled people with very low incomes and few assets.

Some people are eligible for Medicaid because they receive cash assistance; this would be the case for either low income, single-parent families receiving Aid to Families with Dependent Children (AFDC) or for low-income aged, blind, or disabled individuals receiving Supplemental Security Income (SSI).[7] At age 18, adolescents with physical disabilities can apply for SSI (and, therefore, become eligible for Medicaid), even if they are living at home.[8] In addition, noncash assistance groups, such as all young children with family income below the federal poverty level, also qualify.[9]

States can provide Medicaid coverage to individuals receiving state supplement payments (SSP), or they can include people with larger incomes whose medical expenses relative to income are extremely high ("medically needy").[10] In 1991, 34 states extended Medicaid to SSP recipients, and 36 states had medically needy programs for the disabled. Through medically needy programs, states cover many elderly and disabled people requiring nursing facility or home care. A state may offer a more limited package of services to its medically needy population than to its categorically needy population (Congressional Research Service [CRS] 1993, p. 249).[11]

Eligibility for Medicaid is narrow, but the array of covered services in many states is broad. Unlike private medical insurance or Medicare, Medicaid covers preventive care, case management, extensive rehabilitation and day treatment, home health services, medical devices, personal care services, care in nursing homes, and transportation. However, many states have relatively low provider reimbursement and have restrictive licensing policies, thus limiting beneficiaries' access to services.

In addition to care in a nursing facility, states may, under a waiver program, provide home- and community-based services for persons who would otherwise require institutional care. In contrast to the home care benefit, which involves skilled medical attention, waiver services can include a wide variety of nonmedical, social, and supportive services. These waivers are frequently used to serve populations such as the frail elderly—but also people with mental retardation, developmental disabilities, chronic mental illness, or AIDS (CRS 1993, p. 384).

Special work incentive rules are built into the SSI and Medicaid programs for blind and disabled individuals who already are receiving SSI benefits and return to work. Under Section 1619 (a), SSI recipients may continue to have Medicaid benefits, although their cash benefits are gradually reduced as their earnings increase. Once the individuals' earnings rise to the point where they lose SSI cash benefits altogether, they may continue Medicaid coverage, as long as the disabling condition does not improve.[12]

People who lose their jobs and, therefore, their health coverage may find that they are eligible to have Medicaid pay their former employer's premium to continue coverage. The individual must have income below 100 percent of the poverty level and assets below 200 percent of the SSI limit and may not otherwise be eligible for Medicaid. In such cases, the state may opt to pay the premium for continuation coverage. This provision has several restrictions: federally mandated continuation applies only to employers with 20 or more employees, is time-limited, and does not apply to employers that did not offer coverage originally. Finally, coverage is that defined by the private plan, which is unlikely to cover many health-related services needed by persons with disabilities.

Current Medicaid policy addresses some of the employment disincentives for individuals leaving SSI rolls and returning to work. It does not, however, address the motivation to *go on* Medicaid in the first place. This incentive arises because employer-based coverage is unavailable or inadequate and because Medicaid's income test effectively requires that one stop working to become eligible.

Medicaid and Mental Illness

According to the 1989 National Health Interview Survey, 43.5 percent of adults aged 18 and over with serious mental illness received SSI (Barker et al. 1992, p. 7). As a result, in most states these individuals would be eligible for Medicaid. Medicaid financing for mental health historically has been skewed toward institutional care. However, at state option, outpatient services may be included, such as clinics, hospital outpatient departments, partial hospitalization, psychiatric day care, and care from psychiatrists, psychologists, social workers, or psychiatric nurses. Furthermore, states may provide targeted case management, prescription drugs, psychosocial rehabilitation services, and "clinic" services, such as day treatment, family therapy, medication management, psychological testing, and group therapy. The extent of coverage varies considerably by state.

Under Medicaid, states may offer coverage in institutions for mental diseases (IMDs) for persons aged 65 and over and in inpatient psychiatric hospitals for children under age 21. Individuals between the ages of 21 and 65 may receive services for mental illness in hospitals or in nursing facilities, as long as these facilities are neither IMDs nor psychiatric hospitals. Because individuals between the ages of 21 and 65 are not eligible for institutional care under Medicaid, they are precluded from receiving home- and community-based services under a waiver.

Medicaid and Children

The Medicaid program treats coverage for children differently from coverage for adults. The distinctions arise from the Early and Periodic Screening Diagnosis and Treatment (EPSDT) program for children, which was enacted in 1967 as part of the Medicaid initiative to identify and treat children's health problems early. Under the EPSDT program, children may receive services that other groups do not. These services include physical examinations, immunizations, laboratory tests, health education, vision, dental, and hearing care. The greatest change in EPSDT came in 1989 when the law required that *any* physical or mental illness identified during the screens must be referred for treatment; furthermore, the treatment must be covered by Medicaid, even if it is not normally covered under the state's Medicaid list of benefits. Subsequent referrals to health, developmental, or educational professionals must also be reimbursed.

The 1989 change effectively eliminated restrictions on amount, duration, or scope of covered services (as long as the services are medically necessary) and required every state to offer all mandatory and optional Medicaid benefits to children. These expansions particularly opened up many new services for mentally ill and developmentally disabled children. Furthermore, numerous states have been able to shift financing of some public and school health services to Medicaid. Thus, many services in school-based early intervention programs can be reimbursed through Medicaid funds.

Medicare

Medicare primarily serves individuals who were in social security-covered employment but are now either disabled or age 65 or older.[13] Ninety-six percent of the population over age 65 is covered by Medicare (EBRI 1994, p. 5). Medicare is also available for nonelderly people who have been on the Disability Insurance (DI) benefit rolls of the Social Security Administration (SSA) for two years.[14] Overall, 24 percent of working-age individuals who are unable to work and 3 percent of those who are limited in the amount and kind of work they can do are covered through Medicare (see table 1).

In most cases, Medicare coverage is not as broad as that of Medicaid. Medicare has two components: Part A, which covers primarily hospitalization, inpatient care, and home health, and Part B, which primarily covers outpatient and physician services. Medicare does not cover most prescription drugs taken at home. However, Medicare does cover home health services for people requiring skilled nursing and provides for broader mental health services than do most private plans. Generally, Medicare beneficiaries do not pay a premium for Part A, but they do pay a premium for Part B.

Medicare also has work incentive provisions. In the case of a disabled beneficiary who has returned to work and is engaging in substantial gainful employment (beyond a nine-month trial work period), Medicare will continue to provide coverage for three years even after Disability Insurance cash benefits have been discontinued. After three years of coverage, the disabled individual may elect to purchase Medicare Part A and Part B protection. The individual must pay a premium rate equal to the average monthly cost for beneficiaries aged 65 and over.[15] In January 1994, 78,000 beneficiaries were eligible for the buy-in benefit because they were working and their paid Medicare coverage had lapsed; only 450 chose this buy-in option (Department of Health and Human Services 1994). For Medicare beneficiaries with income below 200 percent of the federal poverty line, state Medicaid programs must pay the Part A premium.

Veterans Affairs

The Department of Veterans Affairs (VA) medical care system is the largest in the United States. It encompasses over 150 veteran medical centers and offers a full range of services. However, eligibility rules are complex, and resources are not sufficient to care for all eligible veterans. Wide disparities often result in the levels of care at different centers received by veterans with similar conditions or incomes.

The VA has programs such as hospitalization, blind rehabilitation, care for spinal cord injuries, rehabilitation, prescription services, prosthetic appliances, alcohol and drug dependence rehabilitation, domiciliary care, nursing home care, community residential care programs, hospice units, adult day care centers, hospital-based home care programs, and community outreach clinics. It also has a large outpatient care component that spans examinations, treatment, home health services, podiatric, optometric, dental, and surgical services for eligible veterans. The Veterans Health Administration is noted for its work in geriatrics, spinal cord injury, and substance abuse. In addition, in 1993 the VA cared for approximately 6 percent of the nation's AIDS cases and provided one-third of the nation's care for the chronically mentally ill (Paralyzed Veterans Association [PVA] 1994).

Eligibility rules for veterans' health benefits are confusing. Eligibility requirements for inpatient and outpatient care are different, although, in general, priority is given first to those who need treatment for service-connected disabilities and to those who have disabilities that are 50 percent or more service-connected and who require care for any condition. Some categories are "mandatory" and must be provided services, while others only are served if resources or space are available. Veterans whose incomes are above a specific threshold who do not have service-related needs may be excluded from care. In 1991, three million veterans used VA services, i.e., 12.5 percent of the total veteran population (DVA 1992, p. 66). Ninety-eight percent of these patients had service-connected disabilities or were indigent, and did not have service-connected disabilities. In fact, 25 percent of veteran patients have no other health insurance (DVA 1991, p. 5).

Health Care Reform Proposals

In 1994, Congress debated a number of proposals to reform the financing of health care. Many plans would have substantially reduced the number of people without health insurance or with substantial gaps in health insurance. Access to health care would have been dramatically easier for individuals with chronic care needs, even under those proposals that fell short of universal coverage. As a result, work disincentives and fragmentation of health services would have been substantially alleviated for people with disabilities.

In the absence of major reform, discussions are likely to revolve around incremental changes in existing programs, modifications to the tax code, or small-scale block grants to states. In today's environment, proposals to expand coverage marginally under existing public programs are likely to compete with new demands to reduce the size of the federal government. In addition, closing coverage gaps in a piecemeal fashion for persons with disabilities could perpetuate work disincentives, lead to significant inequities across populations, produce further unraveling of private insurance, or involve substantial public costs.

The array of potential incremental reforms is practically infinite. First, as a society, we should decide how much we are willing to spend, through public and private funds, to improve access to health care. Then we must sort out philosophical differences regarding program structure and priority populations. In this section, possible options for incremental reform and their impact for disabled persons are enumerated, in very general terms. Acute care coverage is addressed, including insurance market reforms and changes to Medicaid, Medicare, and veterans coverage. Issues relating to long-term care are also discussed, including insurance reforms, tax code changes, and new block grant programs.

Access to Acute Care

Acute care coverage could be expanded through private insurance, Medicaid, or Medicare. It is difficult to design a change that only affects those who currently have no public or private coverage. Because private health insurance is voluntary and because different sources of coverage overlap, any incremental modification is likely to have a number of unintended consequences. For example, changes that make private insurance easier to obtain are likely to make it more expensive and, ultimately, will lead to fewer covered individuals. Modest expansions in Medicaid could unintentionally encourage employers to drop coverage and could lead to more employees becoming eligible for Medicaid.

Expanding Access to Private Insurance

Improving access to private insurance means addressing affordability and availability. Individual or small group coverage is frequently not available for people with chronic health conditions; even where it is obtainable, health insurance is often not affordable for moderate-to-low income persons. The insurance reflects the expenses of health care. Therefore, unless these expenses are significantly altered, increasing the voluntary purchase of health insurance requires that the cost be subsidized. Subsidies can be general or targeted through tax deductions, tax credits, vouchers, or premium discounts. It is very difficult to direct subsidies to only those who, without such assistance, would not have health insurance. As a proxy, most proposals restrict subsidies for private insurance to low income populations.

In 1989, for example, the Pepper Commission examined, but rejected, a proposal that would have enrolled everyone with family income below the poverty level into Medicaid, modified the insurance market towards community rating, and provided a sliding-scale subsidy for the voluntary purchase of private coverage (starting at 99 percent of the cost for families with incomes just above the poverty level and declining to zero for those with family incomes above 200 percent of the poverty level). In 1990, such a proposal would have cost approximately $32 billion in new public expenditures and would have reduced the number of uninsured with incomes below 200 percent of the poverty level by nearly 74 percent, assuming 14.4 million individuals enrolled in Medicaid and/or private insurance. Other recent proposals would give individuals the option to enroll in the Federal Employee Health Benefit Program or in Medicare, while providing subsidies toward the purchase of that coverage.

Subsidizing the cost of health insurance is not efficient. People who already have coverage and those willing to buy coverage without a subsidy end up receiving one. Some people eligible for a subsidy will receive coverage from more than one source. Moreover, because of the elasticity of demand among those without coverage, it takes a sizable subsidy to encourage the voluntary purchase of health insurance. In the Pepper Commission example, a subsidy of 50 percent of the cost of health insurance (on average) was assumed to motivate only half of the eligible families to buy insurance (Pepper Commission 1990, appendixes B and D). Assuming that 7.7 million individuals were to enroll, just subsidizing private insurance, could cost $8 billion. A less generous subsidy would lower this figure, but would be less effective at expanding coverage and more likely to apply only to those who would have obtained coverage in the absence of the subsidy.

Subsidizing voluntary coverage also does not resolve today's work disincentive issues. Only proposals mandating that everyone obtain coverage present the opportunity to "delink" employment and health coverage, thereby lessening the motivation to obtain public health care protection by leaving work. However, if private benefits are very limited as compared to public ones, the incentive, particularly for chronically ill populations, would continue.

Reforming Insurance Market Rules

Some policymakers favor changing insurance market rules as a means of expanding coverage without increasing public expenditures. Most of their proposals address the sale of insurance, and some plans deal with the determination of premiums. Health insurance premiums are based on the cost of health care and are affected by the rules associated with the sale of insurance. As long as insurers can deny coverage to those most likely to use health services, the price of insurance will reflect the average cost among those with insurance plus a portion of the cost for the uninsured. Therefore, if people can no longer be denied or excluded from coverage, the overall price of insurance for individuals and small groups is likely to increase.

If new rules address only the sale of insurance, and not the rates, then insurers can selectively price their coverage in order to encourage or discourage specific groups. If premiums are regulated to remain within certain limits, prices for the relatively young and healthy are more likely to increase. Coverage for the sick may expand, but some young and healthy people may drop their coverage due to higher premiums.

New rules regarding the pricing and selling practices of insurers would require a considerable amount of regulation in a voluntary system. Most state insurance departments are not well prepared to undertake this task. The incentive for insurers to avoid high-risk individuals is so strong that merely banning certain practices is unlikely to prevent insurers from seeking other ways, for example, through location, provider choice, or marketing efforts, to avoid high-risk populations. Individuals also have strong reasons to minimize their risk in a voluntary system. Without some limits on eligibility, individuals can wait to buy policies until the moment they need health care, thereby undermining the ability of the private market to sell insurance that pools the cost of health care risks. Consequently, insurance market reforms alone—in the absence of mandatory health care coverage—will not necessarily expand access to insurance and could decrease coverage.

Mandating Private Benefits

In addition to regulating the sale and pricing of health insurance, one could mandate coverage of certain benefits. Mandating broader coverage would lead to higher premiums. For example, most private plans have various restrictions on inpatient and outpatient mental health care in order to limit costs. If the number of days of inpatient psychiatric care were required to be 365, instead of the more typical 30 days, then premiums would increase by 2.6 percent, on average (Congressional Research Service 1988). If reimbursement of outpatient mental health care were raised from the more typical 50 percent of provider charges to 80 percent of charges, premiums would increase by 0.7 percent, on average. Overall, covering mental health care in a manner similar to other health care services would raise private premiums by about 3.1 percent.

Changing Medicaid

Beginning in the late 1980s, there was a series of expansions to Medicaid eligibility and covered services. Benefits added during the 1980s, for example, included home and community-based waivers, case management, and supported employment. In addition, modifications were made to eligibility, income, or asset criteria. New eligibility rules for pregnant women and children, based on family income rather than on receipt of cash benefits, heralded a change in the fundamental principles of the program.

A similar expansion might be considered to provide for the disabled of working age and with family incomes of less than the poverty threshold. Thus, coverage could be extended to 2.8 million people, but with nearly $9 billion in new public costs.[16] Of course, more restrictive eligibility criteria or more limited benefits could lower the cost of this proposal.

Some suggestions are to eliminate the Medicaid program and to enroll beneficiaries in private plans for acute care coverage. This would remove the Medicaid stigma and improve access to private providers. However, many individuals would lose benefits now available under Medicaid but not typically allowed under private plans. Even if Medicaid long-term care coverage does not change, access to many extended services (rehabilitation, assistive devices, social, and supportive services) would be lost in the shift to private plans. While access to such "wrap-around" services could be maintained explicitly through a separate program, in all likelihood such fragmented financing would result in less coordinated care.

Other proposals involve expanding current Medicaid work incentive provisions, by raising the earnings threshold at which Medicaid is discontinued. While these changes would increase the motivation to leave the cash benefit rolls, one must first become eligible for cash benefits, by stopping work, for example, in order to get health and health-related coverage. This increases the pull to obtain cash benefits in the first place. Ultimately, such changes also raise the policy question of why individuals in similar situations, i.e., disabled but working, are treated differently: those who once received cash benefits have health and health-related coverage, but those who never received cash benefits do not.

Changing Medicare

One possible change to the Medicare program would involve eliminating the existing 24-month waiting period for individuals who are receiving DI cash benefits. This would add nearly 628,000 DI beneficiaries to Medicare at an estimated cost of $2.6 billion. Eliminating the waiting period would provide relief for those individuals who have left their jobs without retaining health coverage because their employer did not offer it, because they could not afford the continuation premium, or because the continuation period expired. However, this approach also *increases* the incentive for disabled individuals to obtain cash benefits in order to get health coverage. Thus, a coverage gap would be filled, but the link between cash benefits and health care would be strengthened. This incentive is weaker if the services the individuals need most are extended or long-term care benefits, which are generally not provided by Medicare.

Access to Health-Related and Long-Term Care Services

Expanding coverage for health-related or long-term care services also can be accomplished by adding new programs or by modifying private insurance, public programs, or the tax code.

New Home- and Community-Based Care Programs

Several proposals have attempted to improve access to home- and community-based, long-term care services by creating a new, federally funded program. In most cases, the programs are capped at a specific federal dollar amount and require state contributions. They typically are designed to give states and individuals a great deal of flexibility, and, ultimately, would replace current Medicaid waiver programs.

The president's proposal, for example, included a significant new public program to cover home- and community-based care for individuals with disabilities. Other bills had similar provisions. The president's program would have been state-administered using federal funds and required state contributions. States were allocated a fixed budget, with total budgeted federal spending starting at $4.5 billion in 1996 and increasing to $38.3 billion by 2003. Ultimately, such a program could cover approximately 3 million severely disabled individuals, of whom about 710,000 would be of working age.

Eligibility for the program was based on the need for assistance with three or more ADLs, on severe cognitive or mental impairment, and on special criteria for young children. Under the plan, states had a great deal of flexibility in designing service systems. States had to provide needs assessments and individual care plans. However, not all services identified in the individual care plan had to be offered by the state; in fact, only personal assistance services were required. All other services were at the discretion of the state (for example, case management, home modifications, homemaker and chore assistance, respite services, assistive devices, vocational rehabilitation, supported employment, or mental health) as were limits on amount, duration, and scope of any services offered. Care was offered in the home, in community residential settings, or outside the home. The plan did not provide complete coverage for these services to eligible persons. All services were subject to coinsurance (ranging from less than 10 percent to 25 percent of costs) depending on income, and there was no out-of-pocket limit on an individual's contribution.

How does this proposal compare to Medicaid today? From the perspective of the individual, eligibility and cost-sharing requirements are different. (Eligibility requirements have more restrictive disability criteria but no means testing.) From the perspective of the state, there is more flexibility under the proposal to design services. While Medicaid is an individual entitlement, the proposed program would be an entitlement to states with an overall cap. States could phase out the Medicaid services and instead provide services under the new home- and community-based care program at a higher federal matching rate and with greater flexibility. Because state allocations under the new program would have been based in part on current Medicaid expenditures, inequities across states would have continued.

Changing Medicaid

In 1990, the Medicaid program spent nearly $28 billion (or 37 percent of total costs) covering institutional and community-based long-term care for 2.4 million elderly and nonelderly disabled beneficiaries (CRS 1993, pp.141, 146). This coverage included nursing home care, institutional services for the mentally retarded, care in institutions for mental diseases, home health services, and personal assistance. Short of creating an entirely new program, Medicaid rules could be modified by expanding eligibility through lower income and asset thresholds or through changes to spousal impoverishment rules. For example, one could mandate Medicaid coverage for personal care assistance in all states. If the income eligibility criterion were raised to 200 percent of the poverty level for this service and the asset test were removed, this expansion would cover approximately 10 million individuals with severe limitations (i.e., requiring assistance with three or more ADLs) at a cost of approximately $13 billion. Small, incremental changes may bring relief to narrow segments of the population, but are unlikely to change problems with fragmented delivery across medical care, social services, long-term care, and vocational rehabilitation. Furthermore, only changes in federal mandates would narrow large disparities between states regarding spending levels, reimbursement, and covered services.

Changing Coverage for Veterans

Although many groups, such as the Commission on the Future Structure of Veterans Health Care, have advocated a change in VA eligibility and delivery of services, such initiatives were put on hold during the debate on health care reform. Proposals that provided universal coverage attempted to retain access to special VA benefits for some groups. Other proposals that mandated all individuals to obtain coverage included all VA eligibles as an already covered group that met the requirements of the mandate. Most plans, however, did not address the issue of veterans who are eligible for services (theoretically, all veterans) but who cannot obtain them due to limited resources in their area.

Encouraging Private Long-Term Care Coverage

Some recent proposals have focused on encouraging today's nascent market for private long-term care insurance. The insurance industry has argued that the tax code should be clarified to permit deduction of insurance premiums for long-term care, just as for acute health care.[17] Such a change would affect approximately 17 million individuals and would cost about $0.5 billion to $1.0 billion per year in lost revenues. Others have argued for a tax credit in order to signal the importance of long-term care insurance or to stimulate its purchase. This approach would affect fewer individuals, approximately 3 million, and could cost $0.5 billion to $0.8 billion, depending on the size of the credit. In addition, some have recommended national standards and consumer protection for long-term care policies. In a number of proposals, long-term care policies must meet these standards in order to qualify for preferred tax treatment. In others, policies that failed to meet standards would be prohibited or would face penalties.

Using the Tax Code

Deductions and credits have long been used to either encourage or discourage private actions or to modify inequalities that arise from existing definitions of costs and income. Deductions, generally, are best used to refine the definition of taxable income. They tend to favor taxpayers with higher incomes, who have greater tax rates. Tax credits tend to be more effective at encouraging a particular type of purchase. Most existing credits are not refundable, which means that the credit is limited by the amount of taxes owed. In contrast, a refundable tax credit benefits families regardless of their income, tax rate, or total tax liability. The Earned Income Tax Credit (EITC) is an example of a refundable tax credit.

Tax code modifications can be used to subsidize the cost of insurance premiums, either for health or long-term care. Alternatively, they can subsidize the cost of specific types of equipment or care, such as services currently not recognized in the medical care deduction. The tax code, however, is not a very effective tool for targeting financial assistance to those with few resources or with specific types or levels of disability. New tax forms would have to include measures of assets and types of disability to determine eligibility.

Several proposals in 1994 provided for tax code changes specifically to assist people with disabilities in the work force. One provision extended the existing medical expense deduction to include long-term care services for persons requiring assistance with two or more activities of daily living or with severe cognitive impairment.[18] Such a provision could help the estimated 2.9 million persons needing assistance with ADLs or IADLs (based on the 1989 National Health Interview Survey), but only if they itemize their tax deductions.

The president's plan included a proposal under which disabled, employed individuals could receive a tax credit up to $15,000 per year for 50 percent of the cost of personal assistance services.[19] The credit would give individuals the flexibility to choose services and providers, without constraints that might arise in other programs because of utilization review or low provider reimbursement rates. However, the credit was limited to $15,000 per year and applied only to the cost of personal care services for employed individuals with physical and cognitive impairments, not mental illness. In 1989, approximately 60,000 indi-

viduals needed assistance with ADLs and either worked or were limited in the amount or type of work they could perform. The tax credit
would benefit such people regardless of earnings. Such a proposal also
would help those currently unable to work because of the cost of personal assistance. In 1989, 2.3 million working-age individuals were
unable to work and needed help with ADLs or IADLs; it is not clear
how many of these people would have been employed if part of the
cost of personal assistance had been subsidized. Somewhat more than
30 percent of these individuals currently are covered by Medicaid, the
only existing program that might provide for such long-term care services. The potential employment effect of personal assistance subsidies
for these individuals as well as for those currently without Medicaid is
not clear. For many considering returning to work, the potential loss of
acute care coverage is still a barrier.

Other Initiatives and State-Sponsored Changes

Several other steps could change the financing and delivery of health
care. In the absence of federal health care reform, there has been an
increased movement toward enrollment in managed-care plans. Managed care presents a number of open questions for populations with
chronic conditions. In a fee-for-service plan, individuals can choose
their providers and, to a large extent, their services. In managed-care
systems, individuals often are limited to a panel of providers. The providers receive a set amount per enrollee. By controlling total payments,
health plans may encourage providers to utilize health care resources
more selectively and efficiently and may promote innovations in community-based delivery models. Safeguards may be necessary to ensure
that needed services are not withheld. Furthermore, a smaller managed-care plan may not be able to support a wide range of specialty
physicians, gatekeepers skilled in chronic care management, techni-
cians, equipment, and testing for people with diverse chronic and disabling conditions. There is considerable concern about the ability of
primary care gatekeepers to manage complex cases appropriately and
to refer patients to the specialists and other types of services needed.

States also have been active in changing health care systems, primarily by modifying Medicaid rules. Recently, six states were awarded
large-scale Medicaid waivers (so-called "1115 waivers") to change eli-

gibility, benefits, and service delivery. Proposals by nine other states were pending as of September 1994 (Kaiser Commission on the Future of Medicaid 1994, p. 2). In most cases, the waivers mandate Medicaid coverage through managed-care plans. They also extend coverage to low-income populations who currently are not eligible for Medicaid, but cover them for fewer services than Medicaid beneficiaries have covered. Thus, the implied state preference is to cover more people for a smaller number of services. The impact on persons with disabilities, who frequently require a broad range of services, is not yet clear. Some waivers exclude the disabled, blind and aged from the waiver, others create special managed-care programs for the disabled or for populations with specific conditions, such as mental illness, substance abuse, or mental retardation.

Conclusion

The current health care system, a web of private and public coverage, leaves large gaps for people with disabilities. The most obvious breach is that 17 percent of those unable to work because of a disability and 12 percent of those needing assistance with activities of daily living have no coverage at all. Many others have coverage that excludes chronic, long-term, or health-related needs. These gaps create perverse incentives in employment patterns, particularly for people with chronic conditions who require a lot of care or nonacute care. Some individuals may be trapped in a job because of its health benefits, and others may not want to leave public programs. Employment does not convey coverage automatically; thus, leaving the cash benefit rolls carries the risk of losing one's only opportunity for health care coverage. Furthermore, employment-based insurance frequently does not cover services needed by the disabled.

The opportunity to bring about fundamental change in access to acute care coverage "came and went" for now. Remaining options span a number of smaller, marginal revisions to either the public or private systems. These, however, must stand up to a budget-hostile environment. Furthermore, these incremental steps could exacerbate work disincentives, perpetuate inequities across different groups, or accelerate the decline of private insurance. Recent efforts to overhaul state systems seem to center on spreading a thin public dollar even more thinly across more eligible people—with an as yet undetermined impact on individuals with disabilities. Ultimately, however, only if private and public coverage were seamless, covering most services that chronically ill populations need, would the barriers and employment disincentives completely be removed.

NOTES

NOTE: The views expressed herein are solely those of the authors. They do not represent the official position of the National Academy of Social Insurance, the National Academy on Aging or the organizations that have provided funding for this project. This paper was supported by grants from the Pew Charitable Trusts and the Carnegie Corporation of New York.

*Data from the National Health Interview Survey, 1983-1986 (four-year average). Data are based on household surveys of the civilian, noninstitutionalized population.

1. In the SIPP, activities of daily living are defined as getting around inside the home, getting in or out of bed, taking a bath or shower, dressing, eating, or using the toilet. Instrumental activities of daily living include going outside the home, for example, shopping, keeping track of money and bills, preparing meals, doing light housework, or using the telephone.

2. Similarly, data from the National Health Interview Survey show that, although half of working-age persons have a chronic condition, only 15 percent have a limitation in activity and 10 percent are limited in work (National Institute on Disability and Rehabilitation Research 1991, p. 20).

3. Another 0.9 percent had coverage from undefined plans. Data from the 1989 National Health Interview Survey.

4. Firms with 20 or more employees must extend coverage to former employees for a fixed time period but may charge them the full premium plus 2 percent.

5. Insurers tempt the owners to drop their current policy by offering a lower price, but this price excludes the coverage of any "preexisting" medical conditions. As time elapses and these exclusions are no longer in place, the insurance price increases.

6. In the past, the tax code also was unclear about whether benefits would be treated as taxable income. Since 1989, it has been clarified that the earnings on long-term care insurance reserves can be treated in the same manner as earnings on life insurance reserves, i.e., these earnings are exempt from taxation for insurers and policyholders.

7. Twelve states, the so-called 209(b) states, use more restrictive eligibility standards than SSI policies, either regarding the definition of disability or regarding income and resource limits or definitions. States electing the 209(b) option must allow applicants to "spend down," i.e., to deduct medical expenses from income in determining eligibility.

8. In such cases, parental income and resources are not counted, although the SSI benefit amount is reduced by one-third.

9. Effective April 1990, states have been required to cover all pregnant women and children under age 6 whose income is below 133 percent of the federal poverty level. In addition, Medicaid must expand coverage each year to children under age 19, so that, by October 2001, all children living below 100 percent of the federal poverty level will be covered.

10. In practice, to become medically needy, one must first deplete one's assets to the eligibility standard (i.e., $2,000 for individuals and $3,000 for couples) and then continue to incur high medical expenses relative to one's income.

11. Because the eligibility standard for medically needy applicants must be the same across all applicants (families, children, elderly, and disabled) and because it may not exceed 133 percent of the AFDC payment, very often the medically needy income standard is lower than the SSI benefit standard (CRS 1993, p. 211).

12. The individual's earnings must be less than the combined equivalent of SSI, SSP, Medicaid, and publicly funded personal attendant care benefits.

13. Medicare also covers individuals with end-stage renal disease, regardless of whether or not they work.

14. Disabled beneficiaries include disabled workers under age 65, widows aged 50 to 64, and children aged 18 and over who were disabled before age 22.

15. In 1993, this voluntary premium was $245 per month for Medicare Part A. The premium rate for Part B was $36.60 per month. If the individual returns to the disability rolls within five years (seven years for widows and adult children), there is no two-year waiting period to be re-eligible for Medicare without paying a premium.

16. This estimate is based on the average cost of coverage for those now eligible because of a disability. In this sense, the cost per potential beneficiary is probably overstated. However, this estimate does not include the potential of more people claiming to be disabled than currently measured by random sample surveys. This estimate assumes that both the uninsured and those now covered by private insurance would seek Medicaid coverage.

17. The Internal Revenue Service has argued that legislation, not clarification, would be required.

18. Deductible expenses include the provision of assistance with "activities of daily living" (eating, dressing, bathing, toileting, transferring in and out of bed) or protection from threats to health and safety due to severe cognitive impairment. Services may not be provided by a relative and must be part of a plan of care prescribed by a licensed professional. All deductible medical expenses would be subject to the existing 7.5 percent floor.

19. The 50 percent is reduced by 10 percentage points for each $5,000 in adjusted gross income over $45,000. Services are defined broadly and include personal assistance to carry out "activities of daily living" (eating, dressing, bathing, toileting, transferring in and out of bed) in or outside of the home; homemaker/chore services (e.g., meal preparation or shopping); assistance with life skills (e.g., money management) for people with cognitive impairments; assistive technology services; or modifications to the home. To be eligible, individuals must prove that they have a "medically determinable physical impairment," which has lasted or is expected to last at least 12 months. Furthermore, they must be unable to engage in substantial gainful activity without personal assistance services.

References

Barker, Peggy R., Ronald W. Manderscheid, Gerry E. Hendershot, et al. 1992. "Serious Mental Illness and Disability in the Adult Household Population: United States, 1989."*Advance Data,* No. 218. Hyattsville, MD: National Center for Health Statistics.

Burwell, Brian, Mary Harahan, David Kennell, et al. 1993. *An Analysis of Long-Term Care Reform Proposals: Final Report Prepared for the Office of the Assistant Secretary for Planning and Evaluation, Division of Aging and Long-Term Care Policy.* Cambridge, MA: SysteMetrics, Inc. February.

Congressional Research Service. 1988. *Cost and Effects of Extending Health Insurance Coverage.* Education and Labor Serial No. 100-EE. Washington, DC: Government Printing Office, October.

Congressional Research Service. 1993. *Medicaid Source Book: Background and Data Analysis (A 1993 Update).* Washington, DC: Government Printing Office, January.

Durch, Jane S., ed. 1994. *Protecting and Improving Quality of Care for Children Under Health Care Reform: Workshop Highlights.* Washington, DC: National Research Council, Institute of Medicine.

Employee Benefit Research Institute. 1994. "Sources of Health Insurance and Characteristics of the Uninsured: Analysis of the March 1993 Current Population Survey." *EBRI Issue Brief* No. 145. Washington, DC: EBRI, January.

Kaiser Commission on the Future of Medicaid. 1994. "Statewide Medicaid Demonstrations: Overview of Approved and Proposed Activities under Section 1115 of the Social Security Act." *Policy Brief.* Washington, DC: Henry J. Kaiser Family Foundation, September.

LaPlante, Mitchell P. 1992. "Assistive Technology Devices and Home Accessibility Features: Prevalence, Payment, Need, and Trends." *Advance Data,* No. 217. Hyattsville, MD: National Center for Health Statistics.

National Academy of Social Insurance. 1994. *Preliminary Status Report of the Disability Policy Panel.* Washington, DC: National Academy of Social Insurance, March.

National Center for Health Statistics. 1992. *Prevention Profile. Health United States, 1991.* Hyattsville, MD: Public Health Service.

National Council on Disability. 1994. *Making Health Care Reform Work for Americans with Disabilities.* Washington, DC: National Council on Disability, July 26.

National Institute on Disability and Rehabilitation Research. 1991. *Disability Statistics Report: Disability Risks and Chronic Illnesses and Impairments.*

Report 2. Washington, DC: U.S. Department of Health and Human Services, June.

_____. 1993. *Disability Statistics Report: Disability, Health Insurance Coverage, and Utilization of Acute Health Services in the United States.* Washington, DC: U.S. Department of Education, October.

Paralyzed Veterans Association. 1992. *Strategy 2000: The VA Responsibility in Tomorrow's National Health Care System.* Washington, DC: Paralyzed Veterans Association.

_____. 1994. Personal Communication. October. Washington, DC.

Pepper Commission. 1990. *A Call for Action.* Final Report. Washington, DC: Government Printing Office, September.

Perrin, James, Bernard Guyer, and Jean M. Lawrence. 1992. "Health Care Services for Children and Adolescents," *The Future of Children* 2 (Winter): 58-77.

Ries, Peter. 1991. "Disability and Health: Characteristics of Persons by Limitation of Activity and Assessed Health Status, United States, 1984-88." *Advance Data*, No. 197. Hyattsville, MD: National Center for Health Statistics.

Schlesinger, Mark, and David Mechanic. 1993. "Perspectives: Challenges for Managed Competition From Chronic Illness," *Health Affairs* 12 (Supplement): 123-137.

Smith, Gary A., and Robert M. Gettings. 1991. *Supported Employment and Medicaid Financing.* Alexandria, VA: National Association of State Mental Retardation Program Directors, Inc., September.

Taylor, Ann B., Susan G. Epstein, and Allen C. Crocker. 1990. "Health Care for Children with Special Needs." In *Children in a Changing Health Care System: Assessment and Proposals for Reform*, Mark J. Schlesinger and Leon Eisenberg, eds. Baltimore: Johns Hopkins University Press.

U.S. Department of Commerce. 1993. *Americans with Disabilities: 1991-92: Data from the Survey of Income and Program Participation.* Current Population Reports, P70-33. Washington, DC: Government Printing Office, December.

U.S. Department of Health and Human Services. Public Health Service. 1991. *Healthy People 2000.* Washington, DC: Government Printing Office.

U.S. Department of Health and Human Services. Health Care Financing Administration. Office of the Actuary. 1994. Personal Communication. September.

U.S. Department of Veterans Affairs. 1991. *Report of the Commission on the Future Structure of Veterans Health Care.* Washington, DC: Department of Veterans Affairs, November.

U.S. Equal Employment Opportunity Commission. 1993. Interim Enforcement Guidance, June 8.

U.S. General Accounting Office. 1993. *States Turn to Managed Care to Improve Access and Control Costs*. Washington, DC: General Accounting Office, March.

Weiner, Joshua M., Laurel Hixon Illston, and Raymond J. Hanley. 1994. *Sharing the Burden: Strategies for Public and Private Long-Term Care Insurance*. Washington, DC: Brookings Institution.

Health Care, Personal Assistance and Assistive Technology

Are In-Kind Benefits Key to Independence or Dependence for People with Disabilities?

Andrew I. Batavia
McDermott, Will and Emery
and
Georgetown University
School of Medicine

In-Kind Benefits

In addition to cash benefits, the Social Security system in our country provides a variety of benefits in kind to eligible individuals with disabilities. Eligibility for the in-kind benefits, such as health insurance, is typically contingent upon eligibility for cash benefits under the Social Security Disability Insurance (DI) and Supplemental Security Income (SSI) programs, which, in turn, depends upon inability to work due to a medical impairment. This paper considers whether the system's in-kind benefits, and the way in which they are designed and made available, optimally assist disability beneficiaries to achieve the goals that our nation sets for these programs, and whether there is a better way to fulfill these goals.

The Goal of Independence

There is now a consensus that the goal of U.S. disability policy is to enhance the capacity of people with disabilities to live independently in their communities. This has been the key objective of the independent living movement from its outset in the early 1970s (DeJong 1979, 1981) and was most clearly recognized as a national goal with the enactment of the Americans with Disabilities Act of 1990 (ADA). Disability advocates and researchers have concluded that we must bring the goals and policies of other disability laws and programs, including the Social Security disability programs, in line with the independent living goals of the ADA (National Council on Disability 1986, 1988; DeJong and Batavia 1990).

While there is general agreement that independence is the goal, this consensus may be somewhat illusory because different people mean different things by "independence." The term is often used loosely and ambiguously to refer to two distinct, and often conflicting, objectives. These are:

1. the ability to live in the community and out of institutions, even if this ability is a direct result of government or philanthropic subsidization (which I will refer to as the support goal), and

2. the ability to live self-sufficiently in the community through one's own employment and resources (which I will call the employment goal).

The ADA, with its Title I employment provisions, clearly emphasizes the employment goal. However, both goals address valid objectives of the Social Security disability programs, which cover some individuals who are incapable of work.[1] Each reflects a different objective of the system, and the contrast between them represents the basic tension between the aims of subsidizing those who need assistance and rewarding those who can make the effort to be productive. Ideally, policy decisions concerning eligibility and benefits should be based upon a careful balancing of likely effects on each of these two independent living goals.

Independence and In-Kind Benefits

Most analysts agree that obtaining in-kind Social Security benefits is extremely important to the ability of people with disabilities to live independently, from both the support and employment perspectives. If, for example, individuals who require full-time personal assistance (e.g., attendant care) cannot obtain such services, they will not be able to live in their communities. If beneficiaries will eventually lose their health coverage as a result of accepting employment, it is not in their interest to take a job that does not provide long-term assurance of at least comparable benefits or their cash equivalent.

Advocates often argue that it makes little policy sense to tie eligibility for disability benefits to the ability or decision to work. Individuals with disabilities will need these benefits to live in their communities whether or not they have a job; linking them through employment-based eligibility criteria will only decrease the incentive to work. The disincentive is likely to be particularly strong to the extent that the benefit is not available through employment, as is the case with some in-kind benefits. Despite recent legislative efforts to eliminate work disincentives, people with disabilities remain concerned about eventually losing their in-kind benefits. This concern will persist as long as the eligibility-employment link remains.

In-Kind versus Cash Benefits

Recognizing the importance of in-kind benefits to the ability to live independently also does not inexorably lead to the conclusion that such assistance must be or should be provided in kind. Presumably, if all other factors were equal, the individual with a disability would prefer an added cash benefit to an in-kind benefit of equal value. The cash benefit would offer far greater flexibility for the individual to pursue his or her independent living goals. However, for a variety of reasons, many people with disabilities currently prefer the benefits they receive in kind rather than in cash, and many policy makers prefer to offer them in kind.

From the perspective of the policy maker, who is accountable to the taxpayers financing these programs, a cash benefit does not provide the assurance that the money will be spent in a manner that would satisfy taxpayer concerns. This security is critical to ongoing political support for the program. For example, a cash benefit in lieu of Medicare might be used by a beneficiary for better nutrition or housing. While this may be a rational decision on the part of the recipient, taxpayers may resent this use of program funds, recognizing that they will ultimately still have to pay the bill if the individual becomes ill. Some policy makers do not trust beneficiaries to make accountable decisions.[2]

From the perspective of beneficiaries, an equivalent cash benefit has two significant drawbacks. First, individuals are concerned that a cash payment does not guarantee the ability to purchase the service previously obtained through the in-kind benefit. For example, if private health insurers will not offer coverage at any price to people with disabilities, the cash benefit in lieu of in-kind insurance will be of little use. This problem could be remedied through certain insurance market reforms, such as guaranteed issue (assuring coverage) and community rating (assuring affordability). Second, beneficiaries are concerned that, even with such reforms, there will be a political tendency for the cash amount to be set below the level necessary to obtain adequate services.

For these reasons, cash in lieu of an in-kind benefit is probably not politically feasible in this country and will not be considered further in this paper. However, a system based on vouchers, Medical Savings Accounts (MSAs),[3] or tax credits providing a "cash equivalent" limited to the purchase of specified services would satisfy the accountability needs of many policy makers. With respect to a tax credit, making it "refundable" and therefore available to individuals with no tax liability could equitably provide support for all individuals who require services.

The feasibility of this cash equivalent approach depends largely on whether it can be structured to satisfy the significant concerns of beneficiaries and their advocates. There would have to be some assurance that the voucher, MSA, or tax credit would be sufficient to obtain the needed service over the long term.

In-Kind Benefits and Public Policy

Eligibility and benefits ideally should be based on empirical evidence of how to achieve the independent living goals of support and employment in the most cost-effective way. While several researchers have identified a Social Security disability work disincentive generally (Leonard 1986, Muller 1989, Burkhauser and Haveman 1982), none has specifically considered whether there is a greater disincentive associated with in-kind benefits. Similarly, there has been little study of other implications of providing benefits in kind rather than through cash equivalents. In the absence of such empirical research, we must rely upon economic theory in conjunction with our knowledge of the behavior of beneficiaries.

According to conventional economic theory, receiving disability benefits in kind or through cash equivalents should not fundamentally affect the individual's decision to seek gainful employment, *all other factors equal.* Based on a strict rational choice model, the individual would compare the aggregate value of disability benefits, both cash and in kind, with the aggregate value of a job package, including salary, vacation, and all fringe benefits. If the job's benefits exceed the social program's benefits by a sufficient amount to compensate for the value of the person's labor, the individual will seek and accept employment.

However, it is clear that all other factors are not equal in comparing in-kind benefits and cash equivalents. Many of the benefits in kind currently available to people with disabilities would not be available or affordable to them in the market. The most obvious, again, is health insurance. Health insurers in the individual, nongroup market typically either exclude people with disabilities from coverage altogether or make such coverage extremely unattractive due to specific exclusions and limitations for preexisting conditions (Griss 1988; DeJong, Batavia, and Griss 1989). Whether it is feasible to implement significant alternatives to the current in-kind benefit structure will depend partly on whether such other factors can be made equal through public policy (Batavia 1993).

This paper focuses on three in-kind benefits that are considered very important to people with disabilities: health insurance, personal assistance services, and assistive technology. It examines what disability benefits are currently provided, how individuals are eligible for such benefits, whether these benefits are adequate to allow people to live in their communities, whether this approach is helping individuals to seek work, and how we can restructure eligibility and benefits to encourage independence. The paper's basic premise is that both the support and employment goals are more likely to be achieved to the extent that people with disabilities are able to control their lives. Due to the inherent flexibility of cash equivalents, this form of assistance potentially offers greater control than do benefits provided in kind.

Health Insurance

Access to health care is key to independent living for many people with disabilities. *On average,* such individuals have greater health problems and higher rates of health care utilization than nondisabled individuals (Lubitz and Pine 1986; DeJong, Batavia, and Griss 1989; LaPlante and Miller 1992; Rice and LaPlante 1992). Ironically, people with disabilities also have much poorer access to private health insurance than do other members of the population (Griss 1988; Burns, Batavia and DeJong 1991; Agency for Health Care Policy and Research (AHCPR) 1992; National Council on Disability 1993a; LaPlante, Rice and Cyril 1994).[4]

People with disabilities who are without health insurance, or without adequate coverage, are likely to delay treatment of minor health concerns until they have escalated to major problems. For example, an individual with a spinal cord injury can develop a life-threatening decubitus ulcer (bedsore) in a matter of days without detection and appropriate treatment. If an urgent problem occurs, such individuals potentially compromise their financial ability to live independently. Ultimately, our society often pays both indirectly through uncovered care and directly through the public assistance programs (DeJong, Batavia, and Griss 1989).

How Do People with Disabilities Currently Receive Health Benefits?

The primary public health insurance programs for people with disabilities are Medicare (Title XVIII of the Social Security Act, hereafter, "the Act"), and Medicaid (Title XIX of the Act). Eligibility for Medicare for people with disabilities is based on eligibility for DI. Eligibility for Medicaid is based on eligibility for SSI. Both cash benefits programs, DI and SSI, use the same definition of disability: the inability to engage in any gainful activity due to a medically determinable impairment that is expected to last for a period of 12 consecutive months or to result in death.[5]

When Medicare was established in 1965, it primarily had an acute care orientation and did not focus on the chronic care needs of people with disabilities. In 1972, DI beneficiaries on the disability rolls for at least 24 months were made eligible for full Medicare coverage. This waiting period has been severely criticized, because some beneficiaries have a life expectancy of less than two years and the conditions of others with longer life expectancies may deteriorate if they do not receive the treatment they need in the first two years. In 1992, there were 3.57

million individuals with disabilities enrolled in Medicare, at a cost of $14.3 billion (U.S. Department of Health and Human Services (HHS) 1994, table 8.B2).

Medicaid also was established in 1965. However, unlike Medicare, it had a long-term, chronic care orientation from the outset. Section 1901 of the Act, the introduction to Medicaid, states explicitly that the purpose of the program is to enable states to furnish medical assistance "and rehabilitation and other services ... to help attain or retain capability for independence or self-care."[6] Consequently, from the beginning, Medicaid has been more closely attuned than Medicare to disability issues. In 1993, there were 4.9 million individuals with "permanent and total disabilities" receiving Medicaid, at a cost of $38 billion (HHS 1994, table 8.E2).

Does the Current Eligibility and Benefit Structure Provide Adequate Support?

Medicare now covers a broad set of acute care and rehabilitation services, including inpatient hospitalization and physician services. Also covered are inpatient and outpatient rehabilitation services at a rehabilitation hospital or unit, an acute care hospital, a skilled nursing facility, a Comprehensive Outpatient Rehabilitation Facility (CORF), a therapist's office, or the patient's home. While the Medicare beneficiary's cost-sharing requirements have increased substantially over time (HHS 1994, table 2.C1), most beneficiaries are satisfied with respect to these covered services.

However, Medicare coverage is weak in the areas of preventive or wellness care, long-term and maintenance care, and prescription drugs. It has been criticized for its primarily acute care orientation and its lack of catastrophic stop-loss protection, particularly in light of the increasing chronic and long-term care needs of an aging population (Griss 1988). Several legislative proposals, such as the Medicare Catastrophic Coverage Act of 1988, have been launched to address these shortcomings. Thus far all have been unsuccessful, largely due to the difficulty in financing these expensive benefits in a manner that is politically feasible.

Medicaid coverage for people with disabilities is fairly comprehensive, partly because the federal government requires, as a condition of program participation, that mandatory benefits be provided to those who are eligible as categorically needy (such as SSI recipients).[7] These benefits include inpatient and outpatient hospital services, lab and x-ray services, services in a skilled nursing facility, early and periodic screening, diagnosis and treatment, and family planning, physician, and home health services (Batavia 1989).

Medicaid appears to provide adequate coverage generally, although much depends upon how each state implements its own Medicaid program. While state plans must be consistent with federal requirements, states vary in their rules interpreting these standards and in the extent to which they cover optional services. Some states, such as California, are relatively generous in their coverage. Others cover the bare minimum. Overall, payment rates for Medicaid services tend to be substantially below market rates, and many beneficiaries have difficulty finding providers who will accept Medicaid payment (Griss 1988).

Does the Current Eligibility and Benefit Structure Encourage Employment?

As suggested, despite substantial legislative efforts, there appears to be a continuing work disincentive associated with the fear of losing health benefits. Throughout the 1980s, Congress enacted laws designed to allow disability program participants to accept employment, under certain conditions, without suffering a precipitous loss of cash or health benefits (National Association of Rehabilitation Facilities (NARF) 1988). The major health insurance work incentive provisions are as follow:

- The Social Security Amendments of 1980 allow DI beneficiaries whose disabling conditions continue after losing DI eligibility to retain Medicare eligibility for up to 36 months and to avoid a second 24-month waiting period before becoming re-eligible for Medicare if they become re-eligible for DI within five years.

- The Employment Opportunities for Disabled Americans Act of 1986 made permanent Section 1619 of the Act, allowing SSI recipients to receive cash benefits while gainfully employed and to retain Medicaid eligibility if their income is insufficient to obtain necessary medical services.

- The Omnibus Budget Reconciliation Act of 1989 allows DI beneficiaries who would otherwise lose Medicare benefits after the 36-month extended Medicare eligibility period to pay premiums to maintain their Medicare coverage (i.e., the Medicare buy-in). It also requires states to pay for the Medicare buy-in for certain low-income individuals.

Despite these provisions, in December 1993, only 35,299 of 5.98 million disabled SSI recipients participated in the Section 1619 work incentive program (HHS 1994, tables 7.F5 and 7.A3). Overall, throughout the history of the disability programs, regardless of significant incremental changes in the laws likely to cause work disincentives, relatively few beneficiaries have become employed and left the disability rolls (Muller 1989).[8] This suggests the need for more fundamental, comprehensive reform of our approach to encouraging people with disabilities to seek gainful employment.

How Can We Better Satisfy the Goals of Support and Employment?

As a general rule, the work disincentive associated with health insurance is proportional to both the generosity of the health benefit that could be lost and the likelihood that it will be lost and inversely proportional to the generosity of the health coverage or cash equivalent that would be obtained through employment. Consequently, both sides of the health care equation must be addressed to encourage disability beneficiaries to work.[9] Currently, the program benefit to be lost is substantial, and the employment benefit to be gained varies according to individual job skills and employment opportunities, but would be unavailable for many workers with disabilities.

The best way to deal with both sides of the equation is through policy reform that offers access to coverage whether or not the individual is employed or changes jobs. Developing truly "portable" health insurance was one of the primary objectives of the great health care reform debate of the 103rd Congress. Unfortunately, the focus of the debate was the Health Security Act (i.e., the Clinton plan),[10] which proved to be unduly complex, bureaucratic, unaffordable, and ultimately unacceptable to the American public. Other alternative plans could achieve the objectives of health reform, including the independent living goals of support and employment, without creating a bureaucratic behemoth.

One encouraging approach developed by the Heritage Foundation would offer direct tax credits to all individuals, irrespective of employment status, based upon their health care costs relative to their incomes.[11] Under this proposal, insurers would have to make their plans available to all people including people with disabilities, who would receive the purchasing power to obtain a health plan of their choice (with at least catastrophic coverage). If the individuals accepted employment, the amount of their tax credits would be reduced according to the increase in their incomes. If they experienced high costs in a particular year, the credit would increase, thereby automatically reducing their financial burden.[12]

Another approach, developed by the National Center for Policy Analysis (NCPA), would allow beneficiaries to apply the actuarial value of their Medicare or Medicaid benefits to purchase a catastrophic health insurance plan with a large deductible (e.g., $3,000) and to establish a Medical Savings Account (MSA) with the remaining funds to pay for amounts up to the deductible (NCPA 1995). The MSA could be structured to allow the beneficiaries to accumulate savings from year to year without compromising eligibility. The savings could be used for any of their independent living needs. As with the Heritage proposal, the amount of the government contribution to an MSA could be reduced as income increases. By eliminating or greatly diminishing the link between eligibility and employment, these approaches would significantly reduce the work disincentive.

Personal Assistance

About 9.6 million people with disabilities require the help of another person with basic personal maintenance, hygiene, and household tasks to be able to live independently (Kennedy 1993). The term "personal assistance services" includes aid in the following activities:

- personal or bodily care functions, traditionally referred to as activities of daily living (ADL);

- meal preparation, laundry, light housekeeping, handling money, shopping, and transportation activities, traditionally referred to as instrumental activities of daily living (IADL);

- reader services for blind persons; and

- interpreter services for deaf persons (Litvak, Zukas and Heumann 1987; Nosek 1992; Batavia, DeJong, and McKnew 1992).

Under the "independent living model" of personal assistance, particularly favored by many working-age people with disabilities, the disabled individual actively recruits, selects, manages, and directs his or her own provider of services, known as a "personal assistant."[13] The assistant typically is neither trained as, nor supervised by, a health care professional. The disabled person is a consumer of services, not a patient, and the assistant is accountable to the consumer, not to a supervising nurse or agency (DeJong 1981; DeJong and Wenker 1983). This model was developed by people with disabilities as a reaction to the perceived paternalism of health care professionals giving care under the "medical model" (Batavia, DeJong, and McKnew 1992).

How Do People with Disabilities Currently Receive Personal Assistance Benefits?

The majority of individuals who require personal assistance currently do not receive it under either the independent living or the medical model; they receive assistance through informal supports, such as family, friends, and volunteers (Kennedy 1993, Rutgers Bureau of Economic Research and World Institute on Disability 1990). This informal support model has been criticized because it often fosters an unhealthy dependency-based relationship between the disabled individual and the unpaid caregiver (Batavia, DeJong and McKnew 1992).

In response to these criticisms and to the growing need for personal aid in the population, government programs of paid assistance have been established. The main federal initiatives that offer personal assistance and other home-based services to disability beneficiaries are home health, homemaker, and chore services financed under Medicaid and under the Social Services block grant program (Title XX of the Act); services under Medicare when home-based assistance is associated with a recent hospital stay; and similar services for disabled senior citizens provided under the Older Americans Act.

The independent living model has been adopted by the Department of Veterans Affairs in its Aides and Attendant Allowance Program and by several states in their Medicaid and Social Services programs. For example, Massachusetts, California, and Pennsylvania have incorporated independent living concepts into their interpretation of the federal regulations governing community-based services (DeJong and Wenker 1983; Zukas, Cone, and Leon 1984; Allard and Spence 1986). Other states provide home-based long-term care services under a more medically oriented model using agencies and medical supervision (Litvak, Zukas, and Heumann 1987; Egley 1994).

Does the Current Eligibility and Benefit Structure Provide Adequate Support?

Whether individuals who require personal assistance services receive the support they need under the model that they prefer depends in large part on the state in which they live. In its 50-state survey of all publicly funded in-home service programs, the World Institute on Disability (WID) found that 42 percent did not cover both personal and domestic services, 22 percent do not cover services seven days per week, 50 percent did not serve persons with incomes above the poverty level, and 67 percent did not allow aides or personal assistants to help in personal care involving medications, catheters, suppositories, or menstrual needs (Litvak, Zukas, and Heumann 1987). While some states have since improved their coverage, most still do not conform to the independent living model (Nosek and Howland 1993; Kennedy 1993).

Thus, most states have not responded to the preferences of many people with disabilities for personal assistance services. To the extent that states or agencies have attempted to fund personal assistance services, most have done so in an uncoordinated and nonsystematic manner. Few provide such services in a way that offers consumers maximum control over their lives, optimally supporting their ability to exist independently in their communities (Nosek 1992). Many programs retain strong elements of the medical model, including reliance on institutional placement (Kennedy 1993).

In addition, states typically have not provided adequate funding to meet the substantial need for such services and have developed a variety of rationing mechanisms to limit their financial responsibility. These include eligibility criteria that limit enrollment to those "at risk of institutionalization" or to people with physical disabilities; coverage rules that prohibit funding for certain nonmedical services; rules prohibiting funding for assistants who are related to the recipient; limitations in the number of hours of services covered; and restrictions concerning the site of services.

One reason for such approaches is that states are concerned over "the woodwork effect" (people who are receiving assistance from relatives or friends coming "out of the woodwork" to request funding) and adverse selection (i.e., the tendency of disabled persons to move to those programs and insurance plans that offer the most generous benefits that they need) (Batavia, DeJong, and McKnew 1992). For example, it is generally acknowledged that many younger disabled persons decide to reside in California because it has a comprehensive in-home support services program based on the independent living model.

Does the Current Eligibility and Benefit Structure Encourage Employment?

As in the case of health insurance, the extent of the work disincentive is directly related to the generosity of the benefit. In those states with very generous personal assistance services programs, the work disincentive appears particularly strong. Personal assistance services are not covered under any private health insurance plans available through employment or in the individual market.[14] Consequently, if an individual were to eventually lose his or her personal assistance benefit, he or she would require a very substantial income to be able to pay for such services out of pocket. Without having access to such services, the individual would have to rely on the assistance of unpaid friends or relatives, if available.

How Can We Restructure Eligibility and Benefits
to Encourage Independence?

To meet the need for personal assistance services equitably, and to reduce adverse selection, a national personal assistance services policy is needed (Batavia, DeJong, and McKnew 1992; Nosek and Howland 1993). Such a policy should provide a comprehensive approach to financing assistance services and helping disabled persons to recruit competent, dependable personal assistants. One national model is the Department of Veterans Affairs program, which provides funds directly for personal assistance services based on need to qualified disabled veterans, regardless of employment status. This model would have to be adapted to protect against the woodwork effect in serving the much larger civilian disabled population.

A possible approach would be to implement a system based on tax credits, MSAs, or vouchers, similar to that suggested for health insurance. In one regard, this approach would be easier to apply to personal assistance because there are no significant barriers to purchasing such services through the general market. The primary challenge would be to develop an equitable and efficient mechanism that is not easily subject to fraud and abuse for purposes of determining the appropriate amount of the credit, MSA, or voucher.

Assistive Technology and Durable Medical Equipment

Just as personal assistance services can compensate for lost functional capacity, assistive technology can also help people with disabilities to live independently. In certain circumstances, it can even provide a cost-effective means of reducing the need for certain kinds of personal assistance. Examples of assistive devices used by people with disabilities include wheelchairs, augmentative communication devices, page turners, environmental control units, and amplified listening devices (Seelman 1993).

Estimates from the National Health Interview Survey suggest that about 5 percent of the civilian noninstitutionalized population currently uses assistive devices, excluding eyeglasses (LaPlante, Hendershot, and Moss 1992). About 1 percent of the population indicated that they did not have at least one assistive device that they needed, primarily due to financial considerations. For many of these individuals, the ability to obtain such items would significantly enhance their ability to live more independently and productively.

How Do Disabled People Currently Receive Assistive Technology Benefits?

Medicare Part B covers the purchase or rental of certain devices that qualify as durable medical equipment (DME), such as wheelchairs. In addition, it covers prosthetic devices, orthotic devices, and certain medical supplies. Yet, DME suppliers received only 3.5 percent of all Medicare Part B payments in 1990. Medicare accounted for 17.8 percent of DME, while private insurance paid 10.4 percent, and individuals paid 67.3 percent out of pocket. The vast majority of Medicare DME expenditures are for such medical equipment as oxygen, 34.4 percent; prosthetics and orthotics 18.8 percent; and tube feeding 17.2 percent (Committee on Ways and Means 1991).

States again vary as to the generosity of their Medicaid coverage, although this is generally limited to fairly basic durable medical equipment. While motorized wheelchairs tend to be covered, most other devices that would support independent living are not. Those SSI recipients who are on the Plan to Achieve Self-Sufficiency (PASS) Program may set aside funds to purchase assistive devices without compromising their program eligibility. Also, some state vocational rehabilitation programs provide assistive devices to support an educational and vocational strategy. However, most people with disabilities who need "nonmedical" assistive devices pay for them out of pocket.

Does the Current Eligibility and Benefit Structure Provide Adequate Support?

Medicare does not pay for services or devices "which are not reasonable and necessary for the diagnosis or treatment of illness or injury or to improve the functioning of a malformed body member." Many assistive devices are routinely disallowed because they are considered "convenience items." Motorized wheelchairs are denied to individuals who can operate a manual wheelchair in their homes, even if they would need the motorized wheelchair to transport themselves in their communities (Griss 1988, National Council on Disability 1993b).

As with health insurance and personal assistance, whether Medicaid beneficiaries receive the assistive devices they need depends on the state in which they reside (National Council on Disability 1993b). No state covers the full range of needed devices; items such as environmental control units are virtually never included under state Medicaid plans.[15] Two significant policy barriers to obtaining assistive devices under Medicaid are the requirements that the recipient demonstrate "Medical Need" and obtain "Prior Approval" for the device. Interpretations of these requirements, and the extent of the barriers, vary from state to state (Seelman 1993).

Does the Current Eligibility and Benefit Structure Encourage Employment?

The current system promotes employment to the extent that it provides individuals with the assistive devices they need to seek and maintain jobs. For the most part, individuals do not receive the work-related devices they need under Medicare or Medicaid. Conversely, the eventual loss of eligibility for these programs would consequently not impose a significant work disincentive, except to the extent that needed medical devices, such as oxygen, would be lost. For individuals with requirements for such covered durable medical equipment, the work disincentive is likely to be substantial. Again, the link between eligibility and employment is problematic.

How Can We Better Satisfy the Goals of Support and Employment?

The major difference to be considered in analyzing personal assistance services and assistive devices is that some assistive devices are currently covered through private employer-based health insurance. However, this varies from plan to plan; very few health maintenance organizations (HMOs) cover DME to the same extent that Blue Cross plans do. If other payors do not improve their coverage, Blue Cross may eventually have to cut back to remain competitive. From a policy perspective, this suggests that the playing field should be leveled among different health plans through a uniform minimum benefits requirement. If all private health plans covered DME, the work disincentive associated with such equipment would be reduced.

Another alternative would be to remove assistive technology and DME from the health care financing system and to subsidize them in another manner, such as through tax credits, MSAs, or vouchers. As with personal assistance services, this approach would give individuals with disabilities flexibility in choosing and obtaining the devices they need to live independently. Like personal assistance, it also raises concerns as to how to restructure the financing of services. A major issue is how to determine the amount of the credit, MSA, or voucher.

Conclusions

The benefits that are provided in kind under the Social Security disability programs have a profound effect on the capacity of people with disabilities to live in their communities and to seek gainful employment. An analysis of how health insurance, personal assistance services, and assistive technology are currently provided suggests that they satisfy the support goal to a greater extent than the employment goal. From the low numbers of beneficiaries who have left the disability rolls, it now appears clear that further tinkering with the system's work disincentives is unlikely to achieve independent living objectives.

More fundamental change is necessary. We must reexamine the premises of the current system to determine whether they are consistent with the system's goals. Services that are currently provided in kind could be offered in a number of different ways. No special significance should be attributed to the fact that they are currently provided in kind except to the degree that they would otherwise not be available or affordable to people with disabilities. To that extent, reforms should be implemented to eliminate barriers to an accessible market for such services. The focus must be on meeting the basic support needs of the individual while encouraging self-sufficiency.

The cash equivalent approach advocated in this paper is particularly compatible with these goals for two reasons. First, it is philosophically consistent because it treats people with disabilities in an integrated manner with other people while recognizing, through the subsidy, the additional financial burdens of disability. It thereby implicitly acknowledges that disability is a normal aspect of the human experience. In contrast, the current system treats people with disabilities in a segregated manner, as if they were a separate species. Second, the cash equivalent approach would require less bureaucracy because it would be administered largely through existing structures (i.e., the tax system).

Whether we continue to provide services in kind or through vouchers, MSAs, or refundable tax credits, the issue of eligibility will remain critical. This is particularly true if we divorce the benefits now provided in kind from the present cash benefit programs. Current mechanisms for determining eligibility are grossly inadequate and are at odds with the goal of employment. New approaches, including different definitions and review methods, will be necessary to assure that only individuals with significant functional limitations are eligible for benefits and that these individuals receive the benefits they need to live independently (Batavia and Parker 1995).

Linking eligibility to work is not necessary and is counterproductive to the extent that it creates a self-fulfilling prophecy convincing beneficiaries that they are unemployable. There is no compelling policy rationale for providing benefits in kind, and by doing so we send the implicit message that we do not trust beneficiaries to make decisions for themselves. Alternatively, by providing cash equivalents regardless of employment status and phasing them out as income increases, we can offer people with disabilities greater control over their lives, and we are more likely to satisfy both the support and employment goals.

In pursuing this approach, it is essential to recognize that people with similar impairments and functional limitations can vary dramatically in their need for services and that some mechanism would have to be devised to determine the appropriate amount of the credit, MSA, or voucher. Ideally, this determination should be based on a valid and reliable assessment of each individual's functional capacity and need for services. Unfortunately, we currently have only relatively simple, unsophisticated approaches to assessing functional status, based largely on ADLs that are subject to manipulation (Batavia 1992).

An alternative to basing a cash equivalent on functional assessment would be to use a significant cost-sharing requirement to induce individuals to be cost conscious in their decisions. For example, we could permit a refundable tax credit for a specified percentage of service or coverage costs based on income (e.g., 90 percent for people with incomes up to 200 percent of the poverty level, 80 percent for incomes between 200 percent and 300 percent of the poverty level, etc.) up to a maximum amount (e.g., $15,000 per year). This approach raises certain equity issues that will have to be seriously considered in structuring the credits, MSAs, or vouchers.

It must be emphasized that whether or not a cash equivalent approach will benefit people with disabilities will depend entirely on how it is structured. A poorly designed program using MSAs, for example, could lead to substantial adverse selection that could destroy the Medicare or Medicaid system. Careful attention must be paid to ensuring that a plan does not simply provide a windfall for those who are healthy, depleting the low risks from the general insurance pool and imposing higher costs on those who are less healthy (American Academy of Actuaries 1995).

While systematic reform is necessary, it need not occur all at once. Given the incremental nature of our political system, it would be preferable to achieve these changes in several stages. A first stage might remove barriers to the establishment of a competitive market, in which people with disabilities would have access to services currently provided in kind. Subsequent stages might entail the creation of tax credits, MSAs, or vouchers to offer greater access to these markets and might involve the implementation of demonstration projects to test these approaches.

Whichever specific approach is adopted, and however it is implemented, we must boldly reform our disability programs. A system that does not service the long-term interest of its intended beneficiaries cannot and should not be sustained.

NOTES

1. It is the author's belief that the vast majority of people with disabilities are capable of gainful employment. Individuals with very substantial functional limitations, including respirator dependency, high-level quadriplegia, and mental retardation, have been able to remain productive in the public or private sector. However, it is clear that some individuals, such as those with very severe brain damage, have disabilities that preclude employment.

2. In the worst-case scenario, policy makers are concerned that some beneficiaries may use the cash for entirely unjustifiable purposes, e.g., for the purchase of alcohol or illegal drugs. Such rare

408   Health Care, Personal Assistance and Assistive Technology

situations, which are occasionally revealed through the press, can jeopardize support for an entire program.

3. An MSA is a tax-advantaged savings account, similar to an Individual Retirement Account (IRA), which could be used for certain specified purposes (e.g., medical costs, long-term care, personal assistance services) and could accumulate from year to year (Goodman and Musgrave 1992).

4. People with certain conditions, such as diabetes, spinal cord injury, and acquired immune deficiency syndrome (AIDS), statistically have higher than average health care costs. People with other disabilities, such as blindness, deafness, and mental retardation, have close to average costs, but are often perceived and treated by health insurers (defined broadly in this paper to include commercial insurers, Blue Cross/Blue Shield, managed care plans, and self-insured organizations) as costing more than average. Individuals in both groups find it difficult or impossible to obtain affordable health insurance unless they have access to a group policy.

5. Code of Federal Regulations (C.F.R.) 404.1505, 1995. Washington, DC: U.S. Government Printing Office.

6. U.S.C. Section 1395, The Social Security Act, as amended, Title XIX, Section 1901 (as added July 30, 1965), Public Law 89-97. West Publishing Co. 1992.

7. However, at the time of this writing, Congress is considering legislation that would give states far greater discretion in setting their Medicaid policies unencumbered by federal requirements.

8. While there are numerous possible explanations for the small number of beneficiaries who leave the rolls, I believe that it is a result of a combination of three factors: (1) the substantial psychological investment that beneficiaries must make in initially demonstrating their inability to work in order to establish eligibility, (2) a basic distrust that the government will fulfill its end of the bargain to provide continuing benefits once they become employed or to reestablish their eligibility if they lose their jobs, and (3) an inability to obtain equivalent benefits through employment.

9. One study has found that disabled persons employed part-time are significantly less likely to have any insurance coverage than those employed full-time or not at all, suggesting that disabled individuals who cannot make the transition directly to full-time employment and those who are only capable of part-time employment are likely to have a substantial work disincentive (Burns, Batavia, and DeJong 1994).

10. The Health Security Act of 1993, H.R. 3600 and S. 1757 (103rd Congress).

11. A bill based on this approach, the Consumer Choice Health Security Act of 1993, S. 1743, was introduced by Senator Don Nickles (Republican-Oklahoma) in the 103rd Congress, 1993.

12. Among the advantages of this approach are that it could be designed to offer universal coverage; shift the system from employment-based to household-based, thereby offering full portability of coverage when one changes employment status; provide the type of protection that is most needed, catastrophic and long-term care coverage; stimulate competition among health plans, thereby containing costs while maintaining access and quality; enhance consumers' cost consciousness while maintaining their autonomy and control; and subsidize people who have undue financial burdens (Batavia 1993).

13. Under this model, personal assistance has been defined as "Assistance, under maximum feasible control, with tasks aimed at maintaining well-being, personal appearance, comfort, safety, and interactions with the community and society as a whole" (Litvak, Zukas, and Heumann 1987).

14. It is reported that some long-term care policies are beginning to offer personal assistance services as an option.

15. To the limited extent that they are available to people with disabilities using state funds, it is typically through the vocational rehabilitation system on a discretionary basis.

References

Allard, M., and R. Spence. 1986. *A Policy Analysis of Attendant Services in Pennsylvania: A Discussion of Current Systems and Future Options*. Cambridge, MA: Human Services Research Institute.

American Academy of Actuaries. 1995. *Medical Savings Accounts: Cost Implications and Design Issues*. Public Policy Monograph 1. Washington, DC: American Academy of Actuaries, May.

Batavia, A.I. 1989. *The Payors of Medical Rehabilitation: Eligibility, Coverage and Payment Policies*. Washington, DC: National Association of Rehabilitation Facilities.

_____. 1992. "Assessing the Function of Functional Assessment: A Consumer Perspective," *Disability and Rehabilitation* 14, 3: 156-160.

_____. 1993. "Health Care Reform and People With Disabilities," *Health Affairs* 12, 1 (Spring): 40-57.

Batavia, A.I., G. DeJong, and L. McKnew. 1992. "Toward a National Personal Assistance Program: The Independent Living Model of Long-Term Care for Persons with Disabilities," *Journal of Health Politics, Policy and Law* 16, 3: 525-547.

Batavia, A.I., and S. Parker. 1995. "From Disability Rolls to Payrolls: A Proposal for Social Security Reform," *Journal of Disability Policy Studies*. In press.

Burkhauser, R.V., and R.H. Haveman. 1982. *Disability and Work: The Economics of American Policy*. Baltimore: Johns Hopkins University Press.

Burns, T.J., A.I. Batavia, and G. DeJong. 1991. "The Health Insurance Coverage of Working-Age Persons with Physical Disabilities," *Inquiry* 28, 2 (Summer): 187-93.

_____. 1994. "The Health Insurance Work Disincentive for People with Disabilities." In *Sociology of Health Care,* Volume II. Greenwich, CT: JAI Press.

DeJong, G. 1979. "Independent Living: From Social Movement to Analytic Paradigm," *Archives of Physical Medicine and Rehabilitation* 60: 435-446.

_____. 1981. *Environmental Accessibility and Independent Living Outcomes: Directions for Disability Programs and Research*. East Lansing, MI: Michigan State University, University Center for International Rehabilitation.

DeJong, G., and A.I. Batavia. 1990. "The Americans with Disabilities Act and the Current State of Disability Policy," *Journal of Disability Policy Studies* 1, 3 (Fall): 65-75.

DeJong, G., A.I. Batavia, and R. Griss. 1989. "America's Neglected Health Minority: Working-Age Persons with Disabilities," *The Milbank Quarterly* 67 (Supplement 2, Part 2): 311-351.

DeJong, G., and T. Wenker. 1983. "Attendant Care as a Prototype Independent Living Service," *Caring* 2, 2: 26-30.

Egley, L. 1994. *Program Models Providing Personal Assistance Services (PAS) for Independent Living.* Oakland, CA: World Institute on Disability.

Goodman, J.C., and G.L. Musgrave. 1992. "Controlling Health Care Costs with Medical Savings Accounts." National Center for Policy Analysis, NCPA Policy Report No. 168, January.

Griss, R. 1988. "Strategies for Adapting the Public and Private Health Insurance Systems to the Health-related Needs of Persons with Disabilities and Chronic Conditions," *Access to Health Care* 1, 3-4: 1-76.

Kennedy, J. 1993. "Policy and Program Issues in Providing Personal Assistance Service," *Journal of Rehabilitation* (July/August/September): 17-22.

Kennedy, J., and S. Litvak. 1991. *Case Studies of Six State Personal Assistance Services Funded by the Medicaid Personal Care Option.* Oakland, CA: World Institute on Disability.

LaPlante, M.P., G.E. Hendershot, and A.J. Moss. 1992. "Assistive Technology Devices and Home Accessibility Features: Prevalence, Payment, Need and Trends," *Advance Data* No. 217, Centers for Disease Control, U.S. Department of Health and Human Services, September 16.

LaPlante, M.P., and K.S. Miller. 1992. "People with Disabilities in Basic Life Activities in the U.S.," *Disability Statistics Abstract* No. 3, U.S. Department of Education, National Institute on Disability and Rehabilitation Research, April.

LaPlante, M.P., D.P. Rice, and J.K. Cyril. 1994. "Health Insurance Coverage of People with Disabilities in the U.S.," *Disability Statistics Abstract* No. 4, U.S. Department of Education, National Institute on Disability and Rehabilitation Research, September.

Leonard, J.S. 1986. "Labor Supply Incentives and Disincentives for Disabled Persons." In *Disability and the Labor Market: Economic Problems, Policies and Programs*, M. Berkowitz and M.A. Hill, eds. Ithaca, NY: Cornell University Press.

Litvak, S., H. Zukas, and J.E. Heumann. 1987. *Attending to America: Personal Assistance for Independent Living.* Berkeley, CA: World Institute on Disability.

Lubitz, J., and P. Pine. 1986. "Health Care Use by Medicare's Disabled Enrollees," *Health Care Financing Review* 7, 4:19-31.

Muller, L.S. 1989. "Disability Beneficiaries who Work and their Experience under Program Work Incentives," *Social Security Bulletin* 55, 2: 2-19.

National Association of Rehabilitation Facilities (NARF). 1988. *Incentives to Work for SSI and SSDI Recipients.* Washington, DC: National Association of Rehabilitation Facilities.

National Center for Policy Analysis (NCPA). 1995. *Medical Savings Accounts for Medicare.* NCPA Brief Analysis No. 160. Dallas: National Center for Policy Analysis, April 17.

National Council on Disability. 1986. *Toward Independence.* Washington, DC: National Council on Disability.

_____. 1988. *On the Threshold of Independence.* Washington, DC: National Council on Disability.

_____. 1993a. *Sharing the Risk and Ensuring Independence: A Disability Perspective on Access to Health Insurance and Health-Related Services— A Report to the President and the Congress.* Washington, DC: National Council on Disability, March 4.

_____. 1993b. *Study on the Financing of Assistive Technology and Services for Individuals with Disabilities—A Report to the President and the Congress.* Washington, DC: National Council on Disability, March 4.

Nosek, M.A. 1992. "Personal Assistance Services: A Review of Literature and Analysis of Policy Implications," *Journal of Disability Policy Studies* 2, 2: 1-17.

Nosek, M.A., and C.A. Howland. 1993. "Personal Assistance Services: The Hub of the Policy Wheel for Community Integration of People with Severe Physical Disabilities," *Policy Studies Journal* 21, 4: 789-800.

Rice, D.P., and M.P. LaPlante. 1992. "Medical Expenditures for Disability and Disabling Comorbidity," *American Journal of Public Health*, 82, 5 (May): 739-741.

Rutgers Bureau of Economic Research and World Institute on Disability. 1990. *Towards an Understanding of the Demand for Personal Assistance.* Berkeley, CA: World Institute on Disability.

Seelman, K.D. 1993. "Assistive Technology Policy: A Road to Independence for Individuals with Disabilities," *Journal of Social Issues* 49, 2: 115-136.

U.S. Congress. House of Representatives. Committee on Ways and Means. 1992. *Overview of Entitlement Programs.* 102nd Cong., 2nd Sess.

U.S. Department of Health and Human Services, Agency for Health Care Policy and Research (AHCPR). 1992. *Persons Denied Private Health Insurance Due to Poor Health.* NMES Data Summary 4, AHCPR Publication No. 92-0016.

U.S. Department of Health and Human Services. Social Security Administration. 1994. *Annual Statistical Supplement to the Social Security Bulletin.* Washington, DC: Government Printing Office.

Zukas, H., K. Cone, and J. Leon. 1984. *Descriptive Analysis of the In-Home Supportive Services Program in California.* Berkeley, CA: World Institute on Disability.

INDEX

Aarts, L. J. M., 131, 133t, 142, 153, 160-63t, 343
Accommodation, workplace
  ADA concept of reasonable accommodation, 59, 78-80, 110-12, 118
  after onset of disability, 80-85
  in determination of equal employment opportunities, 110-12
  for disabled in Germany, 144, 149
  EEOC decisions related to, 118
  pre-ADA, 77-78
  proposed tax credit, 87
Achenbaum, W. Andrew, 225
Aid to Families with Dependent Children (AFDC)
  current provisions, 190-91
  effects on work effort of tax rate changes, 199
  family eligibility for Medicaid, 191-92
  financial incentives to leave welfare rols, 214
  Job Opportunities and Basic Skills (JOBS) training, 192-93
  program rules, 190-91
  Unemployed Parent provision, 190-91
  work incentives under, 189
Aid to the Permanently and Totally Disabled (APTD), 226-28
Akabas, S. H., 249
Allard, M., 400
Americans with Disabilities Act, 1990 (ADA)
  application to health insurance, 366-67
  definition of disability, 104
  effectiveness of, 22, 80-83, 103, 123
  employer obligation under, 265
  essential functions and accommodation concepts of, 110-12
  factors in adoption of, 248
  intent and goals of, 1-2, 33, 59, 78-80, 104, 112, 120-21, 210, 246, 389-90
  limitations of, 123

  major life activities concept, 104, 110
  provisions of, 78, 118
  reasonable accommodation requirement, 59, 78-80, 111, 118
Apling, Richard N., 316
Appel, Gary Louis, 199
Armstrong, Timothy, 171
Assitive technology, 402-5
Aylward, M., 153

Bane, Mary J., 70, 89
Barker, Peggy, 360, 369
Barr, Nicholas, 197
Batavia, A. I., 390, 393, 394, 396, 399, 401, 402, 406
Bazzoli, Gloria J., 61, 91
Becker, Gary S., 110
Beedon, Laurel E., 79
Bell, S. H., 268
Bell, Winifred, 199
Belous, Richard, 52
Beneficiary Rehabilitation Program (BRP)
  activities of, 223, 228-37
  investigative studies of, 235-36
  post-BRP SSA and VR spending, 237-40
  questioned efficacy of, 235
Bennefield, Robert L., 6, 105, 107
Berkowitz, Edward, 225, 226, 228
Berkowitz, Monroe, 228, 232, 235, 247, 335, 343
Biddle, Jeff E., 108
Blank, Rebecca, 52, 53, 198
Bluestone, Barry, 42
Bound, John, 61, 91, 113, 204
Bregger, John E., 53
Brown, Diane Robinson, 107
BRP. *See* Beneficiary Rehabilitation Program (BRP)
Burkhauser, Richard V., 50, 64, 83-84, 87, 121, 129, 130, 131, 133t, 160-63t, 392
Burns, T. J., 394

Burtless, Gary, 51, 198, 321
Bushe, Dennis, 199
Butler, J. S., 83-84
Bye, Barry V., 113, 114-15t

Case management
  case manager model, 255-56
  limitations in DI system, 265
  return-to-work as commitment in, 266
  UNUM Insurance Company, 258-60
CDRs. *See* Continuing Disability
  Reviews (CDRs)
Chelius, J., 245
Chirikos, Thomas N., 50, 84
Civil rights approach
  of ADA legislation, 103
  problems of ADA, 112
Clinton administration
  Earned Income Tax Credit, 87
  Health Security Act, 397
Cohany, Sharon R., 122
Cone, K., 400
Continuing Disability Reviews (CDRs),
  180, 346
Couch, Kenneth A., 87
Council of State Administrators of
  Vocational Rehabilitation (CSAVR),
  248
Crocker, Allen C., 361
Current Population Survey (CPS)
  1990, 62-64
  estimates of population with
    disabilities, 61-64
  March supplement, 34
Cyril, J. K., 394

Dabelstein, Donald, 227
Daly, Mary C., 50
Danziger, Sheldon, 197
Data sources
  Current Population Survey (CPS),
    1990 data, 62-64
  Current Population Survey (CPS),
    March supplement, 34

Health and Retirement Survey (HRS),
  80-83
National Health Interview Survey, 34
New Beneficiary Data System
  (NBDS), 119, 169-72
New Beneficiary Survey, 333
outcomes of transitional employment,
  279-80
Panel Study of Income Dynamics
  (PSID), 61-64, 70
Survey of Income and Program
  Participation (SIPP), 62-64
Dean, D. H., 269, 302
Decker, Paul, 273, 275, 277t, 279, 283,
  284, 288, 289, 290t, 293
DeJong, G., 389, 390, 393, 394, 399,
  400, 401, 402
de Jong, P. R., 131, 133t,142, 153, 160-
  63t, 208, 209, 343
Department of Education,
  Rehabilitation Services
    Administration, 240, 298
Department of Veterans Affairs
  adoption of independent living model,
    400
  medical care system, 372
  policy for service-connected disability,
    122
DI. *See* Social Security Disability
  Insurance (DI)
Dippo, Cathryn S., 53
Disability
  ADA definition, 60-61, 104, 110,, 304-
    5
  continued disability review, 180, 346
  defined under Fair Labor Standards
    Act, 324-25
  ecological model, 247-48
  EEOC regulations, 105
  effects on labor market participation,
    10-11
  expanded Nagi definition, 61-62
  factors that may encourage, 264-65
  firm initiatives related to, 254-55

incentives for people with, 267
limitations of, 112-13
measurement of, 90-97
medical or clinical model, 247-48
mental retardation as cause of, 274
Nagi measure of, 60-61
post-1965 SSA definition, 229
recovery from, 75-76
SSI and DI definition, 201, 233
transitory nature of, 113
WHO definition, 104
Disability benefits
allocation agents in European
countries, 151-58
as alternative to unemployment
insurance, 142-43
cash in lieu of in-kind, 391-93
cross-national comparison of, 139-43
differences for older and younger
disabled workers, 172-74
during DI trial work period, 204
eligibility for, 79
growth of costs, 27
incentives for labor force
participation, 79
in-kind, 389-93
paid under Social Security disability
insurance (1969-92), 229-32
partial, 147-48
under Social Security Disability
Insurance, 200
spending for, 248
under Supplemental Security Income
program (SSI), 200-203
Disability Determination Service (DDS)
decisions and rehabilitations (1993),
240
proposed change in responsibility of,
344-45
state-level rehabilitation referral
service, 331-32
Disability insurance
administration in European countries,
157
linking vocational rehabilitation, 224

long- and short-term disability
products, 258-60
proposed incentive-based
reimbursement scheme, 337-43
Disability insurance, SSA
See also Social Security Disability
Insurance (DI); Supplemental
Security Income program (SSI)
Disability management
advantages of, 269
case management under, 255-56
definition and intent, 249
employer practices related to, 252-53
evidence on impact of, 251
Proactive Return-to-Work as, 253
traits of successful programs, 250-51
Disability management programs,
private sector
lessons for public sector policy, 266-
69
Owens-Corning Fiberglas experience,
256-58, 262
United Health Care, 260-62
UNUM Insurance Company, 258-60,
262
Disability policy
focus of, 33
goal of U.S., 389
goals of European countries, 150-51
programs of four European countries,
160-63
recommendations for, 85-88
Disability prevention
employer practices related to, 252-53
UNUM Insurance Company, 258
Disability rights movement, 241
Disability Working Allowance, Britain,
147-48
Disabled persons
ADA criterion of qualified, 110-11
benefits for older, 172-73
benefits for younger, 173
cross-national differences in transfers
related to, 130-34
cross-sectional estimates, 62-64

416

current delivery of health benefits to, 394-97

differentiated by marital status, 174

effect of ADA provisions on, 78, 118

eligibility for targeted jobs tax credit, 321-23

employed in industry (1970-92), 42-45

employment of, 33

employment policy in selected European countries, 146-49

employment testing for, 323-24

employment under special certificates, 324-25

employment with or without workplace accommodation, 80-85

enrolled in JTPA Title II programs, 304-11

health care insurance coverage, 18, 362-66

incidence of health insurance coverage, 362-72

labor market integration of, 85-86

length of workweek (1981-93), 45-47

mortality rates of DI recipients, 171-72

occupations by disability status (1970-92), 42-45

rehabilitation of (1991), 298-301

requiring personal assistance, 398-99

service-connected, 122

SSA in-kind benefits, 389

SSI means-tested benefits for, 5

survey estimates, 105

training or vocational rehabilitation, 117-18

transfer programs for, 200-213

treatment in Europe of, 136-43

use of assitive technology, 402-5

use of health care services, 358-59

using U.S. Employment Service, 319-23

work disabled, 2-9

work effort under DI program, 203-13

See also Nondisabled persons; Work disabled persons

Disabled Persons Act (1944), United Kingdom, 148

Dismissal policy, European countries, 149

Dolan, Robert C., 302

Duncan, Greg J., 108

Dunstan, Shari M., 273, 275, 281, 282t

Durch, Jane S., 361

Dykacz, Janice M., 333

Early and Periodic Screening Diagnosis and Treatment, Medicaid program, 370

Earned Income Tax Credit (EITC)
    intent and effectiveness of, 87
    proposal to extend to disabled persons, 87
    refundable, 381
    as wage subsidy, 214

Earnings
    as basis for disability benefit determination, 172-74
    in calculation of AFDC benefits, 191
    of disabled persons, 50
    marginal tax rates of DI program, 202
    related to onset of disability, 70-77
    of trainees in post-transitional employment, 283-87

Earnings replacement
    DI and SSI programs for, 203
    DI program as, 202
    provided by DI and SSI, 4-5

Economic Dislocation and Worker Adjustment Assistance Act, 1988 (EDWAA)

Education, vocational. See Vocational education programs

Egley, L., 400

Eligibility
    basis in SSI and DI for, 189
    cross-national comparison of disability benefits, 139-40
    determination for DI benefits, 263-65
    DI extended period of, 204-5
    for DI program, 203-4

of disabled persons for Medicare and
Medicaid, 394-97
proposed changes in vterans', 380
SSI and DI tied to ability to work, 201
for state-level vocational rehabilitation
programs, 298
See also Extended period of eligibility
(EPE)
Ellwood, David, 70, 89
Employee Retirement Income Security
Act (ERISA), 1974, 175
Employees with disabilities
access to employer-provided health
insurance, 366
eligibility for workers' compensation,
117
European social insurance coverage,
137-39
Employers
incentives for return-to-work policy,
267
influence on disability policy, 153-56
interest in disability management,
249-50
obligation under ADA, 265
practices related to frequency of
disability, 252-53
pre-ADA workplace accommodation,
77-78
Proactive Return-to-Work, 253
Safety Diligence behavior, 253
Employment
ADA guarantee of opportunities for
equal, 109-10
after onset of disability, 85-86
current health insurance work
incentives, 396-97
of disabled under special certificates,
324-25
effect of trial work period, 206
European policy for disabled, 144
in firms with and without disabilities
(1970-92), 42-45
as focus of disability policy, 33

impact of onset of disability t, 70-77
with or without workplace
accommodation, 80-85
persons with service-connected
disability, 122
with and without disability by
occupation and industry (1970-92),
42-45
work transitions for persons with and
without disabilities, 46-49
Employment, supported, 248
Employment, transitional
benefits to participants, 287-94
costs of demonstration, 281-94
demonstration sites, 278-79, 281-82
measurement of effectiveness, 280-81
nature of, 278
outcomes of demonstration, 281-87
SSA support of, 273
training for mentally retarded, 274-80
See also Transitional Employment
Training Demonstration
Employment Opportunities for Disabled
Americans Act (1986), 396-97
Employment policy
for disabled in European countries,
146-48
for disabled in selected European
countries, 146-49
job slots for disabled in European
countries, 144, 148, 156
Employment services, JTPA programs,
303
Employment testing for disabled people,
323-24
EPE. *See* Extended period of eligibility
(EPE)
Epstein, Susan G., 361
Equal Opportunity Employment
Commission (EEOC)
accommodation regulations, 111, 118
decisions related to functions and
accommodation under, 118

418

disability threshold hiring standard, 110-11
disability under regulations of, 105
post-ADA charges filed with, 85, 103, 121
rules related to access to employer health insurance, 367
Evans, Sara M., 33, 35
Extended period of eligibility (EPE), 202
    DI budget constraint during, 204-5
    effect of, 207
    effect on work effort under DI program, 204-5
    as work incentive under DI, 207

Fair Labor Standards Act (1938), 324-25
Falk, I. S., 224
Food Stamp program
    current provisions, 191
    program rules, 191
    work incentives, 190
Fraker, Thomas, 198
Franklin, James C., 54
Frick, B., 148

Galvin, D., 245, 249, 269
Gardner, Jennifer M., 52
Gardner, John A., 343
Garfinkel, Irwin, 197
Garraty, J. A., 116
Gates, L. B., 249
General Accounting Office (GAO), 240
    BRP efficacy study, 235-36
    evaluation of vocational rehabilitation employment outcomes, 248, 301-2
Germany
    administration of disability insurance, 156-58
    disability policy, 137-39, 141-43, 149, 160-63t
    employment policy for disabled, 147-49, 152
    rehabilitation services, 144
    transfers to persons with disabilities, 131-34

Giannarelli, Linda, 192
Glenn, Andrew J., 87
Griss, R., 393, 394, 395, 396, 404
Gruber, John, 209
Guyer, Bernard, 362

Habeck, R. V., 249, 250, 252
Halberstadt, V., 129, 130
Hall, Robert E., 197
Halpern, Janice, 209
Hamermesh, Daniel S., 108
Handicapped Act, Germany, 148
Handicap (WHO definition), 104
Hanley, Raymond J., 367
Harrison, Bennett, 42
Hartigan, John A., 324
Hashimoto, M., 110-11
Hausman, Jerry, 209
Haveman, Robert H., 64, 120, 129, 130, 197, 208, 209, 392
Health and Retirement Survey (HRS), 80-83
Health care insurance
    ADA application to employer-provided, 366-67
    coverage for disabled persons, 18
    coverage under private, 363
    gaps in coverage by, 362-63
    private long-term care coverage, 367
    proposal to expand access to, 373-75
Health care services
    for children, 361-62
    proposals for reform, 373-83
    proposals to change financing and delivery, 381-84
    proposal to expand long-term care, 378
    used by disabled people, 358-59
    used by substance abusers and mentally retarded, 361
Health care system
    European rehabilitation policy related to, 144
    finance reform proposals, 373
    gaps in coverage, 362-63

Health insurance
  access for disabled, 393-94
  coverage of disabled, 362-72
  proposal to reform, 374-76
  proposed use of tax code to encourage
    purchase of, 381-82
Health maintenance organizations
  (HMOs), 260-62
Health Security Act (Clinton plan), 397
Hendershot, G. E., 402-3
Hennessey, John, 172, 178,333
Hester, E. J., 255
Heumann, J. E., 399, 400
Hill, Martha S., 62
Hirschhorn, Larry, 51
Hobby, Oveta Culp, 227
Holland. See Netherlands, the
Holmes, Stephen A., 121
Howland, C. A., 400, 402
Hoynes, Hilary, 198, 202
Hunt, H. A., 253, 254

Iams, Howard, 171, 175
Illston, Laurel H., 367
Impairment-related work expenses
  (IRWE), 201
Impairments
  disability as physical or mental, 60
  mental, 360-61
  of people receiving DI or SSI, 3-5
  of SSI beneficiaries, 3
  WHO definition, 104
  of work disabled persons, 2-3
Incentives
  in European disability policies, 151-58
  proposed for SSI and DI, 337-50
  for SSA from private sector, 267
  targeted jobs tax credit, 319, 321-22
Incentives to work
  for DI and SSI beneficiaries, 119
  effect of changes in MTR on, 197-200
  expected effects of nondisabled
    programs for, 193-200
  research in transfer programs, 189-90
  for return to work, 177-78
  See also Return to work

Income effect, negative, 205
Independence
  as ADA goal for disabled, 389-90
  relation to in-kind benefits, 390-92
Independent living model, 399-400
Independent Living movement, 248-49
Irwin, Paul M., 316

Jablonski, Mary, 42
Jenkins, William M., 333
Job coach, 278
Job Opportunity and Basic Skills (JOBS)
  program, 192-93
Job placement
  essential functions for disabled, 110-
    12
  under Transitional Employment
    Training Demonstration, 273
  workers with disabilities in European
    countries, 146-48
  See also Sheltered jobs
Job retention
  for disabled and not disabled persons,
    46, 48-49
  for disabled workers, 46
  protection for disabled in European
    countries, 149
Job Training Partnership Act, 1982
  (JTPA)
  employment and training programs,
    303
  persons with disabilities served by,
    304-11
  PICs under, 303`
  SDAs under, 303, 311-16
  targeting requirements, 309-11
  Title II performance management
    system, 311-16
  Title II programs, 303-16
  See also Wagner-Peyser Act (1933)
Johnson, William G., 104, 109
Jones, Nancy L., 33, 103
JTPA. See Job Training Partnership Act,
  1982 (JTPA)

Katz, Patricia P., 38, 48t, 50

Keane, Michael, 192, 197
Kehrer, Kenneth, 198
Kennedy, J., 398, 399, 400
Kim, Yang Woo, 83-84
Kirchner, K. A., 269
Kovar, Mary G., 34
Kubik, Jeffrey, 209
Kutscher, Ronald E., 42

Labor force participation
   among people with work disabilities, 6
   of current disability beneficiaries, 79
   disabled persons (1970-92), 38-42
   effect of disability on, 10-11
   estimate of working-age disabled
      persons, 61-64
   in idea of vocational rehabilitation,
      248
   job retention for disabled and not
      disabled persons, 46, 48-49
   length of workweek, diabled and not
      disabled, 45-47
   persons with and without disabilities
      pre-ADA, 64-68
   persons without disabilities (1970-92),
      38-42
   rates (1970-92), 34-38
   rates before and after 1970, 34-35
   See also Return to work
Labor market
   ADA definition of discrimination in,
      110
   disabled persons in current, 50-55
Labor market institutes, Sweden, 145
Lambrinos, James, 104, 109
Landini, Michael J., 322
LaPlante, Mitchell P., 3, 50, 105, 106t,
   394, 402-3
Lawrence, Jean M., 362
Leon, J., 400
Leonard, Jonathan S., 153, 209, 392
Levy, Frank, 33, 35, 51, 197
Lewin, D., 252
Litvak, S., 399, 400
Lonsdale, S., 133t, 153

Lubitz, J., 394

McCoy, John, 171
MacDonald, Mary E., 224
McKnew, L., 399, 401, 402
McManus, Leo A., 25, 230-31t, 234t,
   268
McNeil, John M., 3, 6, 8, 62-64, 105,
   107
Major life activities, 104, 110
Managed care, 261-62
Marginal tax rate (MTR)
   on earnings in DI program, 202
   for SSI earnings, 203
Marginal tax rate (MTR), transfer
      programs
   on earnings of AFDC and Food Stamp
      recipients, 191-93
   effect on incentives to work, 193-200
   influence on work incentives, 193-20
Masters, Stanley H., 197
Maxfield, Linda D., 169
Means-testing, SSI benefits, 5, 202-3
Mechanic, David, 359
Medicaid
   coverage of children, 370
   current provisions, 191-92
   eligibility and coverage, 367-69
   expansions in eligibility and coverage
      (1980s), 376-77
   health benefits for SSI recipients, 203
   health care coverage for disabled, 18,
      394-97
   Medically Needy state-level programs,
      192
   for mentally ill people, 369-70
   program rules, 191-92
   proposed changes and expansion, 376-
      80
   work incentives, 190
Medical Savings Accounts (MSAs), 392,
   398
Medicare
   Congressional approval (1965), 229

health care coverage for disabled, 18, 371, 394-97
weaknesses of, 395
Mental illness
disabled workers with, 5
incidence of, 360-61
insurance coverage for, 360
Mental retardation
incidence of, 361
SSI special training and job placement for people with, 273-80
Miller, K. S., 394
Moffitt, Robert, 192, 196, 197, 198, 199, 202
Moral hazard, SSI and DI programs, 203
Mortality rates
beneficiaries of Social Security DI, 113-16
persons in New Beneficiary Survey, 171
Moss, A. J., 402-3
MTR. See Marginal tax rate (MTR)
Muller, L. Scott, 119, 120t, 172, 178, 203, 392, 397
Myers, Robert J., 91

Nagi, Saad, 60
Nagi measure of diminished health, 60-61
Nardone, Thomas, 52
Nasar, Sylvia, 45, 54
National Academy of Social Insurance (NASI), 3
National Assessment of Vocational Education survey, 318
National Disability Employment Awareness Month, 319
National Health Interview Survey (HIS), 34
National Postsecondary Student Aid Survey (NPSAS), 317
National Rehabilitation Planners, 251
Negative income tax (NIT) experiments (1970s), 198

Nelson, Barbara J., 33, 35
Netherlands, the
administration of disability insurance, 156-58
disability policy, 136-42, 160-63t
employment policy for disabled, 146-49, 152-53
rehabilitation services, 144
transfers to persons with disabilities, 131-34
New Beneficiary Data System (NBDS), 119, 169-70
findings based on, 175-83
limitations of, 184
New Beneficiary Followup (NBF), 170, 178-79
New Beneficiary Survey (NBS), 169, 179
NIT. See Negative income tax (NIT)
Nondisabled persons
transfer programs for, 190-93
wage subsidies for, 214
work incentives in transfer programs for, 193-200
Nosek, M. A., 399, 400, 402

Occupations with and without disability (1970-92), 42-45
Oi, Walter Y., 110
Okun, A. M., 246
Omnibus Budget Reconciliation Act of 1981 (OBRA), 199, 397
Orr, Larry L., 308
Osterman, Paul, 51, 52
Owens, P., 245
Owens-Corning Fiberglas, 256-58, 262

Packard, Michael D., 175, 176,177
Palmer, Bruce A., 4
Panel Study of Income Dynamics (PSID), 61-64, 70
economic impact of onset of disability, 70-77

estimates of population with
disabilities, 61-64
1986 Health Supplement data, 91-92
pre-ADA labor force participation of
disabled people, 64-69
Parker, S., 406
Parsons, Donald O., 61, 79, 91, 208, 209
Patterson, Jeanne B., 333
Pepper Commission, 374-75
Perkins Act (1984), 316
Perrin, James, 362
Personal assistance
adequacy of current modes of delivery,
399-402
as in-kind benefit, 398-99
PICs. See Private industry councils
(PICs)
Pine, P., 394
Plotnick, Robert, 197
Poe, Gail S., 34
Polivka, Anne E., 52
Poverty related to disability, 72-77
Prediction scale, return-to-work, 259
Prero, Aaron J., 274, 275, 288, 293
Private industry councils (PICs), JTPA
Title II program, 303
Proactive Return-to-Work, 253
Public policy
cross-national comparison of
disability benefits, 134-4
cross-national disability records, 130-
34
equity and efficiency in evaluation of,
246-47
European rehabilitation policies, 143-
49
intent toward disability, 129
related to in-kind benefits, 392-93
Public policy, proposed
for labor market integration of
disabled persons, 86-88
linking DI beneficiaries with return-to-
work services, 24-25, 27-28
modifications to present DI program,
122--23

for rehabilitation and return to work,
24-25
substitute for SS disability insurance,
23
wage subsidy, 22-23,28

Quota system. See Employment

Rehabilitation
cross-national comparison of policies,
143-49
cross-national comparison of policies
f0r, 143-49
decisions of Disability Determination
Services, 240-
defined, 301
mandatory, 335-36
UNUM Insurance Company
assessment, 259-60
Rehabilitation Act (1973)
1992 amendments, 248
vocational rehabilitation program
under, 298
Rehabilitation services
lack of development for disabled, 226-
28
of Medicare, 395
under Social Security Disability
Insurance (DI), 229-33
in Social Security legislation, 224-26
See also Beneficiary Rehabilitation
Program (BRP);
Employment, transitional;
Vocational rehabilitation (VR)
Rehabilitation Services Administration,
Department of Education
information about VR clients, 240
review and monitoring actiivities of,
298
Research Triangle Institute, 199
Return to work
after eligibility period of no gainful
employment, 79-80
of disabled-worker beneficiaries, 181-
83

findings based on New Beneficiary
Survey data, 175-85
post-disability training for, 117-18
Return-to-work concept
case management to promote, 255-56
decline in rates of (1970s-1990s), 245-46
as goal, 266-67
Owens-Corning Fiberglas experience, 256-58, 262
proposals for reform, 348-50
United Health Care, 260-62
UNUM Insurance Company, 258-60, 262
See also Proactive Return-to-Work
Return-to-work services
advantages in providing, 343
estimated market for, 341
existing program, 331-33
See also Rehabilitation services;
Training
Rice, D. P., 394
Ries, Peter, 358
Riley, Gerald F., 113, 114-15t
Robbins, Lionel, 107
Rousmaniere, P., 251
Rupp, K., 268

Sadowski, D., 148
Safety Diligence behavior, 253
Schaffer, Daniel C., 86
Schecter, S., 252
Schlesinger, Mark, 359
Schore, Jennifer, 273, 275, 281, 282t
Schwartz, G. E., 250
Seelman, K. D., 402, 404
Service delivery areas (SDAs), Title II
JTPA programs, 303, 311-16
SGA. See Substantial gainful activity
(SGA)
Sheltered jobs
disabled workers under special
certificates, 325
European countries, 146

Silvestri, George T., 54
Singleman, Joachim, 42
Slade, Frederic, 208, 209
Smith, Vernon, 199
Social insurance policy, Europe, 158-59
Social Security Administration (SSA)
advice related to rehabilitation, 331-32
determination of beneficiary status, 264
Disability Determination Service
(DDS), 331-32
Disability Process Reengineering
Team, 267
in-kind benefits to disabled, 389-93
Old Age, Survivors, and Disability
Insurance, 200-203
planning to link disability insurance
and vocational rehab (1935-56), 224-25
Return to Work system, 331-36
role in disability management, 258, 260, 263
Transitional Employment Training
Demonstration, 273
Social Security Disability Insurance (DI)
benefit calculation, 201
benefits for older and younger
workers, 172-79
as earnings replacement program, 202
effect on labor force participation, 223
federal BRP funds to, 232-33
funding for, 200
growth (1965-92), 229-32
incentive-based proposal for, 343-47
intent of, 210
Medicare coverage for beneficiaries
of, 371
needed reform of, 241
number and age of beneficiaries, 119
post-BRP spending for cases of, 237-40
proposal for incentive-based scheme
for, 337-47

proposed reforms to work incentives under, 210-13
provision, eligibility and benefits, 1, 3-4, 200-201, 203-4, 263-65
recommendations for current program, 122-23
trial work period unnder, 121
work incentive provisions, 201, 206
Social Security System
  disability insurance coverage, 200
Special certificate program, 324-25
Spence, R., 400
SRI International, 198
SSI. *See* Supplemental Security Income program (SSI)
Stafford, Frank, 108
Stanley, Marcus, 304, 308; 317
Stapleton, David, 33, 50
Stern, Steven, 61
Steurle, Eugene, 192
Stubbins,J., 248
Subsidies
  See Wage subsidies
Substance abuse, 361
Substantial gainful activity (SGA), 119-21, 201-2
  for DI eligibility, 203-4
  effect of raising threshhold, 210-11
  under Social Security programs, 233
  as threshhold level of earnings, 201-2
Supplemental Security Income program (SSI)
  criteria for, 202-3
  disability benefits, 3-5
  extension of BRP funding to (1974), 233
  incentive-based proposal for, 347-48
  job placement and special training under, 273
  means testing for, 202
  Medicaid eligibility for beneficiaries of, 368-69
  mentally ill people receiving, 369
  number and age of beneficiaries, 3, 119

payments in post-transitional employment period, 284-87
proposed incentive-based, 347-48
provisions and eligibility, 200-203
work incentives, 207-8, 210
Survey of Income and Program Participation (SIPP), 612-64
Sweden
  administration of disability insurance, 156-58
  disability policy, 136-39, 141-42, 160-63t
  employment plicy for disabled, 146
  employment policy for disabled, 146
  ransfers to persons with disabilities, 132-34
  rehabilitation services, 145
Switzer, Mary, 226-29, 236
Szymanski, Edna Mora, 333

Targeted Jobs Tax Credit (TJTC), 17, 116, 319-21, 323
Tate, D. G., 249
Tax code
  pre-ADA deductions for workplace accommodation, 86
  proposal to encourage purchase of insurance, 381-82
  proposed accommodation tax credits, 87
  proposed extension of Earned Income Tax Credit, 87
Tax credit
  proposed for workplace accommodation, 87
  proposed Medical Savings Accounts, 392, 398
  See also Earned income tax credit (EITC); Targeted Jobs Tax Credit (TJTC)
Taylor, Ann B., 361
Thornton, Craig, 273, 274, 275, 277t, 279, 281, 282t, 283, 284, 288, 289, 290t, 293
TJTC. *See* Targeted Jobs Tax Credit (TJTC)

Towers Perrin, 250
Training
  AFDC Job Opportunity and Basic
    Skills program, 192-93
  JTPA programs for, 303
  in state-level vocational rehabilitation,
    301-2
  transitional employment, 274-80
  vocational education as training
    program, 316
  See also Job Training Partnership Act,
    1982 (JTPA);
    Transitional Employment Training
    Demonstration; Vocational education
Transfer programs for disabled
  eligibility and rules, 200-203
  work incentive provisions, 203-210
Transfer programs for nondisabled
  program rules, 196-200
  tax rate effects on work incentives,
    193-200
Transitional Employment Training
  Demonstration
  costs and benefits of, 287-94
  description and outcome of, 274-87
  for SSI recipients, 273
Trial work period (TWP)
  with DI benefits application, 119, 121
  DI budget constraint during, 204, 206
  effect of, 206
  work effort under DI influenced by,
    204
  as work incentive under DI, 206
Tuma, John, 317

Unemployment insurance, European
  workers, 142-43
United Health Care, 260-62
United Kingdom
  administration of disability insurance,
    156-58
  disability policy, 137-39, 141, 149,
    160-63t
  employment policy for disabled, 146-
    48, 152-53
  rehabilitation services, 145-46

transfers to persons with disabilities,
  132-34
United States
  differences from European welfare
    states, 136
  transfers to persons with disabilities,
    131-34
U.S. Bureau of the Census, 6, 7, 8, 34,
  35, 52
U.S. Employment Service
  aptitude tests, 323-24
  persons with disabilities using, 319-23
  services and funding of, 318-19
  targeted jobs tax credit, 319-23
UNUM Insurance Company, 258-60,
  262

Vandergoot, D., 248
Veterans Administration (VA). See
  Department of Veterans Affairs
Vocational education programs, 316-18
Vocational rehabilitation (VR)
  Britain, 145-46
  with changes in idea of disability, 247-
    48
  DI referral to, 263-64
  under disability insurance, 228-29
  grant-in-aid program to states, 224
  linking diability insurance, 224-25
  money from federal BRP funds, 229,
    232-33
  post-BRP SSA reimbursements to,
    237-40
  by state-level services, 298-302
  Sweden, 145
  as wage subsidy, 116

Wage subsidies
  for disabled workers in European
    countries, 147-48
  earned income tax credit as, 214
  Targeted Jobs Tax Credit program,
    116, 319-23
  vocational rehabilitation as, 116
  workers' compensation as implicit,
    116-17

Wagner-Peyser Act (1933), 318-19
Waidman, Timothy, 91
Weaver, Carolyn, 339
Wenker, T., 399, 400
Wiener, Joshua M., 367
Wigdor, Alexandra, 324
Winkler, Anne, 198
Wolfe, Barbara L., 64, 120, 196, 198,
    208, 209
Work disabled persons
    defined, 2
    labor force participation of, 6
    poverty of, 7
    prevalence of, 7-8
    receiving DI or SSI, 3-4
Work-disabled persons
    heterogeneity of, 5-6, 8, 10-11, 28
Work disincentives
    for disabled persons, 18-19, 52
    related to health insurance, 397
Work effort
    in DI and SSI programs, 203
    under DI program, 203-13
Workers' compensation
    as implicit wage subsidy, 116-17
    United Health Care preferred provider
        network, 260-61
    as wage subsidy program, 116-17
Work experience
    of disability insurance beneficiaries, 5,
        119-20
    of disabled persons, 59
    establishing work history, 50-51

Work history
    establishment of, 50-51
    limitations by age and sex, 105-6
    relation to employment for disabled,
        48-49
Work hours
    effect of disabling condition, 108-9
    persons with and without disabilities
        (1981-93), 45-47
    utility maximizing supply, 107-8
Work incentives
    under current public health insurance
        policy, 396-97
    evidence for disability income
        programs, 208-10
    Medicare provisins, 371
    with proposed reform under disability
        insurance, 210-13
    provisions of DI, 201-2
    relted to health care coverage, 362-63
    SSI and DI, 13-14, 207-8, 210
Work injury programs, Europe and
    United States, 137-38
World Institute on Disability, 400
Wright, Erik O., 42

Ycas, Martynas A., 170, 176, 177
Yelin, Edward H., 38, 42, 46, 48t, 50, 52,
    107
Yu, B., 110-11

Zuboff, Shoshana, 51
Zukas, H., 399, 400

About the Institute

The W.E. Upjohn Institute for Employment Research is a nonprofit research organization devoted to finding and promoting solutions to employment-related problems at the national, state, and local level. It is an activity of the W.E. Upjohn Unemployment Trustee Corporation, which was established in 1932 to administer a fund set aside by the late Dr. W.E. Upjohn, founder of The Upjohn Company, to seek ways to counteract the loss of employment income during economic downturns.

The Institute is funded largely by income from the W.E. Upjohn Unemployment Trust, supplemented by outside grants, contracts, and sales of publications. Activities of the Institute are comprised of the following elements: (1) a research program conducted by a resident staff of professional social scientists; (2) a competitive grant program, which expands and complements the internal research program by providing financial support to researchers outside the Institute; (3) a publications program, which provides the major vehicle for the dissemination of research by staff and grantees, as well as other selected work in the field; and (4) an Employment Management Services division, which manages most of the publicly funded employment and training programs in the local area.

The broad objectives of the Institute's research, grant, and publication programs are to: (1) promote scholarship and experimentation on issues of public and private employment and unemployment policy; and (2) make knowledge and scholarship relevant and useful to policymakers in their pursuit of solutions to employment and unemployment problems.

Current areas of concentration for these programs include: causes, consequences, and measures to alleviate unemployment; social insurance and income maintenance programs; compensation; workforce quality; work arrangements; family labor issues; labor-management relations; and regional economic development and local labor markets.

427